Engaging Autism

Engaging Autism

*Using the Floortime Approach to Help
Children Relate, Communicate, and Think*

⊠ ⊠ ⊠

STANLEY I. GREENSPAN, M.D.
SERENA WIEDER, PH.D.

A Merloyd Lawrence Book

DA CAPO LIFELONG BOOKS
A Member of the Perseus Books Group

Designed by Trish Wilkinson
Set in 11.5-point Goudy by The Perseus Books Group

Library of Congress Cataloging-in-Publication Data

Greenspan, Stanley I.
    Engaging autism : using the floortime approach to help children relate, communicate, and think / Stanley I. Greenspan, Serena Wieder.
        p.   cm.
    Includes bibliographical references and index.
    ISBN-13: 978-0-7382-1028-5 (hardcover : alk. paper)
    ISBN-10: 0-7382-1028-5 (hardcover : alk. paper)   1. Autistic children—Behavior modification.   2. Autistic children—Rehabilitation.   3. Autistic children—Education.   4. Parents of autistic children.   I. Wieder, Serena. II. Title.
RJ506.A9G74 2006
618.92'85882—dc22   2006001814

First Da Capo Press edition 2006
First Da Capo Press paperback edition 2009

PB ISBN: 978-0-7382-1094-0

A Merloyd Lawrence Book
Published by Da Capo Press
A Member of The Perseus Books Group
http://www.dacapopress.com

Da Capo Press books are available at special discounts for bulk purchases in the U.S. by corporations, institutions, and other organizations. For more information, please contact the Special Markets Department at the Perseus Books Group, 2300 Chestnut Street, Suite 200, Philadelphia, PA 19103, or call (800) 810-4145, ext. 5000, or email special.markets@perseusbooks.com.

10 9 8 7 6 5

Acknowledgments

We want to thank Deirdre Schwiesow for her extraordinary sensitivity, talent, and dedication in facilitating the writing and editing of this work. We also want to thank Jan Tunney and Sarah Miller for their very helpful administrative support. A special thanks goes to Merloyd Lawrence for her gifted editing and suggestions.

Most of all, we want to thank the children and families who have allowed us to be members of their teams and who have worked so hard to overcome developmental challenges. Their dedication and creativity are a source of inspiration for the ideas in this work.

Contents

Part III Floortime

Part IV Assessment and Intervention: The DIR Model

Part V Overcoming Difficult Symptoms

Introduction

We Can Do Better

When the pediatrician told Marissa that her beautiful son Sean was autistic, her heart sank to the floor. It took days for Marissa and her husband, John, to confront this diagnosis and to realize its dramatic implications for their beloved, bright-eyed two-year-old child and for their own life together. When they did, and after they had done some research on autism and autistic spectrum disorders (ASDs), the weight in their hearts did not lighten. The information about ASD they gleaned from books and from the Internet was overwhelming, with many different points of view and treatment options. They had to learn a whole new vocabulary just to understand what was going on with Sean, and in the midst of their grief at the diagnosis, they found this very hard to do. Most disturbing of all, they weren't sure they were getting the right advice on how to treat their son. They wanted a treatment program that would give him the best possible chance to make progress and, they hoped, experience friendship, school, birthday parties, dating, sports, college, a career, and someday, having and raising children of his own.

The first specialist whom Marissa and John consulted told the couple that Sean would probably never be able to relate to other people's feelings or to think creatively. The best they could expect was for Sean to learn to behave in socially acceptable ways through a treatment approach that focused on his symptoms and behavior. For example, he could learn to memorize scripted phrases to say to another child, and his parents could encourage him to make eye contact with them by rewarding him with food. In the face of this advice, the couple felt hopeless and helpless. They believed their son had more potential than that, and they wanted him to *want* to relate to them and to think for himself.

Many parents of children diagnosed with ASD feel like Marissa and John. They want a program that will consider their child as an individual, offer personalized treatment, and unleash the child's potential for meaningful communication and relationships. Such parents also want to be a part of their child's treatment plan. They want to help and to hope. This book is written with such parents—and their children's other caregivers—in mind. It presents an approach that can fundamentally change assumptions about autism and ASD and vastly improve the outlook for children with these disorders.

For sixty years, treatments for ASD have focused on the symptoms of the condition, rather than on the underlying problems. As a result, goals for individual children have often been limited to changes in behavior, and the long-term prognosis for many children with the disorder has been deeply pessimistic. Prevailing assumptions about the nature of autism have limited the kind of progress and future expected for these children.

Estimates for the number of children with some form of ASD range as high as 1 in 166. Better futures are now possible for these children. With a comprehensive, individualized approach to assessment and treatment that focuses on the building blocks of healthy development, as described in the following chapters, many children diagnosed with ASD have made progress that goes far beyond what is traditionally described as "high functioning." The formal name for this new approach is the developmental, individual-difference, relationship-based (DIR) model. It is also often referred to as the "Floortime" approach. Floortime is actually a basic strategy within the DIR model. This book explains the DIR approach for parents, professionals, and other caregivers of children with ASD.

The goal of treatment within the DIR/Floortime model is to build foundations for healthy development, rather than to work only on surface behavior and symptoms. With this approach, children learn to master critical abilities missed or derailed along their developmental path—namely, the ability to relate to others with warmth and pleasure, communicate purposefully and meaningfully (first with gestures and then often with words), and, to varying degrees, think logically and creatively. A significant number of children treated in this way have broken new ground, mastering abilities formerly thought unattainable by children with ASD. They have formed warm, intimate relationships with family and peers and have developed sophisticated verbal skills. They not only have mastered academics but also intellectual skills, such as spontaneous thinking, making and understanding inferences, and empathizing with others.

One of the children who has benefited from the DIR approach is a patient we will call Josh. After Josh was diagnosed with autism, his parents decided not to accept the pessimistic prognosis he was given and started their three-year-old on a comprehensive therapeutic program based on the DIR model. Now, at age seventeen, Josh is a happy student in a demanding, regular private school and is exploring possible colleges. He has lots of friends and even a budding romance. He can discuss his own feelings and is intuitive (perhaps even gifted) at reading and understanding the feelings of others. He can discuss and write logical, coherent essays about a variety of topics. According to his parents, his teachers and peers are not aware of his history of autism and see him as a warm, talented teenager.

Another example is David. At two and a half years old, he was self-absorbed, showing no eye contact or apparent pleasure when relating to his parents or his peers. During his evaluation, David spent most of his time in repetitive and self-stimulatory behavior, such as reciting numbers in a rote sequence, spinning and jumping around aimlessly and randomly, and lining up toys and cars, while making little grunts. In many programs, such symptoms would result in a diagnosis with a limited prognosis and a treatment plan focused mainly on stopping this behavior.

However, we saw that David also had strengths: he was able, when extremely motivated, to show what he wanted; to show affection with some hugs; imitate actions, sounds, and words; and to recognize pictures and shapes. We created a comprehensive treatment program based on his unique developmental profile. David overreacted to sound and touch, so we used soft, low-pitched sounds and words in our interactions with him. Because he liked to repeat letters (he had a great memory), we used this to engage him in play. For example, we "made mistakes" such as repeating his "A-B-C" with "C-A-B?" In response, he shook his head and soon learned to say the word "no." Through such games, he became engaged and gradually began talking more purposefully and creatively. After a few years of progress, he enrolled in a regular school, where he eventually excelled in reading and English as well as math. Now he has a number of close friends, a sense of humor, and insights into other people's feelings; his remaining challenges, such as difficulty with fine motor activities and a tendency to become anxious and argumentative in competitive situations, are relatively minor.

Because of a lack of studies on representative populations, we don't know how many children with ASD are in the subgroup that DIR/Floortime has helped reach these levels of thinking and social skills. Of the children we have worked with, however, it is a sizable percentage (see Appendix A). We have also observed that the type of treatment that produces better-than-expected progress in this subgroup also helps children who make slower progress to become warmer, more engaged, and more communicative and reach a higher level of thinking than would have been expected in the past.

Harold, a four-and-a-half-year-old boy with neurological challenges, progressed only very slowly to imitating sounds and words, even with a comprehensive program designed to help him learn oral motor skills. He could say one or two words spontaneously when angry or insistent on getting something, but otherwise had to be pressed to speak. Every utterance was extremely difficult, and he would sometimes stare at a caregiver's mouth to try and form the same mouth movements. His severe dyspraxia (low muscle tone) also interfered with his engaging in pretend play, and he could not use toys creatively, although he did enjoy running around the school yard and the pool with other children.

In the second year of treatment, Harold became able to communicate about what he wanted, such as by pulling his dad over to the refrigerator to find hot dogs. He could even retrieve a few words at such moments—"Hot dog!" and "French fries!" Over time, Harold tuned into more of what was going on around him, using gestures and simple words and making some progress learning letters and numbers. He loved lots of movement and, instead of wandering aimlessly, could now exchange a number of emotional expressions and gestures as part of getting a horsy ride on his father's back or going up and down "like an airplane." As we work with him now, he is still limited in his use of imagination, but has become warm, interactive, and purposeful. We expect his gradual and steady progress to continue. The key point about children like Harold is that, in spite of their neurological challenges, they can learn to relate with great joy and warmth and acquire the most important skills of meaningful communication and problem solving.

Outcomes like these cannot be achieved by programs that work only on symptoms or that accept a fixed prognosis of the child's future potential. Many programs that focus predominantly on symptoms or behaviors rely on the troubling assumption that many children with ASD cannot ever acquire skills for truly intimate relating, empathy, and creative problem-solving.

In contrast, the developmental model described in this book focuses on the underlying deficits that lead to autistic symptoms, rather than only on the symptoms themselves. With help in overcoming these deficits, the child can follow the developmental progression that leads to enjoying relationships and engaging in meaningful communication.

Common wisdom once held that 80 percent of children diagnosed with ASD would still show the symptoms of these disorders many years later. Kathy Lord at the University of Michigan is showing that the old data no longer hold. Our preliminary studies suggest that the prognosis for autistic spectrum disorders must take into account the intervention approach. (Appendix A of this book covers current research in more detail.)

Regional networks of DIR practitioners are now available in most cities and states in the United States and in many cities abroad. The DIR/Floortime model was recently cited by the National Academies of Science (NAS) in their report *Educating Children with Autism* as one of the main comprehensive models supported by current research.

The NAS also acknowledged that modern approaches are moving away from conditioning specific behaviors and focusing more and more on naturalistic (or incidental) learning, fostering the building blocks of healthy development.

In addition, a large field study of the DIR/Floortime model's emotional milestones, conducted by the Psychological Corporation as part of its development of the new Bayley Scales for Infant and Early Childhood Assessment, showed that these milestones could differentiate infants and young children with developmental and emotional disorders from those without such problems. (The Bayley Scales are the most widely used tool for developmental assessment in infancy and early childhood in the world.) The study also validated the ages at which the DIR model predicts mastery of these emotional competencies and demonstrated that—as hypothesized in the model—mastery of the early stages of emotional interaction is associated with language and thinking skills. The results were so encouraging that the Psychological Corporation published the DIR emotional milestones as the "Greenspan Social-Emotional Growth Chart," to be used as a separate assessment tool as well as a component of the new Bayley Scales kit.

In the chapters that follow, we describe the DIR/Floortime approach and show how to enter a child's world and bring her or him into a shared world of relating, communicating, and thinking. Part I presents a new, more accurate way of defining autism and ASD and observing a child's earliest signs, and describes goals for working with children with ASD and other special needs within the DIR framework. Part II shows how families can take the lead in working with their children toward these goals. In Part III we describe the DIR model's Floortime technique and illustrate it in various contexts. Part IV looks at how to create a comprehensive treatment plan and how school environments can be modified to support treatment plans. In Part V we address working with specific problems in greater depth. Appendices A–C present research that supports the DIR model.

Note: The profiles of children at the beginning of each chapter are composites of children we have treated or whose parents have contacted us with questions.

Part I

⊠ ⊠ ⊠

Improving the Prognosis of ASD
Myths, Facts, Early Signs, and a New Framework

Chapter 1

Redefining Autism and the Way We Treat It

Autism is a complex developmental disorder involving delays in and problems with social interaction, language, and a range of emotional, cognitive, motor, and sensory abilities. Specific behavior—such as bodily spinning, lining up toys, or repeating words without apparent purpose or meaning—is often observed as well, but as we will show later, these symptoms arise from more fundamental problems in relating, communicating, and thinking. They are not specific to autism. Language, thinking, and social skills for a child with autism or autistic spectrum disorders (ASDs) vary according to where he or she falls on a spectrum.

Basic facts about the disorder such as causes and rates of occurrence are still poorly understood. As we said earlier, some studies estimate the incidence of ASD to be as high as 1 out of 166. Most also suggest a dramatic increase over the rate estimated a decade ago. While some investigators attribute the higher rate to better identification and diagnosis, many believe there has been an increase in autism and ASD.

Many Paths to Autism

The cause of the increase, like the cause of autism in general, is unknown. A great deal of research supports genetic factors (for example, identical twins are more likely both to have a disorder than are non-identical twins). Historically, the notion has been that these genetic (or more broadly, biological) influences tend to produce the cluster of symptoms associated with autism and ASD. Immunological, meta-bolic, and environmental factors are also believed to play a role. How-ever, no single cause has been definitely shown to produce the disorder. Therefore, we believe the most useful framework for exploring the un-derlying causes of autism is what we call the cumulative-risk, multiple-pathway model, which recognizes that many factors interact to cause the disorder. Genetic or prenatal factors, for example, may make a child vulnerable to subsequent challenges including physical stress, in-fectious illness, and exposure to toxic substances. This newer way of thinking about causation recognizes genetic influences but sees a de-velopmental pathway with many steps, a gradual emergence of the as-sociated problems over time, many variations in the problems, and varying degrees of severity.

A Wide Range of Problems

Autism and ASDs involve difficulties in relating and forming rela-tionships, communicating (whether with gestures, words, or symbols), and thinking. These complex developmental problems can express themselves differently and can appear in different combinations. Not every child under the same general diagnostic label has all of these problems to the same degree. For example, children with Asperger's Syndrome often have large vocabularies and may be early readers, but have trouble using words meaningfully, in an emotionally relevant way. Instead, they may simply repeat words or understand only the dictionary definition of the word. They may also have problems in re-lating with others and in communicating with gestures and emotion.

Another variation is seen in children with severe motor planning problems. Some children have oral-motor problems that make it hard for them to move their tongue and the muscles in their mouth in order to speak. Some children with both severe oral-motor problems and general motor problems may appear to have cognitive disabilities and to lack social skills when in fact they are limited in expressing their abilities and skills by their motor impairments. When we help children with oral motor problems communicate through sign language or other augmentative modes such as computer keyboards, we often find that they understand their world to a much more developed degree than we realized.

Core Problems in ASD

Three core or primary problems characterize autism and ASD. Here are the questions we ask to establish the presence of these core problems:

1. Is the child having trouble with establishing intimacy and warmth? Does the child seek out those adults he is really comfortable with, such as a parent or key caregiver? If so, does he show enjoyment of closeness in that relationship?
2. Does the child communicate with gestures and emotional expressions? Does she engage in a continuous flow of back-and-forth emotional signaling with smiles, frowns, head nods, and other interactive gestures?
3. When the child begins using words, does he use them meaningfully? Are the words or symbols invested with emotion or desire, such as, "Mommy, I love you" or "I want that juice," rather than "This is a table" or "This is a chair"?

If these three basic abilities—establishing closeness, exchanging emotional gestures in a continuous way, and using emerging words or symbols with emotional intent—are not present, we should consider whether the child is showing signs of an autistic spectrum disorder. The degree to which these three core processes or abilities are not functioning in an age-expected manner may indicate, at least initially, the degree of autism affecting the child.

Secondary Symptoms

There are also secondary symptoms, such as the tendency to perseverate (for example, lining up objects repetitively), flap hands, or self-
stimulate (for example, staring at a fan, rubbing a particular spot on
the floor, and so forth). Similarly, repeating words in a scripted way or
reciting whole books that have been read to the child or whole TV
shows she has seen are examples of the disorder's secondary components. Because such symptoms are seen in a number of other kinds of
developmental disorders and thus are not specific to autism, they
should not be used as the primary criteria for making a diagnosis.

Children who have sensory processing problems, such as being
overreactive to touch or sound, but who otherwise have excellent language and relationship skills and can read and respond to emotional
signaling, may be self-stimulatory or perseverative because they get
overloaded; they may be trying to regulate themselves. These secondary phenomena can also be seen in children with severe motor planning problems. Sometimes children with language deficits or very
circumscribed cognitive or learning difficulties may also show some of
these symptoms.

Our new understanding of ASD incorporates observed symptoms
but organizes this information from a developmentally based perspective. In this new way of defining ASD, the secondary symptoms are
kinds of behavior that stem from the core deficits. Some children, for
example, lack the ability to engage in what we call "shared social
problem-solving" with their toys and to play with them in a flexible
way with parents or peers. They are unable to show their toy to a caregiver, flash a big smile, and gesture for a reaction. Rather, they tend to
just line up their toys. Thus, the symptoms reflect and result from a
lack of mastering the core abilities. Having a narrow range of interests
is another such symptom. Because children expand their range of interests through communication with others, when they don't use gestures in continuing interactions to indicate their wishes and needs,
their range of interests remains narrow.

Symptoms such as these may indicate a broader pattern of an ASD, but should not be the sole basis of a diagnosis. The key to making a proper diagnosis—and to knowing what a child's real problems are—is to look at the degree to which the child manifests the three fundamental abilities described above. One of the main reasons for the many misdiagnoses of ASD that are made is that not enough time is spent watching the child interact with a parent or other trusted caregiver. In many evaluations, children are in fact separated from parents and challenged to perform various types of developmental tests in a way that fails to take into account the child's individual differences in processing information. The children thus become stressed and confused, which tends to bring out their lowest level of ability. To make a proper diagnosis, a practitioner also has to see children at their very best; a diagnosis should be based on the whole range of the child's abilities.

Varied Rates of Progress

Over the past couple of decades, children diagnosed with ASD have shown varied levels of progress. Some, described as "high functioning," acquire sufficient language to master a variety of academic subjects such as reading and math (often excelling in memory-based learning), but may nonetheless remain somewhat socially rigid and emotionally isolated. Other children make only very modest gains in language and academic skills, learning to gesture and use selective words. Still others make very little progress. They remain self-absorbed, without functional language, and rely on repetitive behaviors and self-stimulation to cope with their environments.

Yet there are others, such as those described in the introduction, who make unusual progress, advancing significantly beyond the "high functioning" level. Through a treatment program based on the DIR model, they have developed intimate relationships with their families and friendships with peers and have learned to think and communicate flexibly and creatively.

For these reasons, ASD should be viewed as dynamic, not static. A static trait is fixed—the child will be this way no matter what the environment, context, or circumstances. A child's blue eyes are unlikely to change over time or due to changing circumstances; eye color is a relatively fixed trait. Dynamic traits, on the other hand—associated with many factors, including feelings and emotions—are changeable. The three core abilities identified above are dynamic processes: they can and do change—more for some children than for others, and more with certain kinds of treatment programs than with others.

Professionals disagree as to the degree to which these abilities can be favorably influenced, both in general and in any particular child. Our view is that these abilities can change significantly and that a prognosis can be determined by only one factor—the child's actual progress. Many factors—including home environment, treatment program, and maturation of the child's nervous system—influence his or her progress. The only reliable indicator is the child's learning curve over time. The steeper the slope, the better.

Recent studies of how experience, at all stages of life, can change the structure and function of the brain are giving increasing support to the changes seen in autistic children after DIR/Floortime treatment. Newer brain imaging techniques are documenting these changes. They are beginning to offer concrete evidence of the way certain experiences can affect not only the child's ability to relate, communicate, and think, but also the very architecture of the brain.

If there is no progress at all (which would seem to confirm the validity of earlier views of autism and ASD), it is often because the child is not receiving an optimal program of intervention at home, at school, and with therapists. That learning curve can often be improved by providing the child the right help. That slope of the learning curve may change from year to year depending on various factors; the key thing is continual steady progress. So rather than trying to predict progress based on some fixed diagnostic criteria, the idea is to create the optimal program, then watch the child learn and enjoy his progress.

Treatment Options

Available treatment options for autism and ASDs are based on certain underlying assumptions. The DIR/Floortime model is based on the assumption that we can favorably influence the core developmental foundations for relating, thinking, and communicating, even for children with severe problems, by working with the their emotions, or affect. We describe this model in detail in Chapter 4.

For many years, the behavioral model—which did help some children fit into school and home life—was the only model. Today, with the insights we now have into the way the nervous system develops and the way children acquire their core abilities, deeper change and greater opportunities to lead rich, full lives are possible for children with ASD. When practitioners build a healthy developmental foundation, children may also overcome symptoms. When appropriate, therapists may incorporate behavioral approaches into a DIR foundation-building approach: the DIR model is not a single therapy or intervention program; it's a way of understanding how each child is unique and designing and orchestrating a comprehensive treatment program. Based on the needs of the child, the program may have various elements.

Clinicians can also incorporate a number of relationship-based approaches into a broader DIR model by following three principles while engaging in particular activities or exercises. These principles are tailoring interactions to the child's nervous system, building spontaneous interactions, and harnessing the child's natural interests and emotions as part of these interactions. Many practitioners—especially in speech and language pathology, occupational and physical therapy, education, and psychology—have been exploring dynamic interactive approaches. They are demonstrating that interactions geared to a child's unique neurological profile can help the child relate, think, and communicate. For example, oral-motor exercises can help with preverbal vocalizing, gesturing, and imitation, thus facilitating language development. Learning to decode sounds can help "phonemic awareness," a basis for reading.

Yet in spite of this expanding approach, practitioners still tend to focus on symptoms and on only a few of the underlying processing differences. Even though emerging evidence favors a dynamic model, the vast majority of children with ASD have access only to older, static approaches that deal insufficiently with each child's unique developmental profile and potential for growth. Despite their limited success, many of these approaches have remained unchanged for many years.

The following are examples of widely used approaches that are not fully based on dynamic developmental concepts and therefore have not been sufficiently helpful to most children with ASD:

- *Limited educational programs that use repetitive exercises to teach isolated skills*, such as matching shapes, rather than essential developmental building blocks. Such exercises have not been shown to be an essential foundation for cognitive or social capacities or auditory processing and language capacities, and higher level thinking skills.
- *Behavioral approaches* that work predominantly with surface behavior while paying less attention to relationships, individual processing differences, and the building block of thinking.
- *Biomedical approaches* that are not part of a comprehensive program. They may involve various diagnostic procedures and medication without constructing a complementary, comprehensive intervention program. A diagnostician may give parents their child's diagnosis, recommend additional tests and/or a particular medication, and then simply tell the parents to contact representatives of their local special education program.

Many parents and programs are combining elements from naturalistic approaches such as DIR/Floortime and more structural behavioral or educational ones, but without a true developmental road map to orchestrate the program. The DIR model provides such a road map. As will be seen, it shows how to use a range of interventions in a truly integrated manner to promote mastery of the developmental capacities needed for relating, communicating, and thinking (see Chapter 20).

Our research has shown that relating, communicating, and thinking include such well-documented capacities as using language socially, joint attention (playing with a toy and showing it to Dad), theory of mind (understanding the feelings and ideas of another person), reading complex emotional and social signals, and making inferences (creating new ideas). These, we have shown, stem from mastery of a number of more basic building blocks that will be described in Chapters 3 and 4 and subsequent sections (see also, Appendix B). These capacities are not only the foundations of healthy development, they are the very abilities that are compromised in children with autism. That's why we developed a comprehensive model, the DIR/Floortime approach, which uses our knowledge of human development to orchestrate the different components of the intervention program. As will be described in the next section, each step along a child's developmental pathway offers an opportunity to help strengthen the child's core abilities, rather than allowing those abilities to further erode. If a four-month-old child is beginning to show a lack of sustained pleasure and joy, or a four-year-old has not fully mastered joyful relating, we can address the problem at that point rather than waiting. Similarly, we can help a five-year-old use language meaningfully and play creatively. We can look at what biological or environmental factors are contributing to the problem. While it is best to deal with challenges as early as possible, it is *never* too late if we work on true developmental foundations. We can take a proactive approach. The remaining chapters in Part I look in more detail at the myths surrounding autism and ASD and the misdiagnoses that result from these myths. We explain how to identify the signs of ASD—in both infants and children—and how caretakers can address the problems before symptoms appear. Finally, we describe the DIR approach to treating ASD.

Chapter 2

Myths and Misdiagnoses of ASD, Including Asperger's Syndrome

In redefining autism and ASD, we should also clear up the myths around these disorders, because these myths can lead to misdiagnoses.

Inability to Love?

Perhaps the most influential myth relates to the ability of children with ASD to love and form loving relationships. When autism was first identified as a disorder in the 1940s, it was characterized by "autistic aloneness," an inability to form intimate, warm, nurturing relationships. Leo Kanner—known as the "father of autism" for authoring some of the first systematic descriptions of children with ASD—formulated that concept as part of his theory. Since then, the idea of an inability to form intimate bonds or warm, loving relationships has persisted in all subsequent definitions of autism. It is found in the American Psychiatric Association's *Diagnostic and Statistical Manual (DSM)*, in all editions including the current one. Whereas initially children with ASD were thought to have a fundamental autistic aloneness, currently the ability to form intimate relationships is viewed as a continuum. But the notion persists that children with autism will never be able to relate as fully, richly, or as deeply as typically developing children can.

The ability to love, to be comfortable in an intimate relationship, involves experiencing pleasure in emotional closeness with another person. We assume a four-month-old baby's beatific smile at her mother or father reflects a deep, warm sense of engagement that will grow into more and more love and intimacy over the course of the next several months. But when we see a two-and-a-half-year-old child with ASD become scared and run into her grandmother's arms and hold tight, is that any less a sign of love or warmth or intimacy? When we see a four-year-old who has been diagnosed with autism give a big, warm smile when Mommy rubs his back, is Mommy simply an object to him? Or is he experiencing intimacy and counting it as important that it's Mommy who's giving the back rub?

Evidence from our work with children with autism indicates that they feel a personal sense of love, specifically with their mother, father, or other primary caregiver, because other adults often won't produce in the child that same degree of intimacy, or of comfort in a moment of fear or need. In fact, after treatment, the children not only show no sense of aloneness but may become more loving than their typically developing peers. Sometimes parents complain that the children become too dependent: "He won't let me go!" they say. I tell them, "That's great news!" because if a child has been isolated in his own world, nothing is better than to have him want to be with a parent or caregiver "too much." Once children are in relationships, we can gradually help them learn to be independent.

With a DIR/Floortime approach that engages with the child's pleasures, even if they seem perseverative or self-stimulatory, the first element that develops is not language or communication, but a sense of relatedness. It comes quickly, often within the first three to four months of treatment. The fact that relatedness emerges so quickly, even in children who have little of it before, suggests to us that it's there already in some form.

In a recent study (described in more detail in Appendix A), we compared the first part of our initial session with children diagnosed with ASD to the second part of that session and saw significant differences in the children's relatedness from one part to the next. During the session, we coached the parents on reading the child's emotional signals and tuning into his nervous system. For example, if he was hypersensitive to touch and sound, we helped the parents become more soothing. If he had a pattern of self-stimulatory behavior, such as opening and closing a door, we showed the parents how to enter his world and turn the activity into a shared interaction. As we coached the parents, we often saw children who at first seemed self-absorbed brighten up and show robust pleasure and even seek out a parent for affection or play.

So from the first session through the first year of treatment, intimacy emerges and grows as parents are better able to understand their child's nervous system and tune into her world. Almost all the parents tell us about wonderful, warm, intimate moments with their children at home, and say they would like more of these moments and wish their child could verbalize love and warmth. We show the parents how to create such moments by helping the child communicate his emotions more effectively.

This evidence convinces us that the ability to love deeply is present in children with ASD, whether or not it can easily be expressed. In fact, studies are showing that many children with autism can be very emotional but become so overwhelmed by their feelings that they avoid contact so as to control the intensity of their emotions. Other children are very underreactive and thus do not express emotion, because they haven't been sufficiently enticed into the joys and pleasures of relationships.

The confusion about the ability of children with ASD to love and feel strong emotions comes from the fact that many of these children have trouble communicating their emotions. Typically, at four to ten months, children are engaging in back-and-forth emotional interactions through sounds, body posture, and facial expressions: a smile leads to a smile, sounds lead to sounds. In children without developmental problems, this reaches a complex pattern by twelve to sixteen months: they may come up to Mommy or Daddy and reach out their arms, grinning; they may make inviting sounds, even say a word or two; they may giggle and smile, and playfully copy what a parent is doing. There are many exchanges of emotions in a row.

This type of rapid exchange of emotional signals is much harder for children with ASD. We believe this is due to a primary biological challenge in connecting their emotions to their motor systems or motor planning. Because they can't sequence their actions under the guidance of their desires, they may want closeness but can't figure out how to translate that desire into action. In terms of language, even if they can memorize or repeat some words, it's difficult for them to invest words with a feeling, to connect the emotion or affect to the verbal symbols, and say, "I love you" or "Mommy, give me a big hug." We don't believe, however, that this difficulty represents a permanent limitation. With appropriate treatment, children with ASD can not only experience love but also learn to express it.

Inability to Communicate and Think Creatively?

A related myth is that children who have ASD can't learn the fundamentals of communicating and thinking and that the best we can hope for is that they will change their behavior and memorize scripts. As stated in the previous chapter, however, children with autism or ASD can get involved in shared problem-solving and use ideas creatively and logically. Our outcome studies (see Appendix A) have shown that a high percentage of children can reach all the fundamental emotional and developmental milestones.

Once caregivers get past the myths about lack of relatedness and communication and help the child build these skills, undesirable behaviors such as perseveration, echolalia, aggression, and mood instability tend to recede.

Inability to Think Abstractly?

Another, related myth is that children with ASD can't learn to think abstractly and make inferences. We have also found this not to be true. While not all children are capable of reaching the level of abstract thinking (because of the language and cognitive capacity it requires), a follow-up study we conducted (see Appendix A) showed that in a DIR program which worked on foundations and on emotional signaling and cueing, children who made the most progress learned to make inferences, master theory-of-mind tasks, and have empathy. These findings challenge old assumptions and open the door for new research.

Inability to Read Emotions?

Another myth holds that children with ASD can't read the emotions of other children or adults. Earlier research suggested that when children with ASD see expressions of emotion on a human face, they process that information in a different part of the brain than does an individual without ASD. This seems to support the idea that the brains of children with ASD are different. But when Morton Gernsbacher and her colleagues at the University of Wisconsin, Madison, replicated one of these studies, they realized that the subjects of the original study may not have even been looking at the faces of others. When their subjects were encouraged to look at faces, the same areas of the brain that process facial images in subjects without ASD lit up in the brain scans. The subjects were able to process facial expressions in the way that people without ASD process them. In other words, the results of the earlier study reflected the tendency of children with ASD not to look at faces, rather than indicating different brain physiology.

One insight from Gernsbacher and her colleagues' study is that children and adults who overreact to sensation may find it stressful to look at someone else's face too quickly. In fact, when Gernsbacher's subjects looked at the faces of others, they grew anxious. In working with children with ASD, we can help them not only overcome such stressful reactions but take great pleasure in other people's faces and emotional expressions.

This research shows how complex and subtle some of the problems associated with ASD are and how even good research can lead to incorrect conclusions if the investigator doesn't raise all the alternative hypotheses. The most solid evidence about the abilities of children with ASD is that many of these children do develop higher-level thinking capacities. It's easy to say that maybe such children never deserved an ASD diagnosis in the first place, but that would be circular reasoning. These are children who originally met the criteria of the *DSM IV-R* for ASD and who have achieved high levels of abstract and reflective thinking.

Primary Problem or Downstream Effect?

It is easy to assume or conclude that individuals with autism have chronic or fixed deficits related to unchangeable brain differences. However, such conclusions are often based on insufficient data. One of the most difficult questions to answer is whether an observed behavioral, emotional, or brain function difference is a primary problem or a "downstream effect." For example, according to a recent finding from brain imaging, individuals with autism tend to have problems forming connections between the different parts of their brains. As we said earlier, we believe the primary problem in individuals with ASD is a biological difficulty in connecting emotion to motor actions and, later on, to symbols. Our research suggests that emotions link different types of mental functioning. When these linkages are not properly formed early in life, a variety of downstream effects may occur, including difficulty with giving purpose and meaning to actions or words and forming age-expected pathways between the different areas of the central nervous system (see Appendix B).

Because very little research has been done on the development of children showing signs of autism during their infancy and early childhood years, it is difficult to know what is the result of some earlier problem and what is a primary deficit or difficulty. Complicating matters further, much of the research compares children with autism to children without challenges or children with cognitive or language deficits. Very few studies have compared children with ASD to children who do not have ASD but do have the variety of motor and sensory processing problems often seen in children with ASD (that is, very interactive, creative, verbal, abstract-thinking children with lots of motor and sensory problems).

It is best to view ASD in a dynamic framework that considers all the factors that influence the child's development over time. We advocate considering ASD (including Asperger's Syndrome) not as a fixed disorder that you either have or don't have, but as a dynamic process in which certain biological or neurological challenges affect development. The degree of progress possible depends on the amount of neurological impairment, but rather than assuming a fixed disorder, practitioners should try to move each child through the stages of emotional and intellectual development to the best of the child's ability.

Myths About the Value of Repetitive Exercises

The myths surrounding autistic children's inability to develop intellectually have led to myths about the effectiveness of certain treatment programs. Clinicians and parents may be tempted to select a program that focuses on repetitive activities that appear to teach the child specific skills, such as matching or sorting shapes. This temptation is particularly strong when the child seems to be making little or no progress. As the focus on repetitive activities increases, however, the child's progress in engaging or interacting may slow down—or even reverse.

Advocates of repetitive exercises such as matching shapes believe these activities teach children to classify. However, children making very slow progress whom I have observed doing such repetitive practice aren't really learning classification. Although they may learn a specific task they are usually unable to classify a novel shape or color or demonstrate an understanding of the differences between square and round shapes, for example. Equally important, there is no compelling evidence that these sorts of repetitively practiced activities develop the fundamental building blocks of cognition. These particular tasks were originally selected because they were skills that many children could do and it was assumed, therefore, that it would be useful to teach them to children with challenges. Yet the many skills that children without challenges perform easily are quite likely the result of their having mastered important foundations of cognition, language, and social development (see Appendices A and B). We've learned over the years that when children are making little or no progress, the best approach is to redouble our efforts on the developmental basics. More intensive, more skillful work on the fundamentals, taking into account the child's unique biology (as outlined in Part II), helps optimize the child's progress, even if it's slow and steady.

The Myth of a Single Cause

Much confusion still surrounds the causes of autism, especially as more children are being diagnosed with it now than in the past. While some attribute this increase to more accurate diagnoses, broader diagnostic categories, and improved early case finding, others believe it results from autoimmune reactions; environmental stressors (such as lead, PCBs, or dioxins) that are more prevalent than in the past; overexposure to TV, computers, and other technology early in life; and so forth. As we note in chapter 1, research going on all around the world appears to confirm a multicausal model whereby many factors work together to produce cumulative risk. According to this model, multiple paths lead to an ASD. Along each of these paths lie associated cumulative risk factors. We may eventually find that a variety of genetic and other biological challenges are interacting, creating certain types of susceptibility.

Again, it is important to look at causation in a dynamic, developmental framework. The symptoms of autism, such as self-absorption and difficulty with emotional signaling and creative and abstract reasoning, may well lie along a pathway having many different sources. As an analogy, consider a fever or an inflammatory reaction such as swelling. We know that many different causes can lead to fever or inflammation—both are among the body's limited number of responses to an infinite range of challenges. The mind (and the brain) may work in a similar fashion. It, too, may have a limited range of responses to a variety of challenges. It is, therefore, important not only to look at these downstream common effects but to search earlier in the developmental sequence for the critical processes and factors that influence them. As the following chapters show, the DIR/Floortime model offers a dynamic developmental framework to facilitate such explorations.

Misdiagnosis and Inadequate Assessments

The myths surrounding autism often lead to misdiagnosis. Our fundamental premise is that, to determine how a child is functioning and whether he or she deserves a diagnosis of autism, we need to know the child. The typical evaluation process involves structured standardized tests, with only brief observation of the child's interaction with parents or familiar caregivers. Quite often an evaluation begins by separating the child from the parent; then the child interacts mainly with new individuals—the assessment team or the primary clinician in charge of the team. Thus, the team does not observe the child at his best nor see his real ability to relate or even communicate. Instead, they observe, in part, how the child responds to this new set of circumstances, which for some children are very stressful.

For children who overreact to sensation or find transitions and new situations difficult, just the separation from parents can provoke enormous anxiety and cause the child to hide under a chair, go off into a corner, or refuse to talk to anyone. In different circumstances, the same child might talk very nicely with someone. We saw one child in this situation shut down and refuse to talk; he was diagnosed with a severe developmental disorder in the autistic spectrum. Later on in the day, when he saw his mother upset, he asked her, "Why are you having hurt feelings?" He gave her a hug and was interactive and verbal, even eloquent, yet he was unable to show those wonderful abilities during the assessment because of his anxiety at being separated from his mother.

Some may argue that the boy should have been able to cope with the situation more easily, but that's not the issue: he was being assessed not for separation fears but for language and overall developmental problems to determine whether he had an ASD. The clinicians did not see him at his best. That could have easily been remedied by having the child play with his mother for the first forty-five minutes, with the clinical team simply observing the interaction on the sidelines while the boy got comfortable with the situation and the new setting. With his mother he routinely used lots of language and was very interactive. This child's developmental problems had to do with subtle issues.

In our review of two hundred cases evaluated at different leading medical centers, clinics, practice settings, and educational programs, over 90 percent of the evaluations included no more than ten minutes of observing child-caregiver patterns of communication. Most of the assessment was conducted with other adults who were unfamiliar to the child, and the child was observed interacting with parents only while participating in a structured assessment or while the developmental history was taken. In other words, the child's interaction with a parent was never the primary focus for more than just a few minutes.

Parents often observe their child to behave differently in the clinical setting than he or she does at home. Thus, it is important for the clinical team to see videotapes from the home setting, make a home visit, or simply listen very carefully to what parents report. If parents insist that the child's behavior is different at home, the clinical team should continue making observations until a consensus is reached between parents and clinicians. When there is a discrepancy in observations between parents and professional evaluators, the parents are more likely to be right because they have seen the child over longer stretches of time.

Arriving at a consensus is important not only for making a proper assessment but also for planning treatment, because parents and other caregivers will not carry out therapies they feel don't address the problems they see at home. Only parents' reports or clinicians' observations of the children interacting with the parents can reveal how the child actually functions. To make sense of those reports or observations requires expert opinion and guidance, but no sound conclusion is possible without accurate firsthand information. Parents, though not qualified to make medical diagnoses, know their children best. Parents need to trust themselves and their instincts and to find professionals who will take the time to share information and reach consensus with them.

Confusion about a diagnosis may arise when a child who manifests disturbing behaviors or has obvious developmental delays nevertheless scores well on developmental tests. We urge parents and professionals alike not to base conclusions solely on the results of structured tests. Though there is a long tradition of relying on such tests, they are not as revealing as observation. They can be used as part of an evaluation, but not as the sole criterion for determining whether a child is on the autistic spectrum. A common mistake is that children with Asperger's Syndrome have normal or even precocious language skills. Yet a child diagnosed with Asperger's has, by definition, difficulty reading and responding to subtle emotional and social cues and using language creatively and abstractly in a variety of social situations (that is, pragmatic language). This mistake is perpetuated by confusion about how a child performs on structured, memory-based language tasks such as matching pictures to words, defining words, or even doing simple reasoning exercises with words, sentences, and paragraphs. Such structured tasks do not reveal the child's social and emotional use of language, which is central to healthy or typical language development.

It is inaccurate to assume, therefore, that children deserving of an Asperger's diagnosis have healthy language development. Instead, their language strengths, including certain types of memory-based capacities and circumscribed reasoning capacities, should be recognized but harnessed to broaden the child's overall mastery of language, including verbal inferential thinking and pragmatic language. Children with Asperger's Syndrome are often not provided with enough opportunities to practice creative, spontaneous language exchanges with peers and adults. In later chapters, we describe approaches for helping children practice aspects of language that most challenge them.

Recognizing Primary Symptoms

A second, related issue concerning misdiagnosis arises from disagreement over the symptoms of autism and ASD. As discussed in chapter 1, we often fail to distinguish between primary and secondary symptoms. A study done by Nancy Minshew and colleagues at the University of Pittsburgh compared children diagnosed with autism with children without autism. When children from each group were matched for verbal ability, capacity to participate in a standardized test, and performance in processing and responding to test questions, the researchers found that what most distinguished children without ASD from those with ASD were abilities such as making inferences (thinking abstractly and coming up with a new conclusion or hypothesis), reciprocal emotional cueing (socially interacting by reading and responding to another person's signals), showing empathy (understanding what another person is feeling), and trusting in and engaging with others.

No single symptom should ever lead to a diagnosis; however, the absence of the primary abilities outlined in Chapter 1 strongly suggests ASD. As we said earlier, secondary symptoms such as the tendency to repeat action, echolalia, and self-stimulatory behavior are all common in children with ASD but are not specific to ASD. So, in diagnosing autism and ASD, we have to distinguish the primary symptoms from the secondary symptoms. Information available on the Internet about ASD may not always make this distinction. This is understandable; it is not an easy distinction to make. But distinguishing between primary and secondary symptoms is critical to making more secure diagnoses. If the only symptoms are secondary, we can consider alternative diagnoses. Thus a child who is very warm and interactive, who can use even a few words meaningfully, but who overreacts to sensation, stares off into space sometimes, and does repetitive actions may evidence developmental challenges, but not autism.

We have developed a parent questionnaire to assess the functional emotional capacities of children—capacities whose presence suggests healthy development and whose absence indicates a possible developmental challenge that requires a further evaluation. This resource, mentioned earlier, the Greenspan Social-Emotional Growth Chart and Questionnaire, has been field-tested, showing excellent reliability and validity. Published by the Psychological Corporation (see References), it is part of the new Bayley Scales package.

Of course, while we want to avoid a misdiagnosis that ignores a child's true strengths, the secondary symptoms may still require therapy. During a clinical assessment process, a competent assessment team will coach the parents on how to interact with the child in a way that takes into account how her nervous system works. What sensations is the child sensitive or underreactive to? Does she primarily use vision or sound to orient to the world? How well does she plan actions? Can she carry out three-, four-, or five-step action patterns? Clinicians can help parents work with their child's unique nervous system to pull him into optimal interactions. Only then is it possible to see how well he can engage, exchange social signals, and if he has some language, use ideas meaningfully.

Overdiagnosing Autism and Asperger's Syndrome

One of the most common misdiagnoses is to conclude that a child who has strengths in the core abilities (relating, reciprocating social and emotional signals, and thinking creatively and abstractly) is nevertheless "on the spectrum" (has ASD) because he has certain symptoms seen in ASD. Perhaps the child has a great deal of social anxiety and becomes disregulated and has meltdowns very easily. When overloaded, he may become rigid or stubborn. This tendency to overdiagnose ASD is compounded when clinicians study a child's core abilities while he or she is interacting with peers or in busy and noisy school settings, rather than in the ideal, supportive setting of play with a trusted caregiver. The child may have trouble with flexibility, with using his abilities in a variety of age-appropriate settings, and may even become avoidant or have meltdowns in these challenging settings. To see whether an ability exists, therefore, it is vital to observe the child under the most favorable circumstances. If the child can demonstrate it under these conditions, he has the ability. He may have problems that require work, but the diagnosis should be based on his true challenges.

The Vital Role of Observation

We always begin an evaluation by simply observing the child; we conclude by coaching parents to bring out the best the child can do. Every child operates within a wide range of abilities. The key point is that the diagnosis has to be based on the top of the range. If the child can walk sometimes, the child can walk. She may fall sometimes, but she can walk. If the child can relate with others sometimes, he can relate, and we can help him to relate more. Understanding what the child can do at her or his very best is necessary to making the diagnosis.

Often, assessment conditions—noise in the room, a stranger the child has to deal with, various assessment tasks, and so forth—show the child only at the bottom of his range. That's important information: it helps an assessment team understand the child's individual differences and unique patterns. Once a team has identified both the top and bottom of a child's range and observed the primary symptoms we have described here to be present even in a situation comfortable for the child, it may diagnose ASD. Or the team may notice that the child can relate, communicate, and think creatively and abstractly, but not in a noisy environment. It may then assess the child for a regulatory disorder that leads him to lose his abilities under certain conditions of stress—a very different diagnosis than autism.

Often, a team has to follow and work with a child over a few months to see what kind of growth is possible for her. Growth in these cases may result from treatment, but it shows what the child can do in a proper environment and a proper program. Therefore, we prefer to make an initial provisional diagnosis and reserve a more conclusive one until we have seen the child respond to the intervention program for a period of time.

The correct diagnosis informs the selection of the appropriate treatment program, because the program needs to work on the child's primary symptoms. As we explain in greater depth in subsequent chapters, you get what you practice in a treatment program. If treatment addresses only surface behavior, this behavior may improve, but the progress will probably not generalize to the deeper levels of relating, communicating, and thinking, which is what most parents want for their children.

In making a diagnosis, clinicians make a big mistake by thinking only in terms of whether a young child is or is not on the autistic spectrum. The question is much too limiting. Rather, healthy development can be imagined as a scale from one to ten, and a child's placement on that continuum is not fixed. The more a child is fully engaged, showing real intimacy and warmth, with parents and caregivers; communicates with gestures in a continuous flow of back-and-forth interaction; and talks meaningfully (at whatever level), the closer the child is to a ten on the continuum. The child may still have a language or motor problem, but he is moving along a healthy developmental trajectory.

On the other hand, the more self-absorbed and in-his-own-world a child is, the less able he is to get continuous back-and-forth gesturing going, and the more his language is scripted rather than used meaningfully to convey needs, wants, or feelings, the more the child tends toward the autistic end of the spectrum. Again, though, this is a dynamic process. A child who is a four on the developmental continuum—perhaps engaging a little bit but also a bit self-absorbed—won't necessarily be that way always. A comprehensive program may well help the child shift—become more engaged—from a four to a six or even to a nine or a ten on the scale.

So parents who are wondering if their child is on the autistic spectrum or not need to remember that it's not an all-or-nothing decision. If a child has delays, parents need to ask, "How do I make sure my child is moving ahead in a healthy way?" That outlook will keep all doors open for the child's emotional and intellectual growth.

Early and
Ongoing Signs of ASD

*Identifying and Helping
Babies and Children at Risk*

O ne of the benefits of the developmental model described in this
    book is that it encourages early commencement of treatment.
Rather than waiting to see full-blown symptoms before setting up a
treatment program, caregivers and clinicians pay attention to difficulties in the early stages of development. If they spot problems in the
ways a baby learns to look, listen, and move, all together in a rhythmic pattern; and to relate to caregivers; and to read and respond to
emotional signals, they can begin to address them immediately. The
earlier children at risk for or already showing symptoms of ASD begin
treatment—before longer periods of healthy development are missed
and symptoms become more debilitating—the better their chances for
developing normally in the long run.

   Our own research, as well as that of our colleagues, has identified
the core deficits of ASD described in Chapter 1. By observing both
typically developing infants and young children, and infants and
young children on a developmental pathway leading to ASD, we've

defined these deficits. By studying home videos of children who went on to develop ASD and those of children who did not, we have analyzed more fully the essential foundations of healthy development and the core deficits. We've also conducted studies of at-risk and typically developing populations to fine-tune our definitions and analysis. Our observations suggest that the core deficits of ASD express themselves gradually, beginning in early infancy, and can be identified as they emerge. By watching a child's progress toward certain healthy milestones, we can distinguish children developing normally from those with ASD and other developmental disorders. (The Greenspan Social-Emotional Growth Chart, which is now also part of the Bayley developmental scales kit and was validated on a representative population of 1,500 children [see References], can be used to determine an infant or young child's capacity to master healthy developmental foundations.)

In this chapter we describe the earliest signs of ASD, in contrast to the signs of healthy development, and outline the signs of ASD in children of any age. These signs indicate developmental difficulties that families and collaborating professionals can begin working on right away, even while a formal evaluation and intervention program is being organized. (In Part II we spell out what parents can and should do to help children overcome these difficulties.)

Biologically based challenges hinder the progress of children with ASD on the path of healthy functional emotional development. Depending on the severity of these biological challenges, a child with ASD begins to show delays in one of the first four developmental stages. Some master the first three stages before they show signs of a disorder; others get delayed in stage one. Young children who seem to have regressed (who have been developing normally but lose some of their abilities) often show clear problems in the fourth developmental stage, and sometimes show earlier vulnerabilities as well. Table 3.1 outlines the basic developmental stages and the earliest signs of ASD in infants related to each stage. The associated symptoms are also outlined.

Table 3.1 Early Signs of ASD in Infants and Young Children

Foundations for Relating, Communicating, and Thinking	Early Signs of Core Deficits of ASD	Associated Symptoms
Shared attention and regulation (begins at 0–3 months) Calm interest in and purposeful responses to sights, sound, touch, movement, and other sensory experiences (e.g., looking, turning to sounds)	Lack of sustained attention to different sights or sounds	Aimless or self-stimulatory behavior
Engagement and relating (begins at 2–5 months) Growing expressions of intimacy and relatedness (e.g., a gleam in the eye and joyful smiles initiated and sustained)	No engagement or only fleeting expressions of joy, rather than robust, sustained engagement	Self-absorption or withdrawal
Purposeful emotional interactions (begins at 4–10 months) A range of back-and-forth interactions, with emotional expressions, sounds, hand gestures, and the like used to convey intentions	No interactions or only brief back-and-forth interactions with little initiative (i.e., mostly responding)	Unpredictable (random or impulsive) behavior
Long chains of back-and-forth emotional signaling and shared problem-solving (e.g., joint attention) (begins at 10–18 months) Many social and emotional interactions in a row used for problem-solving (e.g., showing Dad a toy)	Inability to initiate and sustain many consecutive back-and-forth social interactions or exchanges of emotional signals	Repetitive or perseverative behavior
Creating ideas (begins at 18–30 months) Meaningful use of words or phrases and interactive pretend play with caregivers or peers	No words, or rote use of words (e.g., mostly repeats what is heard)	Echolalia and other forms of repetition of what's heard or seen
Building bridges between ideas: logical thinking (begins at 30–42 months) Logical connections between meaningful ideas ("Want to go outside *because* I want to play.")	No words, or memorized scripts, coupled with seemingly random, rather than logical, use of ideas	Irrational behavior or illogical or unrealistic use of ideas

Earliest Signs of ASD at Each Stage

Now, let's look in more detail at these signs, which an infant or very young child with ASD will show at one stage or another.

Stage One

A typical infant connects his emotions to his actions and sensations. For example, he sees his mother's big smile and hears her warm voice, and turns his head to see her. An infant at risk for ASD is often unable to form complete links between his emotions and his sensations and motor actions. Signs of this difficulty appear at a number of levels. First, he finds it hard to use movements purposefully to do things like turning to see his mother. Second, he may find it hard to regulate and coordinate movements in general. Movements may lack an organized pattern and may seem random. Third, the infant may have difficulty synchronizing his movements with his caregiver's.

Stage Two

At this stage, infants who can't connect sensory to emotional and motor experiences are unable to engage with others as richly and fully as infants without these problems. They may feel pleasure and experience a deep sense of intimacy, but demonstrating these feelings with joyous smiles and facial expressions and focused, pleasurable interest in their caregivers is difficult. Consequently, such interactions are briefer and the children take little initiative. Caregivers, without the magic of the baby's smile and joyful sounds, may be less drawn in and motivated to keep engaging and playing with him or her. However, if they can intuitively sense the baby's underlying delight (in spite of his difficulty in showing it), they may be able to woo the infant and sustain intimacy.

Stage Three

The delightful wordless dialogue that we usually see at this stage, involving the rapid exchange of facial expressions and other gestures, requires that a baby continually connect a sensation with the emotion the sensation produces and then connect the emotion to an appropriate motor response. Take a simple game: spotting the pacifier in Mother's hand, taking it, looking at it, and offering it back when mother holds out her hand. The baby must link the sight of the pacifier to the emotional response of pleasure or interest and then use the feeling of delight to initiate the motor response of reaching.

This is where we often see clearer signs of trouble in children at risk for autism, because such a continuous flow of back-and-forth signaling and gesturing is too difficult for children lacking the sensory-affect-motor connection. Infants at risk for autism may show fleeting responses and interactions, but find it hard to initiate and sustain them.

Stage Four

Children at risk for ASD almost always show clear signs of difficulty at this stage of social interaction and problem-solving. Even toddlers with marvelous receptive skills such as understanding words and even recognizing letters or numbers may have significant trouble with sustaining a chain of emotional and social communications. At most, they can sustain five or six exchanges, not the thirty-plus often required to solve a problem with someone else. The lack of this basic ability interferes with all the core skills that develop at this stage, including recognizing patterns, forming a sense of self, and beginning to construct and use symbols.

Stages Five, Six, and Beyond

Because children at risk for ASD seldom master stage four, they often do not advance into the creative use of words and symbols. They tend, at best, to use words repetitively or in a rote or scripted manner. Some do not talk at all. Some learn to use pictures or other visual symbols or to type. Higher levels of imaginative, creative, and logical thinking in subsequent stages, however, are possible only if the child learns to exchange emotional and social signals and use ideas in an emotionally meaningful manner.

In the following chapter and in Parts II and III, we offer detailed guidelines for encouraging healthy learning at each stage at the earliest possible time. As Part II reveals, if parents or other caregivers believe a child to be at risk, much can be done while waiting for a formal assessment.

Older Children and Adolescents

The signs of ASD in children beyond the toddler years and in adolescents and adults are similar to those described above. Table 3.2 shows the healthy traits that typically develop at each stage, the signs of ASD, and the associated symptoms.

We encourage parents and professionals who want to strengthen each of the core capacities in older children and adolescents to build on the activities described in Part II. Interactions with the child should be based on observations of what brings him or her pleasure and how he or she responds to touch, sound, sight, and movement. (Also see Part III, especially Chapter 15.)

Early Intervention

As more is learned about the developmental pathways leading to ASD, opportunities will increase for early identification of at-risk infants and young children and for starting treatment programs before severe symptoms and chronic patterns become established. Following are general guidelines for helpful early identification and treatment.

Early identification efforts, including screening, should involve the full range of the infant's emotional, social, intellectual, and related motor and sensory functioning so that risks for ASD and other developmental challenges can be ascertained. This approach prevents specialists from prematurely focusing on a presumed "magic window," that is, a specific behavior or physiologic response that determines a diagnosis. Researchers are nowhere near finding a magic window for ASD. In addition, appropriate screening practices (which look at the full range of expected functioning that is compromised in ASD) provide an important

Table 3.2 Signs of ASD in Older Children, Adolescents, and Adults

Foundations for Relating, Communicating, and Thinking	Signs of ASD (Core Deficits)	Associated Symptoms
Attention, engagement, and emotional interactions The ability to focus warmly on and pleasurably relate to another person and to initiate interactions	Fleeting, intermittent, or no engagement and interaction	Aimless, unpredictable, random, or self-stimulatory behaviors, or self-absorption or withdrawal
Continuous purposeful social interactions and shared problem-solving, including joint attention A combination of gestures and/or words employed as part of a continuous flow of social interaction in order to find something, negotiate, play with someone, or meet a new challenge. This includes joint attention and reading the social and emotional intentions of others.	Only a few back-and-forth interactions, with little initiative taken (i.e., mostly responding), or no interactions at all	Impulsive or repetitive (perseverative) behaviors
Creative and logical use of ideas Ideas used to understand and express needs, wishes, intentions, or feelings. In an older child or adult, this may be seen in meaningful conversation. This involves the ability to connect ideas together logically so that pretend play or conversations make sense.	Inability to use ideas, or ability to use ideas only in a fragmented or piecemeal way (no logical connections)	Echolalia, scripted language, or other forms of repetition of what's heard or seen, or illogical or unrealistic use of ideas
Abstract and reflective thinking The use of higher-level thinking skills, including giving multiple reasons for feelings or events, dealing with degrees of feelings or thoughts, reflecting on one's own and others' feelings and thoughts, and making inferences (drawing new, reasoned conclusions)	Thinking is rigid and concrete, lacking subtlety or nuance.	Exaggerated emotional reactions or avoidance of social and emotional situations (in part due to misperceptions or misreading of complex social interactions)

opportunity to identify a variety of related risks to healthy emotional, social, and intellectual development.

Early identification and intervention programs have a special role in work with infants and very young children. When risk factors or problems are detected early, the intervention program has two goals: to alleviate the identified risk or problems and to facilitate overall healthy emotional, social, and intellectual functioning. If an early intervention program focuses on particular behavior or symptoms but does not encourage—or impairs—healthy caregiver-child interactions that promote overall adaptive functioning, the program could create additional developmental challenges. For example, consider a nine-month-old baby who repetitively touches a toy. Intervention that focuses simply on discouraging that particular type of touching ignores the promotion of healthy, age-appropriate skills, such as exchanging smiles, vocalizations, and other gestures. On the other hand, an approach that seeks to transform the child's problem behavior into spontaneous interactions—for example, making a game out of alternately letting the child touch the toy and covering the toy—would not only help the infant overcome the problematic behavior but also promote healthy development.

The earlier the signs of ASD can be spotted and the earlier appropriate treatment started, the greater the chances of facilitating the foundations for healthy relating, communicating, and thinking—in other words, reversing the core deficits of autism.

Chapter 4

New Goals for Children with ASD

The DIR/Floortime Model

In the past, as we pointed out in Chapter 2, two models guided interventions for ASD. One, the behavioral model, was geared toward modifying surface behaviors and symptoms, such as aggression or noncompliance. Although this approach showed encouraging signs at first, a recent study indicates that children treated according to this model make only modest educational gains and realize little to no social or emotional benefits (see Smith, Groen, and Wynn, 2000, and Shea, 2004, in References). In addition, the model does not sufficiently take into account the individual ways children process information and respond to sensation (e.g., sensory processing and motor planning).

The other approach was to work on circumscribed cognitive skills as guided by the abilities expected at each age. Because it was thought that children with autism and other developmental problems learned best through repetition, they were drilled to memorize certain sequences, such as "This is a square; this is a circle." Although children taught this way could then reproduce a shape in a structured situation, they lacked a full understanding of the shape and what it meant. A child without developmental challenges, on the other hand, is often able to generalize concepts, to apply the concept of a square or a circle to many different squares and circles, and eventually to master geometry.

We have been able to go beyond these earlier approaches. Because every child and every family is unique, with their own special strengths and challenges, we developed an approach tailored to each child and involving families much more intensively than they have been in the past. Our DIR/Floortime model synthesizes the most reliable and current information about how the mind and brain develop and sets new standards of care for children with ASD and related developmental disorders. Three primary insights form the cornerstones of our work with infants, children, and adults:

- *Language and cognition, as well as emotional and social skills, are learned through relationships that involve emotionally meaningful exchanges.*

  We know now that the mind and brain grow most rapidly in the early years as a result of interactions with caregivers. These interactions, as we have described, have several critical features, including warmth and security, regulation, relatedness and engagement, back-and-forth emotional signaling and gesturing, problem-solving, use of ideas in a meaningful and functional way, and thinking and reasoning. Most essential to the development of the mind and brain are multiple interactions that provide a fundamental sense of relatedness. Children who are deprived of this relatedness (for example, in some orphanages) are held back in language and cognitive development and even, in severe cases, in their physical growth.

  Emotions lead development all the way, even to advanced abilities such as abstract thinking. To learn concepts such as fairness, children first need to have had the emotional experience of being treated fairly and unfairly. For example, giving a child a cookie while giving three cookies to his sibling quickly teaches a child what unfairness is. He then can abstract from that experience, creating categories of things that are fair and things that are unfair.

Language, cognition, and mathematical and quantity concepts are all learned through emotionally significant interactive experiences and relationships. In other words, emotions are the forces that enable us to learn. Teaching all children—particularly those with special needs—requires working with them in the contexts of the family and community, because it is within these contexts that relationships and emotional interactions occur.

- *Children vary in their underlying motor and sensory processing capacities.*

  Research in the past two decades has identified the main processing capacities underlying children's behavior. Children differ in their ways of responding to touch, sound, and other sensations; their auditory processing and language; their visual-spatial processing; and their motor planning and sequencing abilities. In terms of the last-named capacity, some children can do only repetitive one-step actions, such as banging a toy on the floor, or only two-step actions, such as putting a toy car in a garage and taking it out. Other children can take the car out of the garage, pretend to take it to Grandmother's house, make a tea party there, then bring the car back with some extra tea for Mommy, who is sitting back at the original house (a complex idea involving numerous steps). Many children with ASD have severe problems with motor planning and sequencing that underlie much of their repetitive behavior.

  Differences in the way children modulate sensation can also be seen early. Children who overreact to sound and touch hold their ears or push away from people who try to tickle them. Other children crave sensory input and want more touch or more noise. And some children who crave sensory input also get easily overloaded, so that it is difficult to keep them engaged. Children who underreact to touch or sound may become self-absorbed. In this way, the biological side of autism is expressed not in some global autistic pattern but through the individual ways children react to and comprehend the various sights, sounds, touches, and movement patterns in their environment and the ways they plan their actions. Work with the child's underlying processing differences can influence much of the child's behavior and help him or her adapt across a broad range of abilities, rather than just developing isolated cognitive skills or behavior.

In addition, by understanding how a child's unique processing profile plays out in his daily life, parents and professionals can tailor the environment to suit his profile so that he can learn. A child who overreacts to sound and becomes overwhelmed in a busy classroom may learn quite well in a corner of a classroom with one other child. Meanwhile, parents, occupational therapists, and speech pathologists can work to strengthen the child's individual processing abilities.

- *Progress in all areas of development is interrelated.*

Historically, the various aspects of early childhood development were considered separately. In terms of motor development, there was a timetable for sitting up, walking, and so forth. A language development timetable predicted when children would make first sounds, first words, then sentences. In different areas of cognitive development, a child should by a certain age be able to search in someone's hand for an object or stack blocks in a certain way. In social and emotional development, the child should, according to schedule, begin to greet others, play with peers, and start pretending.

We now understand that the lines of early development are interrelated. Rather than assessing language skills, motor skills, and social-emotional skills separately, we should look at how well these abilities are integrated in a child, how the components work together as a whole.

Based on research in the past twenty years and on the six core ability stages outlined in chapter 3, we've put together a developmental road map for the "mental team" of language, cognition, and emotions. We have identified the particular motor, language, and visual-spatial processing skills needed to support each stage. Within this integrated developmental picture, we can assess a child's level of development.

The DIR Model

In the name "developmental, individual-difference, relationship-based approach," "developmental" refers to the six stages or levels described in Chapter 3, "individual-difference" refers to the unique way a child processes information, and "relationship-based" refers to our understanding of the learning relationships that enable a child to progress in his development.

The DIR model builds on the three insights articulated above to create intervention programs based on which of the six developmental levels a child has reached, on her individual processing profile, and on the interactive relationships that best support her development. The DIR method of analysis thus enables parents, educators, and clinicians to make assessments and plan treatment programs tailored to individual children with ASD.

Although the DIR model is often referred to as the Floortime model, Floortime is actually one component of a comprehensive DIR-based intervention program. Floortime focuses on creating emotionally meaningful learning interactions that encourage the six basic developmental capacities; Parts II and III of this book explore Floortime more fully. As described in Part IV, other components of a comprehensive DIR program may include semistructured problem-solving activities, speech therapy, occupational therapy, peer play opportunities, and more. The DIR model has helped many children with ASD learn to relate to adults and peers with warmth and intimacy, communicate meaningfully with emotional gestures and words, and think with a high level of abstract reasoning and empathy.

These three cornerstones of healthy development are the basis for the goals we establish for children with ASD. Mastering social situations, acquiring the skills necessary to sit and listen, and learning one's ABCs are worthwhile goals; certainly every parent, clinician, and educator wants all children to attain them. But these situational and skill-specific goals should be addressed within the context of overall emotional and cognitive development. Our DIR model allows us to integrate emotional, social, intellectual, and educational goals for each child.

Stages of Development

Over the past twenty-five years of working with children with special needs, we have defined stages that we call the functional emotional developmental capacities (FEDCs). Tables 3.1 and 3.2 show the first several of these stages. Mastery of these stages is essential not only for normal emotional development but also for cognitive development, higher-level thinking, and a fully developed sense of self. These stages are in many ways the centerpiece of the DIR model: assessment gauges children's progress through these stages, and treatment programs help children master the stages that give them difficulty and return to a healthy developmental pathway, mastering each subsequent stage in turn.

Six primary stages and three advanced stages mark children's development; later stages characterize continuing development in adolescents and adults. This model has opened the door to a fuller understanding of the interconnectedness of emotions and intellect. Most cognitive theories have not explained how to promote the highest levels of reflective thinking, because they have ignored the role of emotion. In the 1940s and 1950s, researchers and clinicians began to look more closely at the influence of early emotional experiences on learning and personality development. Other studies followed that looked at specific aspects of emotional and social experience such as attachment. Building on this earlier research, the DIR framework's road map of the most vital emotional experiences shows, for the first time, how emotions lead to symbolic thinking and, thus, to intelligence. (See *The First Idea: How Symbols, Language, and Intelligence Evolved from our Primate Ancestors to Modern Humans*, by Stanley I. Greenspan and Stuart G. Shanker, in References.)

Newborn infants experience a limited number of global emotional states, such as calmness or distress. Through interactions with their caregivers, they begin to differentiate and elaborate these states; for example, a mother's soothing voice enables the infant to experience pleasure. Through continuing human interactions, infants learn to associate emotions with physical sensations. Every experience a child undergoes has both a physical side and an emotional quality. A hug feels tight—that is its physical property. A hug can also make the baby feel secure or frightened—that is its emotional aspect. A surface feels cold and also feels pleasant or uncomfortable. A mobile looks colorful and is also interesting or disturbing.

Children differ in their perception of sensations. Certain types of touch or sound may soothe one child but overstimulate another. These physical differences—which are present both in children developing normally and in those with challenges such as ASD—influence both a child's physical and emotional reaction to a sensation.

As a parent or caregiver reads and responds to an infant's emotional reaction, interaction begins and development is facilitated. Her developing central nervous system helps her organize patterns. She learns, for example, that her emotional expression leads to a caregiver response. In this way she learns to make responses purposeful, to use these responses as problem-solving tools, and to observe larger and larger patterns. This is how intelligence begins. As we explain in *The First Idea*, these exchanges become more complex, they lead to symbolic thinking and progressively higher levels of intelligence.

Each stage of functional emotional development involves the simultaneous mastery of both emotional and cognitive abilities. For example, a baby learns causality through the exchange of emotional signals: I smile and you smile back. She then uses this knowledge to understand that pulling a string, for example, rings a bell. This early lesson is both emotional and cognitive. Also, a baby must be engaged in a relationship with a caregiver if loving feelings are to become part of an exchange of social signals and if she is to learn to solve problems and see patterns. Emotional ideas—"I feel sad"—precede logical bridges between them—"I feel sad because you won't play with me."

In some cases, a child masters one of these stages of emotional development only partially. When this occurs, emotional development may proceed but in a constricted form. Relationships may be more superficial and less intimate; empathy for other people may be limited to only a few feelings. Brief summaries follow of the stages of emotional development. (These are described in more detail in Part II, along with ways to encourage them.)

Stage One: Regulation and Interest in the World

Within the first few months of life, babies learn to transfer their emotions from their own inner sensations, such as a gas bubble in the tummy, to the world outside themselves. To do that, they have to *want* to look or listen, to pay attention to the outside world. Caregivers entice this desire with gentle touches, soothing voices, big smiles, and expressive eyes—all of which a baby finds emotionally pleasurable. This process begins immediately after birth. Infants only days old react to sensations emotionally, preferring the sound or smell of mother, for example, to all other sounds or scents. They suck more vigorously when offered sweet liquids. The emotional responses produced by different sensations encourage babies to try to discriminate between various sensations. Intelligence is forming as babies use all their senses to perceive the world and find patterns, such as the difference between mother's voice and father's voice.

If early sensations are unpleasant, babies tune out the outside world. Since each baby has an individual response to various sights, sounds, touches, scents, and movements, attentive caregivers can figure out which sensations the baby favors. Some babies are sensitive and require gentle soothing. Some are underreactive and require more energetic wooing. Some need very pleasurable emotional sounds or signals to learn to look or listen.

The focus of this stage is what we call shared attention: to learn and interact socially, children need to be able to focus, be calm, and actively take in information from their experiences with others; from what they see, hear, smell, touch, and taste; and from the way they move.

Stage Two: Engaging and Relating

With warm nurturing, babies become progressively more invested and interested in certain people. From day one, babies begin to distinguish primary caregivers from others. By two to five months, they express preference with joyful smiles and happy coos. When babies become interested in their primary caregiver as a special person who brings pleasure as well as occasional unhappiness, not only do emotional interactions begin to flower, but a new level of intelligence is reached as well. They now learn to distinguish between the pleasures of interacting with the human world and interest in inanimate objects. The pleasure babies receive from their caregivers enables them to decipher patterns in the caregivers' voices and facial expressions that reflect the caregivers' feelings and intentions. Thus begins the journey of learning to recognize patterns and organize perceptions into meaningful categories.

Many parents of children with ASD or other special needs become frustrated when their child is hard to engage. In these situations, sometimes parents are advised to force the relatedness and try to condition the child to "look." We often see parents mistakenly hold their child's head so he has to look at them, or keep touching his face to cue him to look. They do this because they've been told to. But such actions do not promote the desire to look in the child.

When we talk about engaging and relating, we mean doing so from the heart—the way all parents want their child to engage and relate to them. We mean that the child has the *desire* to be part of a relationship. Learning how to help children with ASD with this second cornerstone—as will be described later—not only builds strength in this core capacity but also starts to offset the distressing symptoms related to withdrawal or self-absorption.

Stage Three: Intentionality and Two-Way Communication

By about six months of age, babies begin transforming emotions into signals for communication. For this to happen, caregivers need to read and respond to babies' signals and challenge the babies to read and respond to theirs. Through these exchanges, babies begin to engage in back-and-forth emotional signaling, or two-way communication. For example, a baby smiles at his mother; he gets a smile back, so he smiles again. This is what we call a circle of communication. His smile becomes purposeful: he smiles in order to get a smile in return. Different facial expressions, vocalizations, and gestures become part of this signaling. For children with ASD, this can be a hard milestone to achieve.

A child who has mastered or is mastering this essential skill can begin communicating without words, letting his parents know in a rudimentary way what he wants. A child who is able to make her needs known expresses less frustration through yelling, screaming, and crying than a less skilled child. (Diffused aggression and impulsivity—for example, grabbing a toy from another child instead of pointing to it—are really ways in which the child tries to get her needs met without communicating them.) Mastering purposeful two-way communication also helps keep a child from being repetitive or perseverative, because if she's communicating, she's engaging in continuously new purposeful behaviors.

It is also at this stage of shared communication that logic and a sense of reality begin. By eight months, a typically developing baby can participate in many causal, or logical, interactions. Babies gradually begin to apply these new lessons to perceiving the spatial world and then to planning actions. A baby's eyes follow a rattle as it falls to the ground, or he looks at and touches his father's hand that just hid the rattle. This sense of causality marks the beginning of a sense of reality, which is based on distinguishing the actions of others from one's own: there is a "me" doing something to a "not me." Consciousness also is growing as babies experience their own will and sense of purpose.

Stage Four: Social Problem-solving, Mood Regulation, and Formation of a Sense of Self

Babies make momentous strides between nine and eighteen months. In this stage, they take two-way communication and use it to solve problems. They learn to take Mother's hand, gesture for her to open the door to the yard, and then point to the swing to show they want a ride.

Meanwhile, mother is responding to each of the child's gestures or vocalizations, closing a circle of communication each time. During this stage social problem-solving emerges: children use patterns that involve three or four steps toward achieving a desired result. Later this leads to putting words together in a sentence and to scientific thinking and math. All of this progress is built on emotional interactions that become increasingly complex, leading to higher levels of intelligence. Let's look at each of these new developments in turn.

Shared Social Problem-solving.   Children who take a parent by the hand to search for a toy understand multiple elements of a pattern. These elements include their own emotional needs and desires, the action patterns involved in getting a toy, the visual-spatial aspects of going from ground level to the upper shelf where the toy resides, the vocal pattern involved in getting a parent's attention (a whimper or demanding grunt), and the social patterns involved in working with parents toward a goal. Pattern recognition, or seeing how such elements fit together, is learned even before language develops significantly. Elaborate negotiations or play with others make it possible for a child to experience the world in larger integrated patterns. A child who is withdrawn or finds interacting with others difficult won't experience or fully learn to recognize a broad range of patterns.

Regulating Mood and Behavior.   In daily loving exchanges and struggles with caregivers, toddlers learn to tame catastrophic emotions like fear and rage. In a young infant, anger is explosive and sadness seems global. In stage four, children learn to modulate intense feelings through emotional signaling, or baby-to-caregiver negotiation. Once children are capable of exchanging rapid emotional signals with their caregivers, they can express how they feel with a signal before the feeling becomes too intense. If they are annoyed at waiting for food, they can point at food or make sounds of annoyance. A sensitive mother may quickly gesture back to show that she understands and that she'll get the food more quickly, or that the child needs to wait a minute. Whatever her response, the child is getting an immediate emotional signal in return. He can then negotiate with more signals and further modulate the feeling. Different feelings, from joy to sadness to anger, can become part of fine-tuned exchanges with patient, caring adults.

For a variety of reasons, children may not get this needed experience. Perhaps they have motor problems and can't gesture or signal well, or they have difficulty perceiving their caregiver's vocal or facial expressions. Or perhaps they have caregivers who don't signal back or are intrusive. Such factors sometimes cause deficits in what would otherwise be a fine-tuned interactive system. When children can't express their feelings clearly enough to get a response, or don't get a response for other reasons, they may give up and become self-absorbed. Or their emotions and behavior may become more intense and they may bite and hit. In these latter cases, parents often seek help (sometimes in the form of medication) for the child's "aggression." But with some coaching, parents can learn how to help the child express what she needs and how to read her signals and respond consistently and calmly, and the child often can become a well-regulated toddler within a few months. But without such help from caregivers, the child—left in the clutches of powerful emotions—may become even more aggressive and impulsive or, alternatively, withdrawn and depressed.

Forming the Earliest Sense of Self.   As toddlers go from islands of intentional behavior to whole patterns of multiple problem-solving exchanges, these exchanges become part of their self-definition. The toddler is no longer expressing just one or two feelings and getting a response from a caregiver, but many different feelings and desires. Out of these, the toddler perceives patterns—his own feelings and desires, the caregiver's responses, his next feelings and his actions, and so forth. Over time, these various patterns become identified as an "I" and a "you." An integrated sense of self, interacting with an integrated sense of another, emerges. In other words, happy "I" and angry "I" are now seen as parts of one person, as are "nice Mommy" and "angry Mommy."

Children at this stage also learn how the physical world works: turning this handle causes a clown to pop up out of the box; pushing this object makes a big noise. Seeing the world in patterns increases understanding of how it works and leads to expectations and mastery. Children use this ability to distinguish from among many patterns in the emotional expressions of others those meaning safety and comfort from those meaning danger. They can tell approval from disapproval, acceptance from rejection. Children start to use this awareness to respond differently to people depending on their emotional tone. This ability to decipher human exchanges and pick up emotional cues before any words are exchanged is a supersense that often operates faster than our conscious awareness. In fact, it is the foundation of our social life.

This stage figures prominently in our observations of the developmental pathways leading to autism. Children with autism—even those who have above-average IQs and verbal skills—have difficulty making inferences, empathizing with others, and dealing with other people's emotions. In studying such children over time, we have found that most, including those who seemed to be doing well at first and "regressed" at age two or later, did not fully master the emotional interactions basic to such pattern-recognizing skills. While some of these children could do a little emotional signaling with caregivers, they could not fully initiate and engage sufficiently in shared problem-solving or wordless dialogue to regulate their behavior and moods. They were therefore unable to develop the full range of higher-level abilities. As will be described later, we are conducting research that says children with autism have a biologically based difficulty connecting their emotions to their emerging ability to plan and sequence their actions (see Appendix B). Without the guidance of needs and desires, complex interactions that require many steps are not possible, and actions stay simple or become repetitive. Fortunately, we have found that extra practice with meaningful emotional interactions can help.

Stage Five: Creating Symbols and Using Words and Ideas
By age one and a half, children's motor skills have developed to the point that they can regulate mouth muscles and vocal chords, and their

intellectual skills have progressed to the point that they can begin to use language to express themselves.

To understand and use words and language, children must first be able to engage in complex emotional signaling, which allows them to separate actions from perceptions and hold images in their minds. They must also be able to connect these images with their emotions to give them meaning, thereby forming symbols and ideas. (*The First Idea* describes how this process occurs.) Language ability thus arises because images acquire meaning through many emotionally relevant experiences and exchanges. For example, an eighteen-month-old feels a surge of affection for mother. Whereas at an earlier stage he might have given her a big hug, now he can use symbols to express his affection by saying, "Love you." He can symbolize hitting and screaming by saying, "Me mad!"

Typically people think about using ideas in terms of speaking, using words. But a child can say "car," "table," "chair," and so on without using ideas in the way we mean here. Many children with ASD script, or repeat words over and over again: "car, table, chair, car, table, chair." But by "using ideas," we mean using words, pictures, or symbols meaningfully to communicate something. In general it's much better for children to use single words interactively with meaning than to recite whole sentences or paragraphs they have memorized.

The functional use of ideas and symbols can be seen in imaginative play. At this stage, children use pretend play to symbolize real or imagined events such as tea parties or monster attacks. They also now use symbols to manipulate ideas in their minds without actually having to carry out actions. This allows new flexibility in reasoning, thinking, and problem-solving. Language and the use of symbols become more complex from the beginning of this stage to the end of the following one, moving through the following levels:

- Words and actions are used together to express ideas.
- Words convey bodily feelings: "My stomach hurts."
- Instead of actions, words are used, conveying intent: "I hit you."

- Words convey ideas based on global feelings: "I hate you." The feelings are generally polarized (that is, all good or all bad).
- Words are used to signal something going on inside oneself that makes possible a consideration of many possible actions: "I feel hungry; what do we have to eat?"
- Words are used to convey more differentiated feelings that are not necessarily tied to action: "I'm a little lonely" or "I'm getting frustrated."

The symbolic thinking that leads to language development also gives rise to higher levels of intelligence in many domains, including the visual-spatial arena and the ability to plan actions that serve symbolic goals. It is easy to see why children with a biological difficulty in connecting needs and emotions to actions and words have trouble moving through these stages.

Stage Six: Emotional Thinking, Logic, and a Sense of Reality

At about two and a half years of age, children show increasing ability to connect symbols together logically, making possible thinking and reflecting. A child might ask, "Mommy, where car?" or respond to a parent's "Where is it?" with "Over there!" When you ask, "Why do you want the toy car, sweetie?" the child who can connect ideas logically is able to answer, "Play." That child is linking two ideas together—your idea "why?" with his own idea "play." At this stage, children learn how one event leads to another ("The wind blew and knocked over my card house"); how ideas operate across time ("If I'm good now, I'll get a treat later"); and how ideas operate across space ("Mom is not here but she is close by"). Ideas can also help explain emotions ("I'm happy because I got a toy") and organize knowledge of the world.

Connecting one's own idea to someone else's logically is the basis for a new understanding of reality. Children now connect internal experiences with external experiences, and they distinguish the two—that is, categorize subjective and objective experiences. Emotional investment in relationships enables children to recognize the difference between what's inside them, their fantasies, and the ideas and actual behavior of others. Logical thinking leads to new skills, such as debating, math, and scientific reasoning. Children can now invent things, such as a new game, and play games with rules.

On a typical developmental trajectory, a child masters these first six milestones by age four or five, setting the foundation for the milestones to follow. If the child has ASD or other developmental problems, mastery of these stages may take much longer. For the following, more advanced stages, all individuals—even those without ASD or special needs—have their own timetable.

Stage Seven: Multicausal and Triangular Thinking

From simple causal thinking, children progress to recognizing multiple causes. For example, if a friend doesn't want to play, instead of concluding, "He hates me," the child can think, "Maybe he wants to play with someone else today," or, "Maybe he doesn't want to play with me because I always play Nintendo. Maybe if we do something different he'll come over." Grasping multicausality enables a child to engage in "triangular thinking." For example, he can compare two friends: "I like Pat better than Sam because Pat has great toys." At home, if mother is annoyed, the child can go to father to get attention.

To learn multicausal thinking, children must be able to invest emotion in more than one possibility. For example, they must be able to consider a second friend as a play partner, rather than depend on just one friend. At this stage, children can understand family dynamics in terms of relationships among different people, rather than just in terms of whether they get their own needs met.

Stage Eight: Gray-Area, Emotionally Differentiated Thinking

Multicausal and triangular thinking enable children to progress to understand the varying degrees or relative influence of feelings, events, or phenomena (for instance, "I'm only a little mad"). In school, they not only look at multiple reasons for events but also weigh the relative importance of these reasons. With peers, they can compare feelings that differ in a graduated way and negotiate the politics of the playground, understanding and participating in social hierarchies involving different factors such as athletic skills, academic abilities, likability, and so forth. New ways to solve problems, especially group problems with multiple options, are now possible because children can compromise.

Stage Nine: A Growing Sense of Self and Reflection on an Internal Standard

By puberty and early adolescence, more complex emotional interactions help children progress to thinking in relationship to an internal standard and a growing sense of self. Children can now judge experience. For example, children can say for the first time, "I was angrier than usual." They can look at peers' behavior and say, "It may be OK for them to do that, but it's not the right thing for me."

Children at this stage learn to make inferences and to think in more than one frame of reference at the same time. They create new ideas from existing ones. They can consider the future as well as the past and present. The ability to think in two perspectives at the same time separates individuals who remain somewhat more concrete from those who develop the higher levels of intelligence and reflection that are characteristic of healthy adolescent and mature adult thinking.

After the nine functional emotional developmental capacities are reached, people continue to develop throughout life. Adolescents and adults progress through as many as seven more stages. Seeing the full trajectory of the human journey may help parents and caregivers of children with autism to realize that human development doesn't stop, either for those with or without ASD and other special needs. These stages include:

- An expanded sense of self that includes, for example, family and community relationships
- The ability to reflect on one's personal future
- A stable, separate sense of self (which allows young adults to remain secure when separating from their nuclear families)

- Intimacy and commitment (including long-term commitments such as marriage, home ownership, and a career)
- Parenthood and other nurturing roles
- Broadening perspectives on time, space, the life cycle, and the larger world
- "The wisdom of the ages": a sense of responsibility to the environment and future generations and a sense of perspective on one's place in the grand scheme. (This may be the most challenging of the adult stages because such wisdom must develop while declining physical health and mental ability may cause the individual to regress rather than keep growing.)

Part II of this book addresses how to promote each of the basic stages of development in children with ASD and other challenges, thereby laying the foundation for movement into the advanced stages.

Part II

⊠ ⊠ ⊠

Families First

*How Families Can Use the DIR Model to
Promote Relating, Communicating, and Thinking*

Chapter 5

The "Family First" Initiative

P arents, family members, and other primary caregivers, together with
pediatricians and other primary health care providers, have intimate knowledge of a child's development. With this knowledge they
can spot the first signs of emerging problems—the earlier, the better—
and begin to help children at risk. The "Family First" initiative is a new
effort by the Floortime Foundation (see References) to emphasize and
support the primary role of parents in a child's development. In Part I,
we identified the early signs of ASD and the goals of healthy development. Not offered as a way for parents to diagnose their child themselves, these signs can instead help parents get to know their child well
enough to detect any problems as soon as possible.

This chapter lays out the very first steps parents and other caregivers
can take to start helping children who show problems. A Family First approach enables parents to help the child to learn to relate, communicate,
and think while waiting for a professional screening, comprehensive
evaluation, and the start of educational and therapeutic programs, and
also after such programs are under way. Even if a screening does not identify ASD or other problems, this approach can only strengthen healthy
development. If a child does show developmental delays and an evaluation suggests the need for a comprehensive treatment program, these initial steps parents carry out on their own can be refined and expanded
with the help of an intervention team. Screening, evaluation, and planning of treatment take time. The advantage of a Family First approach is

that children are helped early on when their nervous systems are growing most rapidly. If a formal intervention program is needed, the parents and the professional team can then work together as full collaborators in orchestrating a program to enhance the child's development.

As we have discussed, the children with ASD and other special needs who make the most developmental progress are those who are engaged during most of their waking hours in healthy learning interactions tailored to their unique developmental needs. That's why families must be at the center of any intervention program. The Family First concept is supported by mounting evidence that, as discussed in Part I, certain formative child-caregiver interactions are essential for healthy social, emotional, and intellectual development and that these same practices can prevent or lessen the degree of developmental delay and can facilitate progress in infants and young children at risk for or already showing difficulties, including ASD.

The Family First initiative begins with identifying the child's age-expected abilities or goals (outlined in Part I). Parents and other primary caregivers then focus on working preventively with children at the appropriate stage. Below are brief examples of activities caregivers can engage in with infants and young children to strengthen the building blocks for healthy development. Each of the goals will be discussed in depth in Chapters 6–10.

Many of these activities are what parents do anyway with their children. They are best carried out by building on the child's natural interests and wooing her into the activity. The key is to have fun together; always look for signs of pleasure, such as a big smile, happy sounds, and a gleam in the child's eyes. These activities are most helpful when done for at least fifteen to twenty minutes many times a day when the child is most alert and available. Families may come up with their own activities that meet the same goals.

Stage One

To facilitate *shared attention and regulation*, observe the baby's unique style of hearing, seeing, touching, smelling, and moving. For example, notice what types of sounds (high or low pitches, slow or fast rhythms) help her to look and listen. See what types of touch (gentle and feathery or gentle and firm) help her to be calm, comfortable, and happy. Harness all her senses in enjoyable ways to entice her into the world. Keep paying attention to the baby's unique ways of enjoying the world as she masters the subsequent developmental milestones. (See Chapter 6.)

- *The "look and listen" game:* Face-to-face with the baby, smile and talk to him about his cute mouth, sparkly eyes, and little nose. By slowly moving your animated face to the right or left, try to capture the baby's attention for a few seconds. This game can be played while holding the baby in your arms, or you can hover near her when she's reclining in an infant seat or lying in another person's arms.
- *The "soothe me" game:* Settle into a comfortable rocking chair and enjoy slow, rhythmic rocking with the baby when she's fussy or tired or when you simply want to cuddle her. As you soothingly touch the baby's head, arms, legs, tummy, back, feet, and hands and relax into a lulling rocking rhythm, gently move her little fingers and toes in a "This Little Piggy" game. You can move her arms, legs, fingers, and toes when you change her diaper, too.

Stage Two

To facilitate *engagement and relating,* observe what kinds of interactions— silly sounds, kisses, tickles, or favorite games—bring the baby or child pleasure. Peekaboo and hide-the-toy-under-the-box are visual games that delight most babies, and rhythmic clapping games like patty-cake will especially intrigue babies with auditory strengths. Moving trucks delight toddlers, and imaginative dramas bring joy to most preschoolers. Make the most of the child's "magic moments" of availability and relaxed alertness. Tune in to the baby's or child's rhythms, to his emotions and how he uses his senses and movements. Follow his interests, even if this involves just making silly noises, and you will foster pleasure and closeness. Instead of competing for attention with a toy, become part of it; for example, put a block the child especially likes on your head and make a funny face. (See Chapter 6.)

- *The smiling game:* Use words and funny faces to entice the baby to smile broadly or produce other pleased facial expressions, such as widened eyes.
- *The "Dance with me" sound and movement game:* Try to inspire the baby to make sounds and move her arms, legs, or torso in rhythm with your voice and head movements. You might say, "Are you going to dance with me, sweetheart? Oh, I bet you can—I know you can!" while looking for a sparkle of delight in her eyes.

Stage Three

To facilitate *purposeful emotional interactions*, be very animated as you exchange facial expressions, sounds, and gestures, as well as words and pretend dramas, with the child. Go for the twinkle in the child's eye that lets you know she's alert and enjoying the exchange. Treat all of a child's behavior—even if it seems random—as purposeful. For instance, if she flaps her hands in excitement, you might use this as the basis for an interactive "flap your hands" dance move. If her play seems a little aimless as she pushes a car back and forth, you might announce that your doll has a special delivery letter that needs to be carried straightaway to one of her favorite television characters.

At first, help your child by making her goals easier to achieve. For instance, you may move a bright new ball closer to her after she points her finger and indicates that she wants it. Then, encourage the child's initiative by challenging her to do things, such as putting her teddy bear to bed at night, or climbing onto your shoulders while the two of you are roughhousing, rather than you picking her up yourself. (See Chapter 7.)

- *The funny sound, face, and feeling game:* Notice the sounds and facial expressions the baby naturally uses to express joy, annoyance, surprise, or any other feeling, and mirror these sounds and facial expressions back to him in a playful way. See if you can get a response in return.

- *The circle-of-communication game:* Try to see how many back-and-forth interactions you can get going each time the baby pats your nose and you make a funny squeal or squawk in response. Or see how many times he will try to open your hand when you've hidden an intriguing object inside. Each time the baby follows his interests and takes your bait, he is closing a circle of communication.

Stage Four

To facilitate *shared problem-solving*, create extra steps in pretend dramas. For example, announce, "This car won't move! What shall we do?" Create interesting barriers or obstacles to the child's goals. Work up to a continuous flow of communication. Many toddlers can string together thirty, forty, even fifty circles of communication with your help. Be animated and show your feelings through your voice and facial expressions to help the child clarify her intentions. If she vaguely points to a toy and grunts, you might feign confusion, put on a puzzled expression, and fetch the "wrong" toy. The child's gestures and vocalizations will become more elaborate and perhaps heated as she works harder to make her wishes understood. Increase the child's ability to plan her movements and use her senses and imitative skills in different circumstances, such as through hide-and-seek and treasure hunt games. (See Chapter 7.)

- *The working-together game:* Note the toddler's natural interest in various toys—dolls, stuffed animals, trucks, balls, and so forth—and create a problem that she needs your help to solve around that favorite toy.
- *The copycat game:* Copy the toddler's sounds and gestures and see if you can entice her to mirror your funny faces, sounds, movements, and dance steps. Eventually, add words to the game and

then use the words in a purposeful manner to help her meet a need—for example, by saying "Doll" or "Get up!"

Stage Five

To facilitate *creating ideas*, challenge the child to express his needs, desires, or interests. Foster situations in which he wants to express his feelings or intentions. Encourage him to use ideas both in imaginative play and in realistic verbal interactions. Remember the "words, action, affect" (WAA) guideline: always combine your words or ideas with your affect (expression of feeling) and actions. Encourage the use of all types of ideas; be open to all emotions or themes the child is inclined to explore. Incorporate ideas in the form of pictures, signs, and complex spatial designs, as well as words. (See Chapter 8.)

- *Let's chitchat.* If the child is verbal, see how many circles of communication you can have using words, phrases, or short sentences and focusing on her interests. You can even turn a child's single-word response into a long chat. For instance, if the family is at the playground and the child climbs onto a swing and says, "Push!" you might reply, "Who should push you?" She's likely to say, "Mommy do it," and you can shake your head and say, "Mommy can't now. Who else?" She'll probably turn to her father and ask, "Daddy do it?" and so forth.
- *Let's pretend:* Initially, encourage the child's imagination by helping her stage familiar interactions during pretend play. Then entice her into introducing new plot twists: jump into the drama she has started by becoming a dog, cat, superhero, or some other character, ham it up, and see how long you can keep it going. Challenge her dolls or teddy bears to feed, hug, or kiss each other, to cook or go off to the park and play. From time to time, switch from becoming a character in one of the child's dramas to taking on the role of a narrator or sideline commentator. Your comments will thicken the plot. Periodically summarize the action and encourage the child to move the drama along.

Stages Six and Seven

To facilitate *logical thinking,* challenge the child to close all his circles of communication using ideas, both during pretend play and in reality-based conversations. Challenge him to link different ideas or subplots in a drama. In this way, you help him build bridges between ideas. Pull him back on track by acting confused if his thinking is a little piece-meal or fragmented: "Hold on a minute—I thought you were talking about our neighbor, but now you're talking about sandwiches. I'm lost! Which thing do you want to talk about?" Challenge the child with open-ended questions to help him refocus logically.

If the child avoids responding to your open-ended questions, provide multiple choices of answers. Throw out some silly possibilities: "Did the elephant or the iguana visit your classroom today?" Encourage the child to give reasons for feelings in both pretend dramas and reality-based discussions—"Why are you so happy (or sad or angry)?"—and challenge him to give his opinion rather than recite facts. Debate and negotiate with the child rather than simply stating rules, unless the rule is essential, such as "no hitting."

Challenge the child during real-life conversations and pretend play to incorporate concepts about the past, present, and future. For instance, you might ask make-believe cowboy questions such as, "What are the cowboys going to do tomorrow?" Encourage understanding of quantity concepts: negotiate with the child when he asks you for an extra cookie or an extra slice of pizza, or speculate on how many cups of tea should be served to each doll at the tea party (see Chapter 9).

- *The director game:* See how many plot shifts or new story lines the child can initiate as you play make-believe games together. If the tea party play becomes a little repetitive or lacks direction, subtly challenge the child to thicken the plot by announcing something like, "I'm so full of tea my tummy's sloshing! What can we do next?"
- *The "Why should I?" game:* When the child wants you to do things for him, gently tease him with the response "Why should I?" and see how many reasons he can give you. Then offer a compromise,

such as "Let's do it together," when he wants you to get his toy out of the closet or pick out a new outfit to wear.

These first steps may help parents become aware of any problems or delays and also encourage development at each level. If the child appears to be at risk for ASD, these fundamentals will need more in-depth work. Sometimes children are older when the problems are caught. The following chapters in Part II explore more extensively how families and other caregivers can create experiences to support each stage of healthy development as part of treatment using the DIR approach. Part III shows how such interactions are strengthened through Floortime.

Chapter 6

Fostering Attention and Engagement

Bringing Your Child into a Shared World

Robbie, a sweet-natured seventeen-month-old boy with big brown eyes, had a receptive speech delay that put him several months behind in his development. He also appeared underreactive, tended to repeat meaningless actions when put in unfamiliar situations, and was difficult to engage. His parents tried to interact with him often, but wanted to know what else they could do to help Robbie engage more fully in all situations and learn to communicate his thoughts and feelings more clearly with them.

As Chapter 4 showed, the heart of the DIR/Floortime model, and the first step in helping any child with ASD, is engagement—entering the child's world and helping her enter into a shared world with others. Because difficulty with attention and with engagement are the first core deficits of autism, working with the child on these should be the first goal of parents, educators, and other caregivers.

Engagement: The First Step

Engagement (which follows attention) is critical because most learning in the early years of life occurs through human interaction. Engagement helps a child feel trusting, intimate, and warm—the beginning of social and emotional development. As we said in Chapter 4, a child learns causality and logic—how and why things happen—by signaling to a parent with expressions, sounds, or gestures and getting a response. For this learning to occur, the child has to be engaged. Early engagement is crucial even for the child's physical development—babies who are deprived of this engagement may become listless and fail to thrive.

When a child is isolated in her world, she may seem calm and regulated and even appear to be relaxed and having a good time. But many children who have become verbal have told us that in their preverbal state they felt alone and isolated and were just trying to stay calm. They didn't know they could experience the joy of relationships. Later on, when they had learned to relate to others but regressed temporarily because of stress or overload into a more self-absorbed or self-stimulatory, perseverative state, we would ask them what they were feeling. They would say they felt no pleasure in that more isolated state. Sometimes caregivers think they challenge children too much when they pull them into a shared world, but if done in the right way—with warmth, joy, and trust—the process is pleasurable for the child. An isolated, disengaged child, on the other hand, is not a happy child.

When children experience joyful relationships, many fundamental things happen. Relatedness motivates the child to look and listen, to pay attention to sights, sounds, smells, and other sensations outside herself. If a child does not feel close to you the caregiver, why would she turn toward your voice, listen to what you say, or even try to understand your words? Why would a child be interested in seeing what's on your nose, or how your hair feels, or what color your eyes are—unless she is interested in you?

Being engaged also helps children regulate themselves, because it encourages them to focus on the primary caregiver. Hearing the tenderness and warmth in a parent's voice helps an overexcited child calm down; seeing the parent's warm, gentle smile gives an upset child solace. Once a child has learned to focus on familiar people in familiar situations, eventually she will be able to do this with unfamiliar ones as well.

There's a huge difference between a child looking at you the caregiver because she is conditioned to or because you won't let her look away, and the child *wanting* to look—finding joy in looking. Obviously, if the child wants to be part of a relationship with you, she'll want to look at you at least from time to time. If she averts her eyes because your smile is too bright and it overwhelms her, she still wants to be with you but may be a little more shy and cautious. (Many adults avert their gaze a bit when meeting new people at a party or a gathering until they are comfortable. It's not because they can't be loving or intimate; often shy people are capable of greater intimacy than people who can work the crowd. But averting their eyes at first helps them not to feel overwhelmed.) In general, a child who wants to be part of a relationship looks spontaneously, and if she doesn't look, she may lean into you and enjoy your closeness through touch or sound—through you she takes in the external world.

Engagement also helps give children a sense of purpose or direction in their actions. For example, the child who is in a relationship with you will *want* to reach out to you for a hug or a kiss, or if you put a funny hat on, may reach to take it and put on his own head, because he enjoys the things you do. When you do something intriguing that builds on that pleasure, the child tries to get involved. Rather than jumping around, waving his hands aimlessly, or just staring at a fan, he wants to play with you. She wants to grab your glasses to hear you protest, or wants you to open your hand for a ball. The emotion and pleasure of a relationship make a child's actions more deliberate and purposeful.

When engaged, children have a desire to communicate. Communication occurs in flirtatious interactions, in annoyed or angry interactions that stop short of tantrums, in explorations—all kinds of wonderful things can happen as a child begins using gestures and sounds to communicate. Communication leads to shared problem-solving; for example, the child takes Daddy to the toy area, points up to the shelf, and goes "uhhh, uhhh, uhhh," urging Daddy through gestures to get a toy for her. But none of this happens unless the child is engaged in the world, is part of a relationship, is experiencing pleasure.

Engagement also helps a child figure out where things are in space, because she wants to track Mommy and Daddy visually as they move around the room. This spatial ability helps her figure out that you are on the other side of the door when you leave the room, and that when she can't see the toy, it may be in the toy box.

Then, as a child learns to imitate words, her emotional investment in you and in the relationship gives the words meaning; "Mama" or "Dada" are not just empty sounds; they convey a feeling for Mommy and Daddy because the child has invested all that pleasurable emotion in those two people. To say, "Mommy, pick me up," the child has to know "up," perhaps because she loves being picked up to play airplane. "Mommy," "Daddy," "up," "down," "come," "go"—all these words are charged with emotional meaning through the child's relationship with her primary caregiver. Otherwise, the child may memorize words like "book," and "chair," but the words will be empty, without real personal meaning. The child may label pictures, may be echolalic, may script and repeat whole books without using language in a meaningful, interactive way. True communication occurs only when a child is part of a shared world.

Even something like mathematics is based on emotional engagement. As later chapters explain, a child develops a sense of quantity because he wants a little more or a little less of this or that. Thus the sense of quantity, later systematized by numbers, has emotional meaning; it is related to desire, which in turn is tied to engagement with the world.

When it comes to reading and reading comprehension, a child has to be involved in relationships to understand concepts she reads such as "love," "greed," "competition," and "character." Without being part of a relationship, she might be able to memorize facts or even sound out words. But to comprehend what she reads and then progress in history, literature, science, or other academic subjects, she has to be able to invest symbols with emotional meaning.

Reaching into a child's world and pulling him into a shared world is the foundation for all the progress we want that child to make in emotional and social development, motor skills, visual-spatial skills, academic skills, and pleasure in a lifetime of learning.

Techniques of Engagement

We probably can't make too strong a case for this first step. But how does it happen? Many parents and other caregivers of children with ASD may feel that it's an impossible task. For those who feel discouraged, who feel they have tried and tried without success, we can only paraphrase Will Rogers and say, "I've never met a child—and I mean never—who couldn't be engaged." Over the past thirty years of working with children, researching, and writing, I, Dr. Greenspan (SIG), have always spent at least half my time in direct clinical practice. Of the thousands of children I've seen during my career, I've never met one who couldn't be engaged in some pleasurable way, regardless of the degree of his or her neurological problems. Of course, the degree of language development and depth of intimacy have varied greatly, but I've never met a child who couldn't begin the process of engagement and establish a foundation for pleasure in relating to others and attending to the outside world.

Trying to engage a child who is tuning out or not paying attention can be very frustrating. Sometimes parents just keep talking and playing, essentially talking to themselves and ignoring the child's lack of response. But it's important not to bypass, in the interest of obtaining interaction, the first basic step of getting the child's attention. Discouraged parents often end up losing the feeling in their voice, so the child doesn't get pulled in. What they need to do, rather, is to keep energizing the expectation in their voice. At the same time, they must slow down the rhythm of their movements because fast movement may lose the child with ASD who has tracking problems.

Sensory support—such as an arm placed gently on the child's back, maybe pulsing to match her breathing rate—also helps children pay attention. Sometimes a swing—whether made of Spandex or the care-giver's arms—can entice a child into more engagement by combining movement, firm touch, and expectant sounds. Because it's often help-ful to use all the senses to capture attention, you the caregiver should get down at the level of the child so that she can see and feel you and thus begin to connect what you're saying with your expression and the rhythm of your voice. Once you have the child's attention, you can begin to engage her more and more.

Following the Child's Lead

The first step in engagement is, as described more fully in Part III, also the first principle of the Floortime technique: follow the child's lead, regardless of where his interest lies. But what if a child's interests are unusual or peculiar or are not things we want to encourage? This should not be a concern at this point, because only by joining in the child's interests, by following his lead, do we get a first clue about what he finds important. It may not remain important to him as we pull him into our shared world and new things come to his attention. But initially, the ticket to engaging the child's interest is joining him in his world.

If a child is rubbing a piece of cloth over and over, his mother might simply say, "Stop!" in a harsh voice to scare him out of it, or pull the cloth away or try to move his face to look at her and maybe reward him for doing so with a cookie. Alternatively, the mother could think, "At least he's finding some pleasure and relaxation in rubbing that piece of cloth; let me rub it with him for a second and see if I can enter his world and see how he is feeling." Then she might put the cloth over her own face and see if the child reaches for it. If he does, the mother can make a game of it and eventually entice him to rub her arm or nose with the cloth or even search for it in her hands. Much later on she might speak for a doll who "loves pieces of cloth," and so forth.

If a caregiver tries to distract the child by offering something the caregiver wants her to be interested in, the child may retreat into her own world, feeling the caregiver isn't interested in what she cares about. What do we adults do, for example, when we want to engage a new acquaintance at a cocktail party? We start by talking about what we think interests him or her, and then we may introduce the person to our own agenda. It is the same with a child. Following the child's lead to get a clue about what gives her pleasure and excitement or what makes her calm and relaxed reveals how to approach her and pull her in.

A key point here: following the child's lead need not limit you the caregiver to doing only what the child does. After doing the same thing next to her—rubbing the piece of cloth, say—you might slowly move your hand to where she is rubbing, so that now she is rubbing the hand. Thus, you begin to enter her world through her lead and perhaps entice her into an interaction. You have put a hand over her spot but are still respecting her desire to rub.

Hopefully, she'll start rubbing your hand. But she may not. When I (SIG) tried that with a child who was rubbing a spot on the floor, he moved his hand to the side and started rubbing the spot next to my hand. So I very gradually moved my hand over another inch to where he was rubbing, and he again moved his hand over. I watched his face: he looked a little puzzled and actually gave me a little look—it was the first time he had looked at me—as if asking, "What are you doing?" As he moved his hand away again, I moved my hand ever so slowly toward his, and when I was about to move my hand under his, he uttered, "Uhnnnn uhnnnn uhnnnn!" Although I didn't want to precipitate a tantrum, I didn't mind annoying him because by looking at me for a moment and vocalizing to me purposefully (not just randomly as he had been doing before), he was at least acknowledging my presence and relating to me a little bit, though not yet with much pleasure.

I pulled my hand back a little as though to acknowledge his annoyance and show him that I respected his purposeful gesture. He seemed to take some satisfaction in that; he kept rubbing his spot, and his voice texture changed slightly to a more rhythmic "unnn, unnn, unnn." I joined in with some rhythmic sounds of my own and rubbed next to him for another few seconds. Then I started the pattern again, moving my hand slowly closer, and he made some warning noises. I did this two or three more times, each time a little more playfully with a little more of a smile on my face, and by the fifth time he touched my hand and moved my hand away a little bit. By the eighth time he rubbed my hand when it was on his favorite spot.

Then we got into a cat-and-mouse game in which he actually wanted to rub my hand rather than his spot and I would move it away and then move it back toward him. Sometimes, as he rubbed my hand, I'd close it very gently on his and he'd have to make a sound to get me to open it. So we had a little game going, and during the second session that we did this, I got some little smiles. I had entered his world; he was warmly engaged and acting purposefully. We were nowhere near a continuous flow of emotional signaling and shared problem-solving, but we were on the way. We had taken the first step in the process that gives meaning to actions and words and allows the child to make progress further down the line.

Playful Obstruction

Following the child's lead is only the starting point. Drawing a child into a shared world involves creatively figuring out a maneuver that captures the child's attention, learning what makes her tick, and then challenging her to make a small step into the shared world. One technique for the child who is extremely difficult to engage is to get between her and what she is trying to do, becoming a play object in the child's world. We call this being "playfully obstructive."

For example, during a session, a child was ignoring me (SIG) and his parents, repetitively opening and closing the door. I observed him, and then put my hand on the door, helping him a little bit to open and close it. He didn't like that and made a sound like "Rrrrr!" so I pulled my hand away. But gradually I started getting behind the door. The child used sounds and gentle pushing to get me away from the door; he was now purposeful and starting to interact. As with the boy who was rubbing the floor, I let the interaction evolve very gradually, always sensitive to the child's reactions. In this way, he got not over-loaded but just a little annoyed, always stopping short of having a tantrum. Slowly it changed into a playful interaction in which eventually he said, "No." Later on, he learned to say, "Away" with a great big smile of satisfaction because he was the boss of his door. Just by getting involved with his apparently mindless door routine, I gradually helped this child engage, learn to gesture purposefully, and give meaning to words such as "no," "away," and "leave alone."

By the time a child gets to shared problem-solving, she no longer focuses on the perseverative activity. In each case described above, within six weeks the child had given up his repetitive activities and was involved in more joyful, interactive ones. Once children enjoy engaging with others, they don't need self-stimulation as much. They may continue to do it in times of stress or overload, and not all children give it up quickly. But many do, and they are off to more important things.

Discovering the Child's Sensory and Motor Profile

Entering the child's world involves more than simply intuiting what gives the child pleasure; it's a systematic process. First, caregivers and professionals must learn how the child's nervous system works by taking note of her unique style of hearing, seeing, touching, smelling, and moving. As Chapter 11 explains more fully, children—particularly those with ASD—differ considerably in their sensory reactivity. Some overreact or underreact to certain kinds of touch or sound. Others are sensitive to smells; for example, a strong perfume may lead a child to feel overwhelmed and pull away.

To help children be comfortable in the world, clinicians and caregivers must first learn by careful observation which sensations help children become calm and regulated, which ones overwhelm them, and which don't pull them in enough. Whatever the infant or child's age, you the caregiver need to observe how she responds to different types of touch on different parts of her body. Experiment with different sounds—high- and low-pitched noises, the normal human voice—and different degrees of volume to see which ones draw the child's attention more. Do this with each of the senses. This helps you determine which senses to emphasize as you draw the child into your world.

The next step is to look at how the child comprehends sensations. For example, even before they can speak, some children respond to the

sound of a person's voice as if trying to figure out what he or she is saying. Other children turn away from vocalizations as though they are
overwhelmed and confused. Some babies respond positively to complex vocal rhythms, while others get confused by them but respond
well to simpler rhythms. Older children show a similar range of responses to simple versus complex vocalizations, even before they understand lots of words.

Children also differ in how they comprehend what they see. Some
children like complex visual signals, such as someone's simultaneously
waving his arms, smiling, and moving his head. Other children are
overwhelmed by so much movement and respond better to just a big
smile. Some children do well in a busy environment with lots of children and toys around, while others need to be in an uncluttered corner of the room with just one adult, or an adult and one other child,
in order to play comfortably.

The level of a child's motor planning skills must also be gauged.
The best way to do this is to watch the child play. For example, does
he take a favorite toy car and just move it back and forth—that is, just
repeating one step? If the child goes to a particular room, gets a favorite doll, brings it to Daddy, gives him a big smile, and then gets up
in his lap ready to play with it, that's a five-step action pattern. There
are three basic categories: children just beginning to learn to put actions together, those doing a little more complex action patterns, and
those doing almost as many actions in a row as are needed to solve the
problem at hand.

The kind of activity that engages the child depends on which level she
has reached. For example, if she enjoys horsy rides and is capable of multistep actions, Daddy can go to the other side of the room, pretend to be a
horse, and ask, "Do you want a horsy ride?" and expect her to come over,
jump on his back, and pat him to get him started. On the other hand, if
the child is capable of only a one- or two-step action plan, Mommy may
have to pick her up and say, "I'm going to put you on Daddy so you can
have a horsy ride." Then the child has only one step to do, such as move
her feet, to get Daddy to move. If the child can do only a one-step action,
a parent should begin with simple actions and work up.

Children also differ in the way they respond to movement in space: some children love being thrown up into the air, while others can handle movement through the air only if it's slow and secure. This determines how caregivers play "airplane" with a child, for example. Some children like slow motion, others fast. Some children love to jump and spin—it helps them organize and regulate themselves. Other children are so sensitive to movement in space that caregivers have to move with them soothingly and very gradually.

Every child with ASD or other special needs is unique. (And every typically developing child is also unique—each has her or his own sensory and motor pattern, though generally with fewer extremes.) If caregivers and professionals know the child's pattern—and often they know it intuitively—they can enter the child's world more effectively.

Expanding the Child's Interest in the World

The key to expanding children's ability to be secure, calm, and regulated in the shared world is to meet them first at the level of their existing abilities and then gradually expand out from that base of security. Anytime a child becomes withdrawn or overexcited and irritable, you the caregiver need to go back to the baseline and expand more slowly. Once the child is engaged, you can gradually expand her ability to understand and enjoy a range of sensations and to plan actions. Attempt new challenges slowly to help the one-step-action child become a two-step- and then a three-step-action child. After putting the child on Daddy's back for a horsy ride a few times, Mommy can put the child right next to Daddy, and Daddy—down on the floor playing the horse—can ask, "Horsy ride?" Pretty soon, maybe while holding Mommy's hand, the child may pat Daddy on the back, indicating that she wants to go up on the horsy. Then Mommy can put the child on, and the child may move her legs to get the horse going. So now it's a two-step action plan with a lot of compelling engagement, and even the beginning of communication.

Many innovative techniques have been designed to pull children into relationships and expand their world. Parents and other caregivers and therapists have more success in carrying out these exercises if they use them as part of the DIR/Floortime model and thus take their cues from the child's particular nervous system. Tailoring engagement and play with the child to his unique profile and engaging him to climb the developmental ladder should be part of any technique or strategy. The techniques can be part of spontaneous interactions or part of more or less structured interactions designed to work on specific goals such as language or motor skills.

The Pleasures of Engagement

Many games usually played with babies can be played with older children with ASD to pull them into engagement. Many children, regardless of their neurological challenges, love variations on peekaboo. If you a parent are making funny faces and silly sounds and your child is looking at you, and you then put a napkin over your head, your child may just wander away, but she may take the napkin away to get a look at your face. Many children also love sensory-based play, such as airplane rides or dancing or jumping together. Sometimes holding the child's hands and rhythmically moving her to the sound of your voice as she jumps on a mattress or on a couch can begin engagement.

If a child is very avoidant and walks away every time you the caregiver approach, think, "OK, walking away seems to be giving my child pleasure, so here's my opening." Follow his lead and become an aimless wanderer with him. Assume that whatever the child is doing is bringing him some pleasure, and then see if you can deepen and widen that pleasure and make it part of a human relationship. For example, one little boy wanders aimlessly around the room but is devoted to a particular blanket. He carries his blanket around with him as he moves around the room, so Mommy begins putting the blanket on her head and following him. He responds by pulling the blanket, and she tugs it back a little. Pretty soon he is smiling and playing a little tugging game with her, and then they are both hiding under the blanket together, giggling and laughing.

One of the biggest obstacles to engaging children is the parents' feeling that the child doesn't want to engage with them—rejects them—or is angry with them, causing the parents to want to give up. But a little protest is not really anger, and the two should not be confused. If the child is used to being in her own world, a little protest is natural when someone tries to coax her out of that world. However, I (SIG) have never worked with a child who didn't, at least after a while, enjoy the human world more than the inanimate one. Invariably, even children with the most severe forms of ASD begin to enjoy engagement with another person if it is approached gradually, slowly, with warmth and a light touch.

Once children, with or without ASD, learn the fun of interacting with another human being, it feels so glorious and natural to them that they begin seeking it out more and more. The first week or even month may be difficult, but then it gets considerably easier. So, if you the caregiver find yourself getting annoyed that the child is "rejecting" you, take a break for a few minutes to regroup; then try to be sillier and fun loving as you persist in your task of getting between the child and what she is trying to do so. Try to become the plaything in the child's life. If the child initially treats you impersonally, as a means to an end, in order to get a juice bottle or a toy off a shelf, that's fine. This simple engagement is the first step in falling in love. More emotions will come and gradually you'll see deepening joy and pleasure.

Chapter 7

Encouraging Two-Way Communication and Social Problem-Solving

Claire's parents were at a loss. Their little girl tended to be pas-sive and self-absorbed. She could cuddle a little and sometimes re-spond with a few smiles, but when they tried to talk to her loudly and energetically or tried to entice her to reach for their hands, Claire would only shut down and retreat even more into her own world. They wanted to draw her into real communication, and asked for suggestions about what they could do next.

Preverbal Communication

Communication is central to anyone's work with children who have ASD. Once a child attends to her caregiver, is calm and regulated, and is getting more and more engaged in a shared world, it's critical for her to learn to communicate meaningfully. Although communica-tion is often thought of as the exchange of words ("I'm hungry," "Give me that toy," or "Go out"), it begins at the preverbal level, with ges-tures, as when children show a toy they want or make a sound in response to someone else's sound. It begins very early in life with the first little head nods, smiles, and gurgling sounds and eventually takes off into a rich dialogue of exchanged sounds, gestures, smiles, and scowls—all before words are used to any significant degree.

Even as words are coming in during the second year of life, this gestural language or mutual signaling occurs at a much faster rate and in a more complex manner than the verbal interchanges. It takes a while for the words to catch up, and even after a child becomes verbal, even as adults are speaking, the preverbal or gestural level always goes on at the same time. People communicate with facial expressions, tone of voice, body posture, movements, and so forth.

In fact, most of us trust the preverbal level more than the verbal level. If a stranger says to you politely, "I just need a little help with this map—can you come over here, please?" but his facial expressions, his body posture, and the context suggest danger, you probably will swiftly move away. You'll ignore the verbal part of the situation and pay attention to the gestural part. In assessing political candidates, we attend to their tone of voice and their manner as well as what they say. So using gestures is a basic communication tool early in life and continues throughout life.

The verbal skills children need build on this preverbal level. For words to have meaning and for children to talk and use language successfully, they first need to master communicating with gestures. Even if they are already speaking, children—especially those with ASD—may need help with this preverbal level. Beyond its obvious importance in learning to communicate, mastery of this level is also key to developing social and emotional capacities. Children who can't read and respond to social signals—facial expressions, gestures, body posture—have a hard time knowing what to do and when to do it. Long before children can speak, caregivers let them know what is dangerous and what is safe by a look, a sound, or a tone of voice or by pointing. So a child who is about to put a finger in the electric socket can sense that it's a no-no not so much because she understands the word "no" as because she understands the alarm in Mommy's voice, the grimace on her face, the pointing away from the socket, and being picked up and put away from danger.

Similarly, warmth, acceptance, and love are communicated through expressions and tones of voice. A child gives Mommy a big smile, flirts, and reaches out to be picked up, and Mommy gives the child a big smile back, holds her arms out, and says warmly, "I love you." Before the word "love" is understood, the other, gestural expressions and warm tones communicate love back to the child. Thus he learns about limits or learns about love, all through this preverbal system. Social and emotional capacities, and eventually the ability to read other children's social signals on the playground, are learned first through gestural communication.

How does the child then learn what words mean? In the example above, the child who reaches up to Mommy and is picked up, hugged, kissed, and comforted learns what the word "love" means (typically between eighteen months and two-and-a-half years), because the word comes to summarize all of these interactions that have gone on. Without these exchanges, the child wouldn't know what "love" means. She might be told and might memorize the definition, but she wouldn't feel it, wouldn't grasp its meaning.

Similarly, when a child who has eaten apples and played with them learns the word "apple," he knows all about apples. An apple has meaning for him; it's not just a dictionary definition that says it's round and red. So the word becomes the label for what a child already knows, based on the interactions he has with the world long before he can speak. Children who have been delayed in their gestural level of communication can build it later through multiple interactions at the verbal and gestural levels together, and use it as they master words.

Roots of Cognitive Skills

Cognition and intelligence also build on gestural communication. As we pointed out earlier, the fundamental principle of causality is learned when a baby understands that she can get a smile from her mother by smiling, cooing, and making little gestures. Without two-way communication, children might learn causality in a very limited way by experimenting with the physical world, but not as early or as fully as in this social or emotional way.

Cognitive skills—including those needed for mathematics and science—are also extensions of this basic ability for preverbal communication. For example, a sense of quantity is learned when cookies, toys, and so forth are negotiated early on. Paying attention and problem-solving sequencing are both learned long before the use of words. The basic foundations for intelligence and academic skill require two-way communication, initially without words, early in life. If developmental problems prevent such communication for a child, caregivers and therapists have to get it established as quickly as possible, because weakness at this level tends to hold back higher levels of development and keep the child stuck in self-stimulatory or repetitive behavior.

Communication Delays

Many children with ASD—because of biological challenges in motor planning and sequencing, auditory and visual-spatial processing, modulation of sensory input, and so forth—have a hard time engaging in mutual communication. The foundations for verbal language and for later cognitive and social skills are thereby temporarily derailed until the children get help in communicating. To find out where to start—no matter the age of the child or even adult—clinicians first determine how well she engages with others by observing whether she is part of a shared world or is in a solitary one. They then ask whether she can make facial expressions and hand gestures. Can she show her primary caregiver, even if she can't say, what she wants? Short of using words, can she exchange gestures so as to explore and negotiate? Can she use words?

If the child (or the adult) isn't a two-way communicator with gestures, that is what must be emphasized in working with her. Without two-way communication, all other progress will be difficult. Although therapists can also work on other verbal skills and even some academic skills simultaneously, ignoring this fundamental level will slow their progress, and the foundations of the structure they build will be weak.

Typically, in children without developmental problems, two-way communication begins in the second half of their first year of life and continues more prominently in the second year of life. It's not surprising that when the basic communication and language skills of many children with ASD are evaluated, they are seen to be at a less-than-twelve-month-old level. That's often because the preverbal system hasn't been well established. Some of these children may have isolated words or may identify letters, shapes, or words on a page, but they don't have the fundamentals in place.

For example, a little boy was brought for treatment who talked only in short "fragment islands": he would say "car outside" and then jump to "blue toy" and then "orange shirt." It was hard for his parents and caregivers to make sense of what he said. His communication was intermittent; he would be self-absorbed, then come out with a phrase, and then lapse back into his own world. Following our basic principles, we enticed him into interactions and helped him to gesture and verbalize as much as possible in a continuous flow. Remarkably, by the end of the session, for the first time in his life, he started to make sense and even answered a "why" question.

While this little boy progressed very quickly, most children take more time. Many children use their verbal skills more meaningfully if caregivers and therapists work with them on the basics of two-way communication. A continuous flow of communication is also vital for developing a sense of reality and regulating behavior and emotions. If a child alternates between a self-absorbed world and a shared one, he gets only little samples of reality, not a continuous picture of it. But attending to the world and interacting with it continuously, he gets feedback from his environment. The child can interpret Mommy's stern look or Daddy's gestures, so he can tell when they're getting a little annoyed and he'd better not behave aggressively. This ability in a child to initiate many little emotional and social signals and "read" his caregiver's responses enables him to regulate his behavior, and moods, and emotions. For example, a mother's soothing voice can help her child calm down when he insists on getting a toy right now. Rather than getting upset, he can gesture toward the toy more emphatically; she can indicate with a raised finger that she'll get it in a moment, and so forth. This series of back-and-forth signaling substitutes problem-solving for having a meltdown. Later, this same skill helps the child work in social groups and deal with all the nonverbal and verbal communication encountered in school. Two-way communication helps him think logically as he makes bridges between what he feels and what someone else feels, between what he says and what someone else says. (Of course, we all need to daydream and fantasize occasionally or tune into our own world. But in a verbal or abstract-thinking person, that can be an intentional decision, not simply a reflexive pulling away from the world.)

Encouraging Communication

We can now lay out the basic principles of establishing two-way communication and social problem-solving within our DIR model.

To begin with, as described in the previous chapter, we follow the child's lead, tuning into her interests, emotions, and goals. These have to be known because communication builds on intentionality. The whole goal is to help the child take the initiative. Having a purpose is the first step in meaningful communication.

To get two-way communication going with a child, rather than take her away from a favorite object or activity, the caregiver or therapist incorporates the object or activity into the interaction. With a child who is opening and closing a door, for example, a therapist might put a wedge under the door so the child can't move it. He may ask, "Can I help?" and offer a gesture indicating that he'll push with her. If he is lucky, she might nod, or take his hand and put it to the door, or make some other gesture to indicate assent, in which case he is getting communication going by helping the child meet her own goal. Then we can put some pressure into the push so the wedge gets dislodged and the child can now push the door. Then he'll put the wedge in again, hopefully without the child seeing (there's nothing wrong with being a little tricky if it's in the child's interest).

Or if a child is dancing around the room, a caregiver can offer a hand and see if she'll take ahold of it, and the two can dance—now it's a two-way dance. The caregiver wants the child to take his hand voluntarily. In other words, he does something as simple as offering a hand to her (not actually grabbing her hand), so she has to make that extra step to show her intentionality, to show that she is building on what he is doing because he has built on what she has done. This is called opening and closing a circle of communication. The child opens the circle by her own purpose or intention, by doing what she wants to do. A parent or other caregiver then builds on that by help-ing her achieve her goal. The child in turn closes the circle when she takes advantage of what the caregiver offered and gestures for him or her to help. Then the caregiver tries to get from one circle to another, encouraging multiple exchanges.

As another example, a child we worked with would continually play with his own fingers in a self-absorbed, self-stimulatory way. This gave us a ticket into his world. I put my little finger in his hand and got him to play with my finger. Then I pulled my finger away, but he didn't reach for it, so I touched just the tip of his pinkie. He moved his hand to my hand, and I let him play with it a little; then I would move my hand away a bit and touch his finger and he would grab it again.

Through his seemingly perseverative activity, we generated a bit of communication between us and then built on that. This boy enjoyed a certain kind of firm touch that was not too firm, so I would touch his feet, and he would move his feet closer and would try to catch my feet between his two feet, and so forth. Through this kind of game we brought him into a world of shared interactions, eventually achieving more than twenty circles of communication in which he showed plea-sure and engaged in social problem-solving.

Another way of getting two-way communication going is by being playfully obstructive, as described in the previous chapter. You the care-giver can create obstacles such as a pretend policeman blocking the way of the child's toy car, so the child either has to knock the policeman down or go around him. In playful obstruction, to keep from upsetting the child, you can move in slow motion so he can make a gesture to stop you, which lets him feel the mastery of his own gestures—he's the boss as soon as he gestures purposefully. And now he's enjoying himself, and you've met your goal.

For the child who wanders aimlessly around the room, we have a game we call Moving Fence: I follow the child around and then put my arms around her without actually touching her, so that to get out of the fence and move around the room, she's got to lift my arm, say, "Let go," or gesture in some way. As soon as she does, obviously I follow her initiative.

The number of different ways to get two-way communication going is inexhaustible—simple peekaboo games, hide-and-seek, rhythmic coordinated activities, and so forth. One begins with you the caregiver hiding a cookie or a favorite toy in your hand. The child opens your hand and finds it. Now you take out another little treat or toy, and hide it in one hand, but keep both hands closed so the child has to search for which hand holds it. Now you have two circles of communication. In the third round, you put your hands behind your back so the child first has to go around to your back and find your hands to search. So now we've got four or five circles. Next, you might have a doll hide the cookie in another part of the room, so the child has to search all around the room while you help with clues, pointing here or pointing there. Now you've reached as many as ten circles.

During this game, you can start adding in words so the child has to say "Cookie!" if she's trying to get the cookie. Initially you can cue the child with a word, but then help the child think it through by asking, "Cookie or juice?" First you just repeat the word to the child as she is doing the activity (such as eating the cookie), so she knows what it means. Then you start offering choices, always giving the good choice first and the undesirable choice second, so that simply repeating the last word you said will not bring the result she wants.

The key objective is to help the child become keenly motivated. And that requires returning to the basic principle of following the child's natural interest. You the parent or other caregiver need not stick to the game you start with: whatever the child is doing should be the basis for the next circle of communication, and new challenges can be created around that activity. Getting to a continuous flow of back-and-forth communication is the goal—going from two or three circles, to five, ten, twenty—to the point that circles don't need to be counted anymore because the child can get into a back-and-forth rhythm with you for as long as you're available to help her do it.

Sensory Differences and Communication

The case study described at the beginning of this chapter involves a child who underreacts, doesn't register sound and sensation very well, and because she has low muscle tone, tends to take little initiative. Thus it's difficult for her to point, look, or turn. Children like this are generally difficult to engage; they tend to be easily self-absorbed and are often lost in their own worlds because the sound of someone else's voice or the sight of another's facial expressions don't register very much. It takes a lot of energy and animation on a parent or caregiver's part to get the child even to look in his or her direction. But while this kind of child needs to be challenged and energized, at the same time she might overreact to sound. Working with children with these patterns, one has to find just the right tone and pitch, the right energy level in terms of volume, and the right intensity of expectation. Energy and expectation in the voice are critical for such a child, but the caregiver or therapist's voice need not be loud. Loudness doesn't necessarily convey the expectation; a near-whisper can pack as much energy as a shout. Parents or other caregivers who are low-key, easygoing individuals have got to operate out of their normal character for this child. They have to be very animated, to flirt with the child and entice him to take initiative.

It's difficult to get a continuous flow going with those children who get self-absorbed rapidly. You the caregiver may get a very good interaction at first—you roll a ball, and the child reaches for it—but then you seem to lose her and can't get to the next step. Rather than rolling the ball back to you, the child begins staring out the window. The key here is to become lightning quick at increasing the expression in your voice and actions and upping the stakes. Don't tolerate, even for a second, losing the child. Be observant, and as soon as you lose eye or emotional contact, work to pull the child back in. If the child starts looking at the window, get in front of her and block her view. "You can't run away from me—I'm every place!" is the name of the game with the easily self-absorbed child.

Other children, by contrast, are easily overloaded and get overstimulated by even a light touch. These children may grow irritable or have tantrums easily, or be highly distracted by everything in the environment. The goal of therapy is to help such children be regulated and calm, not by being overanimated with them, but soothing yet compelling and interesting.

Probably the most challenging are children who are so distracted by their own motor movements that they can't pay attention to another person; very active and often avoidant, they may wave their arms and legs in what looks like self-stimulatory and perseverative patterns. As soon as a caregiver or therapist approaches this child, he is off to another part of the room, eluding capture even for a second. One effective technique to help the child be less distracted by his own activity is to try to redirect his movement into a joint movement. For example, as the child is running and jumping, you the caregiver try to catch his hands in yours so that the two of you begin moving together and you are rhythmically interactive with the child at his activity level. Then gradually down-regulate with the child into slower movement patterns and rhythms. This can sometimes help the child settle down into a rhythm with you in which he can gesture and communicate, sometimes even use a word or two. In this way children who have severe motor planning problems and distracting motor activities can be helped to organize and regulate themselves. Then they can engage and get into two-way communication.

Rosemary White, a gifted occupational therapist, suggests giving more purpose or meaning to a child's self-stimulatory gestures. For example, as a child waves her arms, make a "swoosh" sound, or as she jumps, make a "boom" sound. See if she takes note by a look or other action. Arnold Miller has pioneered using elevated platforms. Children with self-regulatory problems can be put on a wide balance beam, a bed, or a very low table. This helps them orient themselves in space and focus a bit; something about struggling with their own postural control and gravity seems to help them organize their nervous system. This can make it easier to get interaction. You the caregiver or therapist can play all kinds of games while the child is elevated (just make sure the ground is soft in case she should fall), or make up games in which you get on the platform with her. If she wants to get down, you can negotiate around that goal. Other children do better when they are moving on a swing or jumping on a little floor-based trampoline.

Helping the Child to Take Initiative

The principle in encouraging two-way communication and social problem-solving is to inspire the child to do something to you the therapist or caregiver—to take initiative, rather than you doing something to the child. Ask yourself, "What do I need to do to get her to want to do something to me?" One little boy was lying face down on the floor in my office, ignoring everyone. His creative mother simply lay down on her child, saying, "Oh, you're sleepy? OK, I'm going to lie down on you." The firm pressure was reassuring to the child, but after a moment he wanted her off. He not only gestured with his arm for her to get off but also said, "Get off!" This child only occasionally used a phrase, and his mother actively built on it to get him to take the initiative, to act on Mommy.

Most children with severe forms of ASD lack initiative. In fact, one of the earliest signs that children are having challenges is that they avoid taking the initiative in social interaction and prefer being responders. Because they may repeat words or identify pictures in a book, they look fine in terms of early cognition and language, but they are waiting, not reaching out to the world. Fortunately, it's never too late to encourage initiative, which makes all the difference in the world.

Getting Communication Going

Key Questions for Parents and Other Caregivers to Ask

1. "Am I following my child's lead by working with her interests?" Always assume that what your child does—even seemingly random behavior—has some purpose for her. Insert yourself into the activity and help your child with it; then begin to make it more complicated.

2. "Am I enticing the child to take the initiative?" Stimulating the child—tickling, verbalizing, vocalizing, and so forth—or doing things for the child doesn't create interaction. Encourage the child to show you where she wants to be tickled—on the tummy or on the back or on the arms. Play dumb and act confused as to where to go, perhaps pointing to two possibilities; accept any gesture on the child's part as an indication of the direction she wants you to go. Initially, treat the slightest little communication as being purposeful.

3. "Do my voice, gestures, and posture show expectation?" If you say, "You *want* the *apple? Look!* I'm hiding it! Here it *goes*—do you *want* it? Do you *want* it?" that's expectation. If you just ask, "Do you want the apple? Do you want the apple?" there's little expectation in your voice. The more animated you are, the more your child responds to your sounds or your facial expressions with something purposeful. Every time the child begins pulling back into her own world, you've got to accentuate the liveliness in your voice (you don't have to get louder) and become more animated—more compelling and expectant.

4. "Am I tailoring the interactions to the child's nervous system?" If a child has low muscle tone and underreacts, are you energizing him? If your child is oversensitive and overreactive, are you being extra soothing? For the child who is a visual learner, are you using extra visual support? Are you emphasizing sounds for the child who has auditory processing problems? Be sure to maintain the rhythm, expectation, and energy in your voice while making your words more distinct.

5. "Am I involving as many senses as possible while I'm tailoring our play to the child's sensory profile?" Appeal to the child's sense of sight, sound, touch, and movement while being sensitive to what upsets and pleases him.

You the parent or other caregiver should entice the child to take initiative. Have something for her to reach for, give her a reason to persist. To that end, it's important to pay attention to what your child is doing, even if you think she's not doing anything. If you treat what she's doing as if it's purposeful, you might then encourage that potential initiative in simple ways, and the child will feel that you're investing in what she wants, rather than distracting her with what you think is interesting. Of course, you'll want to create an environment that's compelling so the child will think, "Hey, that's what I want to do." But let her take that first step and then encourage and support her initiative in every way you can. Once children can communicate in a continuous flow, they move away, as we said earlier, from the symptoms ordinarily associated with ASD. They learn to interact with their environment in a new way, become more regulated, and withdraw, perseverate, or self-stimulate less often.

The first step is always the hardest. Entice your child by, for example, slowly putting his cherished toy or other object of interest in your hand or on your head. As he reaches for it, that critical first step has been taken. A major feat has now been accomplished. The second step is to extend these interactions or circles of communication. Hide his toy in the other hand or in your shirt. Make it easy to get. Next, you and his toy crawl slowly behind a chair, and so forth. When he wants to open the door, offer to help, but he needs to show you where to put your hand and then how to pull it open. Always be thinking of how you can extend or add circles of communication and how you can entice more initiative.

Once your dialogue with the child involves more than twenty consecutive circles, with the child taking the initiative as an equal partner, you have real communication going. Most important, don't be afraid to experiment. Whatever works, works: if the child is taking the initiative and you're getting a continuous flow going, you're doing it right. Practice. The only mistake you can make is getting discouraged and giving up.

Chapter 8

Symbols, Ideas, and Words

Todd, a lively four-year-old boy diagnosed with ASD and slight oral motor problems, used expressive gestures and sounds to communicate with his parents but was still not using any words. His parents wanted to try sending him to kindergarten but felt that he needed at least minimal language abilities for this to work. They wondered how they could help him progress from gestures to words in communicating his needs and desires.

P arents and other caregivers are often pleased once the child with ASD becomes engaged and intentional and learns to gesture. However, they also want this progress to lead to expressing ideas and feelings in words. Once the foundations of engagement and communication are in place, how do children begin creating ideas, symbols, and language and using these to communicate with others?

The First Ideas

The study of human evolution has provided new insights into how language develops in the life of every infant and child (see Greenspan and Shanker, *The First Idea*, in the References). The process is similar for

91

the vast majority of children with ASD and other special needs, even if they have biological difficulties with it. One of the most important components that must be in place for language to develop in children is the presence of ideas in their minds, because ideas give them something to speak about.

We have found that, to have an idea, the child has to separate perception from action. In infants, and in many children with ASD, the two are bound together in what we call fixed perceptual motor patterns; that is, seeing and acting take place automatically. Thus a baby sees Mommy and grabs for her, or hears Mommy's voice and cries for her. Sensory perception and the emotion of the moment lead to immediate action. In many children with ASD, the action might be avoidance or withdrawal: they hear a sound, it's unpleasant because their senses overreact, and they shut down; or they see a fan and stare at it fixedly because the stimulation feels good. Between perception and reaction, there is usually some emotion—fear, anxiety, or self-stimulatory pleasure—but the whole sequence is fixed.

As discussed in the previous two chapters, when babies learn to engage with their emotions, they begin to signal back and forth with others. Preverbal signaling begins to take the place of fixed actions and reactions. The toddler can look at Mommy wistfully and motion or gesture to "pick me up." The parent can give a hand gesture that indicates, "Wait a second," the toddler nods, and they have negotiated. These interactions separate, on one hand, what a child sees or hears and the image created in her mind from, on the other, a fixed action like biting, hitting, grabbing, or withdrawing.

Once freed from automatic actions, the child's perception—what she sees and hears—becomes a freestanding image. The child now has an image of Mother in her mind that is not tied to a fixed action. Initially, such mental images are isolated from each other, but gradually, connections form between the images in a child's mind. The freestanding image of Mother, for example, can acquire meaning through multitudes of experiences with Mother over time. Mother can be gratifying, frustrating, or exciting or can bring the child this or that toy or this or that food. The child can associate all these with Mother and form a meaningful idea of Mother. Everything in the child's life takes on meaning in this way—parents, siblings, blankets, food. This is, in essence, how ideas are born. Once the child can imagine people, objects, and actions, she can consciously remember the past and create wishes for the future.

Interestingly, as children give meaning to objects and people in the world around them and begin to use their imaginations, they may also become more frightened of and sensitive to what they imagine. A child developing in this way may begin acting less confident and needier and may be more afraid if she wakes up in the middle of the night, for example. In the context of symbolic development, this is a good sign; nightmares indicate that the child's brain is experimenting with frightening ideas during sleep. The important thing is to give the child extra support and comfort. Gradually she will learn to distinguish between what is real and what is make-believe.

First Words

This ability to have ideas allows the child to use pictures and to pretend play with dolls   for example, feeding a doll or pretending a doll is Mommy. At this point we parents and other caregivers want to help the child become verbal with his ideas. We want to help him understand the ideas of others by figuring out the sound patterns that others make, to express his own ideas in actual words.

Typically, as children learn to interact with more circles of communication, they vocalize more and gain more control of the fine oral motor patterns involved in movements of the tongue and vocal chords. Words don't come all of a sudden as though a switch is turned on. Rather, in ordinary development, from the child's first few months, more and more complex babbling and sound production emerge in a gradual process, with more and more consonants and vowels, until he starts actually speaking. This may happen later in children with ASD because of motor challenges, but they too gradually increase in their ability to make sounds.

At the same time, the child makes sense of not only hand gestures, smiles, and frowns but also vocal patterns; he learns to decode the sounds that go along with pointing, smiles, and frowns and to distinguish a happy sound from a sad sound from an excited sound. The human tongue and entire oral motor area is capable of generating an enormous range of gestural variations, and the human ear can perceive an enormous range of subtle variations in sound. Therefore, long before words are used to signify shades of meaning, vocal gestures are a vital part of communication. The human brain is a natural pattern recognizer, constantly organizing early communicative interactions. Most children with ASD can develop this ability to recognize patterns, though in some it may be delayed. It requires extra practice, sometimes a great deal of practice, depending on the degree of neurological problems. Often the degree of a child's difficulties won't be known until an optimal intervention program is begun and clinicians see how quickly she can make progress.

Thus as ideas begin to percolate in the child's mind, she learns to decode or recognize sound patterns, make different sounds, control her vocal cords, and imitate sounds that others make. It's not a big leap for the child to start repeating words she hears once she can understand these sound patterns and make these sounds. The child wants to go outside and takes Mommy by the hand and bangs on the door, and Mommy asks, "Do you want to go *out? Out?*" All of a sudden the child says "Ou, ou, ou." Then mommy repeats, "*Out, out*," and the child says, "Out!" and Mommy opens the door and the child goes outside.

Or the child points to juice and says, "Uhh, uhh, uhh," and Daddy says, "That's the juice. Juh, juh, juh," and the child repeats, "juh, juh," while grabbing for the juice. In this way the child not only learns the word "juice" or labels a picture of juice but labels the real juice that she is going to taste, understands what juice is, and relates the word to all her prior experiences of juice. "Juice" is now a meaningful symbol for that child. That's the way words are really learned.

Parents and other caregivers can also help children learn new words by giving them choices so they have to think about what they want.

As suggested in the previous chapter, the child should always be given the good choice first and the weaker choice second: "Do you want to go outside and play, or go to sleep?" The second choice should be a silly choice so if the child is just repeating you (the caregiver) and says "Sleep" because it's the last thing she heard, you'll say, "OK let's go to sleep," and the child will often say, "No, no!" Then you ask, "Well, do you want to go out and play-play or [make a snoring sound] sleep-sleep?" Pretty soon, the child will be getting it.

As the child learns in this way—the way language evolved in humans and the way all children learn language—he or she is acquiring language meaningfully in real situations. The child starts out emotionally invested in communicating and has an idea—"I want that door open." Then we caregivers help her understand and use the word that conveys that intent. When a word is invested with emotion, it has meaning for the child right away and generalizes to other contexts almost immediately. The child can then use the word "open" in a different setting—at school when there is a box of toys to be opened, for example.

All languages, we believe, started off with preverbal gestural communication that included vocal patterns, and these in turn led to increasing vocal interactions. As this interchange connected with emerging ideas, formal language evolved. Just as this was a gradual process during evolution, the emergence of language is a gradual process in the life of each baby and child, and it's an even more gradual process for many children with ASD, who need extra practice.

The Desire to Communicate

What prompts a child to go beyond using words just to meet basic needs to using them to share information? To use ideas and language fully—to be able to say, "Mommy, look at my car," or "Daddy, I'm bouncing the ball," instead of just saying, "Me hungry," or "Give me that"—the child has to *want* to use words to share information. This process occurs in a very interesting way: as a child becomes better at signaling, opening and closing more circles of communication, showing things to his parents, smiling, nodding, and using emotional gestures to solve problems, he learns that he can be close to someone else through emotional signaling. He doesn't have to be held or picked up or kissed to feel warmth, closeness, and dependency; it can occur through an exchange of gestures or words. Hearing a relative's voice on a long-distance call is not quite as good as giving him or her a hug, but it can make most people feel almost as warm as a hug can. This occurs because most of us have become "distal communicators."

The first step toward developing the desire to communicate is use of the gestures themselves; then the exchange of gestures or words helps the child to feel close to people, to feel part of a relationship, and to negotiate and regulate that relationship. As this happens, the child begins to value communication not just as a means to getting a cookie or hug, but because communication itself feels as good as a cookie or hug. Imagine yourself at a cocktail party with someone who is empathetic and warm, who nods and glows as you're talking, and who seems to value your every word. It's not just that the person seems to understand and agree with your ideas; you feel a primary sense of connectedness, a sense of belonging and of being appreciated at a very core level, the same way a four-month-old baby feels when she smiles at Mommy and Mommy gives her a big smile back.

Valuing communication in its own right motivates the child to use words and become a "motor mouth"—talking up a storm and telling you everything under the sun: "Mommy look at that," "Oh, Daddy see what I did," and so forth. In children without special needs, this stage typically occurs between the ages of two and four. In fact, by then many parents wish their children were a little quieter—"Hey, give me a few minutes; I'm talking to Grandma on the telephone." While children with ASD often take longer to get to this stage, we have been able to help them become so excited about their newly discovered words and language that they, too, want to talk about everything they are doing. The first step toward this breakthrough is to invest communication with the same warmth and pleasure that the child feels when she is being held or cared for. The more parents and other caregivers enjoy and work on emotional signaling in combination with the child's language, the more she values communication. She sees that it can serve many different emotional needs—pleasure, curiosity, assertiveness, exploration, and comfort in the face of fear and anxieties—just as it does for most healthy adults.

When communication feels good, children want to imitate their caregiver and learn words quickly. Communication taught through imitation first, without establishing this foundation, is much harder. Obviously, if there are oral motor problems, the child may not be able to pronounce certain sounds, but he certainly tries, maybe replacing some sounds with other sounds. It's fine if the child speaks in his own language initially while you the caregiver work on his oral motor skills—you'll get the hang of what he's trying to say. You can play games in which the child practices different sounds while learning to imitate words.

Sometimes children begin to speak by babbling and using words seemingly randomly. You can help your child learn to speak intentionally by helping her "think." If the child says "car" apparently without meaning, offer her both a toy car and her favorite doll and see which one she reaches for. Emphasize the word for what she wants and for what she doesn't want: "Want *dolly?* Or want *car?*" She will likely say "Doll" or smile and reach for it, or else shake her head at the car or, if you're lucky, say "No car." In this way you help her use words meaningfully rather than by rote. The key to establishing the meaning of words is to create a high-affect interaction—in the example, the child really wanting the doll instead of the car.

Imaginative Play

A child learns pretend play when you entice him to interact with you in make-believe scenarios. You feed the doll and he feeds the doll; your doll reaches out and says, "More hugs." Pretty soon a little story develops with the dolls hugging each other, feeding each other, and so forth. The key is to challenge the child to take the initiative. Pretending helps build a symbolic world by increasing the child's ability to use words and ideas. Initially, children pretend-playing may just repeat things they see at home, which is fine. But they may also apply their own creative twists, even from the beginning. They may start off feeding a doll just like Mommy is, but suddenly may have the doll push the food away and say, "No," causing the parent to wonder where that came from. That is the child's imagination.

Have lots of props available with which to entice your child, especially toy versions of common household objects, so he can play out dramas based on real-life experiences; this is the first place imagination may express itself. Specific dolls or stuffed animals can represent members of the child's family and friends. Also, give the child lots of real-world experiences—nature walks, supermarkets, interactive museums oriented to children, riding on the subway, playing in the sand. Relive some of these experiences with props, and see what the child chooses for pretend play at home.

To encourage pretending, add make-believe elements into the child's favorite activities: for example, if she plays with kitchen utensils, pretend she is a chef (you can be her helper). Start off pretending a scenario familiar to the child. Then you can challenge her to be creative by throwing in your own curve balls: if the child's doll is kissing your doll, your doll can run away and you say, "Your dolly has to find me to kiss me." Suddenly what was a routine now becomes an exciting game where the child's doll chases your doll and captures it. Meanwhile, you continually add in words, inviting the child to respond verbally as well as imaginatively. The key is for you to gesture and talk through your pretend character, whether it's a doll or a puppet or you on all fours pretending to be a horse.

We have developed a curriculum—the Affect-Based Language Curriculum (ABLC)—that systematically teaches language in this way (we discuss the curriculum in greater depth in Chapter 20). The main feature of this approach is that it builds a symbolic world by associating new words and concepts with meaning through real-life experiences that are invested with the child's emotions, *and* through pretend play (which is also emotional) that gives symbolic meaning to the child's inner world. Over time the child gets more imaginative: spaceships go off to the moon, sea monsters scare everyone, or a ballerina impresses an audience.

During pretend play, parents and caretakers should join in the child's interest in an imaginary world. For example, if the child is fascinated with a car, see if she will take a doll for a ride in the car. But speak not for yourself but for the doll. Become the doll and show the child how to enter the make-believe world. This introduces her to new ideas and symbolic constructs. As the doll, ask, "Can I ride in your car? Can I? If you don't say no, I'm going to get into your car." Then put the doll into the child's car, and the child may take "you" for a ride. Then you can make another doll be a police officer and ask, "Where are you going? Are you going to Grandma's house or going to school?" and point to two buildings. The child may not even know what Grandma's house is or what school is, but she can learn this way, and may just point to one of the buildings and go "Uhh, uhh." "There?" you ask. "Well, that's Grandma's house." And you may even have a picture of Grandma right there in the play area so the child can relate the idea to the image of Grandma.

Children who have motor or processing problems have difficulty imagining the world and thus pretending. For children with auditory processing problems, you may need to break directions down into simple, doable phrases. However, avoid talking too slowly or mechanically— rather, use a normal rhythm and inflection so that the child learns to respond to the emotional content of what you say. Children with visual processing problems have difficulty holding images of objects in their minds, making it hard for them to pretend. If such a child moves quickly from one toy to another, help him link images together by reintroducing toys. Also, store their toys in easy-to-see groups, rather than all jumbled up. For children with motor difficulties whose problems with sequencing actions lead to difficulties sequencing ideas, help them practice pretend actions and play out their ideas. Turn activities

such as singing or dancing into performance sequences by adding intro-
ductions, bows, clapping, and so forth.

Engaging with the Child's Interests

Children who crave sensation and like to move around may not sit
still and pick up dolls. Their parents often ask, "What can I do if my
child doesn't want to play with dolls?" In these cases, parents can become the toys. The parent can pretend: "I'm a lion and I'm coming to
your house." Or she can become the child's favorite character from a
book, TV show, or movie; the two can both play dress-up and act out
the drama, exchanging sounds and words.

Parents often say they don't have enough ideas; they can't figure
out what the doll should say, for example. Whenever you the parent
or other caregiver feel stuck, the key is to simply observe the child for
a few seconds and ask yourself what she is interested in: is she trying to
climb on the couch? Is she making one doll hit another doll? Frequently I see a parent trying to teach a child to give the doll a hug, for
example, and the child makes a beeline for the door. The parent then
says, "No, you can't go out. Come back here and play with the dolly,"
and the child has a tantrum. Remember that your goal is to teach the
child to use ideas, not to do any specific pretend play. You can teach
ideas and language at the door, on the couch, or with the doll.

If the child goes for the couch, you know she's interested in that. So
you ask, "Do you want to play on the couch or with dolly?" If the child
points to the couch, you can ask, "Do you want to go under the pillows or climb up on top?" and now you're playing on the couch. In
several minutes the child learns to say, "Climb up!" and you can say,
"OK, we're climbing up on the couch. But what about dolly? Dolly is
going to be very sad. Should we leave dolly on the floor, or bring her
up here with us?" The child may look at the doll. If not, you can get
the doll, have it start to climb up on the couch, and have it say,
"Climb up too, climb up too!" And you can hold the doll out to the

child and ask, "Where should dolly go?" If the child takes the doll and throws it on the floor, you can make a game with that, and so forth.

The idea is to go with the flow, but without giving in to the child's agenda. Her agenda may be just to act without talking, to be self-stimulatory or aimless, or to repeat the same play theme over and over. Instead, stretch the drama by introducing new variations into the child's theme. Introduce a conflict or challenge and use the child's negative response to thicken the plot. Creating conflicts encourage your child to add a new idea to the play. Do this whenever the child's play becomes rote or she tunes out, but don't try to take charge of the drama. You can even exaggerate the child's rigidity ("Yes, boss! All dolls have to march in line, boss!"). Don't worry about seeming negative by introducing conflict; you are challenging your child to grow and become more creative.

As you keep the child engaged and interacting with you in a continuous flow and using more and more ideas and words, she will eventually find all this far more fun than aimlessness or self-stimulation. You're not being mean-spirited by challenging her to learn these things. The key is to follow the child's interests in order to create favorable circumstances for you to teach her. Staying on this course, very gradually and gently, use pretend play to introduce experiences—various sounds, textures, themes, and motor challenges—that are difficult or aversive for your child. (Of course, when the child grows upset or anxious, focus on her favorite sensory experiences to help her calm down.)

Rather than anticipating and satisfying your child's desires right away (by giving her the stuffed bear she always sleeps with, for instance), try waiting a bit until she gives you a word or gesture to indicate her desires; acting as if you're confused about what she wants may help prompt her. By encouraging her to express her desire in words or gestures, you help her to visualize what she wants symbolically, instead of being stuck in the concrete here and now. She thus moves from reacting to thinking, which is a critical shift in development.

In Part III we explore other techniques for imaginative play in the context of Floortime. These techniques always work at the same time on all prior stages: attention, engagement, purposeful communication, and continuous flow of emotional gesturing, as well as using ideas. Tailored to the child's nervous system, such play expands ideas by entering the child's world.

Meaningful Symbols

Parents naturally encourage symbolic development from the very start of their child's life. For example, the teddy bear you put in your infant's crib is his first experience with a symbol that represents your comfort; the child learns that you aren't there all the time, so he carries the teddy bear around with him instead. We use symbols as alternatives to the real thing. But the symbols—whether words, roles, or toys—are embedded in the relationship you have been building from the beginning in caring for your child. Note which toy is your child's favorite, which one he is attaching to; children choose symbols, such as the Teletubbies, dinosaurs, a blanket. We are constantly surrounded by symbols, and whether you encourage it or not, your child probably chooses symbols that have a lot of meaning for him. Those can become the first dolls or toys you use in pretend play; then you can move on to using other toys.

Children indicate with their gestures what they are thinking when they pick up toys. Before a child can say that she wants to go in the car, for example, she may push the toy car along. Or she may feed a baby doll or pick up animals. So you can start out by giving a voice to the toys and activities the child chooses, thereby helping her progress from gestures to language. As you talk for Elmo or the stuffed moose, you also encourage the child to play with you and imitate you. This is where sequencing and motor planning come into play—everything you do should have a beginning, middle, and end. In real life, everything has a sequence: you get up, get out of bed, get dressed, eat breakfast, and so forth.

Watch what your child does with a toy. Does he just push the toy car, or does he take it somewhere? The initial interest in pushing a car back and forth or racing and crashing it evolves into treating the car as a means to an end—for example, driving to the playground, the pool, or the circus. The symbol becomes a vehicle for helping the child get what she wants; symbolic thinking is driven by the idea of what you want or how you feel. Because toys can provide a language that brings a child into the world of symbolic and emotional thinking, we spend a lot of time helping children become active learners this way. (Children who have challenges with manipulating toys and sequencing or with the visual-spatial aspect of finding a destination often prefer playing dress-up because it's easier and more familiar for them to just move themselves instead of a toy; organizing and sequencing both the object and themselves is more complex.)

Exploring Feelings

We want to help children express all their feelings in the realm of ideas, so that they can do more than react physically and automatically to their impulses. Make-believe and pretend play can help children become more comfortable with the whole range of feelings and work through emotional themes. As your child plays, look below her surface actions to the themes being played out, to see what her concerns are and what feelings she may be avoiding. There are many basic themes: dependency, pleasure, curiosity, power, aggression, limit setting, fear, love, and control. Obviously, these themes overlap, and more than one theme may be played out in any given drama: the content of the drama may reflect one theme, while the child's behavior may reflect another.

You can help your child explore feelings within the context of the drama—if a doll is sad, for example, ask if the doll misses her friend who moved away. Help the child to name the feelings that come up in pretend play; until children can put their feelings into words, they experience feelings only as physical impulses rather than as abstract concepts. If you give your child lots of practice separating feelings from actions, it will be easier for her to achieve higher levels of thinking as she gets older. You can also help a child with ASD prepare for new

experiences and anticipate upcoming challenges—such as the birth of
a sibling, a move to a new house, or the first day of school—through
pretend play.

Children should be encouraged to express negative feelings. Don't
take the child's expressions of negative feelings personally, but respond sympathetically so he doesn't get the idea that expressing his
feelings is dangerous. Of course, there should be limits on acting out
(rather than expressing) these feelings. Empathize with the child's
feelings and help him calm down first; then you can negotiate with
him and explain why he can't hit, or whatever the particular action is.
Then, help him talk about the feelings that provoked his behavior.

In addition to pretend play, have lots of reality-based, logical conversations with your child in which you ask (without grilling her)
what her feelings and thoughts are and why she does what she does.
When she asks questions, don't just give yes or no answers; help her
come to her own conclusions.

In summary, when encouraging a child with ASD to develop ideas
and language, there are three objectives:

- Signaling with gestures, to get many circles of communication in
  a row going and to help the child value communication in its
  own right.
- Creating emotionally meaningful situations in which to use what
  you want the child to learn—such as "Daddy," "juice," "open," or
  another new word. Associate the word with an emotional goal.
  In pretend play, if the child likes cars, action figures, or dolls, use
  these to begin imitative play. As you enter the child's world, play
  the role of the doll, the car, or the action figure.
- Using ideas logically, both in pretend play and in reality conversations. Ask questions and then expect, and work toward, a reply
  that answers your question.

Chapter 9

Logical Thinking
and the Real World

Five-year-old Ari had a history of poor motor planning and sequencing and both overreacted to touch and underreacted to sound, which resulted in a tendency to tune out others. Although Ari was bright and affectionate, these difficulties led him to easily become anxious, and he had trouble relating to his peers in kindergarten. He could be logical, but sometimes made statements that seemed completely nonsensical. When he was anxious and frustrated, he would repeat questions over and over, annoying his parents and teachers. Ari's parents wanted to help him be less anxious and more logical and be able to play more easily with other children.

In discussing logical thinking, we mean reality-based logic because sometimes children can be logical but out of touch with reality. A child may make a very logical argument that she can fly because she is just like Superman and Superman can fly. But the logic remains within a fantasy world. Every child, including those with ASD, must learn to understand the world in a realistic logical way. Everyone needs that skill to function at home, at school, at work, and in social situations.

Most adults assume they can be logical; it's very rare that someone assesses his own behavior as illogical, because almost by definition, if he is illogical, he doesn't have the ability to evaluate his thinking or behavior. A person who says, "Gee, I'm behaving illogically," is probably not only logical but also pretty self-aware. A person who is illogical, on the other hand, likely lives in the castles he creates.

Limited and Fully Logical Thinking

Take an adult (we'll call him Mr. Jones) who thinks people at work are whispering mean things about him and telling jokes at his expense. He assumes people intend to hurt him. The reality is that Mr. Jones does get teased a lot, but it is because of his own behavior. He tends to clown around, and also—not on purpose—to knock things over, bang into things, and be socially awkward. People often can't tell whether he's clowning or not, and they deal with it by teasing and joking with him. He often takes it "the wrong way," as his colleagues say, and sometimes gets angry.

Mr. Jones may be highly gifted in his technical work, and others may take his momentary upsets and seemingly illogical behavior as just part of his genius. At the same time, such a person misreads signals and is illogical in complex social situations. It's not unusual for somebody to be highly logical in work requiring scientific or technical skills but illogical in the world of emotional and social functioning or of making political judgments. Rational, logical thinking doesn't necessarily operate the same way in every arena. For full healthy development, we parents and other caregivers would like to see our children become logical in all areas of their lives—in school, work (whether scientific or artistic), and their intimate relationships.

For children with ASD and other special needs, such as the boy in the case study that opens this chapter, their language, motor, or other sensory processing problems make it difficult to achieve logic and reality. It is easier to escape into fantasy. For example, children who find the human voice painful because of its high pitch may withdraw from talking to people, preferring to babble to themselves and daydream.

In a world of fantasy, children can control the characters and the dialogue, and they don't have anyone asking them hard questions such as why, where, or when. They don't have to master new skills like reading, writing, or arithmetic. So it is an easy world to be in. If they are verbal, they can entertain themselves by talking. Some children with these processing difficulties, as many parents complain, talk out loud and babble to themselves in church or synagogue or during school hours, disturbing other children. Or they may tune others out and not fully interact with their parents or peers.

Such a child has difficulty engaging in reality-based thinking, because one of the first steps in becoming logical is to fully engage with the outside world and get to know it. If that is hard for a child because of the way she processes sensation or information, the path to logical thinking may be slower, with more roadblocks. Logical thinking may be achieved only in limited areas (as in our example of Mr. Jones). Once the building blocks are understood, all children can be helped to make progress toward consistently logical thinking.

Rather than being like Mr. Jones, we all would like our children and ourselves to be like Ms. Smith. She understands people. She creates a logical framework for solving the technical problems she faces at work, evaluates her own biases and corrects them in her written discussions, and can judge whether a report contains incomplete information. She can apply these same reasoning skills to her relationships with family, friends, and work colleagues. She can read their subtle signals and interpret what is between the lines. She can do all of this even when she is under stress, tired, or overloaded with work. Rarely falling into the trap of all-or-nothing thinking, she almost always thinks in relative shades of gray in assessing people or looking at probable outcomes for different courses of action. Ms. Smith exemplifies both consistently logical thinking and also the reflective thinking described in the following chapter.

Early Steps in Logical Thinking

How do parents, other caregivers, and professionals help children with ASD make continuing progress toward logical thinking? Steps toward this goal begin very early, as babies start to take in the outside world. Logical thinking requires accurate information; the first step an infant takes is using his senses to take in the world around him and getting a full picture of that external world. This begins in the first three or four months of life.

The second step in logical thinking is engaging the world in an emotionally meaningful way. A baby can look, listen, smell, and taste but choose not to use these abilities because she doesn't trust the world and wants to avoid it. So the second step is willingly embracing the world and trusting both what she sees and the relationships that she has with others who can provide information. This is not easy for those children with ASD who under- or overreact to sensation and need to be pulled into that external world, or whose processing problems make them confused by sensory input. For example, in the case of the little boy Ari, I recommended that his parents be calm, soothing, and reassuring whenever he was anxious and tense. At the same time, they needed to counteract his lagging motor development by energetically bringing him more fully into a shared world, helping him to feel comfortable engaging with others.

The third step is purposeful interaction with the world. This can be as simple as a baby reaching for a rattle and examining it or an older child grabbing a pencil to begin writing when the teacher gives instructions. A child needs to be able to act purposefully in order to understand the world—touching the floor to see if it's hard, squeezing a balloon to see if it's soft. Also, purposeful action is an important step in the development of logic because it usually leads to some reaction. Touching Daddy's nose leads to a sensation in the fingers and maybe a sound from Daddy. Squeezing the rattle leads to feeling a certain texture or hearing a noise. The perceived link between purposeful action and reaction is the beginning of causal thinking and formal cause-effect reasoning, even before ideas come in. This usually begins in the second half of the first year of life.

The fourth step in the development of logic is combining a series of purposeful actions into a pattern, as when a child searches for a hidden toy and gets Mommy to help her. Or the child figures out how an obstacle course works—going over this cube and around this wall and through this tunnel to reach her goal. This requires many problem-solving steps and a number of purposeful actions toward a goal. It is the beginning of higher levels of logic, scientific reasoning, and pattern recognition. So interacting with the child in multiple steps toward solving problems is essential for higher-level critical thinking skills. Children with sequencing or motor problems may find this step very difficult.

The next step is the use of ideas. This is what we often think of as logical reality-based thinking, but it is actually the fifth step in our sequence. At this point children can experiment in their minds. They don't have to search all over the house for that cookie, but can picture in their minds where that cookie might be. They can picture the refrigerator, the cupboard, and the drawer where Mommy tends to hide things. And they can use pretend play to explore ideas—the dolls can find that hidden cookie. So ideas become a vehicle by which children picture the world and play with it inside their heads. As Chapter 8 discussed, this creates a new level of thinking—symbolic thinking—that, in typically developing children, often begins by eighteen to twenty-four months of age.

If using ideas goes well, that child can proceed to the sixth stage, where he builds bridges between ideas. This is the beginning of rational thinking in the traditional sense: children can now combine ideas together logically and engage in discussion and debate. To help children master this stage, caregivers and teachers try constantly to expand their creativity. The more ideas children have, the broader and more elaborate their conversations, and more important, the better thinkers they become.

For example, if you ask the simple question, "What is that?" and the child answers, "That's an apple" or "That's a doggie," that is a logical response connecting her idea to your idea. Initially, a child may answer just simple "what" and "where" questions and perhaps some "who" questions. Or in response to your comment, "I'm going to be a horsy," the child may say, "OK, giddy-up, giddy-up, go!" Eventually, your child will be able to answer "why" questions such as "Why do you want to go to Grandma's house?" with "Because I like Grandma's toys" or "Because she is fun."

These questions can be embedded in pretend play—again, with you the caregiver always talking through the doll or character—or in general conversation. Have a lot of real-life conversations in which you ask the child about his favorite food or what he wants to do, and also a lot of shared pretend play. In both cases, keep the conversation going. The technique, as described earlier, is to follow your child's natural interests, create interaction, generate continuous back-and-forth gesturing, and then build words on that groundwork, with the child using those words meaningfully. There is no one way to do it; the only mistake you can make is not trying.

Meanwhile, you challenge the child to make sense. So if you say, "I'm going to be a horsy," and the child says, "Big tree," and looks outside, it doesn't connect to your idea, and you have to challenge the child to make a connection. You can ask, "Horsy or tree? Horsy or tree?" pointing to yourself as the horsy and then to the tree outside. The child might look at you and make a "no" gesture to the horsy, and then point to the tree; you can ask, "Climb tree or look at tree?" and she may give you a big smile and say, "Climb tree, climb tree," and start banging on the window as though she wants to go outside and climb the tree. Now she is beginning to make sense and connect ideas together.

With a child with ASD, it may take many steps to make this happen. Anytime she jumps randomly from one idea to another, try to bring in logic but without doing it for her. Many parents and professionals think children can learn by copying rather than thinking something through for themselves, but your goal is to challenge the child, not have her memorize scripts. A child who learns only to memorize scripts may, a year later, have lots of scripts but still be unable to have a conversation or think creatively or logically. Children with ASD need more creative and logical thinking challenges than the average child does. Giving way to scripts because they are easier to teach may produce the illusion that the child is saying logical things ("Mommy, go to sleep now," for instance), but it will undermine the child's progress in the future. The child will have a series of memorized phrases, but won't be able to play with peers or converse with a new teacher, because she hasn't learned to use ideas and words flexibly and logically.

At times, the child may memorize whole phrases and use them appropriately. We all do that when we hear certain phrases repeatedly. That's fine as long as the phrases are used in a logical manner. Many children with ASD are fragmented; they are creative and may be using ideas, but they jump around from one idea to another, so their conversation often lacks cohesiveness and logic. For children with ASD who have processing difficulties, you have to make sure they recognize what you are saying so they can connect ideas together logically. Sometimes this means getting playfully obstructive. For example, if you ask a child who is ignoring you, "Where is the car going?" and the child keeps moving the car without responding, you become a police officer who says, "Oh, the car can't move until I know where you are going." Out of frustration, the child may point or say, "There" or "To the house." Thus you help her connect ideas together.

Most children reach this stage by age four. In children with ASD, it may occur later. Often they reach it once they can give answers to "why" questions. In the case of Ari, I recommended that his parents always get him to explain the logic of his statements, particularly when he seemed most illogical, anxious, and repetitive in his language. Rather than explaining things to him, or repeating "yes" or "no" answers, they should challenge him to make sense of his world and his own thoughts. For example, if he asked a question, such as "Are we having dinner soon?" over and over again, they could ask him, "Why are you asking me so many times? Are you afraid that I'm going to forget to feed you or that I will fall asleep?" This would help them understand what is causing him concern. Finally, when Ari made illogical statements, his parents could ask, "Is that a joke or are you serious?" and get him to clarify.

One of the biggest challenges that children with ASD and other special needs pose is helping them to become problem-solvers, to use multiple steps to solve problems, even before they use ideas. If this skill is missing, ideas—even if they come in—won't be very useful. To teach it, parents and other caregivers need to establish a continuous flow of logical interaction with the child.

Distinguishing Between Fantasy and Reality

Many cognitive researchers and theoreticians have thought that once a person can combine ideas and use them in logical ways, he or she is reality based. But, as noted above, being reality based also means appreciating the difference between fantasy and reality. This requires a significant emotional accomplishment, as do all the other stages. Establishing a sense of reality as different from fantasy requires a person to invest the world outside himself with value, interest, and trust.

How do people even tell whether an experience is inside or outside of them? How do we know whether a thought comes from our own brain or from someone else's? How do we know if an apple or a piece of candy is a figment of our imagination—something we have invented—or is real? In dreams, which are all imagination, when we eat that apple, it tastes good. One child who liked to make up stories made up one about going to Disney World when she didn't really go there. When I asked, "Why do you do that?" she said, "Because it feels so good. It feels almost as good as when I really go there." Sometimes, especially for children with ASD, make-believe can feel almost as good as the real thing; that's why they may elect to escape into fantasy.

How do we help children establish the boundary between fantasy and reality? Here are the critical steps: First, starting in infancy, the child has to form relationships with others in the outside world. These others represent external reality. When Mommy sings a lullaby, the sound is coming from outside the child. In this way, children begin to understand the difference between what's inside and what's outside of them. When, a little later on, the child involves a parent in helping him get a toy, he gets further confirmation of the outside world—a person who exists separately from him and who can do things he can't do.

When children begin to pretend-play with another person—perhaps they have the little piggy go, "Oink, oink," and then Mommy says, "Oh, are you hungry, my little piggy—what do you want to eat?"—there is an external voice, an imagination other than their own, interacting with them. This too establishes the difference between what is inside and what is outside. Then, in logical conversations, when Mommy asks, "Why do you want to go outside?" a voice of reality comes from the outside asking the question. It's not the same as doing a puzzle alone or playing a computer game. It is a live human asking a question, judging the child's answer, and saying, "Well, you have to give me a better reason if we are going to go out and play on the slide." Negotiations, opinion-oriented discussions, and debates establish that boundary between the child and the outside world. The more that boundary is established with emotional negotiation—the child and parent discussing the child's emotion to figure out why the child feels that way, to help her figure it out, and to calm her down—the more a sense of self develops. These experiences establish a distinction between feelings inside and those outside the child.

If parents are too punitive, overexciting, or frustrating and can't respond in a regulated, harmonious way, it may be harder for a child to establish that boundary. She may want to escape back into fantasy. A regulated, calm response to each of the child's different feelings in the course of the normal day helps her establish that reality-fantasy boundary. Because of their biological challenges, children with ASD may need extra support in this area.

Thus, with a child who has language but uses that language only in a private fantasy, for example, the key isn't to simply set limits (as many are prone to do) by saying, "Don't babble out loud." The child may just retreat and do it more quietly. The key is to pull that child into the external world, starting with making interaction more fun than escaping into fantasy. If the child says (as many children do), "No, you can't play with me, I want to play by myself," make it a game; sit across the room and negotiate. Ask, "Well, can I sit here?" "No, sit further away." "How much further away?" and so forth.

Every discussion, every circle of communication, brings the child into a shared world. Eventually you the caregiver can ask, "Can I watch you play?" Pretty soon you are the audience watching the child construct her drama and clapping for her. Then you might make suggestions for different kinds of dramas the child can construct. It's now an interactive drama, with you as audience and chorus, and maybe even a character in the play if you prove a good enough audience. That's a way in which you can turn an escapist into a child who enjoys reality.

For a child with ASD, it is especially important to limit TV time and isolated play. Many children who escape into fantasy spend hours and hours a day by themselves; they need to learn to enjoy interactive relationships first. Fifteen minutes alone here and there for a child with ASD is appropriate. We realize that this may be a difficult goal for busy parents, and we encourage having helpers, such as teenagers from the neighborhood, college students, or siblings, to keep the child engaged.

All children need to be helped through the critical early stages of logical thinking so that they can fully engage in life experiences as they get older—including biological changes, more intimate relationships and friendships, and changing group relationships—and learn from these experiences. Children with ASD need extra practice in investing in the outside world through the senses and through trusting relationships, then through problem-solving interactions, then through using ideas, and finally through thinking logically in reality-based ways. With this foundation, interactions in the different spheres of life will keep defining and refining the boundary between reality and fantasy, enhancing the child's ability to think logically.

Chapter 10

Higher Levels of Abstract and Reflective Thinking

Nine-year-old Danny, diagnosed with high-functioning autism, attended a regular third-grade class in a public school, where he had support from an aide. His rote skills were strong and he had a good vocabulary, but he was having difficulty keeping up with the rest of the class in terms of higher levels of thinking, such as understanding complex directions (both written and verbal) for math problems and reading exercises. It was especially difficult for Danny to make inferences, such as figuring out what the boy in a story would do next based on his past behavior. His teachers and parents wondered if they could help him improve these skills, or if he was stuck at this level.

In working with children with autism, intervention programs often don't expect them to advance much beyond the basics of engaging, communicating, and early levels of thinking and everyday functioning. Some are more ambitious. But we have found that many children with various types and levels of ASD can progress not only through the first six stages but also through the additional milestones that we described briefly in Chapter 4, such as multicausal and gray-area

thinking, developing an internal standard, and even abstract, reflective thinking.

Further Levels of Logic

Once children can separate fantasy from reality, and logic from illogic,
they ordinarily progress to multicausal thinking, or conceiving of
events as having multiple reasons for happening: "It's cold outside because the sun isn't shining and because it's wintertime," or "I want to
go out and play because I want to go on the slide and run around and
pick apples off the apple tree." Once children start giving multiple
reasons for events, their thinking abilities become more complicated.
Multicausal thinking—which is just an extension of causal logical
thinking—can be encouraged very simply by asking the child for more
opinions when she answers a question.

Related to multicausal thinking is what we call *indirect* or *triangular
thinking*. This is at work, for example, when a child figures out that in
order to win the Revolutionary War, the United States had to enlist
the help of France, because France was the enemy of England, which
was America's enemy. Similarly, when Eddie wants to become friends
with Johnny, but sees that Johnny won't return his friendship, he becomes friends with Billy—who is already friends with Johnny. Through
Billy, Eddie reaches his original goal.

Some children learn this step naturally: they go ask Mommie for a
cookie, and when Mommie says no, they go ask Daddy. They realize
there is more than one pathway to the cookie. You the parent or other
caregiver don't want to scold them and say, "That's a bad thing to do"
or "You're being manipulative." If children tell outright lies, that's manipulation of a different kind, and you want to teach them to value
honesty. But if they're showing cleverness and learning to solve problems in new ways, that's a valuable skill that will help them become
more abstract and reflective in their thinking. To teach triangular
thinking, go after more than one cause, push for different kinds of

solutions to a problem by challenging the child: "Well, what else can we do? How else can we do it?"

In typical development, multicausal and triangular thinking are mastered by about age seven. Children with ASD may not master this stage until age eight to ten, or even much later. The brain develops into the fifties and sixties, so it's never too late. The attitude we take is that once one level is reached, you go for the next level. So the key thing with children, teenagers, or young adults with ASD is to keep trying for the next level in thinking. You can teach thinking as the child is learning to cross the street, take a train, clean her room, or buy a candy bar (Which is your favorite? Why?) or doing her school-work (What are the reasons a character in a novel acts the way she does?)—all these practical skills can be learned in a thoughtful way or in a simple rote way.

The next level, *gray-area thinking*, involves making comparisons, of-ten on more than one dimension. Gray-area thinking can be broken down into two components: comparative thinking (why broccoli is healthier than cookies) and discussing the degree to which A is better than B or to which one opinion holds more strongly than another. Typically, by age eight, children can understand and express degrees of things: how happy, sad, or angry they are; how much they like A more than B, and the multiple reasons for liking A more than B, and the degree to which the two are different or similar. Gray-area thinking involves the capacity for subtlety and nuance. For example, if a child is reading Mark Twain, you may ask her to compare Huck Finn and Tom Sawyer and tell you why she likes one character better than the other. The child may say, "I like Huck Finn better because he is stronger" or "Huck Finn is smarter" or "Huck Finn is more fun." This is what we call comparative gray-area thinking. The child is compar-ing the two and telling you that one is stronger or wiser or smarter—there is a relative aspect to it.

In gray-area differentiated thinking, the child not only compares two things but also compares them by degree: "Well, Huck Finn is much, much smarter than Tom Sawyer but only a little bit stronger than Tom." Similarly, in giving three reasons for the Civil War—such as slavery, religion, and economic factors—a child engaged in gray-area thinking may give reasons as to the degree of each factor's importance. This is getting into rather sophisticated logic, but if without gray-area thinking, a child (or adult) tends to be left with polarized—"all-or-nothing"—thinking. Many people live in an all-or-nothing world where "it has to be my way or the highway." Many manifest rigid thinking—in which there is only one way to do something ("The spoon goes here!") or only one answer to a question—in politics, in appraisals of history, in misuses of science. But ours is a gray-area world, a world of complexity.

Because of compromised mastery of earlier developmental stages, children with ASD, as well as many others, may get stuck in rigid or polarized thinking. However, by challenging them to expand their emotional, creative, and logical range, we parents, other caregivers, and teachers can help them gradually become more flexible. To stimulate gray-area thinking, we must ask their opinions about things in shades of gray. "I know you want spaghetti for dinner, but how much do you want it? What are your main reasons for wanting spaghetti instead of fish sticks?" Right or wrong answers are not enough; the opinions have to be shades of gray—looking at the relative degrees of things. Children with ASD can become skillful gray-area thinkers if we challenge them to work on it. Many traditional educational approaches go after right and wrong answers. But only reasoned debates—whether about friends, sports, or the causes of the Civil War—help develop gray-area thinking. We don't want to pester the child; we want to be natural. There are many opportunities, both at home and at school, to help exercise subtle, gray-area, reflective thinking.

Many people have not progressed to gray-area thinking. Polarized thinking can be seen in many teenagers and adults, even those without developmental problems. If children are given only facts to memorize—or in the case of children with ASD, scripts to repeat—they never learn to be gray-area thinkers. On the other hand, with debates and exchanges of opinions, children have a better chance of getting to this higher level of logic and reality.

We have one more level of logical thinking to consider: the ability—which usually doesn't develop until the teenage years—for *thinking from an internal standard,* the ability to evaluate one's own thoughts and biases. This ability allows a student to evaluate an essay he has just completed and think: "That was a pretty logical, cohesive essay I just wrote. I made my point strongly, I backed it up, I considered subtlety and nuance, and I brought in all the facts available." Or he might think: "That wasn't such a good essay. I was a little tired, and I didn't have a chance to research everything I wanted to, and my logic, I think, was a little slippery in places." In the emotional arena, a person might think after an outburst, "Hmm, I wonder why I got so mad? I'm not usually that way." An internal standard enables a child to say, "My friends are cheating on tests, but that's not the sort of person I am. I'll see if I can get along with them in spite of not going along with their cheating."

This ability to evaluate oneself, one's behavior, and one's ideas against an internal standard, to have a longer view of a situation than the day-to-day world of peer relationships, allows a person to judge her own thoughts, feelings, and biases. Even among adults this level of logical and reflective thinking is a rare commodity, because it is not easy to acquire. To help children acquire it—especially children with ASD—requires lots of opinion-oriented discussions and respect for the child's developing sense of self. We're so busy telling children whether they've done a good or bad job that we rarely ask them to judge themselves. We need to give them criteria, give them the standards, and help them become their own judges, their own mentors.

Abstract and Reflective Thinking

Historically, higher levels of abstract and reflective thinking—particularly empathy, theory of mind (understanding other people's perspectives), and inference—have been considered beyond the reach of children with ASD. However, as we indicate in Chapter 2, many such children have not only achieved these more advanced milestones but have mastered them with enormous depth and subtlety.

An important factor that prevents children from mastering advanced thinking capacities is the way we teachers, therapists, and parents work with them in educational programs, therapeutic programs, and everyday interactions at home. If we just say, "That's bad" or "No, no, no," we may think we are teaching the child discipline, but we're actually teaching extreme, polarized, all-or-nothing thinking. When a child throws a tantrum or impulsively misbehaves at times, we assume it's because she hasn't been disciplined enough. But it may in fact be because the child has been disciplined in an all-or-nothing way rather than a gray-area way. We can be firm and persistent and teach children values and behavior while also teaching them to have reasoned judgment and gray-area thinking.

Abstract thinking is difficult for all children. The fact that, historically, efforts to help more children with ASD achieve these advanced levels have shown little success reflects in part a failure to challenge them in the right way. They need more practice than other children do, just as children with other developmental problems may need more practice learning to walk, sit up, or use words in the first place.

Using Language to Reason and Think

Children such as the boy described at the beginning of this chapter can show age-appropriate mastery of words and phrases and yet lag their age peers in verbal reflective thinking ability. A child who has an excellent vocabulary, who can accurately define many different words, and who does well in structured language tests may still be unable to reason with words in an age-appropriate manner. The term "age-appropriate language development" refers to the level at which the child is using language to reason and think, as compared to normally developing children.

We see many children with milder forms of ASD, some of whom have been diagnosed with Asperger's Syndrome, who are thought to be age appropriate in their language development, or even advanced because they have excellent vocabularies and can sight-read and sound out text that is three years ahead of their grade level. But when we ask these children to describe more than just the facts of what they read, or try to have a debate with them about what they read, they actually reason at two or more years *below* their age level. This is a significant challenge that needs to be addressed if children are to move ahead in school and beyond. It is largely a result of underlying processing differences. These can be overcome if dealt with correctly, but only if we realize the child has a specific, treatable processing problem, rather than some fixed deficit.

Steps in Achieving Abstract Thought

The first step in achieving the more advanced levels of thinking is to make sure that all of the six basic developmental levels are mastered. You can help solidify these first levels by having long, engaged conversations with the child, using gestures and words, always challenging her to be both creative and logical at the same time. If the child isn't making sense, help her connect ideas by pretending you don't understand. The stages of multicausal, triangular, and gray-area thinking, as well as using logic to evaluate one's own feelings and actions, can then be reached during extended conversations about family activities and relationships, school, and friends and during pretend play dramas.

In every conversation with children who use rote skills but are not yet good abstract thinkers, work on creative thinking and opinions, not facts. Avoid questions such as "What color was the boy's jacket in that story?"; instead ask, "Gee, what did you think about what the boy did? What would you do if you were in that story?" If you know the answer to the question you ask your child, then you're just reinforcing rote knowledge. Ask the question you don't know the answer to because it's an opinion, such as what the child enjoyed most at school that day and why. As long as what the child says makes sense, it's a good answer.

To introduce new abstract concepts to children with ASD, the situations in which you teach these skills must have high emotional meaning. For example, a ten-year-old girl was brought to see me (SIG). She had multiple learning disabilities and cognitive and language delays; some of the professionals who worked with her thought she fell under the autistic spectrum, and some did not. The mother complained that her daughter was very concrete in her thinking and seemed to be at the five- or six-year-old level in terms of understanding abstract ideas and concepts, even though she was very verbal. I asked, "What kind of concepts can't she understand?" "Well, what her father does," the mother replied. The father was a tax accountant, and the little girl did not understand what taxes were.

I said, "Let's see if we can help her understand taxes in the next five minutes." Her mother doubted this was possible. So I tried to create a real-life, emotionally charged situation. I said, "Pretend we have a pizza." We made a pizza out of a piece of paper, and I asked the little girl how many pieces we should cut it into. She decided on six pieces. Her little brother was also in the room, so I said, "Your brother wants to steal your pizza. I'll be the policeman. How many pieces of that pizza will you give me to keep your brother from stealing the whole pizza?" And she said, "I'll give you two pieces." I asked, "How many do you have left?" She counted, saying, "I'll have one, two, three, four left." "OK, you've got a deal," I said. So she gave me two pieces.

"Those two pieces are called taxes," I said. "You have given me two pieces in taxes to protect you from your brother. Now is there anything else you would give me pizza for? Like, to protect you from bad people from another country coming into the United States? Would you pay me to clean the streets? Would you pay me to give you water in your house so you can take a shower?" The little girl replied, "I would pay one piece to keep everything clean." I said, "OK, that's also taxes. Now, if you had lots of pizza, what else would you be willing to have?" She listed other things, such as protection from people with guns and things, and we talked about that as taxes. Then I said, "Mommy, ask her what taxes are." So Mommy asked, "Sweetheart, what are taxes?" And the little girl said, "Taxes is what I would give to have things to help me like police or soldiers." Mother smiled because her daughter now understood the concept of taxes.

I helped this little girl understand the concept of taxes, in everyday language, by creating a highly motivating situation that she could relate to—that is, keeping her pizza from her brother. Similarly, I've helped children write essays—when teachers had told me the children could never master the sequencing of an essay—by starting off with topics that were meaningful to them, such as, "Why I am better than my brother," or, "Why my parents should let me watch more TV." They dictate the essays into my tape recorder and I have someone type them out, and they're organized, sequential essays.

The common principle in the tax and essay examples is that the child has high emotional involvement. When you're arguing a point you feel strongly about, if you can think logically, you use all skills at your command to make your case. We see many children who are failing in school but are street-smart: they are good thinkers and make logical arguments when they are arguing a point having to do with friends, games, or sneakers, for example. But they don't apply this to papers in school. Almost everyone rises to his or her highest level of thinking in an emotionally charged situation.

For this reason, concepts and logical thinking are best taught in two steps: first, create a motivating situation and get the concepts across, and second, introduce new terminology. For example, if a child is trying to master both new words and concepts in a book he is reading so that he can write an essay about them, discuss with him just the basic ideas first. Set aside the terminology and just work on the conceptual part. Once the child has that down, he can learn the related words and work them into a structured essay. It's hard to do both at the same time.

Children can be anxious in a school setting, of course, but if they learn logical thinking through lots of practice at home, even anxiety won't disrupt it. Once children master abstract thinking, they can begin using it when they're anxious —in fact, they can use it as a coping strategy. When children who are good abstract thinkers get anxious or bored at school, they can use abstract logic to defend their interests: "Can I do a different assignment? This one is repetitive and covers what I already know."

Working with new words and concepts is hard, not just because they must be memorized but also because of the sequencing ability required. Most children with ASD and other learning disabilities have motor planning and sequencing problems; they get so lost in memorizing new words that they forget the logic, so they just start guessing. Familiar words and concepts and emotionally relevant situations are the keys. We know kids are great lawyers when they're arguing for an extra half hour of TV or for an ice cream sundae, but they may be incoherent when it comes to writing an essay about a book. If we teach thinking skills in simple, emotionally meaningful contexts, the child will learn to apply them to academic tasks.

The next step in helping children think abstractly is creating multisensory approaches to learning. Teach not just with words but also with images, action, and drama. If a child can't describe to you why you are being unfair, have her show it with a series of drawings or act it out in a drama. Then help the child talk about her drama or drawings.

High levels of abstract thinking, such as making inferences, speculating, and drawing new conclusions, also require the ability to judge one's own conclusions for originality, against an internal standard. To reach this next level of reasoning, a person has to have a strong sense of self, an internal standard from which to reflect. This is both an emotional and intellectual task. The way to help children arrive at this level is to make sure they first master the earlier levels. Then you need to go after judgment and not be satisfied with simpler answers. For example, when a child is expressing great emotion, you can ask, "How are you actually feeling? How does this compare to the way you normally feel? Is today unusual? In what way?" You thus encourage the child to take a step back and observe and evaluate his own feelings and beliefs. This type of critical thinking is so difficult to apply to one's own emotions that many adults can't do it. But the way to start it with kids is to raise the questions.

On intellectual tasks, too, children engage more fully when asked to evaluate the information and reach their own conclusions. You can say to an older child, "Now, be your own devil's advocate. What kind of biases do you have in your essay? Can you argue the other point of view? Which do you think is the more reasonable one, given your own experiences?" You are asking the child to consciously integrate herself into the debate, to evaluate herself, and to argue the opposing point of view. That's a high level of thinking which takes years to do well.

The key to helping children to master abstract thinking, especially children with ASD, is to take your time and go through every step in turn. As you work on each new level of thinking, reinforce the previous levels as well; work on all these advanced levels at the same time. Patience, high emotion, practical, everyday situations—these will promote high-level thinking in children for whom it is not easy. Never assume a ceiling on a child's abilities. Always assume you can get to one more level, and after that, one more level.

Theory of Mind and Empathy

Theory of mind—the ability to figure out how others feel, to take another person's perspective—is an elaboration of the ability to think from an internal standard. If you want to know how someone else feels in a situation, such as being rejected by a love interest, you've got to first ask yourself, "How would I feel if someone rejected me? I would feel sad and depressed." Then you consider alternatives: "But Johnny's acting kind of hyper: he's going up to every new girl in school and trying to meet them. He's not acting sad and depressed. I wonder if he's trying to cheer himself up by just acting the opposite. Or maybe he actually didn't like that girl that much after all; maybe he was just asking her out because of peer pressure."

Empathy is sensing how the other person feels through the way you might feel in his or her situation, but then objectively evaluating your conclusions and considering alternative hypotheses. Empathetic adults can understand how another person feels; their questions, emotional tone, and body posture all convey a sense that they sense what it's like to be in your shoes, without exaggerating your feelings. We all know people who get so upset when we are upset that we wind up calming them down rather than the other way around. That is not empathy. We also have experience with individuals who listen in a sort of mechanical way; they may ask a few correct questions, but don't give the sense that they really understand or care about what we are saying. They want to be empathetic, but don't quite have it at the feeling level. We know still other adults who read people well but use this ability in self-serving, narcissistic ways; so empathy shouldn't be confused with the simple ability to understand where other people are coming from.

Empathy is a difficult skill to learn for all children, let alone for children with ASD, who may not have had enough of the experiences that help them develop it. However, as we have emphasized, we find that many children and adults with ASD and other developmental problems can become highly empathetic and understanding if they have the right kind of learning experiences. Each stage of development provides a chance to create experiences for children that will help them master earlier stages that may have not been mastered the first time around. It's never too late.

Empathy begins with a baby's first loving, warm relationship with a primary caregiver. Without this early nurturing, it's hard to learn deep caring for other human beings; you have to experience empathy to bear it toward others. What happens next is critical. By eight to nine months, a baby learns to read and respond to different emotional signals, such as Mommy's smile or frown. This is the beginning of the baby's knowing that another person is separate from him so he doesn't get overidentified with that other. In addition, the baby learns to quickly read and respond to the other person's emotions. These are foundations for empathy.

Then, by eighteen months, children typically are playing with other children, taking turns going up the slide, and giggling together at a shared joke. They aren't just knocking each other down as you might see with two fourteen-month-olds, or crying when the other gets upset; now they are actually sharing humor together. This reflects the ability not just to react to feelings but also to participate in cooperative endeavors in which two or more people may copy and identify with each other and share each other's sorrows and joys.

Next we start to see the first signs of altruism: a child goes up to her mother, for example, and pats her on the arm if she looks upset. This isn't quite empathy, because empathy requires understanding intellectually as well as emotionally how another person is feeling. But it is certainly a step in that direction because the child—whether she is copying observed behavior or truly feeling it—is now trying to help the other person feel better.

The next big step is the stage of shared meanings, which occurs when pretend play and the use of words come in—between eighteen months and two and a half or three years of age in typical development. Now children get involved in shared pretending with parents or with other children. They are now at the symbolic level of words and ideas, sharing feelings through pretend play, and are beginning not only to feel empathetically but to think empathetically. Empathy requires an extra step, where the child can think in a cause-effect way and reason about how another person is feeling. When the child can ask, "Mommy, why are you mad?" she can separate her internal world from your world, but still be concerned about yours.

If that initial stage of empathy goes well, children move into a yet more complicated stage where they can explore multiple reasons for feelings and begin perceiving shades of gray. Their empathy expands as they enter into what we call playground politics—becoming part of a social group at school and looking at how they fit into a social hierarchy with other children. Who's the angriest? Who's the most popular? Who's the best soccer player? Who's the best at math? Sometimes it's very painful for children to feel that they are not as good as other children in certain things. As I like to tell parents, it's far better for children to feel disappointed or dejected now about not being the best at everything than to learn it for the first time at age nineteen through rejection by a boyfriend, girlfriend, or a good friend. First-time disappointments are harder to deal with in the late teenage years.

Being part of a social group allows children to broaden their capacity for empathy. We can help our children to expand their empathetic range and their ability to identify beyond what they experience immediately.

Can they empathize with children who have different skin colors or different religious backgrounds, for example? In this regard, placing children with ASD and those without together in integrated classes can enable each one to understand the different abilities of the other.

Some children with ASD can progress through all of these levels of empathy, but they have to go step by step. As they become more self-aware, they can size up the group at school and confront that very painful realization of being different. "Mommy, why can't I talk as well as Johnny or Suzy?" or "Why do the kids make fun of me?" or "Why is it easier for me to learn spelling than it is for the other kids?" Facing these differences is the first step in self-definition and can lead to disappointment and sadness, as well as satisfaction. But without disappointment and sadness, a child can't have joy or an identity, because a sense of self is created by what I call boundary-defining feelings—feelings that tell us who we are.

To truly empathize with another person's joy, sadness, or humiliation, we need to have experienced each of those feelings ourselves, at least to some degree. It is not surprising that many adults who had ASD and other special needs as children achieve a high level of empathy or enter the helping professions, because often they had to struggle more with challenges or feelings of disappointment than their peers did. That can deepen one's sense of humanity. It is hard for a child to deal with these challenges, but with the support and empathy of a family, the experience can be a real asset for the future.

Finally, there is yet another level of empathy—the ability to empathize reflectively. This means having an organized sense of self, knowing who one is, going through these self-defining experiences of happiness and joy, sorrow and disappointment, and then being able to understand a range of feelings in others and compare them to one's own feelings. Empathy embraces all emotions, and parents should support the exploration of negative emotions as they arise in play so that the child has an opportunity to understand them more deeply.

When it comes to assessing your child's progress in these higher levels of thinking, remember that life is always in the gray zone, so you should never ask, "Has my child truly mastered this or that milestone?"

Rather, you should ask, "To what degree has my child mastered the milestone?" For example, a child who is walking a little bit and then falls and stumbles and gets up is walking some of the time, not all the time. Some children require a little more support to master a skill; they may do it when we encourage and challenge them, but won't take the initiative. So instead of demanding an all-or-nothing answer, try to understand in what way the child has mastered logical or abstract thinking or empathy, and how deeply: with or without support, some or all of the time.

Chapter 11

Unique Biologies, I

Experiencing the World
Through the Senses

All children—typically developing children as well as those with ASD and other special needs—are unique in the way they experience the world through their senses. By tailoring their care to these individual differences, parents, therapists, and other caregivers working with children on the autistic spectrum can help these children—even those who are very rigid or want exact predictability in their experience—to develop and become more flexible.

Even before we're born, many environmental and genetic forces affect how our central nervous systems and physical bodies develop. After birth, as our bodies begin to mature, we continue to be subject to all sorts of influences that nurture, inhibit, and otherwise contribute to these variations. In children at risk for ASD, genetic, prenatal, and even early postnatal influences tend to express themselves in terms of differences in the way these children react to sensations, organize movement, and process and comprehend what they hear and see. We call these individual differences in the way children take in experience and plan and execute actions their "unique biologies." We need to work with these whenever we start treatment for children with ASD, whatever their age.

Following our DIR model, we look at each child's stage of development and individual processing differences and then create learning relationships geared to these factors. These differences are tied to the stages of development in the following way: children are born with sensory and motor systems, but these systems need to be hooked up and working together. What helps those sensory and motor patterns connect at higher and higher levels is emotion. In other words, a child's sense impressions get connected to her actions through her emotions—what we call her affect—very early in life. For example, when a baby moves her head to look toward the source of her mother's voice rather than away, it is because her mother's voice is pleasurable to her.

But if that baby is hypersensitive to sound, the normal human voice may be unpleasant to her, and therefore she may have a hard time coordinating her senses and motor patterns and may even get overloaded and lapse into panic mode. It's analogous to an adult who gets scared and goes into a fight-or-flight reaction. In situations of extreme fear, stress, or overload, there are a number of "catastrophic reactions" that relate to primitive levels of our nervous system.

On the other hand, if a child underreacts to sound, he may not hear his mother or father calling to him, for example. He has a hard time connecting the sensory pattern of hearing with the motor pattern of looking, which would be guided by the pleasure of hearing a parent's voice. A child with a motor planning problem (who can't sequence his actions) can hear his mother's voice and want to turn to her, but can't organize his response. So he looks off to the other direction by mistake, doesn't see his mother, experiences no exchange of smiles, and isn't motivated to seek out more warm connections. A child who craves sensation may be so active that there is almost no time for him to connect sense impressions, emotions, and motor activity.

By focusing on the special way a child understands information coming in and plans the response that goes out, we can help children with their processing difficulties and eventually turn those difficulties into strengths. In this chapter we discuss the most common processing problems in children with ASD. In the following chapter, we discuss more severe visual and auditory impairments and how parents and caregivers can work with these challenges.

Auditory Processing and Language

"Auditory processing" refers to the way we hear information and comprehend what we hear. To understand what we hear, we have to decode it—that is, discriminate between different sounds, such as high or low pitch—and make sense of the sounds in terms of the words and ideas being conveyed by another person. Language includes auditory processing and expressing thoughts, ideas, and responses to others. The most prominent processing problems we see in children with ASD are in the realm of auditory processing and expressive language. Sometimes children can't make sense of the information coming in. Other times they can't express what's going on in their minds. Some children with autism have trouble with both. Many typically developing children also have difficulties with auditory processing and language. (Our Affect-Based Language Curriculum [ABLC], described in Chapter 20, addresses language development.)

Some children, even as babies, can recognize complex rhythmic patterns such as "bump bump be dump bump, *bump bump.*" These infants brighten and become more alert at the surprising taps at the end. In contrast, other babies (even those without any special difficulties) are confused by this pattern and seem not to respond to or process the rhythmic sounds. Adults, too, have differences in auditory processing and language: some lucky ones can listen to a lecture and remember most of what was said, while others can remember only the first and last sentences and need to read and study the material again at exam time.

Difficulties in auditory processing may contribute to other, seemingly unrelated, issues. For example, a child diagnosed with a disruptive behavior disorder may be unable to understand directions, which leads her to become easily frustrated, thereby aggravating her aggressive behavior. It is important to note that many children with ASD who have auditory and language difficulties can show the complexity of their thinking and their imagination through drawing. We have to find every avenue to represent thought: for many children one avenue may be gestures, and this is why playing charades strengthens a child's ability to show you what she's thinking. We encourage parents to find Marcel Marceau videos because children love seeing how much can be conveyed through mime. For other children, drawing pictures of what they're going to do that day helps them face challenging situations.

Finally, if a child has an auditory processing problem, we recommend that the parents arrange for an audiological exam to make sure the child's hearing is competent for all frequencies; children who seem to hear fully may not perceive sounds equally in all frequencies, and audiologists can help with this problem. In the following chapter we address in greater depth biologically based hearing deficits.

Motor Planning and Sequencing

"Motor planning and sequencing" refers to how we act on our ideas or in response to what we hear and see. This ability can be seen emerging in infants who try to see where a voice is coming from. While it may seem that they are responding automatically, there are actually quite a number of steps to the process. First, they must register the sound and find it interesting. Then they have to organize their muscles to move in such a way that they can turn toward the sound. Next, they have to physically turn their bodies, coordinating and sequencing the muscle movements so that they go in the desired direction. Finally, they have to look for the person possessing the voice and actually recognize that they've located the face the voice comes from. Later, at age sixteen months or so, a child can take his mother by the hand, walk her to the refrigerator, and point to the food he wants. This requires many more complex actions in a row, again sequencing motions and using emotions to get what's desired.

This type of motor planning and sequencing is also the underpinning for a later ability called executive functioning, or the ability to execute a series of actions leading to a specific goal. It is, for example, the seven- or eight-year-old's ability to solve problems and stay on task, following through until the problem is solved. This is difficult for many children—not just those with ASD but also those with attentional learning problems. We all vary considerably in our executive functioning ability.

Visual-Spatial Processing

In the first few years of life, children learn through their actions, through hands-on doing. They learn in this way long before they have words—you don't need words to think. The visual-spatial world is primary. Children with ASD and other special needs whose eyesight is normal may still have problems with the visual-spatial abilities that organize the visual world and help us make sense of things—how objects operate in relationship to our bodies, for example, and how patterns are formed. These abilities lead, eventually, to higher-level academic work such as solving math problems or analyzing a text or image. The first sign of problems with visual-spatial processing can occur when babies have a hard time focusing on a parent, or moving their eyes from a rattle to a parent's smiling face and back again (what we call joint attention).

As they get older, children with visual-spatial processing difficulties may have fragmented thinking, be unaware of other people's body space, or may relate in an aimless rather than purposeful way with their physical environments. When they do develop words, they may speak in a fragmented, piecemeal way, rather than in a logical, cohesive way. They may drop something and not notice it, may not be able to find where anything is, or may knock over a glass when they're reaching for something else. Clearly, problems with visual-spatial processing have an enormous impact on a child's day-to-day functioning.

We have collaborated with Harry Wachs, a pioneering developmental optometrist who worked with child psychologist Jean Piaget and together with Hans Furth extended Piaget's theory of cognition into the realm of visual-spatial thinking. Visual-spatial processing can be divided into six basic abilities, starting with understanding one's relationship to one's own body, moving to the world of objects outside one's body, and then progressing to the relationships between objects inside oneself, and eventually to concepts such as one-to-one correspondence and conservation and higher levels of visual-spatial symbolic reasoning. We have worked with Dr. Wachs to further elaborate his processing concepts and relate them to the DIR model.

Although presented sequentially here, ultimately these abilities develop simultaneously. Typically, aspects of each develop during the first six years of life, while each also builds on earlier abilities.

Body Awareness and Sense

The first visual-spatial ability is body awareness—understanding the different parts of yourself and where you are in space. This begins at birth, when the baby finds her hand, puts it in her mouth, and realizes she can do it again and again. Awareness of the mouth—the most important organ for survival at this stage, when the baby is nursing—is crucial. In the first year of life, as the baby becomes more and more capable of purposeful movement, she also becomes more and more aware of her own body. Through countless little experiences each day—touching the side of the crib, holding a rattle, nursing, playing with her own toes—the baby begins to form a mental map of her body. As she begins to move by rolling and crawling and, later, creeping or pulling herself up to stand, she understands that she can have some control over her body in relationship to her environment; she can move through it. For example, she can crawl faster to see Mommy when she comes home from work.

So the first awareness is that of one's own sensations and movements. But some babies who are at risk for ASD don't develop this body awareness because of the way their nervous systems are wired. Also, if a baby isn't picked up often and held upright, if he doesn't get the experience of standing or being placed on his feet, or sitting and knowing he can be upright against gravity, it's very hard for him to begin moving more independently. For these babies, experiencing frequent rhythmic interactive activity and the pleasure that goes with it, in earliest infancy, can be extremely helpful. It can also be helpful for a four-year-old who isn't yet fully engaged and doesn't have much awareness of his body. If we can woo children into rhythmic activity, they can really enjoy it, which sustains their effort at keeping it going.

After infancy, body sense manifests itself in purposeful movement (such as rolling a ball back and forth with a caregiver), followed by an awareness of where the body boundaries of self and others lie, how the body affects others in space and time, and how to use the body for coordinated actions. Often children with ASD reach for the parent's hand to do something, rather than using their own hand. They lack the awareness that they can hold and turn something. Somewhere along the line, they learned that their parents' hands can do it better, and they have not gotten practice using their own hands as functional extensions of their own bodies. Much work is needed to help children overcome this difficulty. We can play hand games such as patty-cake and clapping games that encourage the child to use her two hands in space at once. Or we can encourage her to lift the top off a container to get some toys she wants, or pull on a bow to open up a package. We want the child to use two hands and bring them together to the midline (the center of the body). This provides a foundation for the later ability to cross the midline in order to perform such tasks as writing.

As we move, we experience sensation in our bodies. That sensation is affective in nature; it brings an emotional reaction. The sensation may be bland, indifferent, or exciting, as in a perfect tennis shot or the perfect dance step. The more pleasurable the emotions that we can harness for children who have trouble with body awareness, the more this awareness will emerge.

Location of the Body in Space
This stage involves understanding the parts of one's body in relationship to each other, and locating the whole body in its environment.

Babies begin to move in space, then understand that objects and people move in space in relationship to themselves. As toddlers, they begin purposeful movement in relation to other moving or moveable objects (chasing a puppy or stacking blocks), then learn to plan movement before taking action; ultimately they learn to be team players.

The child with ASD and visual processing difficulties who has trouble knowing what his hands can do might not be able to pick up the block and put it somewhere. Children with ASD who are a little older and still lack body awareness and an understanding of where they are in space need to have a lot of movement, to climb and run out on the playground, to practice targeting (throwing a ball to Mommy or to a friend), and to play all the typical childhood games. Games such as Giant Steps, Red Light–Green Light and relay races, and Twister and Duck, Duck, Goose are very important.

Children with ASD generally take much longer than other children to understand sequences of action: it's not always obvious to them which direction they should run in, for example. Parents can help by serving as their child's partner in these games. Rather than tell a child how to do something, take her by the hand and say, "Come on, let's go." As her body is guided through these activities, the child begins to develop the ability to locate her body in space. One thing that can get in the way of children learning this is expecting them to do it too quickly. Encouraging a child to watch one of these social games several times before joining in can make a big difference. One little girl with ASD really wanted to play London Bridge, but couldn't quite get it, so her very creative mother videotaped the child's siblings playing the game. The little girl watched the video and within a few days was able to play London Bridge herself. Help the child to observe by pointing out what other children are doing and be patient and encouraging.

Relationship of Objects to Self, Other Objects, and Other People

Very early, babies experiment with the effect they can have on objects (dropping toys out of the crib) and on people. By one year old, they also develop rudimentary "object constancy"—for example, pulling a scarf off Mommy's head to see her face. As toddlers, they deliberately affect objects in space—moving a toy car faster or slower, for instance. They also realize that symbols can take the place of real things and people.

As they get a little older and become more aware of people and objects in their environment, children learn to play or run around without bumping into them. While they are developing this awareness of the boundaries between self and other, they may have trouble staying in line, which is why we see little painted footsteps on the floor in many nursery schools. Children who lack body awareness at this stage often have a hard time with depth perception as well: they don't walk up steps with alternating feet, for example, because they can't quite figure out where their feet are in relation to the stairs. Or they may drop things without noticing, often irritating adults who don't understand the child's difficulties.

Between age three and five, children begin to understand social rules and can play games that are more systematic, such as musical chairs, board games like Candyland, and team games like T-ball. They can also apply some of these developmental skills to daily life: they take off their shoes and know to put their dirty socks in the hamper, and can get ready for a bath and get their pajamas out of the drawer. Children with visual processing difficulties often benefit from having visual cues or other strategies to help them with these daily life tasks, such as laying clothes out separately—instead of all in a pile—so they can remember what they need and the order in which to put them on.

This ability to sequence—to solve a problem that has multiple steps (and may incorporate objects, as in the examples above) requiring ingenuity and creativity—requires a child to have an intention or idea, put together a plan of action to carry out that idea, and then follow through on it. As soon as we begin seeing problems with sequencing, we need to give the child extra practice and recruit the other senses—for example, talking a child through a process if he can't easily order what he sees. At the same time, we need to increase the child's interest in what he is doing, because it is easier for a child to sequence when he is strongly motivated.

Conservation of Space

Newborns' concept of the dimensions of space is limited. After a year, a child begins to experience space as three-dimensional and understand that although her own movement through space makes the environment seem to change, space isn't moving; she is. This is "conservation of space," a foundation of visual-spatial abilities. When toddlers are afraid to go down slides, for example, they may have a problem with conserving space; they don't understand that the distance from the top of the slide down to the ground is the same as from the ground to the top of the slide.

Children who have challenges with this stage may actually close their eyes as a ball comes toward them or cringe in a pretend sword fight. They can move forward, attacking another person in the sword fight, but retreat when they are attacked. This stems from an inability to focus, to have their eyes work together. Many children with ASD rely on peripheral vision and have difficulty converging on and tracking things that are moving in front of them. This disability is one of the factors that contribute to the poor eye contact many of them have.

Children with visual-spatial processing challenges may have difficulty with the ability to combine space and time that typically comes at this stage. The practice they require to develop in this arena pays off in unexpected ways: learning how to catch and throw a big Nerf ball, for example, cultivates the same abilities to judge speed and distance that keep a child safe when she crosses the street. Practice also leads to the body awareness needed for coordinated actions. To ride a tricycle or a bike, children have to know that they can use different parts of their bodies in different ways. Children who ride their bikes or scooters and crash into people or parked cars are usually not doing it on purpose; they need more practice coordinating their different body parts. We can't emphasize enough that children with ASD have more difficulty with these abilities and need lots of practice every day.

The more children want to avoid these kinds of activities because of their difficulty, the more they need to do them, and the more we have to make the process fun for them. Help a child who's avoiding an activity because it's hard or takes too much energy by going down to a simpler level—starting with simple, fun steps within a child's range and creating games around it. Then you can slowly help the child move up the visual-spatial developmental ladder.

Visual-Logical Reasoning

As they are learning cause-effect reasoning, children often try to use toys as if they are real—for example, trying to put on doll clothes or ride in a toy car. Rather than telling the child that the toy is too small or that it isn't real, parents should let the child try it, because it's only by trying that children begin to get a sense that their foot doesn't fit into the doll's boots or that the toy dog won't bark. Then they can begin to use the toys symbolically in pretend play and understand that they are imitations of the real thing. This is a big developmental step.

Children also begin to use logical thinking to solve problems and plan actions, such as setting the table. This also involves the ability to reason. The use of space is now coupled with an understanding of *why* things are arranged or organized in a certain way. Simple participation in daily life activities—whether cooking, putting away the groceries, or washing the car—gives the child practice organizing what he needs and where he has to place objects. This is the stage when children begin to draw or represent visually some of the things they actually see. Children also learn a more advanced level of object constancy—the understanding that just because they can't see something doesn't mean it doesn't exist.

Representational Thought

By the end of year two, typically, children make a dramatic leap in their ability to represent thoughts or desires through words, sounds, gestures, pointing at pictures, and so forth. Representational, or symbolic, thought is the last basic visual-spatial ability, and it is essential for higher-level thinking. Gradually children become more accurate and purposeful in what they represent, using language or scribbling images on paper. They also begin to see the relationships between objects, allowing them to make conceptual groupings of like and unlike things. In addition to the techniques described in earlier chapters, activities to help children develop symbolic thought include having them draw a copy of your "secret code" designs in order to sneak into a toy castle, for example. Then you might have them draw diagrams of how the toy soldiers are going to fight each other or enact a scene from a favorite book.

Sensory Modulation

The last processing area that makes up a child's unique biology is the ability to modulate or regulate sensation as it comes in. For example, many children with ASD overreact to sensation, so that light touch (which is ordinarily very pleasurable to a child) might feel like someone running sandpaper over their skin. In terms of sound, the ordinary human voice may feel like loud screeching. In the visual arena, bright lights, lots of color and movement, and even sunlight can be overwhelming.

At the other extreme, many children underreact to certain sounds, touch, or sights. For example, some children hardly register that you're there when you talk to them or barely register being touched. Such children may retreat because they don't feel connected to the world. Other children crave sensation; they seek out movement, touch, or sounds. Children who both underreact to and crave sensation may run around banging into people to get extra sensory input. They may underreact to pain, not registering it as intensely as other children do, in which case they seem impervious when they fall or bang into things. Still other children are overresponsive to touch and sound and yet crave sensations, thereby overloading themselves. Understanding how children experience and modulate sensation is key to helping them develop.

Daily Variations and the Range of Abilities

Children vary from day to day in terms of their unique profiles. Some days they are more or less sensitive to touch or sound than on others. Children have good or bad days just as adults do—a tennis player may

play like a pro one day and feel like a klutz the next. It's the same nervous system, the same body. Maybe you got a little more sleep last
night; maybe it's something you ate yesterday. Often you can't find
any explanation for the change.

The important point is that all human beings vary considerably
from day to day in the way their nervous systems work. In children
who are just learning to walk, that variation determines whether they
fall or walk on a given day. When babies are learning to engage with
others, these variations may affect whether they stay engaged and respond to us or drift off into their own worlds. In all humans, but especially in children with ASD, these variations in functioning always
affect the most recently learned abilities because they are still the
most vulnerable. We should expect this variation as natural and not
worry about it.

Therefore, the question is not "What can my child do?" but "What
range does my child operate in?" Processing abilities, like other skills,
operate within a range or sliding scale. At the top are the abilities
children have in the best moment of their best days. The bottom represents the level children can still reach at their worst times. This
range can be very wide. For example, children who on their best days
can make sense of directions and navigate around the house may seem
confused and lost in the house on another day. These two extremes reveal the developmental range in which the child operates.

Once a child's range has been identified, the goal is not to keep the
child at the top of the range, because that is impossible, but to move
the whole range up the developmental ladder, so that the new bottom
is where the top had been. It's just as important to work with children
when they're at peak performance as when they're struggling, because
then we help them advance developmentally and master higher levels
all the time.

When children are inconsistent in their abilities, parents often say,
for example, "Well, she managed to do that puzzle once last week, but
not since then." Rather than worrying that the child isn't always operating at the top of her range, parents should focus on meeting the child
at her current level (in any given moment) and helping her move up

the ladder. Take a child who, operating at the bottom of her ability range, seems to bump into everything and can't find her toys. You can engage her in a slow treasure hunt around the house or play with a large beach ball that she can follow easily. Recognizing the child's whole range and tailoring your interactions to the level of the moment allow you to help the child move up the scale, no matter what the situation or daily variation brings.

The Importance of Matching Rhythms

One of the first ways newborn babies interact with others is by matching rhythms of movement, emotional expression, and vocalization with the caregiver. Children at risk for ASD have a difficult time achieving this harmony, in part because their nervous systems differ from other children's. In establishing this important rhythm, first match the child and then vary the rhythm to help him regulate. For example, if you're working with a sensory-craving child, you'll start off by imitating him to capture his rhythm, but then you'll adjust it to a slower, more soothing and organized rhythm. For a child who is underreactive and self-absorbed and can't register sensation, after first matching her rhythm, you can introduce more animation into your voice to get her attention. If the child underreacts but is easily overstimulated, as soon as you get her attention by energizing up, you might then immediately become more soothing.

Many caregivers do this intuitively with their babies. With a four-month-old baby, a parent may speak animatedly to get the baby's attention, then try to maintain it by becoming more soothing. It's like an orchestra conductor who leads the band to play loud, then soft, and then loud again. So first match the child's rhythm, but then adjust it to maintain engagement, attention, and (if the child is at this stage) back-and-forth communication, whether with gestures or words.

To get the attention of an underreactive child, avoid grabbing her head and forcibly turning it toward you. As we said earlier, you want her to *want* to look at you because you are exciting, enjoyable, and interesting. Animated sounds coupled maybe with tapping her on the shoulder or playing cat-and-mouse with her hands or feet will draw her attention. Or you could walk your fingers toward the spot she seems to be staring at—into her field of vision—to engage her. You could provide some nice deep pressure via hugging her or gently squeezing her hand or leg, to help her feel more in her own body. Make sure you are in front of her rather than behind her, so it's easier for her to grasp her visual-spatial relationship to you. If it feels as if she is collapsing on you, then her muscle tone may be low that day.

Children show us their own solutions to their sensory processing system challenges. It's up to us to recognize the solution and figure out a way to expand on it by making it interactive. For example, an underreactive child who is lying on her tummy and pushing a car back and forth is seeking support from the floor. To engage her, lie down on the floor in front of her, and, as she pushes the car around aimlessly, you can either meet her with another car, crash your car into hers, or push it further away. Once she's engaged and begins to get more mobilized, you can start moving her up the ladder, using her sensory needs to guide the interactions.

For children who want to move around but have motor problems that cause you to worry they may fall, a solution is to work in tandem with another caregiver, such as a spouse or babysitter. As one of you holds the child's hand or just stays nearby to catch her if she falls, the other one can interact with the child—having treasure hunts, playing peekaboo or hide-and-seek, or setting up problem-solving challenges such as obstacle courses. In this way you can get interaction and social problem-solving going without worrying about the child's safety. The idea is to create safe situations and safe environments (maybe even padding the floor and removing sharp-edged furniture to safeguard against injury if the child falls) so you can relax and have more fun with her.

Often we look for a way to reach a child—the magic key that will unlock the hidden door—when all the while the child is showing what he needs by his actions and the way he's processing what comes his way. We need to observe what children are doing to help themselves in the moment and then figure out how to meet them there.

One strategy that helps caregivers learn how to match rhythms with a child is coaching one another. Sometimes the person on the sidelines can see what the person actually interacting with the child misses. The observer can make concrete suggestions, pointing out that the caregiver might be a little more energetic or more soothing or might try holding hands, and so forth. Or the sideline observer can convey the rhythm he thinks will work with the child. Thus instead of just giving a suggestion here and there, the coach actually tries to get into the mind of the person working with the child through a commentary: "OK, now you've got her. Now you've got her. Now try this—take her hand now—I think it's going to work. Oh, you've got her! Look at that eye contact! Look at how the two of you are going!" The rhythm of the observer's voice guides the rhythm he is trying to create between the caregiver and the child; he is demonstrating the rhythm he thinks is going to help the caregiver enter the child's rhythm. So it's a three-way rhythmic exercise. The person who is coaching may be no more skilled than the person doing the actual work—maybe even less skilled—but has the benefit of gauging the rhythm more easily from the sidelines.

Caregivers may or may not enjoy coaching. Either way, it's important for them to keep a constant rhythm going with their voices and movements. Often, I'll see parents, educators, or therapists become silent and just wait when they don't know what to do next. This is not the best strategy. If you don't know what to do or what to say, just describe what the child is doing. Let's say she's hopping around the room, and you're trying to decide whether to be playfully obstructive or to entice her with a toy. While you're thinking about which strategy to use, you can say to her, "Oh, there you go jumping. What a good jump that was. I see that jump! Boy that was a great jump! What are you going to do now? Oh, I see you're going after that toy. What a great toy that is!" The child is hearing the rhythm of your voice and sensing the rhythm of your emotion, and you and she are connected because you are matching your rhythm and voice to the child's movement. So you're providing a sense of connectedness, even while the child is doing her own thing.

Children with auditory processing challenges especially need to hear the rhythm of a voice. So, rather than not talking, you might repeat what you say, and emphasize it. For example, if the child is standing on the stairway, you can ask, "Do you want to go up? Up? Up? Here, let me show you. This is up. This is down. Which do you want? Do you want to go up?" The point is to keep the child in rhythm with you, adjusting your rhythm to the child's. The same process applies to facial expressions: your expressions and movement patterns can be slower and more emphasized for the child with visual-spatial processing difficulties.

With children who are somewhat verbal but slow to process auditory information or formulate responses to questions, a common issue is how to give them enough time to respond while still maintaining the relatedness and the rhythm at a reasonable pace. The best way to address this is to maintain a rhythm through gesturing. As the child is formulating a response, you gesture to her encouragingly with smiles and your hand and body movements and by nodding your head in an expectant way—coaxing the words out of her. What you'll find is that as you do that, she will begin moving in rhythm to your movement, which will actually help her formulate the response. Sometimes you can repeat the question just to reorient the child, using different words.

If the child still can't come up with an answer, you can offer multiple choices in an empathetic way: "Gee, that was a hard question—it's hard to think of the answer. Let me give you a couple of choices." As we mentioned earlier, whenever you give choices, offer the desirable one first and the less appealing second. That way, the child can't just repeat the last thing—she has to make an effort to say which she prefers.

Turning Weaknesses into Strengths

As each potential problem is mastered, it can become a strength. For example, the overreactive child can become intuitive, empathetic, and sensitive to other's needs. Individual differences can either be the source of a problem or an unusual gift depending on whether or not they are nurtured and fed. The way we interact with children helps determine their potential, because their brains and minds are not fully developed.

As children move up the developmental ladder, mastering each of the basic emotional milestones, they learn to work with their unique biologies, rather than being ruled by them. For example, children who reach the point of a continuous flow of shared problem-solving can now signal to you with gestures or facial expressions that your voice is too loud, instead of escaping or shutting down to deal with the noise. Once they have words, they can regulate their environment to suit their needs by saying, "Mommy, that's too noisy" or "Daddy, I need a hug now" or "I want to run around outside!" They can do this even before they have words once they get twenty to thirty circles of gestural communications in a row, thus achieving what we call coregulated emotional interactions. This means the child is initiating as much as the parent is, rather than just reacting to the parent. Instead of just running around aimlessly, the child can pull Daddy from his chair and gesture to be picked up and play the airplane game. And once the child learns to use ideas, whenever he realizes, "Whew, I'm overloaded!" he can be purposeful and intentional about controlling or responding to his environment. He now becomes an active partner with his parents or other caregivers, taking the initiative to solve the problems of his own biology.

Self-Talking

Children who have auditory processing and language difficulties often engage in self-talking. This can be simply thinking aloud or a defense against engaging with others, which may be difficult. For example, children who have a hard time processing what other people are saying and tend to be self-absorbed may find it easier to talk to themselves. Self-talking can be an elaborate way of daydreaming out loud to tune out other input. Try to discover what in a child's processing profile makes self-talking an easier option than interacting.

To tailor interactions to children who tend to self-talk, we first observe and interact with them, trying different things. If they underreact and become self-absorbed because they don't find the environment compelling enough, or if they have auditory processing problems that make it easier for them to focus on their own ideas than on someone else's, or if both characteristics are present, we have to talk to them in simple terms, but with high energy and enthusiasm: *"Hey! What are you doing?" "What would you like?" "Look at this!"* Keeping it simple, energized, and compelling helps to bring them more and more into the interaction they need.

In a school setting, a child who self-talks and has a profile of underreactivity to sensation as well as auditory processing problems might need to operate in a small group of two or three children, with the teacher, an aide, or parent volunteer to assist. Alternatively, the child might need one-on-one interactions to keep the environment as compelling as possible. Not until children can communicate well with another person can they learn in a large group. If they have auditory processing issues and are self-talking, they are probably still mastering two-way communication and need small-group or one-on-one learning to help them enjoy relationships. With a solid foundation, the self-talking will correct itself.

The following chapter explores visual and auditory deficits and how to help children master emotional and intellectual milestones when they are unable to see or hear. Parts III, IV, and V look further at how unique biologies can be addressed through Floortime, educational programs, and treatment of specific symptoms.

Chapter 12

Unique Biologies, II

Visual and
Auditory Challenges

Two unique biologies require deeper exploration: visual and auditory deficits. How can we help children who are unable to see or hear? How can we enable them to use their other senses and their emotions to develop a sense of self and achieve emotional and intellectual milestones? In this chapter we provide guidelines for working with children with a range of processing challenges in a particular sensory capacity. Whichever sense we are addressing, and whether the deficit or processing challenge is mild or amounts to an inability to take in sensations through that channel, the principles of intervention are the same:

1. Strengthen that channel as much as it is humanly possible given medical and biological knowledge
2. Use the other senses to create the awareness and understanding of the world that ordinarily would occur through the impaired channel
3. Get all the available senses working together as a team
4. Help the "team" of senses to master each of the developmental milestones

Working with Visual Deficits

Many children are born with varying degrees of visual difficulties. Our DIR model of intervention can help children with ASD who also have visual deficits (as well as those without ASD) master each stage of emotional development while at the same time developing their ability to comprehend experiences fully, even those experiences that would ordinarily be taken in through sight. (Parents who suspect that their baby has trouble seeing should consult their pediatrician and, if necessary, a pediatric ophthalmologist.)

A baby's basic interest in the world begins, ordinarily, through all the senses—sight, hearing, touch, taste, and smell. A baby turns toward her mother's voice and looks at her big smile and the twinkle in her eyes. But what about a baby who is unable to see? How do we help that baby develop a sense of the spatial world?

If you move to the left or the right while talking to your baby in warm, inviting tones, and—although she cannot see—she follows and localizes where you are through sound, she is constructing a "visual map": a sense of where things are in space. If she turns toward the sound of your voice but cannot yet reach toward you, you can take her little hand and put it next to your mouth so she feels your mouth moving. She can then "see" where that sound is coming from through her experience of touch. You can do similar things with smell for slightly older babies—putting an interesting scent such as lemon juice on your hand so the baby can take an interest in the smell and locate your hand in space.

The idea is to begin with the child's primary asset—his emotions or affect—and help him take an interest in the world outside himself and then utilize all his working senses to help him construct a spatial road map. With an older, fifteen- or sixteen-month-old child who doesn't have this spatial road map—who doesn't seem to know where things are even though she's been negotiating the house or the room for a while—you can do the same kind of exercise but at the level of the child's motor skill. For example, you can coax her into little "Can you find me?" games by giving treats such as kisses or snacks when she finds you. Now she is motivated to create a spatial road map as well as to take action.

At each stage, the principle is the same—for newborn babies, with whom we work to prevent developmental difficulties from occurring, and for older children, who need to master the developmental milestones. With the second stage, engagement, the baby or child needs to experience warmth and pleasure through sound, touch, smell, and rhythmic movement to get a mental picture of a joyful parent beaming at her. So when a father gives his three-month-old daughter a big joyful smile while talking rhythmically to her, the baby hears the joy in his voice. She may even smile back, but since she can't see Daddy's smile, he has to take her hands to his face so she can touch his mouth and get a kiss on her hands. This way she'll get a sense of where the pleasurable sound is coming from. Daddy might have a different smell than Mommy has, so the child begins to create a multisensory image of a loving caregiver and falls in love with this image.

Let's look at an example of a child of three who has ASD and a severe visual impairment and is self-absorbed and aimless. To help her become more connected and engaged with you and with the world, you can use the same kind of exercise: getting into rhythmic, back-and-forth vocalizations, even just making silly sounds at each other, and then having her touch your face to understand where those joyful sounds are coming from. At this age the child may have some motor control, so you can entice her to reach to you. For example, you can put a favorite textured toy that she likes on top of your head and guide her hand up to it, and then she may reach to touch it again. By getting the child engaged with you, you help her create a visual spatial map.

At the third stage in our sequence—purposeful two-way communication—we typically see a baby reaching for something in Mommy's hand, taking it, and handing it back. This is particularly difficult for a child without sight, who can't see the necklace that Mother is dangling for him to play with. We have to let the baby know that the objects exist through touch: Mother can put the necklace in the baby's hand, then slowly move it next to her face, so the baby who is now purposeful is going to reach for it if he likes the texture of the necklace. The mother can use the back-and-forth babbling typical of this stage and connect it to the baby's reaching, directing him with sounds: "Here it is! Here it is!" The baby, localizing the sound, begins to reach toward the sound and discovers that when he reaches, he gets that necklace he wants or the rattle he likes.

In reaching toward the sound, the baby is being purposeful. He takes the necklace from Mother, then Mother asks, "Oh, can I have that back?" and touches his hand. Mother may take the necklace back and then move to the baby's other side and offer it again so he'll reach for it. This little game combines vocalizations, movement, touch, and maybe also taste and smell (this should be done with all kinds of objects, including food), so the baby is exercising all his working senses together but also using each one individually.

It is important to go for a range of emotion. The child can't see facial expressions, but she can mirror the emotion in her parent's voice. Be especially animated in the way you use your voice, because the child is learning the subtleties of emotional expression—joy, surprise, or annoyance if she bites or scratches—by the sounds that go along with those facial expressions. If the baby grabs her mother's hair and pulls, the mother can say, "Ouch, that hurt!" bringing the baby's hand to her face so she can feel that people have a different facial expression, as well as a different vocal tone, when they are upset than they have when they are happy. Thus through touch, sound, and movement, the child senses the emotions of the other person in order to fine-tune her own emotions as part of two-way emotional signaling.

The same pattern works well for an older child with ASD and visual deficits who hasn't yet mastered this signaling. With a two-, three-, or even four-year-old, you can create the same kind of interactions, geared to the level of the child's intellectual and emotional interests. The toy or the treat you use might be different, or you can use actual words if the child is verbal. But the goal is the same: back-and-forth communication involving sounds or words, touch, and movement. For example, with a child interested in a little airplane, you might keep the airplane moving while you ask, "Where is it?" Your voice indicates where it is, and the child reaches for it. She takes it, and you say,

"Oops, it has to come back to me, I'm over here, it has to come back and land over here," and see if she can land it in your hand. That way, you're facilitating two-way communication within a spatial road map.

At the next level, shared problem-solving, you want that same sense of collaboration and the exchange of even more subtle and complex emotions. The goal is to have all the emotional themes of life—including dependency, closeness, assertiveness, exploration, and even anger—expressed through fifty, sixty, or seventy circles of emotional interaction. As part of that, the child learns to unify all his senses, to put together all the information he's getting through sound, sight (if he is able to see at all), touch, smell, movement. This helps him integrate the different circuits of his brain.

In the first year of life, many areas of the brain work in isolation. By the second year, these areas are forming connections with one another. These connections can be promoted in children with ASD by getting the whole mental team working together, orchestrated by the child's emotional interest. If the child is not able to see, you have to create even a richer array of experiences through the other channels to get that shared problem-solving going. For a slightly older child who is able to walk around, games such as "search" and "treasure hunt" can be adjusted for visual deficits by, for example, using a toy that makes a distinct sound such as a squeaking doll or a music box. Or Daddy could play the toy, hiding and making a funny sound. Then the child goes searching around the room for Daddy, with Mommy as a partner, looking in three or four places until she finds where the sound is coming from. Moving left, right, forward, backward, she creates a movement picture of the room.

When she finds Daddy, it confirms where Daddy is in her mental map. The joy of discovering that Daddy has the Cheerios or M&Ms or the vibrating toy the child enjoys touching adds further pleasure to the discovery. This interaction, in addition to the interactions with Mommy as they are searching for Daddy, gives the child practice in exchanging lots of vocal and emotional signals: "You're close!" "Oh, now we're far away. Where can he be?" Even if children don't have a lot of words yet, they can often understand vocal intonations; they understand the cues of "hot" and "cold" even if they don't really know what the words mean. If the child is playing without a partner, the parent who is hiding might be in a constant back-and-forth signaling, "Nope, you're going farther away . . . I'm over here, here I am!" and the child may vocalize back and giggle and laugh, exchanging lots of emotional signals while improving her motor and language skills. In this way, the nervous system can fully develop, even though the child doesn't have sight.

The problem-solving interaction also helps the child regulate his mood and behavior. Ordinarily, at this stage children develop the ability to feel close to their caregivers from far away; they look over at a parent's smiling face while they're playing on the other side of the room, rather than having to sit in the parent's lap. They can be independent yet still receive nurturing and support through distal communication. In other words, they begin carrying the security blanket inside themselves through what they see. Children who can't see or can't see well can learn to do this through what they hear, but their caregivers have to be more animated and continuous in their vocalizations.

If your child is playing with blocks while you are across the room looking at a magazine, and the child is not very interactive, you want to be continuously vocal. If the child is basically relational and you want to promote a little independence, then you can periodically make animated comments such as, "Boy, that's a cool tower you're building!" The child hears your voice and through your voice feels close to you. Occasionally you can say, "Can you come over here and give Mommy a little hug?" In that way she uses her hearing to know exactly where you are and uses her motor system to get there, gets the hug, goes back to play with her blocks, hears your voice reassuring her, and has a sense of where you are in space and that you are approving what she is doing.

At the next stage, creating ideas, we need to make sure that the symbols, the ideas that are forming, are multisensory. For a child of any age with visual challenges who hasn't mastered pretend play, we want to help her create an imaginative world through all the other senses. A parent can take the voice of a character from a book, tape, or TV show or cartoon that she reads, listens to, or watches with the child, describing the action to him. Or she can be a made-up character or a little dog, cat, or some other animal. Or the parent can take on the voice for a doll or stuffed animal—something with lots of texture and big features that are easy to figure out through touch.

Talk for the toy and then ask the child a question, prompting him to pretend. (With two caretakers, one can even be behind the child, modeling for him how to talk through the toy.) "Here's a car! Let's go for a ride. Can you put Teddy in the car?" Help the child to put the bear in the car, then ask, "Oh, where is he going to go? Is he going to come to me? Where am I?" encouraging the child to push the car toward you. The idea is, again, to use touch, movement, sound, and words to create imaginative dramas that take into account space. The keys to helping a child with visual deficits take this developmental step into the world of imagination and play is to make the toys interesting from a tactile point of view and to keep the vocalizations rich and animated.

Sometimes it's difficult for parents and other caregivers to put themselves quite in the child's shoes if they don't share the visual deficit. In that case a parent can do a little exercise in which he keeps his eyes closed while he plays with the child, so that he may see that it can be fun to get into imaginative worlds through touch, sound, smell, and taste. Sometimes we project onto the child more anguish or more frustration than the child actually feels, particularly a child who has had a visual deficit from the beginning of life. Such a child has come to know the world in ways other than sight and may even have a heightened understanding of the world through her existing senses that we don't have; we want to help the child develop pride in that.

At the next stage, connecting ideas together, we can do much through verbal conversation, but we want to help the child connect up the spatial world too. She learns to move the car from the dollhouse to the doll school or to build a little town. Where are the dolls going, and why? We want to help the child answer "why" questions: "Why does Barbie want to go to school?" or "Why is Elmo cold?" We want to help the child connect the logic of words with the logic of spatial connections. Again, all of this seems much harder for children who are not seeing. How do they learn higher-level spatial concepts such as quantity? Again, through touch and movement. The child can touch two pennies and then five pennies. She's moving her hands, and there is a longer movement pattern when touching five pennies than when touching two. The child creates a mental picture of what five pennies look like versus two, and she enjoys it when she gets to keep all the pennies.

So we want to introduce concepts of quantity, connections of one part of space to another part, and lots of verbal dialogue with "what," "where," "who," "when," and "why" questions to help the child connect ideas together. We do that through pretend play and in logical conversation. As we move into multicausal and then gray-area thinking, we remember to address the child's spatial thinking as well as her verbal thinking. So if she is learning shades of gray, for example, you can approach it verbally with questions such as, "Why do you like to play with Johnny more than with Eloise?" and "How much more?" But you can also approach it spatially: "How much applesauce do you want?" Give the child three different bowls so she can touch them and feel the difference in size and tell you which bowl she wants her applesauce in today. When you do this exercise with something the child cares about, she invests size and dimensions of quantity with her emotions.

There is also what we call big-picture thinking—seeing the whole forest rather than just the trees. As a child with visual deficits goes through the higher levels of thinking, we can promote big-picture thinking by encouraging the child to sum things up. For example, if the child is telling you about his day at school—that the teacher gave too much homework and another child was mean—we might ask, "Gee, how would you add all that up? What was your day like overall?" "Well, it was just a bad, bad day, Mommy." Or there might be good and bad things, so the child says that overall it was OK. That simple statement, adding it all up, helps the child put the pieces together in a larger whole and become a big-picture thinker.

Finally, as children with visual deficits move through higher levels of thinking, we want to keep developing their motor and spatial abilities. So, as the child is, say, using Braille to read or listening to books on tape, we want to keep working on basic skills such as balance, co-ordination, and left-right integration and on spatial problem-solving. Children who can't see can still learn to play checkers, for example, with special boards that allow them to picture the board mentally through touch.

Working with Hearing Deficits

Many children are born with severe hearing deficits; sound doesn't register for them, usually for a clear biological reason. As with children with visual deficits, the challenge is to help those with hearing deficits become full emotional and social interacters and to develop all of their cognitive skills in spite of the hearing loss, using other senses to master the six stages of development.

At each stage, the hearing-impaired child has more difficulty than a child without this deficit would. A newborn baby learning to attend and regulate ordinarily uses sound. Instead, a hearing-impaired baby needs to use vision and touch. Using a soothing tone of voice won't work (though of course you want to talk to the baby so she gets used to seeing people communicate that way), but you can use a soothing head nod and a soothing touch and rhythm to convey the same kind of warmth and regulation. When you are helping your baby learn to coordinate motor and sensory input, again you can use touch and vision and even experiment with different smells. Children can become very sensitive to the different gradations of pleasure and intimacy through these other sensations.

Purposeful two-way communication can be developed through exchanging objects, facial expressions, different kinds of touch, or all of these. Similarly, in shared problem-solving, since you can't use sounds to stay in touch with the child from across the room, you have to keep in touch visually. You need to be more animated in your facial expressions—the angry "no-no" look, the joyful "Ah-ha, that's wonderful!" look, and everything in between. Your child can also learn to

regulate his mood and behavior by the way you hold his hand—
gently, pleasurably, or firmly (to set limits). You need to be more animated, more demonstrative, and subtler in the way you engage the
child using her senses other than hearing.

When it comes to using ideas and symbols, the same principles hold
true. Obviously this stage is going to be harder for a child who can't
hear, but she can symbolize with pictures and through pretend play.
For hearing-impaired children who are learning to read mouth movements and to vocalize, it's especially important for parents to be very
animated with their mouths. Eventually they can start teaching the
child to make certain sounds by imitating mouth and tongue movements.

If a child with a hearing deficit has been given cochlear implants,
caregivers are often told to stand behind the child or hide their mouths
to force the child to use her hearing and not her other sensory modalities. In our view, this is counterproductive because healthy experience
is multisensory. Each system supports every other system, and every
symbol has a visual, tactile, olfactory, movement, and (for a hearing
individual) auditory aspect. So if one of those channels is blocked, all
the other channels should be allowed to work. For the child with a
cochlear implant, you want to combine her new experience of sound
with all her other senses so she has a rich, multisensory image. Otherwise we're creating an artificial problem, thereby adding to the difficulty that children with ASD have with integrating the different
senses. We might spend short periods of time isolating the child's hearing for specific exercises, to help her learn to detect and discriminate
sound, but the child's main experience should integrate all the senses.

Often it is assumed that a child with a major sensory deficit is likely
to be self-absorbed. This doesn't have to be the case, but the risk is
there. Heightening the other sensory experiences can go a long way toward minimizing the risk. Make sure you are in front of the child and
that he can take in visually your animation, and be sure to use great
feeling in your touch to convey the affect, so he has the extra information he needs to see and feel what he isn't hearing.

Sometimes when the child has a major sensory challenge, the parents stop communicating through that modality. If the child is deaf, the parents might eventually stop talking to her. But it's very important for caregivers to continue talking to maintain their own energy, to maintain their own way of conveying emotion and caring, whether or not the child hears it or not. That rhythm or vibration, along with touch, signs, and expressive looks, will help woo the child into the next step in joint communication.

The goal is to provide experiences that support the child's ability to achieve and successfully negotiate all the emotional milestones and that use all the child's working senses, together with her emotions, to construct a full sense of self and age-expected social and intellectual abilities.

Part III

※ ※ ※

Floortime

Chapter 13

Floortime as a
Family Approach

*A family had two children. Eight-year-old Anna had a mild form
of autism and required lots of energy from her parents to keep her
engaged and interactive. Thirteen-year-old Darcy, a bright girl,
was doing well in school. Whenever their mother was working with
Anna, preparing a meal in the kitchen, or doing chores around the
house, Darcy—instead of focusing on her homework—would vie
for Mother's attention. The mother wondered how to help Darcy
and Anna together.*

R ather than talking about a child with special needs, we should
talk about families with special needs, because when a child has
uneven development—whether the cause is ASD or a severe language, motor, or other problem—the entire family has a challenge.
Families have two primary ways of responding to a diagnosis of autism
or other developmental problem. The positive response is to take the
crisis as a cue to organize everyone in the family and the community
to rise to the occasion, to find new ways of coming together and new
constructive solutions. Certainly, many families and communities do
just that in a crisis.

Unfortunately, a different response all too often gets in the way of the constructive one. The stress of the situation can lead to a narrow focus and rigidity. Just as children who have ASD or other special needs can be rigid as a way to cope, families sometimes react the same way. We see this in the larger world, too; a crisis can cause polarization, an "us versus them" mentality, in a community.

Becoming rigid, anxious, polarized; focusing in on a few details; and limiting one's perspective is, of course, a common response to stress that goes back to early human ancestors. In fact, in most healthy families there is an ebb and flow between these two patterns. We are all more constructive on some days—solving problems collaboratively with spouses and even with extended-family members—and are rigid, combative, and undermining on other days. While working with a child with ASD on the developmental milestones, or while engaging in the Floortime techniques described in the chapters that follow, it helps for parents and other caregivers to consider their own patterns.

Strengths and Weaknesses

The difficulties and demands of raising a child with ASD take extra work to keep the balance tipped in the constructive direction. Staying constructive requires understanding the strengths and weaknesses of each of the major caregivers—parents, grandparents, teachers, therapists, siblings. We all have natural strengths, and each of us has an Achilles' heel. In one family, for example, the mother was very nurturing and read the signals of her little girl very well, and so was able to create lively gestural dialogues. When the mother got nervous, however, she became overprotective and didn't challenge her child enough. When she was unsure of herself, instead of perhaps challenging her daughter to take the initiative by coming over, opening her fingers, and finding the little toy in her hands, the mother would open her hand and literally put the toy in the girl's hand, which took away from the child the chance to act and solve a problem.

Interestingly, this played out in her marriage as well: when she became upset and unsure of herself, she did what her husband described as "smothering" him, and that led him to feel resentful. When we discussed it, it turned out that the mother often did that when she was feeling resentful herself. It was her way of coping with her anger—nurturing the other person in an aggressive way whether he or she wanted it or not. As we talked about this pattern and the mother began dealing with her frustrations more directly, she was able to entice and challenge while remaining nurturing. With her natural caring attitude, she became gifted at Floortime.

The father in this family was a computer expert and a very orderly person; he ran a large division of a big company and managed a number of people, so his organizational skills and systematic thinking served him well. In the family, he was the one who organized all the therapies and services and negotiated very effectively with the school to help get his daughter what she needed. But in his Floortime play, when his little girl wouldn't do what he expected her to do, he got bossy and insistent. Instead of remaining playful and saying, "Oh, I bet you can't find Daddy! I'm going to hide! Where am I?" he would start ordering her: "Look over here!" Then the little girl would tense up and become more self-absorbed and self-stimulatory, jumping around and staring at lights.

Through coaching, we helped the father remain flexible with his daughter. He in fact had a wonderful playful side; he could relax, grow funny and mischievous, and challenge his daughter in a playful way, such as by putting on funny hats and ducking behind different objects so she would run around the room trying to find him, getting lots of circles of communication going in the process, which delighted both of them. At such moments the little girl became interactive, warm, and engaging and began to use a few words. But when he stiffened up and got autocratic, she regressed.

To help the child through the steps outlined in Part II and apply the Floortime methods in the chapters that follow, the first job of a family is to figure out the relative strengths and vulnerabilities of each caregiver.

Families can do this by themselves or with the help of a clinician. What's critical is for the main caregivers to sit down at regular times and ask the difficult question, "What are our strengths, and what are our vulnerabilities?" Parents and other caregivers whom we work with are able to do this well, particularly when we directly ask them, "When the going gets rough, when you're under stress, what do you tend to do? What happens?" If the person can't answer, we explore some of the common reactions: "Well, do you tend to withdraw, to get bossier or more aggressive, to get overprotective, to get more fragmented and nervous and kind of lose sight of your goals?" There aren't that many possibilities, so I'll just reiterate them. Obviously, the constructive things you can do are to become more soothing and regulating, more nurturing and warm, more interactive and facilitating, more verbally supportive, more creative, and more collaborative.

Most of us when frustrated are going to have responses from both columns. Therapists can help caregivers walk through these characteristics (as well as others), or caregivers can do it themselves. If a parent has trouble coming up with his or her own characteristics, we may ask the spouse what he or she thinks of as the other spouse's strength and vulnerability. Often the spouse will get it right away; rarely have we found a family in which spouses don't know each other's strengths and weaknesses.

Once we identify a caregiver's strengths and weaknesses, we look at how they play out in two situations. First, we look at the characteristics in terms of the child's progress through the developmental milestones. How do these patterns enhance or get in the way of optimal interactions? How do they help or hinder the calm, regulated attention necessary for the child to relax, attend, and focus? How well can parents facilitate warm, nurturing engagement, depth of intimacy, communication with gestures and facial expressions, and long chains of social and emotional signaling as part of problem-solving?

The second issue to consider is how the parents' traits play out in their relationship and in the family pattern as a whole. The same pattern that may undermine the work with the child—for example, the father becoming autocratic rather than more playful—may also show up when the parents are alone having dinner or going over bills or talking about the child's school. Father may become frustrated, then a little too bossy, and then mother becomes resentful, and so forth. If the spouses are at war with each other, it's very hard to provide the nurturing interactions that a child requires. More often than not, the same Achilles' heels will play out in multiple ways with the child, with other children in the family, and in the parents' relationship.

When the family is together, how much intimacy is there? How much communication is there? How much shared problem-solving is there? Is there creativity and imagination in words or pretend play? What about logical thinking—connecting ideas together, making sense of each other's words, and opening and following through on ideas and discussions, as opposed to just changing subjects all the time? If during the family's dinnertime a little child says, "Blue car, blue car," and someone asks the child, "Where is the blue car, sweetheart?" and the child points and says, "I want to play. No eat—play," now the family has made sense of what could have been viewed as just a random comment.

When parents and other caretakers work individually with a child, they may support the child's development, whereas when the family is together as a unit, there may be distractibility, self-absorption, fragmented conversation, concrete rather than creative use of ideas, and poor capacity to make sense out of things. If family members always talk in parallel or at cross-purposes with each other, if the parents undermine each other, or the siblings are competitive with one another, there may be difficulties.

Families of children with ASD, as well as other families, need to notice how well they're promoting the first six emotional milestones in the children, and then the higher levels of gray-area and reflective thinking. Once caretakers have identified these family patterns, it's not too hard to see how they play out in other family relationships, because we're creatures of habit and tend to do the same things over and over under stress. We repeat the patterns when we're unsure, uncertain, and anxious, and often have learned these patterns in our own families of origin. It's helpful (though not essential) to understand the family history of these habits. How did we get to be autocratic or over-protective when we're under stress? What in our own families led us to be that way?

The next step for parents is to work around weaknesses and play to their strengths. How do we do this? For those who are tennis players, it's a bit like working around your backhand; if you have a better fore-hand than backhand, you tend to try to use your feet and hit more forehands. At college, those who are good at literature and poor at math tend to take more literature than math courses. We work around our weaknesses and play to our strengths in these and other situations, and the same principle applies to a family caring for a child with ASD. Spouses who know each others' weaknesses should avoid stirring them up. And they should be aware of their own weaknesses and not give in to them.

Returning to the family example discussed above, the father who becomes more autocratic and orders people around when he doesn't get his way can become aware of this tendency and notice that, when his daughter is being difficult and negative, his voice gets more stri-dent and commanding. Then, through conscious effort—even though it doesn't feel natural not to order her around when he's angry—he can take a step back. Even though he's thinking, "She's being spoiled. I can't cave in to her. She's got to learn to deal with discipline and with the realities of the world," he can learn to say to himself, "Gee, she's only two-and-a-half. We've got twenty years to help her deal with the realities of the world. It doesn't have to be right away."

If caretakers rationalize continuing their old patterns, we remind them that this will only dig the hole deeper. The child will continue to be more difficult. As this father becomes aware of his tendency to be an autocrat, he can work around it. The overprotective mother in this family can, when she sees herself doing too much for the child, try to catch herself: "Oh, there I go again." She may still do it, but only for a few minutes instead of hours. Once you catch yourself, you can make a compensatory change by playing to your strengths. Father can say, "I've got to turn the switch and become playful," and make a conscious effort to do so. Mother says, "I've got to turn the switch and become more challenging." It may not be easy the first several times. But by the fiftieth time, you'll get the hang of it and switch the pattern easily. The learning curve can be surprisingly fast if you keep asking yourself, "What am I doing?" Sometimes spouses can help by just reminding each other, "You're being the general again," "You're being the 'feeder' again." Try to come up with one word that your spouse can use as a signal when you're digging yourself into a hole. Set aside time to discuss these issues; the key is to let the spouse share his or her concerns first and then offer advice. It's important for each spouse to be empathetic, not patronizing. This will be very helpful as you apply Floortime techniques with your child.

Bringing Out the Best

This gets us to the next principle: Bring out the best in each other, your spouse, or any other caregiver. Typically, we tend to dig the hole deeper. Let's look again at the example of the rigid father and the over-stuffing mother. (In no way do we mean to stereotype the mother and father. In many families it's just the opposite, with the mother being the rigid autocrat and the father overprotective. There are other patterns, too, and infinite variations on all the patterns.) If the father is being rigid, the mother gets angry at him for upsetting the little girl and becomes critical and micromanages him: "Don't do that!" That makes Father even more tense and autocratic, and then everyone is angry at each other, and everything deteriorates. Or vice versa: Mother is doing too much again for the child, and Father feels alienated that he's not getting any nurturing from Mommy himself, so he becomes critical of her or withdraws, and then she just hovers more, because that's her way of dealing with anxiety—and the pattern intensifies.

Instead of asking yourself, "How do I put my spouse's face in their own mess and make them admit that they're the problem in the family?" you can ask yourself, "How do I bring out the best in my spouse (or grandparent or teacher) so that they can work better with my child?" Even if you're divorced, these same principles hold because no matter what legal battles you're involved in, no matter how much you may be angry at your spouse, he or she is still the mother or father of your child for life. Treat your former spouse like a valued relative and follow these same principles. Obviously, it's going to be harder to do, because you have to separate the divorce issues from the world in which you come together around your child or children.

If your wife is being rigid and you know she does that when she's feeling insecure, try to help her relax and be more playful. Maybe you join the play a little bit and use humor: "OK, boss! We better listen to Mommy because she's in charge!" and so forth. Or you may have a little supportive chat with each other about these principles after the play, perhaps with a back rub and some ice cream. Each spouse knows the ticket to the other one's heart—what's going to make his heart melt and help him relax. In that mood, he will reason with you, and you'll be able to bring out the best. So don't take the bait; often, when people are being critical, anxious, and controlling, what they need is warmth, nurturance, and security to get them relaxed, because their behavior comes from feeling nervous and tense. If a parent hovers, he may be feeling insecure, thinking that somehow, if he were a better provider, his little girl wouldn't have these problems. Being reassuring, supportive, and letting him feel valued as a spouse will help him relax.

If one thing doesn't work, another thing will. The families that do come together in the most constructive ways tell us, "Actually, Susie's challenges brought us closer together as a family." You can just feel the connection and the working partnership; the family has discovered something new in life that opens their hearts and makes their relationships deeper and more meaningful than they are in many families. Instead of being preoccupied only with the kids' soccer games or the family vacation or where little Johnny and Susie are going to go to college, they relate around deeper issues—intimacy, warmth, empathy, and caring. In these families, the parents experience the same feelings of frustration, anger, and disappointment that typically arise when parents learn that their child has ASD, but as they go through these feelings and discuss them with each other, they draw closer to one another and become more connected.

We are not saying any of this is easy. Sometimes, instead of supporting one another, the spouses can't help but dig the holes deeper by attacking each other, micromanaging, being critical. Families that have a hard time finding greater connection are often stuck in expectable frustration, anger, disappointment, or just exhaustion because the feelings don't get worked through. If it's hard for a family to deal with the challenge of a child with ASD, it's fine to get help. If a couple has tried to analyze their strengths and weaknesses and play to their strengths, but it's just not working—there's conflict and they're still pressing each other's buttons—it's time to get help.

You could get help from the person who is guiding your child's therapy (various specialists are described in Chapter 20) or from someone whom the therapist or friends or colleagues refer you to. It could even be a close friend who's good at this kind of thing. The important thing is to find someone who can help you understand your patterns as a family and as a couple within the framework described here. Tell this person that you're trying to figure out your strengths and weaknesses and trying to bring out the best in each other. Sometimes we perceive what the other person is doing as an attack when it is just his or her way of coping with uncertainty and anxiety; we personalize it. Maybe that third party can help you remove some of the roadblocks.

Time for Parents

When couples are having difficulties (and even when they're not), it's important for parents to have time alone with each other to regain the intimacy of the marriage. You will see in the chapters that follow why we call this Floortime for parents. If parents are afraid to leave the children with babysitters and don't have family around to help, everyone can sometimes be stressed out and exhausted; there's no time to nurture each other by going for a walk, having dinner together, or going out to a movie. Frequently couples are just running around, leading parallel lives—taking the kids to doctor and therapy appointments, dealing with the school system, and coping with the symptoms that can accompany ASD (finicky eating, poor sleeping patterns, behavior control problems including aggression and self-injury). All this stress, coupled with a lack of intimacy, can even increase the risk of divorce.

Intimacy is the fuel that keeps the soul going, and if that's missing in the marital relationship—if there's no time together to be warm and nurturing and talk to each other—the spouses don't feel secure inside, don't feel valued as people. These feelings come from your relationships with your good friends and especially with your spouse. If you don't get it, you don't have it to give to your child. A child's progress with a DIR/Floortime program requires parents who are emotionally very available. If their emotions are drained by marital strife; by anger, disappointment, or depression; or by exhaustion from their workload, it's very hard for them to provide their child what he needs. The heart of Floortime is the warmth and nurturing that you're conveying to your child so he will want to play with you rather than retreat into his own world. You can only go on your reserve tank for so long. So it's very important to create time each week—ideally several times, but at least once a week—to go off alone with your spouse. Work hard to find somebody you can trust—a relative, older sibling, or babysitter—to take over even just for a couple of hours so you can go for a walk or out for a quick bite to eat. It's good also to have an hour or half hour each evening, or at least three or four times a week, after the kids are asleep to come together and talk and tune into one another.

Time for Siblings

Siblings of a child with ASD have challenges of their own, as in the family described in the case study that opens this chapter. The sibling reaction that everyone talks about is jealousy or resentment, because often the child with ASD receives so much attention that a brother or sister naturally feels lost in the shuffle. But there are other reactions too: anxiety anyone may feel about a family member having a problem; or worry, particularly in young children, that the same thing could happen to them, that they could become autistic. Some siblings, especially older ones, may become very protective of their little brother or sister with ASD, which inhibits normal, age-appropriate sibling rivalry; thus a five- or six-year-old can become a little Mommy or Daddy too quickly. That can lead to an inability to express ordinary assertive and competitive feelings in life. Other children take the opposite tack, becoming very impulsive and aggressive with their sibling with challenges, almost disregarding the other child's vulnerability because it's too scary to recognize. This can result in the child developing a more self-centered attitude overall.

While sometimes one feeling, such as fear, can masquerade as another feeling, such as embarrassment, it's also natural that the siblings might feel embarrassed in front of their friends by the child with ASD. They may expect their friends to make fun of them because they have a sibling with a problem. Parents may be critical of this reaction, and yet they themselves can get embarrassed very quickly if their child with ASD is spinning around in a supermarket, causing other people to stare, or doing some kind of self-stimulating behavior when company is visiting the home. If parents experience embarrassment, the sibling can be assumed to experience it a hundred times as intensely. While not admirable, it's a very understandable feeling to have.

Any and all of these are reactions to be expected (of course, each family will have its own unique pattern), and the more often parents become aware of them and talk to each other about them, the more likely the family can get to that deeper level of understanding that brings everyone closer together and solidifies the family unit. You'll want to set up plenty of opportunities for siblings to talk about their feelings and for you to let them know that you empathize and to answer any questions they have (particularly if the sibling is younger than the child with ASD): it's important to explain the situation to the sibling in terms appropriate to his or her age.

You also want to draw the sibling into the effort to help the child. Some families don't want to burden the sibling with the issues of the child with ASD. But that's a *big* mistake. If you don't pull the sibling into the family challenge—and this is a family challenge—the sibling feels excluded. You're not doing him or her a favor. What we hear, especially from older verbal siblings, is that when they're not involved, they believe that their parents "don't think I know how to play with little Susie," as one sibling said. "They think I'll hurt her," or "They feel I can't do a good job, so they don't let me play alone with her." This makes the sibling feel excluded. It's the parents' job to help the sibling feel included in a constructive, not a burdensome, way. As we mentioned, you don't want to make the sibling into another adult by giving him or her too many responsibilities, nor do you want exclusion.

One way to achieve this is through group Floortime, as described in Chapter 15. If the child without ASD is older than the child with ASD, the parent can coach the older child in how to get circles of communication open and closed. The older child can learn how to do Floortime and, after a number of weeks, may be a spontaneous play partner with the child with ASD, and the two can play when you're busy cooking dinner and doing other things. Sometimes, you can ask siblings who are significantly older than the child with ASD (for example, a nine-year-old with a four-year-old) to babysit and pay them modest wages, as practice for babysitting jobs they might do for others later. With a nine-year-old, a parent would still be in the house, of course, but the older sibling learns through babysitting how to play and interact with the younger child and gain a source of pride and a deeper sense of empathy. This is similar to integrated classroom settings in which children without special needs partner with children with ASD, and—because it's challenging to pull in a child who tends to get self-absorbed—learn how to empathize and relate and practice social skills; it's a very constructive experience for everyone.

Of course, you don't want to involve siblings without challenges to the point that they don't get to play sports or do the other activities they need and want to do. Often a sibling may be feeling needy and vying for your attention, such as Darcy in the chapter's opening case study. Each parent should spend at least half an hour a day with the sibling, letting her be the star. This can be Floortime, a planned activity, or just hang-out time, but she is the center of attention, whether you are riding bikes, going for a nature walk or out for an ice cream, talking, or playing games together. It's helpful to do this before the child settles down to her homework; otherwise she won't get any purely enjoyable time with you, and a power struggle may develop around the homework. The child can catch up on her homework over the weekend, if necessary.

Children who are old enough to be verbal can also benefit from "problem-solving time" every day (this can also benefit children with ASD who become verbal, as we describe in detail in a later chapter). This can take place during dinner, in the car, or while sitting on the couch. During this time, you can play a game we call Thinking about Tomorrow, in which you talk about the good things that will happen the next day but also the challenges the child might face—such as doing her homework, feeling jealous of her sister, or being teased at school. You help her visualize the situation and the feelings she will have. If another person is involved, the child can also picture her or his feelings. Then have the child describe how she would normally act in this situation, such as nagging mother if she is feeling jealous of her sister. You can actually ask the child, "What is the best way you have of getting my attention when you feel I'm paying too much attention to your little sister? What is the cleverest thing you have ever done?" An eighth-grader is going to enjoy bragging about how she's outsmarted you. Then you ask what other things she can do, other than pestering you or procrastinating on her homework. Perhaps even ask her what she'd do if she were the parent—she might surprise you with a good suggestion. In this way she starts to see that she has options, and feels supported.

We always recommend that kids—whether or not they have ASD or other challenges—have at least four play dates a week, so that their main source of companionship begins shifting from parents to peers. If they have only one or two play dates a week and Mommy is the chief playmate, the pattern of neediness continues. But with more play dates, peers become more important for fun. Mommy is still important for security, warmth, and problem solving, but not for going out and riding bikes together.

Finally, there should also be a lot of family time so everybody feels that they're part of this mission together. Sometimes the whole family can just have fun together—Mommy and Daddy and the child with

176   ENGAGING AUTISM

ASD and the brother or sister all on the floor—and then the family's goal is to just facilitate as much interaction between the siblings and between parents and the sibling and the child with ASD as possible. Everyone's at a different developmental level, but you can try to find some common drama, some common way of having fun together. It could be dancing to music, playing Duck, Duck, Goose, or having a scavenger hunt. And you may switch gears from catering to the young one to catering to the older one and letting the young one try to imitate and learn from the interaction.

When a family is having a great time together, playing, cooking, or taking a walk, there will normally be lots of attention and engagement, gesturing, interaction, and solving problems together. Something as simple as planting bulbs or decorating a birthday cake involves using ideas creatively and logically and even thinking reflectively. Each child will be at a different level of development, but if everyone is participating, everyone is benefiting. The younger ones are engaged and interactive, older ones can debate articulately, and parents will see all kinds of interests and talents in their children that might not emerge otherwise.

The key point is to look at how you're doing as a family—whether you've worked around your weaknesses, are supporting each other's strengths, are bringing out the best in one another, are involving the siblings of the child with ASD in a constructive way but also supporting their independent lives. If there is too much conflict and tension, ask yourselves, "Why are we having difficulties?" and look for the answers in the context of your strengths and weaknesses and how well the whole family is mastering the emotional milestones. Get help if the problems are too much to handle, and give yourselves time and plenty of chances to regroup.

If you try to be perfect, you're trying to be nonhuman. This is especially true for a family with a child who has ASD or another serious developmental challenge. The most important human quality you have as a family is your warmth, spontaneity, and emotionality; if you try to be perfect, you're going to be rigid. All families have both strengths and weaknesses, and life is an ongoing process of keeping these in balance.

Chapter 14

Floortime

What It Is and What It Isn't

A mother wanted to do Floortime with her self-absorbed, six-year-old son, Brandon, to help him become more engaged. Brandon had a narrow range of interests; he tended to get intensely preoccupied with his toy soldiers to the exclusion of other games and activities. In a consultation, we observed that the mother's attempt to gain Brandon's attention consisted mainly of intruding on his activity by, for example, helping her three-year-old son, Scott, break into a toy castle Brandon had built. Inevitably, Brandon would get upset and withdraw. We showed the mother how to follow Brandon's lead and interests and help him break out of the cycle of repetitive play.

Floortime is at the heart of both our DIR model and a comprehensive program for infants and children with a variety of developmental challenges, including ASD. As we discussed in Part I and discuss more thoroughly in Part IV, a comprehensive program includes working at a child's emotional developmental level, creating learning relationships tailored to his individual processing differences in order to move him up the developmental ladder. This program includes not only Floortime but also different therapies, education programs, counseling support for parents, and intensive home and school programs, as well as other learning opportunities such as play groups, music lessons, gymnastics classes, and so forth. Floortime is at the heart of the home component and can be woven into many other parts of the program.

Floortime is both a specific technique—in which for twenty or more minutes at a time a caregiver gets down on the floor to interact with the child—and a general philosophy that characterizes all daily interactions with the child. Let's look at what Floortime is and what it isn't, and explain why it is the cornerstone of the DIR model and the developmental process.

The Two Goals of Floortime

Floortime has two main goals. Sometimes these two work together easily, and other times they may appear almost in opposition, but both must always be considered. One goal—by far the more widely known and followed—is *to follow the child's lead* or harness the child's natural interests. Why do we follow the child's lead? After all, historically, educators have long held that adults can't just allow children to do what they want to do, because children are creatures of instinct who would never become socialized if we just followed their lead. But in Floortime, we take our cue from the child because a child's interests are the window to her emotional and intellectual life. Through observing the child's interests and natural desires, we get a picture of what she finds enjoyable, what motivates her. If a child is staring at a fan, rubbing a spot on the floor over and over, or always walking on her toes, these might seem actions that we want to discourage. But something about the behavior is meaningful or pleasurable to the child.

Therefore, we always start off by asking the question, "Why is my child doing that?" To say simply that it's because he has this or that disorder doesn't answer the question. The child may have a disorder or a set of problems, but he is not the disorder or set of problems. He is a human being with real feelings, real desires, and real wishes. If children can't express their desires or wishes, we have to deduce what they enjoy from what they are doing. So in Floortime we begin by following the child's lead and joining him in his own world.

The second goal is to bring the child into a shared world. However, we don't want to pull her in kicking and screaming. We want her to *want* to be in the world with us. For a variety of reasons, a child may have elected to be self-absorbed, aimless, or seemingly withdrawn into her own world. Thus the rationale for the first goal: a child feels closer to you if he sees that you can respect and participate in what interests her. We described ways for fostering attention and engagement in Chapter 6, such as wandering about a room with a child to share in his aimless wandering. As the child starts giving you some curious or friendly glances, instead of looking annoyed or running away from you, that's the beginning of a shared world.

Once the child enjoys participating with us, we can begin helping her master each of the basic abilities of relating, communicating, and thinking that we described in Part II. Our ultimate goal for bringing children into a shared world is to help them become empathetic, creative, logical, reflective individuals.

How does "following the child's lead," the first goal of Floortime, help the child master these critical developmental milestones? This gets to the real substance of Floortime. For each of the six core capacities and the three advanced levels of reflective thinking, we've worked out a number of strategies that begin with following a child's lead and then continue with enticing the child to really want to learn this new, wonderful ability.

For example, if a child always wants to play with his favorite toy instead of interacting, we may use the strategy described earlier of being playfully obstructive: we can gently scoop the toy up, put it on our head and make silly faces, and see if he will reach for it. We could then show him that we are putting it outside the door. When he bangs on the door to get it back, we ask, "Should I help you?" And pretty soon he's taking our hand and putting it on the doorknob. Eventually, he's saying "Open," to get us to open the door to get that favorite toy.

So now, through following the child's lead, we have mobilized not just attention, engagement, and purposeful action, but problem-solving and even the beginning use of words. These strategies are useful even for a child who is aimless or avoidant.

Some children have a narrow range of focus and have a hard time integrating attention to people and things at the same time. To help a child with this problem become more interactive with more flexible attention, caregivers should join his play and become one of the characters in the drama, rather than simply intruding into the child's play as happened in the case study at the beginning of this chapter. This can encourage a continuous flow of creative dialogue with the child.

Sometimes all that is necessary is to help a child toward his own goals. If a child is moving a truck back and forth and we make our hands into a tunnel, he may look at that, give us a big smile, and move the truck right into our tunnel. Now we have shared attention, engagement, purposeful action, and some problem-solving. Eventually we may introduce the word "truck" and he may repeat it. We can even give him choices: "Do you want to move it into the tunnel or into the house?" He may respond, "Hou—," and point toward the toy house. Then we have thinking occurring along with the use of words.

In Floortime, we follow the child's lead to enter his emotional world, then create a series of opportunities and challenges to help him move up to higher levels of relating, communicating, and thinking. While challenging children to master new milestones, we are always trying to strengthen and broaden their current abilities. If they can be a little purposeful, we want them to be more purposeful. If they can open and close three or four circles of communication, we want to increase that to eight, and then to ten, and on until we get to more than fifty. If they have a few words, we want to stretch these into conversations.

In doing all this, of course, we have to tailor our strategies to the child's individual processing differences, as described in Chapters 11 and 12. We also need to pay attention to ourselves as caregivers. What are our natural strengths and weaknesses? What do we do easily? A high-energy person is great for kids who underreact and need a lot of energizing and wooing, but that person may have a harder time soothing the child. A calm person may be a great soother for hypersensitive children, but have a hard time energizing up for an underreactive child. If a child avoids us, do we take it as a personal rejection and either shut down and stop trying or get too intrusive and try to force her to pay attention to us? Asking those difficult questions, we can then fine-tune our strategies to meet the child's special sensitivities and needs.

Floortime Learning

Floortime is not about doing a right or wrong thing; it's a process in which you and your child are always learning. Following the child's lead doesn't mean commenting about or just imitating what he is doing; it means getting in there and interacting with him on the basic level of his interest. Because you have to give the child a reason to want to play with you, it's important to start out by observing for a few moments so you can discover what his true interests are. Those interests may go beyond his specific behavior. For example, he may be lining up toys, but his broader interest might be to create order or fixed patterns or a certain design. If he is setting his toys in a straight line, you might offer another toy for his line, or playfully challenge him by putting a toy at a right angle to his line with a big smile. In either case, you might get a nice interaction. Once he sees that you are not going to stop him or pull him away, he might pause and look, after he puts another toy in the line, to see if you'll put the next toy in the lineup. So think of yourself primarily as a player.

Once a child can stop worrying that you are going to interfere with what she wants to do, she will let you join in and play because playing together is actually more fun. Help the child do what she wants to do. Break a motor problem down into little pieces, for example, if the child wants to open a container, find a toy, or reach a shelf. Depending on the child, you may use toys in the interaction, or you may just use yourself and some very simple objects. If your child loves to run and climb, you can make that interactive by being a human obstacle course—she will figure out what you are doing and begin to work around it. You're looking for the moment when she realizes, "Oh, this is a game!"

After a Floortime session is over, step back and analyze what happened. Try to think about what it is that gets in the way of the flow of interactions. (As we noted in Chapter 13, if both parents are available, each can take turns coaching the other.) Are you using visual cues and strategies? Is your tone of voice lively and energizing or soothing and quiet? Remember, your voice is probably the most powerful tool you have to cue your child. Whether or not the child understands the words, the message comes from the tone, rhythm, loudness, and pacing of your voice. Find out how it is you stay connected to your child.

One of the most important things is to meet the child at his current developmental level. Parents often are disappointed that their child isn't playing the way they think he should be. If that enters your mind, it's an indication that you are not following the child's lead enough. To help the child be more purposeful, we want to treat what he is doing as purposeful. Start out by helping him to do what he wants to do, then try to expand on that with him. If he is playing with a car and suddenly starts to move on, you might see if he wants to have some other cars, and before you know it, you'll be building a garage together. Worry not so much about what you do next as about staying within what your child already started; this is critical if you are going to bring more depth and elaboration to that activity or interest.

Using Objects and Symbols in Floortime

Fostering engagement and a continuous flow of interaction is always a primary goal of Floortime. So is helping the child to interact with objects and people together and to create symbols or ideas.

Children often love specific objects or toys, such as a dinosaur they use for everything. Accept your child's objects. Whether it's Barney or a Sesame Street character or a teddy bear, your child's plaything will give you some indication of her emotional life and what she finds meaningful. When the child is ready to use toys in Floortime, you can focus on generating the interactive flow around that particular toy. It could be as simple as making a slide. If you put a figure on top of a slide, you can inevitably get a child to push the figure down the slide. Think about the favorite toy as a friend that you can use to play with together.

Once the child is playing with a toy, see if you can help the child to give it symbolic meaning. For example, as your child is eating, talk for a favorite doll and ask for food: "Feed me, please!" One day your child may delight you by putting food near the doll's mouth. With this kind of prompting, the child might begin to elaborate his play around familiar experiences, incorporating dollhouses, doctor kits, tool kits, and so forth. But be sure that the child chooses it, so that it is meaningful to him. Then you can introduce something that responds to what your child did. The magic words in elaboration are, "What else? What else can we do?" The real goal is to keep that interaction going. Take a good look at whether you are providing all the support the child needs in terms of his specific processing abilities, regulatory system, and interest and initiative and also in the way you respond yourself. If your child is distracted, you want to be sure you're not the one distracting him. Try to see what makes him get stuck. Trust that this is a process—there is no right or wrong answer—and if something doesn't work, just follow the child's next step, and you'll have another chance to get a more elaborate game going.

Don't worry about the content; we can't move the content ahead of the process. We won't get elaborate symbolic stories and much pretend play in any form unless we get a nice lively interaction going first. Rather than pushing the child up the developmental ladder, focus on deepening the level where the child is already, because that is where he'll have the most ability to become fully engaged. There is no rush in Floortime. If you're not sure what to do, step back and see what your child is up to, reconnect, and then expand on that connection. We mobilize children's development by being players with them.

When Floortime Seems Too Difficult

The main reason parents avoid doing Floortime or avoid emotional interactions with their children is that, deep down (often not consciously), they fear they can't do it. Often parents tell us, once we've stripped away some of the surface defenses, "No one ever played with me this way, and I don't think I can do it. I think the best I could do is just change my child's behavior." Other parents get stuck during Floortime; they feel they have used up their bag of tricks and that nothing they do seems to work.

My advice in these situations is always the same: Don't pressure yourself to do so much. Whenever you feel stuck, take a step back, relax, and observe what the child is doing. The child may not seem to be doing much; she may just be playing with her own fingers. But that is something. A child is always doing something. Ask yourself how you can build on it. Joining one of your fingers with hers, or any other strategy that helps your child relate to you, could work. For children who are extremely challenging, sometimes the best way to start a relationship is through simple, sensory-based play, such as lying on the floor together, rolling over each other, and making funny noises, or simple holding and rhythmic rocking. There's no substitute for warm, joyful relatedness.

What this all boils down to is finding something you and your child can enjoy together. Often that requires exploring which rhythmic movement, touch, or sound game is mutually enjoyable. While you may not love crawling on the floor with your child, you'll enjoy his pleasure in this shared activity. Once you get that joyful relating going, don't be afraid to incorporate things you know he loves, such as a favorite toy, food treat, or game. You can provide several options and then the child can choose among them.

Ultimately, as we discussed in Chapter 7, you want to challenge the child to take the initiative. For example, if the child enjoys riding around on your shoulders, after doing this for a bit, you might stand still and challenge her to gesture, make a sound, or somehow indicate where she wants you to go before you'll go anywhere. When giving the child a back rub, let her show you where to rub—arms, back, or tummy.

Whenever play is repetitive, vary what you do. This challenges the child to vary what he does, even if it's within the same basic action or the same basic game.

Once the interaction is moving forward, and there is attention, engagement, and purposeful communication with gestures and maybe words, then the goal—and this can be the hardest thing to achieve for children with ASD—is to get the child interacting and communicating for ten to fifteen minutes at a time. We see many children with ASD who are already reading, doing math, and using long whole sentences but who can't have a long shared conversation.

The Floortime Checklist

To summarize, Floortime involves following the child's lead and pulling him into your world, then going beyond that by challenging him to master each of the developmental levels. It requires paying attention to the child's individual processing differences and nervous system, to family patterns, and to your own personality (to learn how you need to stretch to work with the child).

Floortime Checklist Questions to Ask

Is he:

- engaging with toys (objects) or me?
- reacting or initiating interactions?
- opening and closing a few circles of communication or heading toward a continuous flow?
- labeling or creating his own new ideas in play conversations?
- marching to his own drummer or responding to my ideas as well as his own?

Chapter 15

Floortime All the Time Everywhere

Creating Learning Environments

Three-year-old Emily, who had a mild form of autism and motor delays, was spending an hour and a half in the car twice a week being driven to her occupational therapy sessions. Her mother wanted to know how she could make use of this time to encourage interaction with Emily.

Within our DIR model, the motto for working with children with ASD and other developmental challenges is "Floortime all the time everywhere." This means that Floortime should be done often—eight or more times a day for twenty minutes or more at a time—and in many settings. Floortime can of course be done anywhere in the house. On nice days it can be done in the backyard. It can also be done in the supermarket and at the playground. It can be done with other children—siblings or peers—or just with an adult. It can be done at any time of the day, after supper, in the bathtub, or cuddling in bed. It can be done when you're exhausted at the end of the day and all you want to do is lie down on the floor, and the child has had a full day of school and doesn't want to do anything but sit and stare at the wall. It can be done in the car, on short or long trips. Floortime can also be incorporated into many five- or ten-minute intervals here and there when you're doing laundry, washing the dishes, tinkering in the backyard, or shopping. It can be done in pretty much any situation. So it's Floortime all the time, everywhere.

Including Siblings and Peers

How do we create Floortime in these different settings? One of the main opportunities is with peers or siblings. Parents often say, "I can't get any time alone with Johnny or Susie for Floortime because little Sally or little Timmy is there all the time." Well, that's great! As we pointed out in Chapter 13, siblings and peers can help a great deal; in fact, we recommend four or more play dates a week with peers so children can learn to use their interactive and communication skills with peers. When siblings or peers are present, you have group Floortime. Initially, it's better to keep the group small; start with just one other child, so there are three of you—one adult and two children. Later you can add another child. If you have a big family, both parents can participate—or you can bring in a helper or pay an older sibling to act as a babysitter—and divide the children into two groups.

In group Floortime, give each child a turn being the leader, so that the child without challenges is motivated to get involved and have time with Mommy or Daddy. The leader chooses the toy, or activity, and then you the parent or other adult try to bring the other child into the interaction as much as possible. For example, if the leader is just jumping around aimlessly, you say, "OK, we're playing the jumping game." And then you put on some music and jump rhythmically with the child, encouraging the sibling or the peer to jump too.

If the child with ASD jumps away from you, you might ask the sibling to hold your hand and create a little circle around the child. If the child in the middle wants to get out, you can say, "If you want to get out, you have to pick up our arms." So he has to either jump under, pick up, or break through your arms (you can make it very easy for him). He may now gesture purposefully or make a sound like "pick up arms," and pretty soon everyone is giggling and having a good time.

If it's the other child's turn to take the lead, and she—let's call her Susie—wants to move cars or trucks into a toy house, but the child with ASD, Johnny, wants to wander away, how do you keep him involved while little Susie gets to be the leader? This can be challenging. First of all, it can be helpful to put up barriers that will keep the child from leaving the room. Then, as Susie moves a car toward the house, you have to challenge or encourage Johnny to come look at the car. If he ignores you, you can say to Susie, "We've got to get Johnny to help us open the door to the house, because we can't get your car in there without some help," and then put the house in front of Johnny and say, "Push this door open please, push this door open." You can encourage Susie to talk to Johnny and say, "Push, push, push," and ask her to show Johnny how to do it. Susie pushes, and if you're lucky, maybe Johnny will copy her. If Johnny still tries to wander away, you can get in front of him and ask Susie, "Should we show him how to push the door open?" with Susie doing the leading. If you try three or four times, and Johnny continues to evade you, you might finally have to open the door yourself, saying, "This time I'll do it," so Susie can put the car in the house. But then you can try to involve Johnny in the next thing that Susie wants to do.

Sometimes you'll succeed, sometimes you won't. You're not going to help a child with ASD be a cooperative player overnight. But over time, as you help a sibling engage him and as you challenge him with playful obstruction and try to make it fun, you'll get more engagement. The goal is not to get the child to open that garage door or even to get him to talk. The goal is just to get him to relate to his sibling and to you. So if you and the sibling are blocking him and he goes around the two of you, then he is beginning to relate to you both. That's the first step. Over time, he will relate more and more, and pretty soon he will be smiling and giggling and then imitating what his sibling is doing. It's a slow process; the key is to keep innovating and not get discouraged.

One way to strengthen interaction between two siblings is to ask each of them to be the messenger to the other throughout the day. If you want to give a child something, have the other one take it to him, and vice versa. That will help the child with ASD tune into his sibling, because the sibling is bringing him what he wants. Another idea is to have various toys or activities around that require two participants, so that each child learns that it is more fun to play with the other child than to play alone. Older, more sophisticated children who may not enjoy these kinds of activities as much can be paid to babysit their sibling with ASD and can be taught how to do Floortime as part of this "employment."

Floortime in the backyard or on the playground is likely to involve a lot of gross motor activity—running, climbing, going on slides. Here too, the key is not just doing an activity but fostering human involvement. Who is going to help Johnny up the ladder? Or when Johnny gets on the slide, you and Susie can block Johnny so he has to say, "Let me go" or "Ready to slide," or has to point so that your arm moves up and he can go down the slide. Pretty soon, he is engaging with you and Susie. Then, as Johnny is about to go up the ladder, suddenly Susie may rush to go up too, and now they have to use gestures and facial expressions to decide who gets to go first. All this draws Johnny into relationship with you and other children as he goes up and down the slide, which he may love to do.

Floortime in Different Settings

Even the supermarket can be a setting for Floortime. Many kids love to ride around in the cart, so you can make the ride dependent on the child directing you where to go. You can encourage her to point or make a sound to tell you which aisle to go down and indicate which groceries she wants taken off the shelves. If the child isn't likely to make a scene, there's no harm in taking cans you don't need off the shelf; ask the child to help you put them back. And you can see what kind of noise a can or box makes as you knock it with your finger a little bit. All kinds of interesting things can go on in supermarkets; the key is to encourage your child to be intrigued and insert yourself into the activity.

On a car trip, a parent or an older sibling can ride in the back of the car with the child, playing games with him. They can look at books together, the child encouraged to point to a favorite picture and make sounds to go with the picture, or they can play with finger puppets. If the child is more interested in looking out the window, follow his lead and comment on passing sights. Hold your hand against the window and let him push it away so he can see.

When it's only you and your child in the car, your first responsibility, of course, is to drive safely, and the child should always ride in the back seat, but you can still talk to her, sing with her, and play sound games or other car-time games. In fact, the advantage of being in a car is that your child is a "fixed audience." If she is verbal, you can do some of the traditional games such as the one that starts with "I went to the zoo and I saw a . . ." And you say "zebra," and she'll say "a bear," and you say, "a zebra, a bear, and a giraffe," and so forth. You work on memory, going back and forth and getting silly about all the different animals. And you can play this game to practice other categories that are meaningful or of special interest to the child, such as trains or food.

A related car game, but one that can be played anytime to help children learn to visualize, is "Picture this." You start by describing a favorite animal, toy, person, or place and seeing if the child can picture it in his mind and guess what you are thinking of. For example, "Picture this: he has four legs, is brown and shaggy, barks, and loves to jump all over you when you come home!" The clues can be simpler for a child with emerging receptive or language retrieval challenges, or more complex for a child with stronger abilities. Using personal cues that draw on the child's experience of the object, place, or person adds a special emotional quality to the game. So picture Daddy coming home, or the places you and your child had fun, or the special package Grandma sent, or a favorite character from a story. Personalizing learning brings in the affect connection that can improve the child's processing ability. Where possible, encourage your child to take his turn and describe something for you to guess. (Don't forget to play dumb so the child gives you another clue or just enjoys your being wrong!) If necessary, be your child's partner and use a photo or picture to help him describe something or someone for the other parent or a sibling to guess. The ability to visualize is an important tool for dealing with separation by picturing the person missed, for comprehending a book by picturing each scene to better understand the sequence of events, and for dealing with anxiety by preparing the child for the situation he has to cope with.

Other car-time games can enhance visual-spatial abilities, such as spotting a certain kind of car or anything else that might be en route. In a variation on the old Punch Buggy Red game, have your child tap the person sitting next to her or nudge the front seat when she sees, for example, red cars. Adding the physical gesture enhances the fun and coordination of doing two things at once. Looking out the car window is also an opportunity to help your child notice things and learn the reasons behind what she sees. For example, the fire engine's siren tells everyone to get out of the way so it can pass quickly. To start, you might just help your child notice that you're getting off the road or that the fire engine is in a rush. Later, you might wonder aloud where it is going and why. Similarly, notice the tow truck helping the broken-down car, or the patrolman who pulled someone over, or the giant truck delivering food to the store. These opportunities for incidental learning many children just pick up from comments you might make here and there. But the child with processing challenges does not always tune into these observations or comments automatically, and it is useful to notice, ask questions, and talk about the experiences you encounter incidentally day in and day out. Later, your child can report what she saw to you, and you can help your child become a better reporter, especially if the event or sighting was novel or exciting and invested with the affect of your earlier conversation.

On long drives it is also useful to listen to audiotapes of stories. Tapes are usually quite animated with cues and sound effects. Start with a familiar story so the child learns to listen to the tape; then add new stories. You can stop the tape and talk about it, asking, "What do you think is going to happen next?" Or ask your child's opinion about the main idea. This is also a good opportunity to briefly explore and

reinforce pure listening, without pictures. Some children need en-
couragement to listen to a tape like that; if you stop and start the tape,
you can get some interaction around it and help the child become engaged. You can even tell your own stories, beginning with "Once upon
a time . . ." and having your child finish that thought. Then you add
to his ideas, and the two of you go back and forth, adding on and on.
These stories need not make sense but are fun and reinforce the back-
and-forth elaboration.

The important thing is the enjoyment. A conversation about what
is coming the next day or something that just happened can promote
empathy. For a child who is less verbal, you can have a bag of sensory
toys in the back of the car, and ask him which one he likes best and
then encourage him to do more with it. Other children love to be on
the road, and they memorize the route and get upset if you take a different route. Capitalize on this visual strength by having the child
point out different license plates or speed limit signs and so forth, and
challenge him to tell you how they are different; lots of incidental
learning can occur in a car. If these kinds of activities are too distracting for you, play it safe and let your child listen to music. Or do motor
activities such as drawing on an erasable board, and you can talk at
red lights or at other times when you're not too distracted. Or sing
along together—any type of interaction is good.

Floortime can also happen when the child is in the bath, particularly if she likes water. Obviously there are many toys that can go in
the bath and all kinds of games that can be played with soap—most
children enjoy a bit of splashing! At bedtime, you can look at picture
books or do quieter play, such as "This little piggy goes to market."
The activity should be relaxing but interactive. Remember to encourage the child to lead and interact. What picture book does she want to
look at? Perhaps you can then pick a new one in order to expand her
repertoire, but do not be reluctant to reread favorite bedtime stories
you have enjoyed together. You can insert small challenges by changing the words your child has memorized or reading the book upside
down or skipping a page. This will inevitably get your child's attention
and make her your teacher! As your child develops, reading books be-

comes a wonderful way to learn ideas and figure out motives and feelings. But from the start, choose simple picture books whose story connects one page to the next so that your child begins to recognize the beginning, middle, and end of an idea or theme.

At the end of the day, when you're really tired and the child is exhausted from school, you can lie down and relax together. While lying down, you can, as at bedtime, do things such as rubbing the child's back or moving his little toes. Even a very quiet, soothing activity can engage the child with you. Lay out some pillows for him to rearrange; or if you're giving him a massage, let him show you what he wants, putting one or the other foot up to be rubbed. These little purposeful interactions build into big ones, and that's what you're looking for. In Chapters 6 and 14, we discussed several strategies for creative interaction with even the most withdrawn or perseverative child. These strategies can be used in all the settings we have discussed here.

Floortime and Everyday Activities: Getting Your Child to Work and Think

It is also valuable to incorporate day-to-day, real-life activities—such as preparing food, cleaning up, or getting ready to go outside—into Floortime. These are opportunities to help a child understand the reasons you do things and the sequences needed to carry them out. As soon as your child shows interest in, or has to do, something that's a part of daily life, you can introduce the reasons for what you are doing. For example, when the child gets out of the tub, instead of automatically wrapping her in a towel, you might just pause for a moment and say, "Gosh you're wet. What do you need?" She might look for a towel, point, or grab it on her own.

You might start out asking, "Are you cold?" so that later your child might tell you, "Hurry Mom, get the towel, I'm cold!" Remarkably, we often do things for or tell children what to do but do not mention the reason for our actions. Does your child know why you put the milk in the refrigerator, or why you lock the door, wear a seat belt, or tuck her in tightly at night? There are countless opportunities throughout the day to help your child learn the reasons while they are actually engaged in the activity. You might mention the reason to begin with, but next ask the question and see what your child is thinking. Do not get stuck on the "why-because" pattern, which often occurs when children are not ready to answer a why question. Other ways to get at the reason would be to ask, "How come . . . ?" "What if . . . ?" or "If . . . then what would happen?" Or just start with getting your child familiar with the language of thinking by using phrases such as "There must be a reason" or "What a great idea!" when relevant to an action or feeling she has. For example, "You get mad when Mommy says it is time to clean up. Is that the reason you are throwing toys?" Or, if your child wants to play birthday again for the tenth time, "Oh, what a great idea! Birthdays are your favorite idea! How come?" Even if your child cannot yet discuss the reasons he loves birthdays, you are helping him enjoy the idea of a birthday and all it symbolizes. Perhaps, you can next explore "what you love best about birthdays" and offer choices to help elaborate.

Another way to harness the child's engagement is to change the usual way you do things. Children get familiar with routine, and we don't always give them a chance to do some of the work themselves or to participate as much as they could. Novelty and surprise help them become more active, so you can make little "mistakes" such as giving them a fork when they need a spoon or sitting in their usual chair. The idea is to create novelty to get them to do some problem-solving or express their preferences.

Problem-solving sequences are good for developing motor planning skills. The goal is not so much to create problems as it is to let your child encounter problems, such as opening a package to get something he wants. You can encourage your child to practice sequences of actions by putting him to work; ask him what he'll need if you're going to the park or the pool, for example, and have him pack his own little backpack. Every child knows what goodies are in Mommy's bag but not always the reason. When your child really wants to go somewhere, ask him to "get ready!" So if he wants to go to the pool that he loves, help him choose items to pack by asking him questions: What if you want to dry off? What if you get thirsty? What if you get hungry? It is very sunny—how will you keep from getting a sunburn? What if your clothes get dirty or you need to change your diaper? Each and every thing you usually bring along has a reason. Your child will learn to find what he needs and bring it over and, if he talks, will tell you why you need it. You can start with just two things and expand as your child begins to take over and not only remember but also tell you what he needs for the pool and why. The same would be true if you ask if he is ready for school (pack his teddy and snack) or to go to the park on a cold day (get his coat and boots). The Are You Ready? game can be applied to all purposeful behavior and ideas, from taking a bath to getting the toys needed for play.

Similarly, children usually enjoy real work that is purposeful and meaningful to them. Just as almost all children love to cook and prepare food with you—learning the sequences, measures, and how-to of cooking—they can enjoy other tasks as well, especially if there is a sensory component to it. In helping with washing the car or cleaning windows, a child can learn the sequence of steps for doing these tasks, practice the necessary motor skills, find solutions for problems that may occur, and experience satisfaction with the results.

These day-to-day chores are also opportunities to develop negotiation and conflict resolution skills, especially when working or playing with you, a sibling, or other children. For instance, instead of insisting that a child take turns or share, encourage him to start trading or make deals. While taking turns can sometimes be appropriate, sharing usually means giving up what you have to someone else. Start negotiation by encouraging trading. If the child wants something you have, what's he going to give you in return? If you don't like the trade, what else can he offer to get what he wants? In this way, your child has the opportunity to put himself in your shoes and think about what you like! For the more verbal child, help her tell you what she wants and the reason she does not want to share. See if she can understand how her sister will feel. Respect her reason not to want to give something up, and encourage the children to solve the problem. Ask them, What else can we do? They may come up with something you did not think of, or you might discover a retaliation in process.

Of course negotiations, ranging from simple trades to complex deals, need to be geared to the child's developmental level. Negotiations can take many forms and are best practiced with a secure adult who acts like the friend you want your child to play with. Let your child experience the feelings of not always being able to get what he wants just because he requested it or said the magic words. Instead, help your child learn the different strategies and possible outcomes when he is with peers or even siblings. This will encourage him to trade, or find something you might like better, or ask you if you could do it together, or learn to wait until you are through, or perhaps not be able to work it out and not get what he wants now. Such negotiations can also be done with another child on a play date when you may have to initially mediate the trade. Social rules change rapidly once a child starts school and must learn to deal with hearing "I got it first!" or losing a toy to another child when he leaves it on the classroom floor.

Think of yourself as your child's partner when she is involved in any group game or social ritual. Even better is to get a sibling or peer to be the child's partner, so your child can practice the interactions that will later occur at school or in the park, when you might not be there. Partnership is key to making "Floortime all the time everywhere" rewarding for both you and your child.

Research shows that when we provide children with emotionally relevant learning experiences—in which they are involved and interested and care about what they are learning—they want to learn. Brain-imaging studies show that while people are engaged in those kinds of learning experiences, all the different parts of their brain are working together to master the experience. We have observed that children who learn in this way are much more capable of generalizing what they've learned to other, different situations. A child who learns how to be social in fun and emotionally engaging learning environments at home will *want* to be social and will be able to do it at school or at home, with his grandparents or his peers, because he can generalize what he learned.

Everyone wants children to use ideas meaningfully. But this requires investing an image such as a table or chair, Mommy or Daddy, with emotional meaning. To achieve that you have to create learning experiences that build on the child's emotional interest. This is not easy for the parents, teachers, or therapists of a child who is withdrawn or aimless or who runs away rather than toward people. The first step is to go back to the goals, described in Chapters 6 to 10, of mastering the basic developmental capacities, taking one step at a time, starting with the levels the child has already mastered. Then, we have to create two conditions in the learning environment, whether it is at home or at school.

The first condition requires tailoring the interactions to the child's individual processing differences, as we described in Chapters 11 and 12. For example, if a child overreacts to touch and sound, placing her in a noisy room with lots of kids talking all at once is very likely to overwhelm her. She won't be able to have a pleasurable and meaningful learning experience in such a setting. Instead, she is more likely to be thrown into panic mode—fragmented in her thinking, frazzled, and just barely able to keep from falling apart. Similarly, if the child underreacts to touch and sound and we are structured and formal and keep our energy low, we won't be able to generate any real pleasure, engagement, or motivation in that child.

For another example, if a child is strong in visual learning but weak in taking in and understanding words, using lots of words (no matter how clearly and simply spoken) without much visual support is likely to confuse him. Even getting in front of your child when you want to tell him something, so that he can *see what he hears* through your gestures, facial expressions, pointing, signing, or holding the object you are talking about, increases his comprehension markedly. Your moving to get your child's visual attention and even preparing him for something you want to say will increase his auditory attention and comprehension; for example, "Susie, I want to tell you something!" or "David, did you see this . . . ?" A child who's confused is likely to feel anxious and may either pull away or become fragmented and impulsive. Tailoring learning experiences to the child's unique nervous system functioning is the first condition we must meet to foster a strong learning environment.

The second condition involves creating pleasurable emotion around each challenge so that the child wants to learn. When a child is withdrawn, highly negative, or avoidant, we can easily feel helpless and frustrated. If he won't look at us during interactions, it seems easier to try to force him to do so by, for example, holding his head. Even if we succeed in forcing a child to look at us, however, she hasn't necessarily learned anything. We may scare the child into looking or hold her head so she has to look, but if she doesn't want to, that child certainly won't look at Grandma unless we're there saying, "Better look!" The fact is that forcing a child to look at you is the best way to get a child to *not* want to look at you.

Emotion always comes before behavior. The child needs to enjoy relationships with parents, peers, and teachers in order to learn. So, rather than focusing on the behavior, we focus on the underlying emotional state. When the child finds pleasure in relating and learning, the behavior improves. Many techniques for creating enjoyable interactions are discussed earlier in this chapter and in Part II. Motivating the child requires imagination and persistence. However, while many parents and educators tell us, "That's too hard, I can't do it," we have never met a parent or educator who couldn't motivate a child and do it almost brilliantly after a while. The reason is that it becomes fun for the adult, too. Once you get the hang of it, it's more fun than you might have imagined. But you've got to be willing to struggle with it a little bit in the beginning.

Clinicians and researchers are developing a range of approaches based on teaching children fundamental abilities through their natural interests. The DIR/Floortime model provides a comprehensive and systematic framework for these approaches. We show how it works in a school setting in Chapter 21. At home, once children can engage with their caregivers, interact with gestures in a continuous flow, and begin to use words, they need opportunities for playing and communicating with peers. It's important for children to learn to use words and gestures and develop relationships with peers at the same time they are learning to do these with adults. If they wait, this learning will be more difficult later on. The reason some children's thinking skills move ahead of their peer-relating skills is simply because we give them much more practice with the former.

For these reasons, as pointed out earlier, we recommend that once children are of school age, they have four or more peer play dates a week, in addition to school. The greater degree of intimacy in one-on-one play dates enables children to become better at reading the subtle emotional signals of peers. All children differ in athletic and academic skills and the way they dress; some children are more physically awkward than others because of poor motor skills. Children, we find, accept all those differences pretty well in each other and tend not to consider a child weird or unusual as long as he can understand and exchange emotional signals easily. Play dates incorporating Floortime give children with ASD extra practice with their emotional signaling.

Floortime at School

Schools tend to be very structured and to put a high priority on compliance and limit setting, rather than on engaging, interacting, problem-solving, and thinking creatively and logically. In Chapter 21 we will show how school settings can teach specific skills as part of broader developmental goals. A parent evaluating schools for a child with ASD can look for programs that use the same principles that we recommend for the home environment: creating learning interactions tailored to the child's individual differences and harnessing the child's natural interests in spontaneous and semi-structured ways.

For a child with ASD who is becoming verbal, it's very helpful to have a group setting where other children are interactive and communicative and will react and respond to him. That's why we prefer all children with ASD or other special needs to be in integrated or regular educational settings with an aide or a helper. Whether the helper is a parent or hired caregiver, the goal of that adult and of the teacher is to facilitate interaction between the child or children with ASD and the others. Instead of parallel play or self-absorption, we want the exchange of emotional signals or gestures, or any sort of interaction, with other children. If having a parent there gives the child more confidence in playing with other children, then that's terrific. If, on the other hand, the parent encourages the child only to sit in his or her lap, then maybe an aide would better facilitate the child's playing with peers.

In an integrated setting, the caretaker may want to give the other children some sort of context for the challenges faced by the child with ASD. The general rule is to tell the other children only what they can already observe. For example, if a child is in a wheelchair, the other children see that. So it's nice if the teacher or the parent says, "You know, Suzy needs a wheelchair because she has a hard time walking, and we're going to need you guys to help us sometimes to wheel her from one place to another and to make it easier for her to get around." And if a child isn't verbal, you can say, "Johnny is just learning to talk, and you all can help him by talking a lot to him." Just tell them what they will observe on their own, in a way that will facilitate interacting with the child who needs extra help.

Parents will also want to look for a school that focuses on the building blocks of academic and social skills—the ability to attend, engage, interact purposefully, solve problems, and think creatively and logically—not on rote learning. These build an overall understanding of the world. Academics and social skills follow. For a child with ASD especially, we recommend one-on-one and small-group (two to four children per adult) learning opportunities. This is essential for tailoring learning interactions to a child's individual differences and developmental levels. One-on-one time can involve an aide, a teacher, or even highly interactive and interested volunteers. To teach the child, a teacher or aide needs to understand how a child operates in terms of processing sensations and what the child's interests are. In a group of eight to ten, let alone twenty to thirty children, such understanding and observation are virtually impossible.

While it's useful for schools to teach compliance, respect for others, and social rules such as waiting one's turn, for children who are just trying to master engaging with another person and other fundamentals, schools need to focus on the building blocks. These other efforts put the cart before the horse. Instead, one-on-one interaction and work in very small groups helps these children master basic skills, which will naturally lead to social skills.

Parents also need to look for and encourage coordination and partnership between school and home. Everyone needs to be on the same page working together. Ideally, educators need to watch how parents interact with their children, and parents need to watch how educators interact with those children.

Clearly, the basic principle of "Floortime all the time everywhere" is helpful for all children, not just children with ASD and other special needs. When we do Floortime all the time everywhere, in a spirit of warmth and fun, we are promoting children's relating, trusting, engaging, communicating, and thinking. Eventually we can even help them learn to make judgments about things and evaluate their own feelings and thoughts: "Gee, what do you think about that little tantrum you just threw? Was that something you like to do or don't like to do?" Such approaches help kids move up the developmental ladder regardless of whether they have challenges. In a sense, then, Floortime can be all the time everywhere for everyone.

Chapter 16

The Hardest Part of Floortime

Following the Child's Lead and Challenging the Child at the Same Time

One of the questions parents most frequently ask about the Floortime approach, and one of the main sources of confusion, is: "How can I follow my child's lead and at the same time challenge him to learn new skills or new abilities?"

Our view is that following the child's lead and challenging him are two sides of the same coin. Sometimes one or the other seems easier, and we can be tempted to focus only on that one, but both are central to the DIR/Floortime approach. As we've explained, the DIR/Floortime approach is based on the idea that emotion is critical to the growth of the mind and brain. Following the child's lead means following his emotions. We ask, "What is of interest to this child? What gives him pleasure?" Whatever it is, the child's interest is our clue, our window into what he's feeling. So we watch closely to tune into his emotional world. Once we figure out what he's interested in, we use that to draw him further up the developmental ladder we described in Part II.

To do that, we have to challenge the child, and that brings us to the other side of the coin. If you simply follow a child around who is, let's say, pushing a toy car, and you push another toy car with the child, you may get a look or two from her, but not much is happening in terms of her learning new skills. On the other hand, if the child is interested in a toy car and you put your hand over the car, and she pushes your hand off to get the car, there's an interaction between you two, and you're mobilizing the third stage of functional emotional development, namely, two-way communication. If you take the toy car and put it on your head and the child gives you a big smile and reaches for it, you're mobilizing both engagement and two-way communication.

We build on the child's interest to help him move up the ladder of shared attention, engagement, two-way communication, shared problem-solving, and creative and logical use of ideas. That requires not just following the child's lead but also challenging him. So, when we say, "Follow the child's lead," we don't mean simply copying or imitating the child. We mean taking the child's cue in order to build new interactions and experiences. Every interest of the child—even aimless wandering—can be turned into an interaction and a challenge that helps him move up the developmental ladder. To follow his lead and challenge him at the same time, you can start by joining him in aimless wandering, but then become a little doggie that gets stuck in front of the child's legs, so he has to go around you.

Following the child's lead—understanding his interests—tells you the best way to challenge him. If the child is playing with a paper airplane and you decide to challenge him by having him learn to put square blocks in a square hole and round blocks in a round hole, that lesson doesn't challenge the child in an area that interests him. If you hand him a square block and point to the square hole, the child is likely just to throw it on the floor and ignore you. Even if the child does it, perhaps because he's been trained to be obedient or compliant, nothing much is happening between the two of you. On the other hand, if the child is moving his plane back and forth and you make another paper airplane and fly it into the path of your child's, the child has to decide whether to go around you, go over you, or crash into you. This way, you're challenging the child to be purposeful, logical, and interactive by the clue you get from his interests.

If the child is playing with a block, you can make a little cup with your hand and say, "Oh! Mr. Hand wants the block!" If the child puts the block in your hand and gives you a smile, you're getting engagement and you're getting interaction; eventually, you may hold the block sorter in your hand and see if the child wants to put the square blocks in the square holes and the round blocks in the round holes.

You can teach a child almost anything when her natural interest gives you that window of opportunity. The point is that following the child's lead enables you to get her attention, to get her emotions activated and harnessed to help her through a challenge that moves her up the developmental ladder. Avoid simply repeating what the child is doing—though you might do that for a minute or two just to get your bearings and allow the child to feel that you're in tune with her. Also avoid inventing a challenge of your own that is not related to the child's interests. You can, of course, make available toys or activities that you think might interest the child.

Following the child's lead facilitates Floortime because the child shows us what he cares about if we observe what he is moving toward—we don't have to guess. The question then becomes how we insert ourselves into the child's interest to get the challenge going. As we've pointed out in previous chapters, some of the best ways to become part of the child's interest include "becoming the toy," being playfully obstructive, and being the receptacle for a particular toy that the child wants to put somewhere. The key is to become part of the child's interest in a way that gives him either a problem to solve or a desire for more of the experience. Children are remarkable in their ability to do what they want to do, even if it seems a purposeless activity, such as walking around in circles. Whatever it is, we need to treat it as purposeful so we can connect to it.

Sometimes the child's response is simply to undo what you've done to obstruct him; but that's getting interaction going. Caregivers often worry that the child will get mad or reject them, but these are valid emotions and they give us a way in. When the child figures out, "Wow, I can sneak under Mom's arm and get the toy," he's doing something purposeful. Or if he gets mad and makes a sound that means "You're getting in my way!" and glares at you, you're getting that flow of inter-action going. Of course, we never want to challenge the child so much that he has a tantrum or gives up his activity in despair; we want to keep the challenge playful.

Following are a few examples of how to use this approach of follow-ing the child's lead and challenging him at the same time.

Building on Attention

Caregivers often try to interact with a child before they actually get her attention. A caregiver may be talking to a child, trying to get her to search for a hidden object or do some other activity, but the child is clearly looking around elsewhere or is too distracted by her own motor movements to pay attention. Even with a child who is capable of shared problem-solving or using some words and ideas, we can miss those opportunities because we don't get the child's attention first.

Sometimes all you have to do is get in front of the child and say, "Sweetheart!" with expectancy in your voice. "SWEETHEART! Are you going to listen to Mommy, *or* are you going to move that car around? SWEETHEART! Which is it? The car or Mommy?" You may have to put your hand gently over the car (very slowly so you don't provoke a meltdown), so the child looks at you, and he may shake his head and pull the car away, but you've got his attention.

In eliciting the child's attention, as we described in Chapters 11 and 12, you want to adjust the sensations you offer—vocal pitch, cadence, visual animation, firmness of touch, and so forth—to the child's unique biology. Some children, even if they have auditory pro-cessing problems, respond better to a faster vocal rhythm, repeated several times, because slowing down can have the effect of taking out the emotion and rhythm in your voice. One example of how parents use cadence instinctively to challenge a child is when they play little chase games and say things like, "Here I co-ome. I'm-gonna-get-you!"—conveying affect and expectation through fluctuation in the voice and physical movement. Children connect the rhythm to the pleasurable anticipation of the chase, the gentle tickle, and the bear hug that are coming.

If the child has motor planning and sequencing problems that make her wave her arms around in a way that distracts her, you can gently hold her hands and move her arms in rhythm with your voice, thus making a game of shifting the rhythmic patterns. This way you're following her lead of moving her arms, but you're also challenging her to take the lead in the "dance," to show you the rhythm she enjoys. If you're moving slowly, she may try to speed it up, or vice versa. Now you're in a rhythmic interaction with each other, and she is taking some initiative, rather than just moving in a disorganized way on her own. Similarly, children who need to move in space attend more to any challenge to interact when they're in a swing, perhaps a spandex swing that supports them with some firm pressure.

So focusing on a child's sensory system and using the sensory and affective experiences that will gain his attention has to be the first step, even if he is already quite verbal. Otherwise, if the caregiver tries to have a conversation with the child when his attention is elsewhere, the adult may feel discouraged and give up. The parent or caregiver may have to work for five minutes to get him attending and engaged, and then can bring the child into an interactive conversation.

Building Engagement

At the second level, we follow the child's lead—what gives the child pleasure—to encourage engagement and relating with others. Whatever the source of pleasure is for the child, we don't compete with it, whether it's a stuffed animal, a rattle, or a book; we don't try to force the child to look at us or go through the motions of relating. The goal isn't mechanical looking, but intimacy and the enjoyment of relating with another. So, we use the child's interests; we join the child's object of desire so we and the object become one. If the object is a book, in addition to looking at the book with the child, a parent can put the book on his head or hide it behind his back. He can sit on it, so the child has to push him over to get it. (Of course, the parent makes it relatively easy for the child to do so: the goal is not to really frustrate the child, although a little bit of frustration sometimes piques the child's interest.) The idea is to get the little grin that says, "That's funny." For example, if the object is something that can go in your mouth, most children will be amused or intrigued if you put it in your mouth; they'll want to take it out, and you can have a little game around that. Be playful, as if you were a slightly naughty child yourself.

To build engagement, challenge the child to do something active to you. A common mistake is to *do to* the child—tickle him, move his face, and so forth—to get him to react to you. Instead, we want to woo and entice the child to take the initiative in the interaction. As you challenge the child, if you find that he is getting frustrated, it's important to empathize with him: "Uh-oh! Oh, that's not what you wanted!" The words you use are not so important as the message that you care and understand. This will keep the child going even when he's frustrated because you've crossed that line from novelty and amusement to setting a challenge that seems too hard for him.

Keep watching his reactions so you can move back and forth between challenging him to get a toy, for example, and helping him feel successful. If you're holding the rocket ship up too high for the child to reach and he gets discouraged and starts to give up, you can change your position and say, "Oh, now you can reach it!" Although you're challenging him, you also want the child to feel that he can win by his engagement with you. Give him enough time to respond, but not so much that there are long pauses in the action; if he doesn't seem to know what to do next, you can cue him a bit.

Extending Two-Way Communication

At this stage, the goal is to help the child become a truly purposeful partner, opening and closing many circles of communication. For example, you can challenge the child to point to something she wants, take it from you, and give it back, until you get a continuous flow of back-and-forth communication. Again, to generate this, you want to help the child take the initiative. It's not real two-way communication if you just tickle a child ten times in a row and he giggles ten times in a row. Each new circle should be somewhat different from the prior circle: the child smiles and you smile back; you stick out your tongue, and he makes a funny face; you make an even funnier face, and he makes a big sound; and so forth.

Observe what interests the child: a doll? funny noises? jumping on Mommy? playing with the light switch? flushing the toilet? Then ask yourself, "How do I turn this into interaction, with my child taking initiative?" Let's take a simple example. Small children love doors. In my office there is a door to the waiting room and another door that goes into my living room. Invariably, children want to explore the room and see where the doors go. They almost always try to open the door to my living room. It's typical that the caregiver will say, "No! You can't do that"—which ends the interaction and misses the opportunity.

We try not to say "no" unless the child is about to hurt himself or someone else or damage something. Instead, as we've described in earlier chapters, we create interactions around the child's desire to go out the door. Perhaps the father puts his foot in front of the door so it can't readily open. The child starts pulling and can't open the door, so the father offers—either with words or actions—to help the child, for example, by offering his hand so the child can take it and put it on the door knob. The father may make a gesture indicating "Open door?" and the child nods his head, and now we have two-way communication. And maybe the father indicates that the two of them need Mother's help, so the child goes to get Mother and brings her to the door, and so forth. The end result may be just going out to the waiting room—thus allowing the child ultimately to succeed. After playing in the waiting room for a few minutes, the child himself wants to come back to the main play area. If we can't let the child go into the waiting room for some reason, we may finally have to try distracting him with another toy or say gently, "No, no, we can't do it now, but maybe later." Even if the child has a tiny meltdown at this point, we've gotten ten or more circles of communication, and the child has taken initiative. All of this builds on following the child's lead and challenging him to move to the next developmental level.

This kind of interaction offers a great opportunity to develop gestural communication: knocking on the door, turning a key if there is one, playing with the handle and pulling on it, and so forth. What makes the playful obstruction work is always conveying to the child that you understand and support her intent—which is to open the door—instead of trying to stop her or being disapproving or anxious. This supportive attitude encourages the child to keep taking the initiative to get what she wants, which leads to our next stage.

Initiative and Shared Problem-Solving

The goal at this stage is to help the child take initiative in solving a problem with you. The example above showed the beginning of this process. Let's look at another example: a child playing with a toy action figure. If he puts it down for a minute to look out the window, you can put the toy up on the shelf. When he turns around to find his toy, you can ask, "Where did it go?" and look surprised. The child may look at you and then around the room a bit for the toy, and if he doesn't find it, you may say, "Huh! I think Mr. Toy ran up on the shelf!" and point toward it. Once the child sees it and perhaps reaches out or moves toward the shelf, you can hold out your arms out and ask, "Well, how are we going to get it?" Thirty circles of communication later, the child may have taken you to a chair that the two of you can move so that he can climb on it to get to the toy, or may have gotten on your shoulders to reach for it. The more easily the child gets frustrated, the easier you should make the challenge, for example, by putting the toy on a low shelf that he can reach by himself (perhaps by standing on a little stool).

Whatever the challenge or problem you create, it should build on the child's interest and make it necessary for her to use a continuous flow of interaction with you to solve it. In other words, you use the child's interest in a toy or activity and set up multiple barriers to the child's achieving her goal that require shared problem-solving to surmount. Or you may simply help the child reach her destination or objective in a way that requires her to take the initiative in interaction with you. For example, if she wants a ride, you can be a willing horsy, but one that doesn't move until the child pats him on the back. You can even get into a signaling system with touch—two pats mean go, one pat means stop—so the child can control this horsy who doesn't know what to do.

When we talk about creating a "problem," it's not a question of just setting up a lot of little obstacles. We want children to encounter problems in their natural environment. Even in day-to-day kinds of experiences, we can trigger the child's emotion by surprise. If the child wants a cookie, what if the cookie jar is empty? Can he work with you to solve that problem? Or if he's packing his backpack to hurry to the pool, what does he want in his lunch? He'll work to solve that problem because he wants to go swimming. So you don't have to work so hard to figure out how to create a problem out of thin air; you just work with the child's intent.

We want to stress that progress comes from getting the child to take the initiative. The biggest mistake we see is telling the child what to do or doing something to her to provoke a set response, rather than challenging her to take the initiative or to solve a problem with you. Initiative is often the missing piece in children with ASD, even in highly verbal children. They haven't learned to take the initiative in problem-solving, which is an essential building block of later thinking. So we can't ignore this stage.

Encouraging Creative and Logical Thinking

In stages five and six, the goal is to again follow the child's lead, now challenging him to develop and elaborate pretend dramas and then to build bridges between ideas. If the child is playing with a baby doll and pretending to feed the doll, you challenge the child to make the drama more complex. You might join the drama by becoming the baby and talking for it: "Oh! I like that—give me more!" or "Oh, no, no, no!

Don't want the soup! Want the cookie! Give me the *big* cookie!" This way you enter the drama and challenge the child to build on his scenario without telling him what to do. You can create all sorts of fun interactions around pretend play that deepen the plot the child has begun.

Once the child is using ideas creatively, we want to challenge her to think logically and make sense, whatever her age (in typical development, this step occurs more and more between ages three and four, but in a child with ASD it may occur then or later). If she is playing with teddy bears, you can enter the drama by asking, "Where's the bear going in that car? Mr. Bear, where are you going?" One technique that works well is for the caregiver to use two voices, that of the toy ("I'm a hungry bear! Where are my crackers?") and that of a coach ("The bear's still hungry! Let's help him find the crackers!"). You don't have to flood your child with questions to get interaction going in a drama; instead, use different characters with lots of affect to keep the child engaged. Your child will learn to switch roles herself once she gets into it.

Alternatively, if you're just chatting with the child, asking what he wants for lunch or which book he wants to read at bedtime, and why (whatever the discussion topic), focus on helping the child to elaborate on what he is saying while being logical. One good way to get the child to give you more words is to play dumb: pretend you understand less, instead of finishing the child's sentences for him because you think you know what he's going to say or because he's saying it wrong. Rather than worrying about the child's grammar, focus on facilitating an exchange of words or short phrases (or often symbols, such as pictures, if the child has oral motor problems). In this way the child develops pragmatic language. Once the child can hold a fifteen-minute spontaneous, creative, logical conversation, you can start correcting grammar if it seems necessary. But initially, challenge the child to be a chatterbox, to be more imaginative, and to make sense.

Chapter 17

Working with Older Children, Adolescents, and Adults with ASD, I

A Lifetime of Learning

WRITTEN WITH HENRY MANN, M.D.

Fourteen-year-old Tony, a good-natured boy with Asperger's Syndrome, was doing fairly well in a regular classroom setting. However, as he began to go through puberty, Tony started to have more difficulties with making simple decisions: he often froze up when asked to choose between playing a game inside or going outside. He was relying more on scripted language in new social situations and was also becoming much more negative. Tony's parents wondered if these behaviors were typical of puberty or if their son was regressing developmentally, and what they should do.

W orking therapeutically with older children, adolescents, and adults with ASD poses many challenges. The most significant challenge to overcome is the myth that children reach a developmental plateau beyond which improvement can only be minimal. In fact, during the teenage and adult years, the brain and nervous system are still developing. The areas of the brain that regulate emotions, sequence ideas and actions, and influence abstract thinking and concept building continue developing into the fifties and sixties. (The expression "use it or lose it" applies to the continuous development of abilities.)

Because of this myth many therapists, in treating older children, adolescents, and adults, teach only superficial skills and routines instead of trying to support and strengthen the patient's basic developmental and processing capacities. Diagnoses of ASD, mental retardation, or other conditions can mislead caregivers into limiting their expectations for older children and adults. Reliance on standardized tests that may not be appropriate for a particular child's learning profile can lead to an assumption that the child's disability is not amenable to change. A diagnosis that implies limits (such as mental retardation) should be made only after a child has participated in an optimal program for at least three years and has made no intellectual or developmental progress. Prematurely identifying a child with a chronic disorder carries with it resignation to the status quo rather than fostering an approach that encourages the child's ability to develop.

Learning challenges are often related to problems in processing information through one or more of the sensory pathways—visual-spatial, sensory-motor, or auditory. In the DIR approach, we work on whichever pathways give the child trouble, while strengthening the others. Each of these pathways may have many components, with different strengths or weaknesses. This approach demands more of parents and therapists, but it gives hope for many children and adults previously labeled as too developmentally impaired to be helped to a significant degree. Helping adults go from aimless, nonverbal, self-injurious behavior to purposeful interaction with others, pleasure in relating to others, engagement in simple problem-solving interactions (such as signaling to get food or a game), and even use of signs or words is a huge gain. Even if they still have enormous limitations, the quality and meaning of their lives have grown significantly, along with their skills.

Age and size can stand in the way of good care for older children, adolescents, and adults. Older and larger individuals do not generate in caregivers the same nurturing and protective urges as little children do. A caregiver's response to an angry, agitated, or negative adolescent is generally quite different from his or her response to an angry three-year-old. If a three-year-old boy wants to go out into the snow with his shoes off, we attempt to persuade and support him and firmly help him to make the correct decision. If a seventeen-year-old boy angrily demands to go out into the snow with his shoes off, we have quite a different response. Fear of consequences and lack of control inevitably affect caregivers, whether they are family members or staff at schools, rehabilitation centers, and other institutions. The reaction is based on the objectives of setting limits and maintaining containment and restraint, rather than trying to engage those in their charge and to help them understand and want to cooperate.

Basic Principles in Working with
Older Children and Adults with ASD

The basic approach of our DIR model applies also in the adolescent and adult years, with certain adaptations. The example that follows illustrates principles involved in evaluating and treating adolescents and adults with ASD.

Jim, a thirty-year-old man with ASD and many associated developmental difficulties, lived at home and spent all his time with his mother. She was familiar with the DIR model, and described her son as warm, sensitive, and adept at reading other people's nonverbal cues. Nevertheless, though she had worked to engage him, by age twenty Jim's two-way communication abilities were still minimal. When he became frustrated or worried, he would often scream, leading the mother to assume that something was wrong and that Jim needed her help. In an effort to help him, his mother attended a symposium on using typing to teach language, and over the following ten years she taught Jim to use a typing program. Eventually Jim was able to explain that he had screamed because he was overwhelmed with frustration about his difficulty with word retrieval: "Words would not come, and all I could do was scream," he typed out. By age thirty, Jim could go to a museum and then, using the typing program, describe the pictures he had seen, or he could go to a party, come home, and describe it, along with his uncomfortable feelings while there.

It took Jim ten years of working with the typing program before he was able to verbalize his feelings. To teach him to type and to use simple meaningful phrases—such as "No car," "Buy cookie," or "Go to sleep, tired"—Jim's mother worked slowly and laboriously with him, bringing out one word at a time. Jim had low muscle tone, so his mother held his forearm as he typed. Jim's progress toward simple verbal expressions by age thirty illustrates how appropriate interventions begun at any age can, if pursued consistently, lead to unexpected progress.

Jim's mother also helped him with other challenges, such as learning to engage in pretend play. She herself was uncomfortable with pretend play, and Jim's low muscle tone and difficulty with two-way communication interfered with the development of his skills in this arena. However, once Jim began using words, he went from being almost completely self-absorbed to seeking others out and saying, "Come sit with me." He began to engage in (limited) spontaneous pretend play with his father, such as pretending to be a character from a cartoon he enjoyed. Jim also began to read simple books aloud to his mother. Whenever she asked him how he learned to read, he would answer, "I learned by myself."

Jim's mother was concerned about how to soothe him. He particularly enjoyed listening to music, and she found that he responded best to the music on some of his favorite videos. Her most frequent problem was dealing with Jim's frustration at not being able to say the words he wanted to use. Clearly, Jim was struggling with the same issues a three- or four-year-old child has who is just becoming verbal, is still working on gestural communication and engagement, and has some splinter skills in terms of ability to read a little bit or at least recognize some words. This is not an unusual picture. The point is that we can make interventions with a thirty-year-old man that are comparable to what we might do with a three- to five-year-old child.

The first principle of intervention with adolescents and adults is to work with the basic building blocks in the context of each person's interests. In this regard, working with Jim is somewhat different than working with a young child, because Jim has some of the interests of an adult, such as music. Also, since he is a little more set in his ways, he can't be engaged as easily as a young child can. However, we need to work on the same building blocks with Jim as we would with a child who has the same developmental profile. So if we are working on pretend play and Jim doesn't want to get down on the floor and pretend, we might set up an informal improvisational theater program at home or participate in an improvisation class with teenagers or other adults with ASD. Playing different roles in a drama enables individuals to learn to improvise, be more flexible, practice uncomfortable situations, and think more creatively. Integrating a developmental approach into an age-appropriate activity would allow Jim to build foundation skills in a comfortable environment.

We also recommend building on Jim's interest in music to promote imaginative play. One of his parents could listen to music with him and then begin to dramatize the music. Jim could be asked to select music to fit his mood, such as a vigorous march or a soft, soothing melody, which would give a clue as to how to proceed with the drama. His parents could dramatize the music and the story with action figures or pictures. The use of pictures might be particularly helpful with Jim, or other individuals at a similar stage here, because they allow quick recognition and interaction and they support language development. Because Jim has particular difficulty with expressive language, we want to give it as much use as possible; practice with sequencing imaginative pictures would help. Jim could cut out pictures that interest him from magazines or books and use them to tell a story. He could also use photos of people, pets, and other things in his everyday life. Pictures might also be helpful to him if they are available when he is agitated and upset; he could point to them to quickly indicate his concerns. If the images were used in dialogue in both pretend and real situations, the picture system would help Jim start to speak.

The second principle is to keep moving sequentially through the stages of development outlined in Chapters 6–10. Unfortunately, treatment of many older children, adolescents, and adults often stops when they have achieved a partially developed language system. Much more work is needed if the individual is still unable to appreciate and make gradations of thought and feeling. Individuals who are still at the concrete stage are vulnerable to being impulsive or to having tantrums because they cannot understand concepts of relativity (shades of gray), time, or quantity. They can't anticipate the future well enough to plan and be patient.

Techniques, such as those described in Chapter 10, to help Jim learn relativistic thinking might include asking, when he is feeling angry or upset, "How upset? A little bit? A lot? A whole lot?" and spreading out our arms to indicate the extent of the feeling. If Jim is unable to anticipate the future very well, we could ask questions that project into the future about a subject he finds emotionally interesting; for example, "Do you want a chocolate chip cookie now and vanilla ice cream tomorrow, or ice cream now and a cookie tomorrow?" Then we might move to hypothetical thinking about possibilities (which is more difficult) by asking questions such as, "Do you want to eat one cookie now or wait and maybe get a double ice cream cone later?" Learning to anticipate is crucial to social and emotional self-regulation.

Most adults who remain in special-needs programs rarely advance intellectually above the ten- to twelve-year-old level because of the limitations of our educational approach to these individuals. Many of them could progress far beyond the level of concrete thinking, yet our curriculums fail to challenge them to do so; treatment approaches tend to reinforce concrete thinking.

In Jim's case, we would recommend, in addition to continuing the dedicated work that his mother initiated in terms of facilitated writing and speaking and using pictures to develop gray-area thinking, working with his interest in music to strengthen the earlier developmental building blocks of engagement and gestural language. While at times

Jim might prefer to be alone, at other times he might accept a parent's offer to listen to music with him, starting with just sitting quietly together in the room to build basic shared attention. Concurrently, his parents could get him out into the community more by taking him to music stores and helping him make selections, including negotiating around the selections (meaning that he should have to make choices between one CD and another); this activity would motivate him to talk about his feelings and interact with others. It would build more nuanced thinking as well as enhance his ability to interact with others.

The third general principal in working with older children and adults is to create emotionally meaningful contexts for learning. Often a child with ASD learns some speech and can answer "why" questions but is unable to master abstract concepts. This limited, concrete understanding of the world persists into adolescence and adulthood. We see this situation not only in individuals with ASD or Asperger's Syndrome but also in those with cognitive delays, mental retardation, or severe learning disabilities. A common underlying factor in all of these cases is the presence of processing problems, which makes gray-area or reflective thinking difficult. The key to progress, as we discussed in Chapter 10, is to use abstract concepts in emotionally meaningful contexts.

For example, justice is an abstract notion. We continually refine our sense of justice through experiencing situations that are fair and unfair. We can give children a dictionary definition, but this approach would not get us very far. But if we create make-believe situations such as one in which a girl's brother gets a lot of presents and the girl gets none, the girl will quickly say, "That's unfair." Justice is being treated fairly. With an emotionally meaningful example like this, children or adults will get the basic concept. Then they can refine it through other experiences.

Every concept, such as love, has a simple definition and then more complicated meanings that are gradually acquired over time, through more and more emotional experiences. To a young child, love means hugs and kisses; to an adult it means hugs, kisses, and also warmth, caring, desire, devotion, and compassion. Concepts of dimension, which are both physical and mathematical, also become more complex as we get older. When we are very young, there is "big" and "little," but with experience, we come to understand height, length, width, depth, and concepts such as "three-dimensional."

The more severe the processing problems, the more powerful the emotional meaning of the learning experience has to be. The importance of finding an emotionally meaningful context increases when we are attempting to teach gray-area thinking and reflective thinking. Here, without the strong motivation provided by a context such as a school conflict or a future birthday present, progress might be impossible. The ability to think abstractly and with nuances is crucial to individual development; without this ability we cannot understand other people's motives, and we can understand only a limited amount of academic material. Individuals with only memory-based reading and arithmetic skills will be limited academically.

Peer Relationships

Another basic goal of working with adolescents and adults with autism and developmental challenges is to help improve the extent and quality of their relations to peers. Children diagnosed with Asperger's Syndrome who are sufficiently verbal and academically skillful to be in a regular class but cannot get along appropriately with other children feel isolated and alienated. They can become very sad and depressed. They are aware enough to want to have friends and to be part of a social group, but they are also keenly aware of their lack of acceptance by others. Teenagers and adults with similar developmental disabilities may experience the same feelings.

For example, Donald, a fifteen-year-old boy, was in therapy with a psychiatrist for severe depression and withdrawal following the death of his grandfather. He had previously been seen by another therapist, who had diagnosed him with Asperger's Syndrome and had treated him with a combination of antipsychotic and stimulant medication. According to that therapist, Donald was very difficult to engage and generally interacted with little emotion. He could speak, read, and understand language fairly well and could do his schoolwork with the support of special education classes and an individual tutor. Although he was hypersensitive to sound and touch and had low muscle tone and problems with fine and gross motor coordination, the family had not been able to obtain adequate occupational and physical therapy services for him. His new psychiatrist discovered that Donald's greatest concerns were the loss of his grandfather and his lack of friends. For several years prior to his grandfather's death, Donald had daily telephone conversations with his grandfather that lasted up to an hour and a half. His grandfather had in fact been attempting to fill in for the social contact that was otherwise completely lacking in Donald's life.

The psychiatrist saw Donald weekly or semiweekly for therapy sessions and talked with him daily on the telephone for five to ten minutes. As part of these sessions, the psychiatrist offered Donald an opportunity to engage in role playing. Donald welcomed this chance. Often the psychiatrist would play the role of a highly verbal, obnoxious, and playful adolescent (the kind Donald had the most trouble with at school). The goal for the conversations was to engage Donald and to educate him in the nonverbal aspects of teenage communication, both face-to-face and on the phone. With four months of this approach, Donald's initial, extraordinarily flat and depressed emotional tone changed. The pace, rhythm, and range of emotion in his speech improved and became closer to that of other adolescents his age. Within the next five months he began, for the first time in his life, to have some limited friendships and a girlfriend and to start work in a volunteer position at a local hospital. The psychiatrist encouraged these relationships and also lots of "practice" with real peers on a daily basis. (The topic of facilitating peer relationships in adolescents and adults with ASD is addressed in greater depth in the following chapter.)

Medication

While some older children, adolescents, and adults with challenges require medication, it is often used as a substitute for working on the basic developmental building blocks. Medication can be helpful as an adjunct to therapy if the patient is overwhelmed by anxiety, depression, or fragmented thinking. Unfortunately, as noted above, adolescents and young adults who become easily frustrated, aggressive, or in any way threatening to their caretakers usually end up with medication-based treatment, with the fundamentals of a developmentally based approach left far behind—along with the individual.

Later Developmental Stages

Some adolescents and adults with ASD and other challenges have relative mastery of the six early developmental stages described in previous chapters, but have limitations in the more advanced stages described in Chapter 10: triangular thinking, gray-area thinking, and thinking from an internal standard.

Along with an expanded interest in their world, children also show more fears and anxieties at this stage. Adolescents and adults who move into triangular thinking may suddenly become more manipulative. This development can cause anxiety for caretakers, but parents and therapists should support these individuals throughout this period, helping them to learn judgment and also to reduce their anxiety about their newfound assertiveness. We also need to help them to keep the grandiosity and expansive thinking typical of this stage at a realistic and manageable level.

Puberty and ASD

A big change occurs in the adolescent years within the teenager's body. There is growing interest in sexuality. Aggression is more dangerous at this time because the adolescent body is getting bigger, muscles are developing, and hormones are changing. Testosterone increases in boys may affect the quality of their aggression. A teenager's changing body can be very frightening to him.

Adolescence is hard enough for children with no processing difficulties, who have mastered all the prior developmental levels. How does it affect children who are very concrete and just have the bare minimum of verbal concepts, who can answer "why" questions but cannot do gray-area and triangular thinking? What about children who cannot even answer "why" questions yet? What happens when the body, sexual interests, and levels of aggression change in children with weaker processing and reflective abilities? Without strong visual-spatial processing, a person cannot develop a body image very well. This is when caretakers begin to have many concerns about an adolescent's or adult's propensity toward aggression or sexual acting out.

The development of sexual interest and acting out in adolescents with ASD who may be functioning developmentally as three-, five-, or seven-year-olds can be very difficult for caretakers. It should be addressed in the context of that particular child's developmental level. We may tell a simple "birds and bees" story to one child, while for another we may need to emphasize that while people like to touch their bodies in different places, it is a private activity and there is a place and time to do it. For the fifteen-year-old who is at a seven- or eight-year-old level, we may use a book with pictures and explanations about how the body works as a basis for some discussion. Discussing how to protect oneself from being exploited sexually or from getting diseases is no different than any other discussion about self-protection; it should be addressed to the thinking level of the individual.

Regarding Tony, the boy in the case study at the beginning of this chapter, our suggestion to the parents was not to make it an either-or situation. All children experience upsets during puberty because of the physical and biological changes occurring. Friends and teachers are also making more social demands on them at school, and academic work is more difficult, and families are expecting more from them. They also struggle with wanting to be on their own while still feeling the need for care from their parents. If they have developmental problems, they need more care and more help, yet they also want more independence. Therefore, they have more conflicts over their own neediness; they want to cover it up and deny it, and that makes them more oppositional.

In adolescents with ASD, all these issues are exaggerated. The key is not to treat puberty issues separately from developmental issues or to brush off problems as puberty related, but to deal with the aggression, acting out, or anxiety in its own right. This means staying calm and regulated yourself and inviting the teenager be a collaborative problem-solver with you. Respect the child's need to be independent while slipping in the "chicken soup" on the side. In other words, meet the child's dependency needs with warmth, nurturing, and support, through activities such as long rides in the car, listening to him talk about how he's feeling, hanging out with him and listening to his music, and playing the games he wants to play, and let him pretend to be more independent than he really is.

The most important—and the hardest—thing to do is to maintain a nurturing relationship with developmentally delayed adolescents and young adults. Because they are larger physically and not as cuddly and warm as younger children, parents and other caregivers often hold back nurturing, warmth, and intimacy. When this happens, the adolescent's or adult's need for basic security and dependency isn't met, so the individual seeks reassurance in other settings. They may be drawn to substance abuse, risky sex, or dangerous relationships and activities. There are other ways than cuddling to help adolescents and adults with ASD feel the security and warmth they need, such as long walks, cooking meals, or going to the movies with them, depending on their interests.

Moving into adulthood—whether the individual is living at home, on her own, or in a sheltered setting—there is often some separation from parents. Other relationships—friendships or sexual relationships—take over some of the parental function. These transitional relationships can be quite chaotic because adolescents expect so much from the other person. Although adolescents with developmental problems may want these relationships, they may become more depressed, anxious, and fragmented as they struggle with the inevitable conflicts. Caretakers need to be aware of this turmoil and provide more support during these times.

Some of the issues of adulthood—including forging a career, having intimate relationships and a family of one's own, entering middle age, and coming to grips with the aging process—may be relevant for some individuals with milder developmental problems. The additional struggles posed by ASD must be recognized, and support will be needed, whether from the nuclear family or counseling. Each individual will have unique abilities and challenges and be interested in these adult stages of development to varying degrees. Each person deserves individually tailored support on a *continuing* developmental journey.

Adults with Severe Developmental Problems

The issues and techniques described above relate to individuals with mild to moderate difficulties. In contrast, adolescents and adults who cannot relate at all and whose behavior appears aimless, aggressive, and disorganized often lack even the ability to put together a sequence of three or four gestures. If we can help them to move from aimless activity to engagement and then to the use of simple purposeful gestures to communicate, we can add considerably to their quality of life. The next step would be to help them begin to solve problems and interact with five- or six-step sequences, so that they can, for example, take us to the kitchen and show us what they want to eat. We can then try to help them reach the early symbolic developmental level of using a few pictures or words to communicate.

We may be tempted to give up on individuals with profound developmental problems because of our own reactions to their limitations. They may seem not to respond or may display a great deal of aggression (toward others or themselves) as well as much disturbing and aimless behavior, so their caretakers may resort primarily to physical restraint or medication. The DIR approach has been applied to chronically institutionalized adults with severe developmental deficits, with promising results.

One patient, thirty-four-year-old Peter, was institutionalized at age five with a diagnosis of mental retardation because of his failure to develop language or even nonverbal communication skills. As a child, he had frequent uncontrollable rages and required full-time one-on-

one care. As Peter grew, so did his capacity for dangerous attacks on other patients and staff. Over many years he was given large amounts of psychotropic and mood-stabilizing medications, but did not seem to respond well. He needed a very high level of care until the introduction of Risperdol to his medical treatment, which led to a decreasing intensity and frequency of rage reactions to frustrating situations and changes in schedule.

Peter was not able to function past the very earliest developmental stages. He could focus on various objects that might interest him, such as cans of soda, pieces of paper, and pens, which would inevitably end up in his mouth. There was no noticeable engagement with staff or others throughout his time in residential care, and he showed little or no evidence of two-way communication. In addition, he also did not seem to understand others' complex gestures or words. His day-to-day life consisted of being cared for and passively accepting directions.

When a clinician initiated the DIR approach with Peter, using simple imitation of all Peter's movements and sounds, Peter rapidly began to focus his attention on the therapist. This technique is one that mothers naturally use to engage their babies' attention in the first months of life. It was appropriate for Peter because the first therapeutic task was to engage his attention and then build on this to help him relate and finally interact in some purposeful way.

To explore what might be helpful for Peter, he was seen for twenty- to thirty-minute Floortime sessions twice monthly. (The infrequent sessions were due to the limitation of the clinician's schedule; more sessions would have been helpful.) The goal was to learn how to capture his attention, to create opportunities for emotional engagement and two-way communication, and then to share these insights with the staff so they could work with Peter on a daily basis. Peter responded very quickly during the first Floortime session; at one point he even leaned toward the clinician and almost touched heads with him. In the second session he showed what was probably a reaction to the first meeting by coming into the meeting room and turning his back to the clinician for nearly ten minutes. Eventually he sat next to the clinician, but looked away and almost never allowed the clinician to engage his attention. Whenever it was clear to him that the clinician was attending to him, he dropped his gaze or turned his body.

The third Floortime session showed almost the reverse. Peter came into the meeting making loud guttural sounds. The clinician responded with a similar sound and a friendly tone. For about ten minutes they sat next to each other making these sounds. Peter did not build on the clinician's sounds, but his persistence and occasional look of real interest in this activity was a clear indication of fleeting involvement and engagement.

Over a series of sessions, Peter increased his repertoire of sounds to include short combinations of consonants and vowels in a somewhat rhythmic pattern, which the clinician imitated. He appeared to be more engaged and aware that the clinician was picking up on whatever he produced. During some sessions he was openly interested in the clinician, taking the clinician's eyeglasses or pens and putting them in his mouth and moving close to the clinician. These two- or three-minute periods of engagement were usually followed by withdrawal for an equivalent amount of time or longer. However, over time, the periods of intimacy increased from about twenty seconds to three or four minutes. In one dramatic session, Peter included other staff in the Floortime interaction, responding equally well to two staff members. He exchanged looks, had some fleeting smiles, and exchanged objects.

It was observed that Peter was very sensitive to light touch and sound and that his visual-spatial abilities (here, finding things) were much more developed than his auditory ones (he never followed verbal directions). Staff members began daily Floortime sessions with Peter, supervised by the clinician. The sessions would begin with simple imitation of Peter's behavior to get interactions going. The staff members were careful not to intrude on his sensitive tactile or auditory systems, and used lots of gestural animation to appeal to his stronger visual problem-solving skills. Though they were initially skeptical of the process, the staff became enthusiastic and fully engaged in learning about Floortime.

Peter's ability for engagement increased; in one Floortime session with a staff member, Peter maintained his attention on the staff person for the full twenty minutes. Peter also increased the complexity of his use of sounds, so that a typical Floortime session consisted of the purposeful exchange of a wide range of sounds and variations in volume. He also began to gesture purposefully, for example, vocalizing and moving his hand toward a desired object. The staff began saying, "We can read him." Exchanges of looks and little grins became commonplace. Eventually Peter was able to approach a staff person, vocalize, and indicate with an arm movement his desire for some food. This rate of progress indicated that Peter might ultimately begin to use language to communicate. Finally, Peter's overall mood improved with this treatment. Before the DIR therapy began, each spring Peter would have one to two months of extreme agitation—becoming aggressive, sleepless, and irritable. After the start of the program, he still had considerably increased energy during the spring, but did not have periods of agitation and depression.

Another patient, named Alice, a fifty-nine-year-old woman with severe motor problems, had been placed in a large residential center when she was a child, after a diagnosis of autism and profound retardation. She avoided contact with others; was withdrawn, nonverbal, and gaze-avoidant; and showed a complete indifference to her surroundings, to staff, and to other patients. She had frequent episodes of crying and whining that appeared unrelated to any external circumstances. A nurse's aide, Kim, showed an interest in learning the DIR/Floortime approach and asked to work with Alice. Kim was supervised while she initiated contact with Alice and engaged her attention, at first by simply mirroring Alice's gestures and sounds. Within several sessions, Kim was consistently able to engage Alice's attention, and she began working with Alice three times a week in thirty-minute Floortime sessions.

Alice responded to these sessions by beginning to reach out for Kim and making eye contact with her. After several months Alice started to become attached to Kim; she showed pleasure when Kim entered her room and would reach out for Kim's hand and bring it close to her head to rub the side of her face. After never being observed to smile or show signs of pleasure for many years, she began to smile spontaneously. Her episodes of crying and whining decreased. After several more months of regular Floortime, Alice started to reach out for and make eye contact with other staff and to show signs of recognition of others. Within six months, many staff members who at first did not support the Floortime approach began to use some of the techniques to engage Alice themselves.

With severely challenged adults, as with all others, the first step is to encourage attention, engagement, and two-way purposeful interaction. Gains in these basic foundations can make an enormous difference in an individual's emotional and social adaptation.

Chapter 18

Working with Older Children, Adolescents, and Adults with ASD, II

Creating Learning Communities

O ur goals for older children, adolescents, and adults are similar to those for very young children: to maximize learning and human development. For individuals with special needs or severe developmental problems, overcoming processing challenges can be a lifelong goal, and in many respects, a lifelong opportunity for mastery. It's the same for someone trying to develop competency in a particular skill, whether it's reading, playing tennis, ballet dancing, or playing guitar. We all receive pleasure from moving forward in one or another capacity. In a sense, the human organism is characterized, we believe, by the ongoing need to learn new skills, to master its environment.

For individuals without special needs, certain basic skill levels are often at their peak at relatively early ages, whereas for those fields that require more experience there are longer learning curves. In adults with ASD, the learning curve for the basics, such as language and thinking skills, doesn't peak at an early age, but continues into the forties, fifties, and even sixties. Our hunch is that the learning curve for individuals with processing problems extends longer into the adult years. What that means is that we parents, professionals, and policy makers have to create challenging learning communities, relationships, and educational programs for these individuals throughout their life spans.

The question is how to do that. Our school systems put great effort into early education, but by the time children with ASD are teenagers, and certainly by the time they graduate from high school, there are few formal community- or state-supported educational programs set up to develop the abilities of our young adults with developmental delays. Often, parents create their own programs, sometimes with a focus on vocational approaches if the individual is capable of mastering an occupational skill. But social relationships, basic reasoning skills, and language abilities in adolescents and adults with ASD have been addressed only by pioneering individuals and programs, not universally. This chapter suggests a model for such programs. Many may immediately condemn such an endeavor as too costly, but it actually costs more to do nothing, simply caring for individuals at their current level of development, than to help them become contributing members of society or their own learning communities.

A Model Learning Community

A true learning environment works constantly on strengthening individuals' processing skills, while at the same time helping these people move up the ladder of functional emotional developmental levels discussed in earlier chapters. Such an environment provides a day-to-day interpersonal context in which individuals can build these skills in ways that are appropriate and meaningful to their interests and their developmental age (as opposed to their chronological age). A twenty-two-year-old may have the interests of a twelve-year-old, so the way to approach him is through those interests. On the other hand, a thirty-year-old may have the language skills of a six-year-old, but some of the interests of a thirty-year-old—such as music or art; so the way to approach her is through those types of activities. Thus each goal has to be approached through the varied interests of the individuals in a learning community.

Such communities should also facilitate social interaction. An adolescent or adult with ASD may isolate himself because he's oversensitive to noise or doesn't have the skills to negotiate the simplest of social gestures, but deep down he may have a longing to be close to other people. We have never worked with a child, teenager, or adult who didn't have a desire to relate to others. The key thing is working with each individual's nervous system so that the process of relating becomes enjoyable and meaningful for that person, rather than obnoxious or aversive. Beyond one-on-one relationships, these communities should foster social networks and group activities.

For example, in Bethesda, Maryland, the Imagination Stage has groups for children with special needs, including Down syndrome, ASD, Asperger's Syndrome, and other conditions. All of the children are partially verbal, and in some of the acting groups, they are integrated with other children who have no developmental problems. The children write, produce, and perform their own plays several times a year, and in the process build a strong and supportive social network. Children play different roles depending on their abilities, and everyone seems to enjoy participating to the degree that he or she can. Drama is a particularly fruitful activity for individuals with ASD because it draws on many of the basic developmental capacities (engaging, gesturing, pretending) and because a play requires that all of the participants, both onstage and off-, have a close working relationship.

After a production at the Imagination Stage, I (SIG) noticed the performers—all with severe language and motor or other problems—talking about the party they were going to have. In their early twenties, these individuals showed the excitement of teenagers about getting together. It was delightful to see the pleasure they had in being part of a group and the sense of camaraderie that had developed.

Finally, learning communities should provide the opportunity—for those who are able—for meaningful work, as well as meaningful learning. The work should be learning based. For example, many individuals with special needs who may not be ready to live or attend college on their own, nonetheless have skills they can contribute, such as computer operation, gardening, or administrative support. Individuals may have special gifts in certain areas, even though they may be limited in others. Individuals with more skills may be able to earn money by helping to care for individuals with fewer skills. Incorporating opportunities for work also enables communities to be at least partially self-sustaining.

A learning community may include individuals ranging in age from sixteen to ninety-five, at different skill levels, requiring different levels of support. Just as we have communities for the elderly that allow individuals to live on their own and enjoy the recreational benefits of the setting while also offering assisted living for those who require support, we can have similar communities for adults with a range of developmental challenges. Individuals who require very little or no support, just a little bit of structure, may live alongside individuals who require graduated levels of support.

The staff (including, part of the time, some of the higher-functioning individuals) would be trained to do two things: fostering ever higher levels of social and intellectual development within the context of emotional developmental stages, and strengthening all the processing capacities. Just as in our programs for young children (described in detail in Part IV), part of each day would be spent on strengthening each of the core processing abilities, while supporting the overall development of intellectual and social skills based on the individuals' interests.

A heavy emphasis on activities such as drama, dance, art, music, and gardening facilitates the development of motor, sequencing, visual-spatial, and (if there's talking involved) verbal skills. Such activities are often highly pleasurable to individuals with ASD or other developmental delays. In addition, individuals with severe language problems often have a well-developed sense of music or appreciation of the visual arts, so the activities play to natural strengths. Other activities might include computer games and working on computer skills, depending on individuals' interests and skill levels.

Another part of the day may be spent mastering our six fundamental levels of development in learning interactions and then going on to the higher levels of thinking. Obviously, such learning communities would require that the staff be thoroughly trained in promoting the developmental levels in all interactions throughout the day, as well as in special sessions. (Depending on individuals' needs, staff might have four to eight sessions a day for work on the fundamentals.)

For those capable, another part of the day would be spent on work or occupational training (either inside the community or outside, for those able), in the context of the individual's natural strengths. Individuals could earn income for the work, offsetting some of the cost of their care; some communities might even have businesses, such as a bakery or organic garden, that generates income for the community. To the extent the work is done in the community, it would develop a sense of collegiality, mutual support, and community identity and involvement.

Five Principles for a Learning Community

Programs may be structured to meet these goals in many different ways. However it's done, there are five principles to remember:

1. Learning communities and learning relationships must provide opportunities for individuals to develop throughout their life spans. Societal responsibility should not be age-related, but development-related. Our society has focused on providing education for children and adolescents (and young adults in state-supported colleges) based on the notion that young people should achieve certain educational outcomes before we send them out on their own to make their way in the world. Doesn't it make more sense instead to think of our responsibility as a society as getting all individuals to a certain developmental level? If for some individuals that takes a lifetime, so be it. That's our society's obligation—to provide that lifetime of effort.

    Current programs for the elderly and other individuals who can't fully care for themselves (such as those with developmental delays) often end up simply warehousing individuals. From a purely economic perspective, it costs more in the long run to warehouse people than to run proper programs for them. It's also wise from the point of view of the human spirit to see our responsibility as hinging on the developmental level of individuals, not their age or a certain number of years of schooling. As long as a person has not yet mastered a certain developmental level—and we would say that's the level of reflective thinking, at which people can be self-evaluative, reason problems through, and begin moving toward self-sufficiency—we should have some community responsibility toward him or her. This doesn't mean that families don't have a big responsibility; rather a family-community partnership can help those families less financially able to provide these kinds of learning opportunities and relationships for their children.

2. Learning communities shouldn't be focused predominantly on concrete "living skills," forgetting the developmental foundations for thinking and social relationships. Historically, we've made an arbitrary distinction, saying "OK, we'll teach people academic skills like reading and math. If we don't think an individual can learn those skills, we'll give up on that and just teach the person how to take a bus or cross the street without stepping into traffic." What's missed when we make that distinction is that both sorts of skills—taking a bus or crossing the street *and* doing math or reading—require thinking. We shouldn't set limits based on the specific skill. Rather, we should work on the developmental fundamentals in multiple contexts—both knowledge-acquiring contexts and life skills contexts. Taking a bus and going shopping can be taught as creatively as writing an essay comparing two novels. Both life skills and academic skills can be taught through memorization or in a thinking way, and rote memory is a far less effective way of teaching, though it may seem easier initially.

3. In promoting both academic and life skills, all the processing areas should be strengthened as well.

4. An individual's patterns of avoidant, antisocial, or unusual behavior are related to his unique nervous system and shouldn't be taken as indications that he can't become more flexible or doesn't want

to interact. We have to be respectful of these unique features but always work toward more flexibility, recognizing that nervous systems are by their nature plastic and that improving the environment can increase flexibility. So learning communities should always assume the potential for growth and increased flexibility, and create environments that promote them.

5. Most people naturally want not only to relate to others but also to belong, to share a group identity. In learning communities, we can create these group identities through shared activities, whether work or recreation, that also allow self-expression and a sense of accomplishment. Individuals with ASD or other developmental delays may need support, but may also have certain skills that enable them to create useful software programs or beautiful drawings, for example. While working with special needs, we have to be sensitive to and encourage special talents that help individuals contribute to the group.

At present, it's obviously going to take a very large effort from the private sector among parents of individuals with special needs to help create programs that follow the model outlined above and to demonstrate that the model works and is financially achievable. Then we have to develop a grassroots effort among representatives at the community, city, state, and national levels to promote the view that public responsibility for individuals with special needs should last an individual's lifetime or until he or she achieves the developmental capacity for self-sufficiency.

A Case Study

The story of an individual who has thrived in a program we created along these lines illustrates the progress that can be made. A thirty-two-year-old man we'll call Robert had never spoken and tended to isolate himself and follow certain routines. He stayed in bed for a large part of the day and didn't interact with others except to indicate with some loud grumbling sounds when he was hungry. His devoted mother had been taking care of him without much hope of seeing Robert advance (Robert's father had died). After she consulted us, we involved Robert and his mother in a learning relationship and began building a learning program for Robert to participate in that took advantage of existing resources in his community.

First, we worked only with Robert and his mother, to build engagement and a more complex system of gestural communication and get into more problem-solving sequences. Since Robert's main form of communication related to getting fed, Mother played a little dumb to extend those moments when Robert was negotiating for some of his favorite foods, helping him progress from gruff vocalizations to actually pointing and making hand gestures to indicate what he really wanted. Mother would bring the wrong thing in, and Robert would shake his head; eventually he began taking his mother to the refrigerator to show her exactly what he wanted. In this way we built a more complex system of preverbal communication, moving gradually so as to challenge Robert without aggravating him, since he could easily have meltdowns, and he was a large man and his mother was small and frail.

As Robert became more purposeful in his communication and as these negotiations around food became longer and more complex, Robert began brightening up a bit. We began expanding their interactions, using pictures so Robert could point to the type of food he wanted. Because Robert could make certain sounds, we then brought in a speech pathologist to work on some oral-motor activities with him. Slowly but surely, Robert increased the range of sounds he could make and the number of pictures he could use to communicate in his negotiations for food.

We discovered that Robert enjoyed listening in his room to the music his mother played. As he became more communicative, he began to indicate whether or not he liked certain pieces of classical music. We also noticed that his visual memory was quite good and that he had strength in visual problem-solving. For example, he could figure out where things were in the house, such as a CD he wanted to hear, or where his mother had hidden his favorite cookies (he tended to overeat). We wondered whether he could perhaps use these skills to learn to read. So we began putting words under the pictures he was using and encouraging him to vocalize a few simple words for the foods he wanted, such as "milk" or "juice." Although he said them in a shortened way, "muh" and "juh," he actually memorized some of the words under the pictures. We worked with him to learn to sound words out and, over many months, he became a bit of a reader. Then we began working with augmentative communication and symbol boards, and over the next year he actually learned to type a few words, and developed a slightly larger vocabulary of simple words and phrases.

As he progressed, Robert became more engaged and interactive. And so, because he liked music, his mother got him involved with a local arts program for young adults with special needs. He began by going to listen to music, but ultimately got involved, since he was fairly strong physically, in doing some backstage support work for one of the dramas in this program. He actually began looking forward to spending time several days a week at this arts center, listening to music and participating with the drama group's backstage crew.

Over a five-year period, Robert became a much more engaged, interactive individual who could sequence, solve problems, and have lots of gestural interactions. He could use simple phrases and words, as well as manipulate the images on a symbol board, to communicate basic needs, and he enjoyed his involvement in the arts center group. Robert also became much more flexible at home, rarely having tantrums anymore when he didn't immediately get his way, and actually helping his mother with chores and other activities. In that time span, he expanded his functional capacities by about 300 percent.

It is still an ongoing adventure for Robert, and he continues to make progress in the program we created for him. We've continued to work on his language skills and motor planning and sequencing skills and to capitalize on his visual-spatial memory and processing skills. He had underreacted to sensation and had low muscle tone, but also had selectively overreacted to certain noises and sounds. He's now more flexible with these sensory differences and can cope with a greater variety of environments.

Robert's learning community is not a residential center, organized in one physical place, nor does it need to be. A learning community can be built around the individual. All communities should have arts and other programs like the one Robert attends, coordinated with residential care for those who need it, as not all parents can be as available as Robert's mother is. Within a given town or city, different components of a learning community may be in different locations, but the involvement of any individual should be organized around the developmental principles discussed above: strengthening processing skills and the fundamentals of development while facilitating meaningful peer-to-peer relationships, creative expression, and (if the individual is capable of it) meaningful work.

Part IV

⊠ ⊠ ⊠

Assessment and Intervention
The DIR Model

Chapter 19

Assessment

The DIR/Floortime Approach

A lthough making a definitive diagnosis of ASD should generally wait for sufficient observations of the child's capacity to learn over time, assessments and evaluations to determine the need for an intervention should be done quickly. A two-year-old child showing the signs of problems discussed in Chapter 3 requires *immediate* attention, not a wait-and-see attitude, because each developmental step builds on the last. Waiting until the child is a little older or clearly shows an ASD tends to make therapy more difficult and may affect the ultimate outcome, as the child falls further and further behind and misses more opportunities. This is especially true for deficits that stand in the way of a child's learning to attend, relate, communicate, play, or think.

It is possible to work on basic developmental abilities while continuing over time to make the observations necessary for an appropriate diagnosis. (If needed for insurance purposes or access to services, a provisional diagnosis can be made.) Guiding the intervention program is the important distinction between circumscribed problems that do not derail a child's progress in relating, communicating, and thinking, and more substantial challenges that do interfere with these core processes. For example, a mild articulation (speech) problem in a toddler who relates with others and communicates nicely with purposeful gestures (bringing a book to her parents, for example) is a significantly different case than a toddler who can't use any social gestures to show you what she wants even if she can repeat words. The latter child's development is more likely to be deeply affected.

Before and along with any professional assessments, parents can and should observe their own child and identify where he stands in relation to the six fundamental stages of development laid out in the chart in Chapter 3 and described in Chapters 5–10. To summarize again, the questions to ask are:

1. Does the child enter into a state of shared attention?
2. Does he engage with you with warmth and intimacy?
3. Is he able to interact with you in a purposeful way—to nod yes or no or show you with a hand gesture or a sound what he wants?
4. Can he open and close many circles of communication in a row and solve problems with your help?
5. Can he create ideas and put intentions, desires, wishes, feelings, or goals into words, pretend play, or pictures?
6. Can the child combine ideas logically?

Of course we want to notice and record behaviors such as lining up toys or repeating everything someone says without actually understanding it—or scary behaviors such as banging one's head or just running around aimlessly in circles. But we also have to ask where the child is in terms of the six fundamentals outlined above. We need to identify which of these fundamentals the child has mastered fully, which she has learned only partially, and which she has not learned.

Next, parents should observe how their child reacts to sensations and how he plans actions. Does he crave or get overloaded by touch, sounds, or sights? Which ones? To what degree can he comprehend what he hears or sees? Does he do the same action over and over, or does he put a number of different actions together in a row?

Then observe his learning relationships. To what degree can you or his teacher meet him at his developmental level and tailor interactions to his unique needs?

As we pointed out in Chapter 5, this is not a technical assessment that only a professional can make but one every parent can handle by making these observations and answering these questions. The clinician may see the child for a couple of hours, but parents see the child for hours and hours every single day for years. Professionals can help parents ask the questions, but parents have to answer them. If they are unsure or if there is a difference of opinion, the professionals can observe with them until parents and professionals come to some consensus.

Among the most important features that the DIR model brings to the treatment of ASD are early identification and prevention-oriented intervention, as well as a comprehensive individualized focus. These features require an intensive evaluation with attention to many areas overlooked by older treatment models. The DIR model contains four essential areas for evaluation and intervention:

1. The child's progress through the stages of emotional development
2. The child's individual differences in the way her nervous system works, with a focus on how these differences affect the way she processes experiences and plans responses
3. Interactions between the child and her caregivers, family, community, and the larger service system
4. A team approach to intervention in which experts in the areas relevant to the child's deficits work together to optimize her progress

The DIR Approach to Assessment

An appropriate assessment is lengthy and complex, requiring a number of sessions with the child and family and consideration of all of the DIR model's components. Parents should seek an assessment that includes the following six elements:

1. Two or more forty-five-minute clinical observations of the child interacting with her parents or other caregivers or both, including the clinician "coaching" the child to elicit her highest level of

functioning. (If there is a discrepancy between the parents' report and the clinician's observations, more than two sessions are required.)

2. A pre- and postnatal developmental history and a review of how the child is currently functioning

3. A review of the interactional patterns of the parents (or main caregivers), including the identification of strengths and vulnerabilities as well as personality and family and cultural patterns

4. A review of all current interventions, educational programs, daily activities, and related behavior and interaction patterns

5. Consultation with specialists, who may include speech pathologists, occupational and physical therapists, visual and developmental specialists, educators, and mental health professionals. Structured tests may be used in addition to clinical evaluation, not routinely but as needed to understand specific functional areas in more depth.

6. A medical evaluation to rule out concurrent or contributing medical disorders and to help pinpoint biomedical contributions to the child's functional impairments. A biomedical expert—usually a physician from developmental pediatrics, child psychiatry, or pediatric neurology—should do the proper blood tests and physical examinations, often including a twenty-four-hour or extended-sleep EEG (electroencephalogram) to further identify any specific physical contribution to the disorder. It's especially important to rule out a progressive developmental disorder related to metabolic or genetic factors.

The evaluation may involve one person—a child psychiatrist, clinical developmental psychologist, developmental pediatrician or pediatric neurologist, or other specialist who's trained to do a whole evaluation—or it may involve a whole team of people, including a speech pathologist, occupational or physical therapist, mental health professional, and developmental pediatrician. Either way, the completed evaluation should yield an understanding of the child's strengths and vulnerabilities in the areas described above.

The Child's Profile

A thorough assessment results in an individualized profile that captures the child's unique developmental features and serves as a basis for an individually tailored treatment program. The profile should include all areas of functioning, not simply those more obviously associated with disturbing symptoms. For example, a preschooler's inability to symbolize a broad range of emotional interests and themes in either pretend play or talk is just as important, if not more important, than his tendency to be perseverative or self-stimulatory. Similarly, areas of special strength may also be critical to the intervention program. For example, strong visual-spatial thinking capacities may help a child with severe language problems to interact with others, learn, and reason.

A complete profile enables the clinician to consider each functional challenge separately, explore different explanations for it, and resist the temptation (unless all alternative explanations have been ruled out) to assume that difficulties are necessarily tied together as part of a syndrome. For example, children with motor problems often flap their hands when they become excited or overloaded. Many conditions, including cerebral palsy, hypotonia, and dyspraxia, as well as ASD, involve motor problems and, at times, hand flapping. Yet this symptom is often assumed to be uniquely a part of the autistic spectrum. Similarly, over- or underreactivity to sensation is present in many disorders and developmental variations, not just ASD. Because the profile captures the child's individual variations, children with the same diagnosis may have very different profiles, and children with different diagnoses may have similar profiles.

Watching for Processing Problems

A special feature of the DIR profile is the focus on unique biologically based processing challenges. This focus enables clinicians and parents to consider the underlying processing patterns that help the child master the fundamentals, rather than looking only at symptoms or behavior. It is also important to look at how far the processing problem influences all areas of the child's life. For example, the same visual-spatial and motor planning problems that may make planning and organizing schoolwork difficult may also make it difficult to interpret other people's facial expressions and body posture, leading to social and emotional misperceptions.

When children take in sounds, they also have to decode (make sense of) those sounds. Then, after hearing and comprehending, they need to take those same skills and use them on the outflow side to communicate what they want. They have to be able to make sounds and, eventually, to form intelligible words. (Children who have trouble with outflow because of motor difficulties, meaning they can't make the sounds with their tongue and mouth, can often learn to type out what they want to say or use various electronic supports, such as a voice-output device (a machine that talks when they press buttons labeled with symbols). They can also use pictures, various hand signs, or a sign system. The new diagnostic system that we call the ICDL-DMIC (the *Interdisciplinary Council on Developmental and Learning Disorders Diagnostic Manual for Infancy and Early Childhood*) presents a developmental approach to all the processing areas (see References).

Other basic processing abilities include visual-spatial processing (understanding what is seen) as described in Chapter 12. When a child sees Mommy or Daddy, does she recognize them? Can she put the eyes, nose, mouth, arms, and legs together and form an image of a whole person? Even if a baby can see the whole pattern, she may still be unable to recognize Mommy or Daddy. At some point, the woman with red hair and blue eyes who is there every day smiling at her becomes "Mommy"; the baby gives her meaning because of all the feelings and experiences associated with the visual image. For visual images to acquire meaning over time, the brain has to be able to put experiences together with what is seen.

Another component of processing is motor planning and sequencing, the ability to carry out physical actions based on an idea or desire and a plan on how to achieve or satisfy it. Playing also involves motor planning. Some children with ASD can do only one- or two-step actions such as banging a toy on the table or moving a car back and forth. Other children can do four- or five-step actions; they can take the car, roll it to Mommy, then roll it to Daddy, then put it in the little house, then roll it back to Mommy again. The more actions you can take in a row, the easier it is to solve problems, because problem-solving involves lots of actions in a meaningful sequence. Multiple-step action is necessary for independent and interactive day-to-day tasks such as dressing, eating at meal time, and playing. Later, this capacity is called executive functions, the organizational skills necessary for school and work.

Finally, how does the child modulate or regulate sensation? Does he over- or underreact to basic sensations such as touch and sound and movement in space? For some children, even the normal human voice can be overstimulating, while other children hardly react to it. If the human voice irritates the child because it sounds too shrill, thinking, relating, and communicating are more difficult. Similarly, an over-stimulating environment can overwhelm a child and make it too difficult for him to discriminate and differentiate the world around him in order to think, relate, and communicate.

These processing capacities support the six foundations for relating, thinking, and communicating. So we have to know a child's strengths or weaknesses in these areas; otherwise we won't know the underlying reasons for the child's difficulty with the fundamentals.

A Child's Profile over Time

Any child's profile must be periodically updated. These ongoing clinical observations and updated profiles then serve as a basis for revising the child's intervention program. A child's "functioning" involves her ability to develop over time in various learning contexts. Thus, observing how a child responds to interventions that foster engagement and interaction reveals more about the child's ability to relate than a one-time evaluation of how she relates to the clinician in an office. Similarly, the child's ability to gesture and use words purposefully is best assessed by observing her at home, in school, and—if she is highly motivated and provided with developmentally meaningful interactive opportunities—in the clinician's office.

Observation over time is especially relevant to diagnosing ASD. We have observed a group of children who met the *DSM IV* criteria for autistic spectrum diagnosis. Within a comprehensive, developmentally based intervention program, they quickly became warmly related, interactive, and verbally communicative. Within one year, for example, many in this group of children became quite engaged and interactive, overcoming their perseverative and self-stimulatory patterns. After two years, many of them used language flexibly and creatively, though still with delays. If we had waited for a year and observed the response to intervention before making a diagnosis, we would have diagnosed this group of rapidly improving children with language disorders and motor planning problems, rather than the autistic spectrum diagnosis they initially manifested. Their challenges were secondary to their processing difficulties, which derailed interaction and resulted in difficulties relating and communicating. With comprehensive DIR-based intervention, many in this group have since developed excellent language and learning abilities as well as a solid capacity for relating to others, including peers, with warmth, empathy, creativity, and a sense of humor. In their later school years, when they had problems, these were more circumscribed, involving motor planning and sequencing.

Other children we have worked with who initially also met the criteria for autistic spectrum diagnoses made much slower progress, and one and two years into the intervention still met the criteria for ASD, though with greater capacity to relate and communicate. Still other children made extremely slow progress, continuing to meet the criteria for autism after many years. While each of these groups had different presenting profiles in terms of developmental abilities (for example, relatedness, motor planning and sequencing, and visual-spatial processing), by far the clearest difference between the groups was the way they responded to an effective intervention program. The most accurate

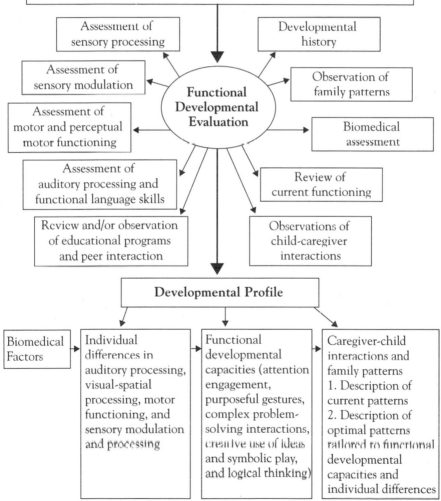

method of making a proper diagnosis is, therefore, to observe a child's progress while fostering his development with an optimal program.

With this approach in mind, parents make better decisions about assessment and treatment for their child. All the major U.S. cities (and many abroad) have professionals trained in the DIR/Floortime model who can help parents coordinate an appropriate assessment (see www.floortime.org and www.icdl.com for more information).

Chapter 20

A Comprehensive
Intervention Program Using the
DIR/Floortime Approach

While there are many different approaches for treating children with ASD, there is also a need for a comprehensive program. As an analogy, if somebody has heart disease, one approach might involve a specific medication. But that medication is only one part of a comprehensive program that may also involve diet, stress level reduction, and other specific interventions. So how do we develop a comprehensive program for a particular child? How can parents choose the right program for their child, one that promotes the most growth and development?

These questions are critical because the program and approach selected for a child with ASD has enormous influence on how she will progress. This does not mean that, even with the ideal program, every child will progress to the level we wish for her; other factors, including neurological ones, obviously have an influence. But we can never tell what a child's full potential is unless we have an optimal program for her.

The most basic difference between the major approaches is in their goals. Developmental approaches such as DIR/Floortime strive to help children build healthy foundations for relating, communicating, and thinking. In contrast, behavioral approaches (the most intensive of

which is ABA–Discrete Trial, developed by Ivar Lovaas) work on changing surface behaviors with structured tasks. In the most recent study of
behavioral approaches—the only one to use a true clinical trial design
(randomly assigning children to different interventions)—Tristram
Smith (a colleague of Lovaas) showed that these approaches produced
only modest gains in educational areas and little to no gains in emotional and social areas, compared to control groups. And even in terms
of the structured educational gains, only 13 percent of the children studied achieved the high-level educational outcomes that were claimed for
a much higher percentage in earlier studies (see Smith, Groen, and
Wynn, 2000, in References). Also, a review in 2004 of all studies on
ABA approaches by Victoria Shea showed that the original claims for
their effectiveness have not been replicated (Shea, 2004, in References).

Behavioral approaches, when successful, may change specific behaviors, but because they rely on repetition and highly structured
learning, most children who learn tasks with this approach may perform the tasks only in the way they practice them. Therefore, they
may not develop fundamental cognitive, language, or social capacities.

In contrast, what are broadly termed "developmental relationship
approaches" tend to use naturalistic learning—that is, learning through
interaction and discovery. The results are improvements in social
interactions—engaging in imaginative play, forming friendships, getting comfortable with dependency and warmth, and the like—as well
as advances in thinking abilities. This is not surprising, because these
approaches tend to work with foundation skills such as engaging, relating with others, and reading social signals, and to practice these in
spontaneous learning interactions.

The qualities most parents want from their children—a desire to
seek the parents out, love, warmth, engagement, and initiative—can
be taught, but they have to be taught through spontaneous interactions that follow the child's lead, rather than by a memorized script.
Relationship approaches, as pointed out earlier, also help to develop
higher-level thinking skills; you can't teach judgment or reasoned
thinking by requiring memorization, providing scripts, or changing
specific surface behaviors.

Interestingly, many of the more structured approaches that were origi-nally founded on behavioral principles are moving toward the use of spontaneous learning situations. And autism treatment in general is moving toward developmental relationship–based models. In a report on educating children with autism, the National Academy of Sciences cited ten models, including both the DIR/Floortime model and ABA–Discrete Trial. Three of the models were developmental relationship-based, two were strict behavioral, and four were mixed. The review cited all ten as having some supporting evidence, but noted that no one approach has definitive supporting evidence and no comparative studies have been carried out (see Appendix A).

The DIR model offers a framework to help parents and profession-als create a comprehensive program. DIR dictates no specific inter-vention, but offers a systematic assessment to create a comprehensive program that addresses relationships, specific behaviors, the creative use of ideas, and the various processing areas. It can help families and educational and therapeutic programs do what many are already doing more effectively—that is combine different intervention strategies. Many programs are using both naturalistic (developmental) and struc-tured (behavioral) interventions. The key is to tailor these interven-tions to the child and orchestrate them to build healthy foundations for relating, communicating, and thinking. The DIR model enables us to meet this goal and not fall into the trap of simply doing a bit of this and that in a nonintegrated manner. In addition to helping the family tailor the approach to the child, it helps resolve family problems that may interfere with that. The key is not to fit the child to the interven-tion, but to fit the intervention program to the child and the entire family.

Comprehensive approaches address the fundamentals as well as the surface problems. The surface problems or behaviors often get our at-tention because they make the child look different out on the play-ground or in the restaurant; You've got to address both.

The most important thing about the DIR model of intervention is that it is tailored to the individual child. Even though two children share a common diagnosis and show many of the same symptoms, each has a unique pattern of weaknesses and strengths. The treatment must be molded to fit that unique pattern. It must also be comprehensive, addressing each and every deficit—both secondary and primary. Finally, it must be intensive. This involves working with the child—or at least interacting in a developmentally appropriate way—during most of his waking hours. This is necessary because a child with ASD is often unable to have meaningful learning experiences on his own. Most children with these disorders are not offered sufficiently comprehensive or intensive interventions. (Such an intensive approach is not intended to overwork or stress a child, however. The child's state of mind is considered, and the activities recommended are part of playful interactions in which the child's interests and initiative are followed.)

The DIR intervention program is organized around the answers to the following basic questions: What are the problem behaviors? How is the child doing on the fundamentals of relating, thinking, and communicating? How is the child doing on her processing capacities, and what are the contributing factors (including biomedical challenges) affecting these capacities? What experiences work and don't work to help the child, and how capable is the family of doing the things that work? Once we answer these four questions in an assessment, we can have an idea of what a child needs. We also know the degree of work needed on family issues, such as marital, sibling rivalry, and financial problems, so that the family can do what works. Families differ in terms of their resources—how much they can or want to do themselves versus how much they want or need professionals to help them with. There are differences in terms of available programs, schools, and professional services. We need to take all these factors into account as we tailor the approach to the specific child and her family.

The DIR model helps to systematize many helpful assessments and interventions currently used, and emphasizes elements of a comprehensive approach that are often ignored or dealt with only superficially. All the elements in the DIR model have a long tradition, including speech and language therapy, occupational therapy, special and early childhood education, and Floortime-type interactions with parents. The DIR model, however, expands on these traditional practices by further defining the child's developmental level, individual processing differences, and need for certain types of interactions and by incorporating them into a comprehensive program in which all the elements can work together toward common goals.

The primary goal of the DIR-based intervention program is to enable children to form a sense of themselves as intentional, interactive individuals; develop cognitive, language, and social capacities from this basic sense of intentionality; and progress through the six fundamental developmental stages and the more advanced ones. The DIR approach can be conceptualized as a pyramid (see the diagram). Each of the components of the pyramid build on one another and are briefly described below.

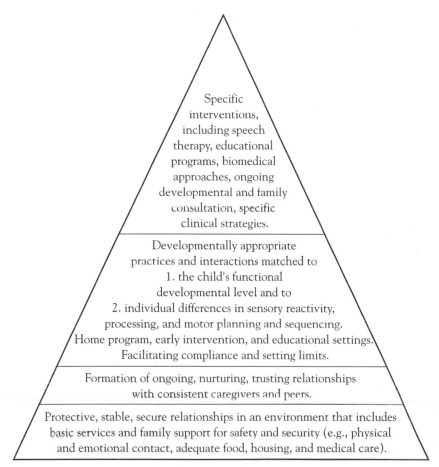

Specific interventions, including speech therapy, educational programs, biomedical approaches, ongoing developmental and family consultation, specific clinical strategies.

Developmentally appropriate practices and interactions matched to 1. the child's functional developmental level and to 2. individual differences in sensory reactivity, processing, and motor planning and sequencing. Home program, early intervention, and educational settings. Facilitating compliance and setting limits.

Formation of ongoing, nurturing, trusting relationships with consistent caregivers and peers.

Protective, stable, secure relationships in an environment that includes basic services and family support for safety and security (e.g., physical and emotional contact, adequate food, housing, and medical care).

Intervention Pyramid for Children with ASD

Stable, Secure, and Protective Relationships

At the foundation of the intervention pyramid are the protective, stable, developmentally supportive relationships and family patterns that all children require. This foundation includes physical protection and an ongoing sense of security. Some families provide this easily; others require a great deal of support or therapy in order to stabilize and organize these basic functions. Extreme poverty and chronic states of fearfulness threaten this first requirement, as do relationships within the family that are abusive, neglectful, or fragmented. Some families require counseling to explore family patterns and interactions in order to help them face the major challenges of coping with a child with ASD and the changing relationships between spouses and siblings that this entails.

For this basic foundation to develop, psychiatrists, psychologists, or social workers may be needed who are trained to assess family needs, develop alliances, solve problems, advocate on behalf of families (for social and economic support), and provide family counseling and family or personal therapy.

Ongoing, Nurturing, Trusting Relationships

At the second level of our pyramid are the ongoing and consistent relationships that every child requires for emotional and cognitive competency. Children with ASD and other special needs, who often have difficulty relating, require even more warm, consistent caregiving than do typically developing children. Their caregivers, however, often find it difficult to sustain intimate relationships with them because it is so easy to misperceive their child's intentions. Understanding problematic behavior as children's attempts to cope with their difficulties or as reactions to being overwhelmed by them can often help caregivers get past these misperceptions and move on to more creative and empathetic ways of relating to their children. For example, children who are hypersensitive to touch may reject the parents' comfort and care when they cry. This is very painful to parents. For such a child it may be important to avoid light touch and to use deep pressure to help her feel more comfortable. Similarly, the child who has difficulty comprehending words may become confused and avoid communication. She may benefit from pictures or gestural signs to understand her environment.

As we explained in earlier chapters, almost all human learning occurs in relationships, whether in the classroom, home, or clinic. To bring about this learning, relationships must foster warmth, intimacy, and pleasure. The regulatory aspects of relationships (for example, protection of the child from over- or understimulation) help the child maintain pleasure in intimacy and a secure, alert, attentive state that permits new learning and development to occur. Supporting a child's ability to relate to others requires time, consistency, and understanding. Family difficulties or frequent turnovers among child-care staff or teachers may undermine the progress of a child who is just learning how to relate to others.

Developmentally Appropriate Practices and Interactions

At the third level of our pyramid lie developmentally appropriate practices and interactions adapted to the individual differences and developmental needs of the child with ASD. Children generally are happier, less stressed, and make more progress when involved in developmentally appropriate interactions and activities. In fact, these can constitute the most important factor in their growth. Such activities and interactions must be available at home, school, and therapist's office. Regrettably, a child's tendency for self-absorption, perseveration, self-stimulation, impulsiveness, or avoidance often elicits attempts to alter the immediate behavior rather than build interactions that both promote growth and alter the problem behavior.

Children without special needs naturally play on their own or with peers, siblings, or parents using developmentally appropriate toys, games, puzzles, and so forth in a constructive, growth-facilitating manner. Children with ASD, however, because of their processing difficulties, may find it very hard to interact with people or toys in a way that facilitates their development. The activities chosen by the child may *not* be developmentally appropriate or facilitating. These include hours of TV watching, perseverative behavior, repetitive computer games, and the like.

Developing healthy practices for the child with ASD involves using the child's individual profile to design interactions that are pleasurable and developmentally meaningful. For example, a four-year-old may have the functional capacities of a typical two-year-old, understand visual-spatial experiences better than auditory ones, and be oversensitive to sensations. The focus for such a child will, therefore, involve work on engaging, gesturing, and beginning to elaborate symbols with lots of visual support and pretend play—all within the context of being very soothing and regulating.

These activities often require one-on-one work with the child. Parents must decide how much they can do on their own and how much to enlist the help of volunteers, hired students, or others or—if available—home visitors through community-, county-, or state-supported intervention programs. The home-based component of developmentally appropriate interactions and practices can be divided into two parts: Floortime interactions based on following the child's interests, and structured problem-solving interactions.

The Home Program

Typically, the foundation of a comprehensive intervention is the home program, which involves the following elements:

1. *Floortime interactions:* parents and other caregivers engage in Floortime social and learning interactions for twenty minutes or longer, often eight or more times a day. They follow the child's lead, tailor interactions to his unique differences, and foster the six fundamentals—attention, relating to others, two-way communication, problem-solving interactions, creative use of ideas, and logical use of ideas—at the highest level the child can reach. Beginning with the skills the child can do or is ready to learn to

do, parents keep working up the ladder until the child eventually learns to use ideas logically, then reflectively and with inference and creativity. Some people will give this a different name—"family fun" or "play." (See Parts II and III for a comprehensive look at Floortime.)

2. *Peer play:* once the child begins to be interactive—that is, enters into a continuous flow of back-and-forth communication with adults—parents can try for four or more peer play dates a week, because we want the child to learn to communicate with his peers as well. It's very important to do this in the beginning so the skills generalize into the peer world quickly. If we wait until the child is older, then it's much harder for him to learn to relate spontaneously to peers with humor and joy (though even then, with a great deal of practice, children can master spontaneous exchange). Initially the parents have to orchestrate the interactions and games (see Chapters 13 and 15). The goal is to help children rub shoulders with each other, to communicate with gestures and words. The need for peer play occurs at about the same time that children should be integrated, often with an aide, into a regular preschool program or be part of a special integrated program.

   Peer play is especially important once children master preverbal problem-solving and are beginning to use ideas intentionally and spontaneously. At this point, children need to practice their emerging skills not only with adults but also with other children at a similar or higher developmental level (that is, children who are interactive, somewhat verbal, and imaginative). However, the playmates need not be the same age as the child. For example, if a child is four and a half years old but has the developmental capacity of a typical three-year-old, he might enjoy the company (and vice versa) of three-year-olds.

3. *Problem-solving interactions—motor, sensory, and visual-spacial exercises:* These interactions harness the child's emotions but involve semistructured situations so as to facilitate mastery of specific processing abilities and emotional, cognitive, language, and motor skills. The adult takes the lead in these interactions, which

can focus on learning imitative skills, new words and concepts, motor planning and sequencing, or spatial reasoning. Designing this program involves the help of some of the specialists described later in this chapter, along with a specific curriculum for this component of the home program. The various skill-building exercises described above can also be carried out at school, and parents may want to have helpers assist with Floortime.

(The balance between spontaneous learning elements and the semistructured and structured elements depends on the child's profile and needs. For example, with a child who is just learning to open and close circles of communication and has little language, we might do half semistructured and structured work and half spontaneous work; whereas a child who already has lots of words and is very interactive may develop new language and social skills almost entirely through Floortime.)

Following are areas to be addressed in structured activities.

- *Work on motor, sensory, and spatial skills:* We generally recommend three or four physical workouts (of twenty minutes or longer) a day, with motor and sensory exercises (running, jumping on a trampoline or mattress, and spinning), deep pressure, some perceptual motor exercises (throwing, catching, kicking with big Nerf balls, reaching for moving objects), and obstacle courses and search games such as treasure hunts and hide-and-seek that require visual-spatial thinking.
- *Work on balance, coordination, and left-right integration:* exercises to improve these skills can include walking across a balance beam, standing on one leg with eyes closed, catching and throwing with both hands, or drawing with both hands on two separate sheets of paper at the same time.
- *Rhythmic activity:* this includes many games such as pattycake and dancing to music.
- *Modulation practice:* the child moves fast to slow, talks loud to soft, and so forth.

- *Visual-spatial exercises:* these include search or treasure hunt games, catching and throwing, and activities geared to the abilities described in Chapter 11. (See also www.icdl.com for a description of a new visual-spatial curriculum, and Furth and Wachs 1974.)

We may do these skill-building activities in structured ways or spontaneous ways, such as while the child is pretending to be a fantasy figure (a movie star or super hero).

Home Language Program

A DIR-based home language program is founded on developmental principles and models of how language is learned. Most children, even those with ASD, can learn language through interactive experiences that strengthen their capacities to relate and communicate in a developmentally based sequence related to gestures, vocalizations, imitation of words and songs, and so forth, in which language is driven by their interests and desires as well as by problem-solving. The new *ICDL Diagnostic Manual for Infants and Young Children* (DMIC) spells out this sequence within the six foundation-building blocks described earlier, including auditory processing and, in some cases, the oral motor challenges, which derail receptive and expressive language development. In the DIR model, language is supported in each of the components based on affect and engagement (that is, Floortime), problem-solving interactions, peer experiences with role models who communicate and play interactively and symbolically, and speech, language, and other therapies. Visual strategies to support comprehension and augmentation may also be used for the child who cannot yet produce the sounds and words for speaking.

The Affect-Based Language Curriculum

We have formulated a specific curriculum based on the DIR model: the Affect-Based Language Curriculum (ABLC). This curriculum is designed to be implemented by caregivers at home. The ABLC is based on the fact that emotion (or affect) is critical for many elements of language acquisition and use. Without affect and engagement as a basis, a child will have a hard time developing purposeful and meaningful language. The ABLC involves a series of structured and semistructured activities done with high affect and motivation so that they generalize quickly; it combines the best of the structured approaches with the emotional approaches to lay the foundations for relating, communicating, and thinking. A similar curriculum for visual-spatial thinking skills, motor planning skills, and sensory modulation capacities will be available shortly. Others who work within the DIR model have developed their own language curriculums.

In the ABLC, caretakers create an environment where the child is pleasurably engaged in the specified activity before she is taught a new language skill. Also, at every step, the adult establishes and maintains circles of communication with the child. The ABLC approach combines both structured and spontaneous, dynamic, emotionally charged inter-actions and divides the child's time into a number of steps. These steps include systematic instruction, which tends to be more structured and involves practicing specific skills, such as oral motor capacities, prag-matic language skills, and learning of new concepts and words. The cur-riculum is accompanied by applied Floortime, in which what's learned in more structured ways is practiced in dynamic contexts, and by regular Floortime, which emphasizes spontaneous usage. These steps give chil-dren the opportunity to master both the building blocks and more ad-vanced components of language. The ABLC also focuses on traditional elements of language, such as phonology, syntax, grammar, and seman-tics, but goes beyond the traditional approaches by addressing reflective and abstract thinking. Parents and caretakers may learn to do the ABLC with their child by reading the ABLC book (coauthored by Diane Lewis, MA, CCC/SLP, and available through www.icdl.com).

Setting Limits, Facilitating Compliance

Setting limits and facilitating compliance can be difficult for parents, clinicians, and teachers. In Chapter 25 we discuss the most productive ways of addressing these challenges.

You Get What You Practice

We want to emphasize again that you get what you practice. For example, we recognize that some children need help with social skills, such as reading the emotional signals of a peer to know whether or not he or she wants to be approached. How does a child learn to be a good social partner and read those signals easily? Here is where the approach is crucial. If we practice very structured approaches—such as teaching that when one sees a new person, one says "Hello" and offers one's hand for the other to shake—and you give the child a series of structured questions or comments she can say as well as opening social gestures, that's what you are going to get. The child will go and greet peers with, "Hello, my name is so-and-so. What do you want to play? I would like to play this-or-that."

That may seem fine to an adult who is trying to encourage a child to engage in peer play (and may be appropriate for some formal adult settings such as church or synagogue), but when the child gets out onto the playground, how do you think the other children will respond to that? If they are used to more spontaneous interactions—a little smile or smirk, a joke, a teasing comment—they aren't going to respond very well to the child who is overly structured. You may think, "Well, I could never teach my child to be so spontaneous and joke and fool around," but in fact, we have seen many children with ASD learn to be spontaneous and warm, have a sense of humor, and join the crowd in a way that is fun for everyone. However, you have to practice those skills. Among children who, as part of our program, have four or more peer play dates a week—in which the parent or other adult facilitates spontaneous interaction between the child with ASD and a peer who can interact, read signals, and be spontaneous—we have seen hundreds make remarkable progress in learning to be spontaneous, to giggle and chase, and have fun.

As we said in Part I, you have to know what your goals are, because you won't get goal B by practicing goal A. The same thing holds true if you want to help children think creatively and abstractly and make inferences. The principle "You get what you practice" generally seems to hold up; the key is knowing how to create that practice. And the key to that is understanding the developmental pathway to any specific skill—such as math literacy, which has to be learned through the child's emotional investment in quantity, for example—and then practicing the steps on the pathway so the skill is achieved as part of healthy, adaptive development.

So, as a parent, when you select an intervention program, look at what the child is actually going to be doing for hours a day and ask, "Is that what I want to teach?" That's a commonsense question, but we often don't ask it in quite that way. For different goals, different approaches are helpful. The more structured approaches can be helpful for very specific and concrete goals. But they are not as good, we find, for helping children enjoy relationships and become more involved in the world and learn to express love, because that comes from the heart, from the inside. These things can't be controlled by external reinforcers.

Specific Therapies and Educational Strategies

At the apex of the pyramid are specific therapies or educational techniques to overcome particular challenges. It's important to distinguish between a specific technique looked at in isolation and one that is part of an overall comprehensive program. Often someone points out that technique A or technique B has not been proven in its own right to be helpful. They look at particular motor-based exercises or sensory processing exercises, for example, and ask, "Do these techniques cure autism?" Of course, it's silly to even suggest that they could! But the fact that children with autism may have motor planning and sequencing problems or may over- or underreact to sensation has been documented in hundreds of studies. Therefore, such problems should be addressed as part of a comprehensive program, and in that context, a particular technique may be quite effective.

We often recommend specific professional therapies, depending on the needs of the child. If a child is working on the basic developmental capacities, the parents may need someone to coach them in doing

Floortime activities. A clinician trained in the Floortime approach can serve as a coach and may also help orchestrate the entire program. The ideal person would have a strong background in working with children with severe developmental problems and their families. It might be a clinical psychologist, child psychiatrist, or developmental pediatrician—but it also could be an educator, speech pathologist, or occupational therapist with special training in the DIR/Floortime approach.

If the family lives in an area where there are no trained DIR/Floortime clinicians who can help them, the parents may read additional books such as *The Child with Special Needs* or our ICDL Clinical Practice Guidelines, or study the new parent versions of our training videotapes (available at our Floortime Foundation website, www.Floortime.org or www.icdl.com), for guidance in creating Floortime interactions at home.

In general, it's most effective for the child's therapeutic team—including parents, educators, coordinator, and specific therapists—to meet regularly to design goals for the program, including the semi-structured aspect of developmentally appropriate at-home practices.

Often half of the child's available time at home may be spent on spontaneous, Floortime-like interactions (including peer play), and the remaining time spent on semistructured problem-solving activities. This may seem to require that all the child's waking time be spent in "therapeutic" interactions; in fact, it is simply tailoring all the child's interactions to her profile. In successful Floortime, the child simply experiences the interactions as fun; after a while, this mode of interaction comes naturally to the parent or caregiver, who also experiences it as fun and emotionally satisfying.

If there are language or auditory processing challenges, or both, a speech pathologist should be involved. Speech and language therapy is helpful for preverbal and all types of symbolic communication (involving words, pictures, signs, and so forth). It can also be especially valuable for oral-motor work and related expressive language challenges. (See also the description of the Affect-Based Language Curriculum, above.)

Occupational or physical therapy, or both, is helpful for motor problems, motor planning and sequencing difficulties, low muscle tone, and sensory modulation and processing challenges. Typically, if the problem

has more to do with severe low muscle tone and coordination, including conditions such as cerebral palsy or a developmental syndrome, a
physical therapist is involved. If the problems center more on sensory
modulation and reactivity, or motor planning and sequencing, an occupational therapist is more likely the appropriate choice. If necessary,
both a physical therapist and an occupational therapist can be involved,
though some physical therapists are trained in occupational therapy
strategies and vice versa.

For some children, additional programs involving art or music, or
sensory-motor physical activities such as gymnastics, swimming, bike
riding, and sports lessons, are appropriate. Finally, if the original evaluation reveals that a child has visual-spatial processing difficulties (as
described in Chapter 11), an expert in this area would be an important
member of the team. Again, when these therapies are done in a DIR
approach, everyone working with the child addresses the six fundamentals while pursuing specific goals of a particular processing area.

Many programs for children with ASD do not provide an adequate
level of intensity of either language or occupational and physical therapy. We have found that three or more individual thirty- to sixty-
minute sessions per week are often required for each of these therapies,
in addition to consultation about integrating the therapies with the
home and educational programs. If that number of sessions is not possible, the specialist can provide guidance for the caretakers to carry out
the day-to-day activities themselves, demonstrating the activities
while the child and parent are in the session and providing parents
with a weekly home program of recommended activities to follow up
on the therapies.

Biomedical Approaches

A number of biomedical factors should be considered when creating a
comprehensive intervention program for a child with ASD. First, it is vital to have a comprehensive pediatric medical evaluation to rule out
known physical illnesses. Such an evaluation should include referrals to
specialists to evaluate specific aspects of physical functioning, such as gas-
trointestinal problems if there are questions about them. As part of a

comprehensive evaluation, a neurological evaluation and appropriate assessments should be considered in order to identify contributing factors
and rule out other syndromes. It is especially important to rule out progressive neurological disorders (for example, genetic syndromes). As part
of this evaluation, an extended-sleep EEG is often helpful, to discover or
rule out subtle irregularities that may not be identified in a standard EEG.
Such a finding can inform the selection of an appropriate medication.

Some children with ASD may benefit from biomedical interventions. In general, except in the treatment of a specific medical or neurological disorder, we recommend first working with a comprehensive
program to determine the child's growth curve. If the child is making
good to excellent progress, we advise continuing with the program and
being very cautious in considering biomedical interventions that are
not for specific medical or neurological disorders or problems. But if
the child is in an optimal program and is still not making good
progress, it may be appropriate to look at biomedical interventions, including medications to improve overall functioning and ability to learn
and progress. For each child, parents and physicians need to carefully
weigh the benefits versus risks or side effects.

If parents and physician do decide to make a biomedical intervention, they should monitor the child to see if the new measure improves
her learning curve. If there are side effects or other negative effects,
they may reconsider that particular intervention. It is often unwise
to increase a dose that has not proven effective, hoping for a positive
result. In my (SIG's) experience, it works better to cut back on the
medication or stop it for a while and consider alternatives. Because
each child is unique, however, only the family and their physician can
make those determinations.

The key thing with trying a medication or other biomedical intervention is to look for improvements in the functional emotional developmental capacities, rather than only improvement in a particular
symptom. The question is whether the whole mental "team" is working
better with the medication or other approach being tried.

There are many types of biomedical interventions, and the research
to back them up ranges from isolated anecdotal reports, to systematic

reviews of large numbers of cases, to clinical trial studies. The different interventions also pose varying benefit-to-risk profiles. Some approaches, such as elimination diets that substitute healthy alternatives for certain foods, have little to no side effects, while certain medications may have considerable ones. It is vital to determine the child's "baseline" in his functional emotional capacities and symptoms and then look for changes. For example, increased irritability or self-absorption should raise questions about the particular intervention, whereas improved engagement, interaction, and communication may confirm that the approach is helpful.

Perhaps most important to remember is the importance of continuing with an intensive, comprehensive daily program, as outlined in this book. While exploring biomedical interventions, families and physicians should maintain the core program even though it may be difficult to do both. For a consideration of specific biomedical options, parents should consult with their child's physician (see also www.floortime.org).

Behavioral Analysis

Some children do have serious problematic behavior. If the overall approach is not helping in terms of those behaviors—if the child is injuring herself, for example, or her behavior makes it hard for her to interact with others—then we should analyze the cause of this behavior. (There is a difference between behavioral analysis, or looking at what is supporting maladaptive behaviors, as a supplementary measure, and a structured discrete trial intervention program that focuses on changing behaviors without working on the fundamental building blocks.) Behavioral analysis can be part of the overall DIR/Floortime program, as can specific exercises from different behavioral programs, including discrete trial approaches. The key is to include these, if needed, as part of a comprehensive DIR/Floortime program in which the specific analyses facilitate a continuous flow of back-and-forth interactions and support initiative and creativity and other foundations of healthy development. (See Part V for more information on working with specific problematic behaviors.)

Educational Strategies

Education begins with the developmental basics of attending, relating, communicating, and thinking. As children begin the more formal elements of their educational programs, the basics must always be strengthened, alongside learning reading, writing, math, and other subjects. Mainstream and special educators are a critical part of the team. For some children, they join the team early, as the children work on the basics. Educators generally focus on "cognitive" and academic skills, but the role of the special educator needs to be broader, focusing first on the developmental capacities. These are the first academic skills because without them there can be no further academic progress. (See the following chapter for more information on educational programs.)

The DIR Model, an Integrated Approach

Thus, rather than promoting a "one size fits all" approach, the DIR model advocates many approaches working in combination with each other, while offering a method of analysis that allows tailoring the approach to your child's goals. Seeking out a "simple" solution in which families take little responsibility won't work for complicated problems. A complex problem calls for a complex approach. Professionals from the mental health field, developmental pediatrics, pediatric neurology, social work, and so forth can be coquarterbacks with the family, helping to put together a comprehensive plan for the child.

The program need not be expensive. At its heart is the home program. Ideally, the home program is combined with the necessary therapies, but if the school system or insurance won't support specialists, then we recommend that parents use specialists as consultants rather than seeing them weekly or several times a week. For some families, the professionals we've mentioned are available only once a month or once every few months, sometimes even only through telephone consultations because of where the family lives; yet in spite of those limitations, many such families and their children thrive. Some of the best progress has been made in areas of the country where there's nobody within a three-hundred-mile radius of the family who can provide special services. But the family has—through reading, telephone consultations, and periodic consultations with the organizing clinician or with some of these specialists we've described—put together a program to help the child develop and have daily fun and enjoyment. It's that daily program that counts.

When a Child Makes Little or No Progress

If you try an approach and it doesn't work—the child makes little or no progress—it's important not to get discouraged, but rather to seek a re-evaluation, with the professional who originally saw the child, if you have faith in that person, or else with a new professional. Keep trying to find an approach that works. We rarely see a case for which we can't figure out the right mixture of elements in a comprehensive program. The key thing is to persist and follow through.

In such cases, it's first useful to review the biomedical workup and make sure no stone has been left unturned, that there are no known physical factors contributing. As discussed earlier, an extended-sleep EEG should be included to identify subtle irregularities that may be treatable; this may prevent more serious difficulties later.

Often, if a child seems to be making little or no progress, there is a natural tendency to select methods that may give an illusion of progress but that actually weaken the child's potential for long-term gains. Clinicians and parents may be tempted to try a program that focuses on repetitive activities that teach the child to do something, such as matching or sorting shapes. As the focus on repetitive activities increases, however, parents and clinicians may notice that the child's abilities to engage and interact (however minimal already) remain static or are even decreasing. A colleague recently shared with us just such a dilemma: "We have to do something to help the children be ready for preschool, and they're learning to sit and match shapes, but they're less related and interactive." Our colleague believed it was a choice between cognitive and relationship gains, but is it really?

Advocates of repetitive activities feel that they teach a child specific skills, such as how to classify. As discussed in Chapter 2, because the child so trained is unable to demonstrate a full understanding of the differences between square and round shapes, he more likely has learned a specific task, not classification. Nor is there compelling evidence that repetitively practiced activities such as sorting or matching shapes builds language or cognition. Because these are skills that many children can do, it is sometimes thought useful to teach them to children with ASD. But many skills we observe typically developing children performing easily are the result of their having mastered basic foundations of cognition, language, and social development. Recent neuroimaging research which suggests that repetitive learning involves the basal ganglia rather than the higher cortical centers raises the question whether it's wise to focus on precortical types of learning when the child's main challenges may lie in fully using their higher cortical centers (see Bayley, Frascino, and Squire, 2005, in References).

Consider development as a tree with many branches. If the trunk grows in a healthy manner, a variety of branches grow and flourish. Thus, nurturing the tree trunk (the foundations) is critical.

Cognition, language, and social-emotional development all stem from the same trunk or foundation. Parents and clinicians need not make a Solomon's choice between relationships on one hand and cognitive and language skills on the other. Fostering the foundations fosters the rest. When children are making little or no progress, the best approach is to double up efforts on the basics. Children with special needs vary in the degree of their neurological challenges, which may be expressed in the way (and degree to which) they over- or underrespond to sensations, have difficulty comprehending sights or sounds, and encounter problems in planning actions. More intensive and skillful work on the basics, taking into account the child's unique biology, will help optimize the child's progress, even if it's very slow.

Some children do require more structure. For example, the child who has a hard time making sounds may require more structured practice with oral motor activities to help her control the muscles in her mouth. Such a child may require higher motivation to learn to say "ope" as she is trying to open a door to find a favorite toy. The Affect-Based

Language Curriculum, described above, provides extra structure for children who require it to learn language skills, while keeping the focus on the fundamentals of relating, interacting, communicating, and thinking.

When, out of frustration, we take our eyes off the true foundations for learning and focus on repetitive, isolated skill building, we may experience a short-term sense of relief because, after all, as a colleague told us, "she is finally learning something." Two years later, however, the same child may be able to do only the tasks practiced and only in the settings where she has practiced them. Again, "You get what you practice." The form by which we teach children determines how they learn.

While some children make rapid progress in all areas in a comprehensive, intensive DIR program, others make slower progress—some at a steady but modest rate, others at a very slow rate. We work constantly to improve our strategies to enable all children to make more progress. In the meantime—as we have been reminded over and over again—it is essential to keep our eyes on the foundations and resist the temptation to create an illusion of progress. A large number of children who have made extremely slow progress but who have continually worked on the fundamentals are now warmly engaged, happy, interactive youngsters who can use short phrases and have conversations—answering, for example, "what," "where," and (with a little multiple-choice help) "why" questions. They show minimal to no perseveration, self-stimulation, or self-absorption. Many of these children have also been able to master the early stages of reading and math. Although their progress is slow, it's considerable, given the degree of their original neurological challenges.

Integrating Other Approaches into the DIR Model

Finally, as we noted earlier, the DIR approach is inclusive and can incorporate specific techniques from a range of relationship-based interventions, as well as behavioral strategies, depending on the needs of a particular child. Generally, these techniques fit within the semistructured component of the intervention, as described above. (Once a child can learn dynamically through interaction, the need for structured learning decreases considerably.)

Many useful strategies have been formulated within a number of frameworks, including social stories, role taking and turn taking, social skills groups, exercises to support "emotional intelligence," theory-of-mind tasks, semistructured relationship and social development exercises, and a range of incremental learning exercises. Parents and clinicians find many of these specific exercises helpful in promoting relationships, socialization, and thinking. These strategies can be considered, depending on the needs of the particular child and family. Similarly, as indicated earlier, highly structured behavioral exercises for teaching imitation, for example, can be used as part of a comprehensive DIR program.

The key point to remember, however, is that, to be incorporated into the DIR model, these problem-solving interactions should:

1. Be part of a continuous flow of back-and-forth interaction and communication;
2. Involve the child's emotion, either naturally or in response to a challenge;
3. Be tailored to the child's individual processing profile; and
4. Be keyed to the child's developmental level.

For example, if the child plays a game in which he has to guess what the other person is thinking, and this is done as part of a pattern of warm relating and ongoing back-and-forth emotional gesturing, using lots of ideas connected together, and is tailored to the child's nervous system, the child may learn a particular skill while strengthening his developmental foundations and higher levels of thinking. In other words, a wide variety of semistructured skill-building and problem-solving activities, such as setting up scenarios to teach the child to read social signals ("Am I looking at you, or am I looking at my book?"), can be incorporated into the program, as long as you work with the child in a Floortime context.

⊠

Chapter 21

Educational Approaches That Promote Thinking, Communicating, and Academic Progress

Nine-year-old Joanna, diagnosed with autism, had been doing well in a program that combined homeschooling and time in a second-grade classroom, where she had a supportive teacher and a tutor who used a Floortime approach. However, the school district wanted Joanna to move up to fourth-grade classes, in a new school building with a new teacher. Joanna's parents wondered whether this was the right placement for her and how they could work with the school system and the new teacher to create the best educational program for their daughter.

Evolving Views of Autism:
Three Educational Approaches

The history of treating autism presents an image of children some-what out of control—running around aimlessly, banging their heads against the wall, repeating everything they hear, or simply shaking in a corner alone. This image of self-absorbed, self-stimulatory children did not reflect the reality of ASD; many children with ASD probably weren't diagnosed because they didn't show these more extreme behaviors. Because they were thought to be hard to educate, children with ASD were largely untreated or were treated without much understanding of their challenges.

Then the behavioral approach (ABA and Discrete Trials) emerged, based on the understanding that some behaviors symptomatic of ASD could be influenced by rewarding desirable behavior and ignoring undesirable behavior (and early in the movement's history, sometimes using negative reinforcement). With this approach, the image became that of a child sitting at a desk learning to comply with requests and put blocks in differently shaped holes, match shapes, or repeat sounds or imitate gestures. The understanding now was that children with autism could learn appropriate social behaviors in a scripted, memorized way, but not engage in spontaneous and creative social interactions and thinking.

The challenge that has emerged over the years from the behavioral approach is to help children take a learned behavior from one situation and generalize it to other situations—in particular, a new one they don't anticipate. This requires creative and reflective thinking and judgment—skills difficult for many children receiving intensive behavioral treatment approaches to learn. These approaches left many children limited in their development.

With the new developmental approaches we describe in this book, the picture of autism has changed again. We now see it as a continuum on which all children can become warm and related and purposeful though they may have different degrees of language and thinking capacities, depending on the degree of the original neurological impairment and the type and intensity of their intervention program.

Our schools are struggling with which of these three images of ASD to embrace and how to integrate the image they embrace with traditional notions of education. Historically, education has been geared toward teaching specific skills such as reading, writing, and arithmetic; how does that work with children who come into school with deficits in their ability to relate and communicate with others or to think meaningfully? To be part of the school environment, a child has to be able to relate to others. Reading, writing, and arithmetic require the foundation skills of thinking and communicating; it is not easy to integrate children who do not have these foundations (typically mastered before a child starts school) into the classroom environment.

Some schools and educational programs have embraced behavioral approaches, believing they could at least get children behaving in a school-appropriate manner—sitting at desks, carrying out tasks, matching shapes, and counting the number of pictures in a box and matching it to a number on the other side of the page. This approach makes it easy to measure progress: a child can now match six more shapes than she could two months ago, for example. But does this approach really help children overcome the core deficits of ASD and learn the skills they need? Given the new understanding of children with ASD, the job of schools should be to help children relate to others in a meaningful way, use language and ideas creatively, and become abstract and reflective thinkers, as well as master academic subjects.

The Building Blocks of Knowledge

This mandate represents a new way of thinking about education in general, because many children besides those with ASD need work on these same fundamentals, including children from deprived backgrounds and those with processing or learning disabilities. In fact, as we work on reversing the core deficits of autism, we are developing better approaches for children with learning disabilities, attentional problems, impulse control problems, and executive functioning difficulties, as well as very selective problems in writing essays or in performing in math, physics, or science classes. The insights we are gaining can be applied across the board, but implementing these insights requires an evolution in the way we conceptualize education—from teaching facts that can be memorized and regurgitated, to a truly developmental approach based on the building blocks of knowledge.

Jean Piaget was the father of the constructivist approach to learning, based on the theory that children construct knowledge through their experiences with the world, as opposed to memorizing facts from the world. This approach enables children to have true knowledge, which includes knowing facts but puts those facts into a conceptual framework. Piaget took only the first steps in understanding the development of thinking. In particular, he didn't figure out the role of affective or emotional interactions in building the capacities to think, communicate, and socialize. (See Greenspan and Shanker 2004.)

Thinking can be difficult for children with autism or learning disabilities, and it can be even harder if they are encouraged to regurgitate facts. But they can learn to think with an appropriate approach.

How can schools move beyond approaches that have the appearance of education but don't necessarily provide the fundamental building blocks of knowledge? A school or educational program that addresses our current understanding of the treatment of autism relates closely to the home program described in Part II: the school day needs to be tailored to the child and the child's needs.

The first thing we need to do is to profile children to find the degree to which they have mastered healthy relating, communicating, and thinking. Do they need to work on relationships? On reading emotional signals? On creative play? On logical thinking and applying logical thought to academics? If we try to teach logical thinking to a child who is not yet able to engage in reciprocal social interactions, for example, we are trying to build the upper story of a house on a very weak foundation. We can sometimes work on a number of building blocks at the same time, but we can't ignore the primary ones in favor of the secondary ones.

Then we need to understand where children are in terms of processing information—auditory processing, sensory modulation, visual-spatial processing, and motor planning and sequencing. For example, a child who overreacts or underreacts to sensations may have trouble taking in information, because she gets overwhelmed. If a child can't plan and sequence actions, she can't solve problems. If a child can't discriminate among sensations—what she sees, hears, touches, tastes, smells—she can't make sense or categorize.

With a child's profile in hand, the school can begin to tailor an approach. Children who are working on the fundamentals of relating require a one-on-one approach; to put children who lack these fundamentals into a group where they passively sit and watch is simply wasting their time and may dig the hole deeper for them in terms of making progress. An aide, teaching assistant, teacher, parent, or volunteer may need to work one-on-one with the child to promote social interaction between the child with special needs and the other children and to help the child master each of the fundamental developmental levels.

During a lesson, for example, when the teacher is explaining something, the aide can have quiet conversations with the child, gesturing and exchanging information using thinking skills, helping the child reason and answer "why." If the child is working quietly at his desk doing a math lesson, the aide may make sure the child understands the lesson by having him use manipulatives and explain why he is doing what he is doing; then he is learning language and social skills as well as math reasoning. During recess or free-play time, the aide may help the child play with peers. The aide can encourage the child to speak up in class, or signal the teacher to ask him a question. So the aide's role is to facilitate interaction and higher functional emotional levels, not to redirect the child or set limits, unless of course the child is getting into hot water.

Earlier chapters have discussed how to mobilize attention, engagement, two-way communication, and a continuous flow of back-and-forth problem-solving. With the help of aides, a school program can work on these fundamentals in two ways: spontaneous Floortime interactions that follow the child's natural interests in a play environment, and semistructured problem-solving opportunities for mastering the four processing areas. For example, to help a child sequence more actions in a row, a teacher or aide may set up little obstacle courses that the child has to move around, through, or above in order to get a desired object, such as a favorite toy. The child can be urged on with warm gestures and supportive vocalizations, helping her not only to practice attending, engaging, and purposeful action but also to increase the number of actions she can take in a row. Similarly, to work on visual spatial processing, the aide might take a favorite object and hide it with the child watching, so she has to navigate space to get to the toy. Eventually, the adult hides it without the child knowing where it is, so she has to search in three or four places to find it, which helps her understand how spaces are organized.

To work on the ability to discriminate sounds, exercises such as using simple words that enable the child to get what she wants can help her perceive those words again. For example, if she wants a little doll, the teacher can hide it in his hand and say, "It's in my *hand*, in my *hand*," and show her his hand. This way she learns what the word "hand" means in a personally meaningful way. If the child is fairly engaged, the teacher can play little imitative games, starting with sounds the child can make, like "ee-ee," and then moving on to "ba," "da," and so forth, with the child and teacher looking in a mirror together so the child can imitate the way the teacher's mouth moves. Many developmentally oriented speech pathologists have versions of such problem-solving approaches to language, as well as the more structured ABLC described earlier, that encourage meaningful use of words for communication.

These one-on-one, spontaneous, and semistructured learning situations need to characterize the educational environment for the child who is working on the fundamentals; they can't be done in a large group, but one or two other children can be partners. As a child gets used to interacting with peers in the classroom, he may enjoy some of the classroom rituals, but that is less important at the moment because children need to become continuous social problem-solvers before they can benefit from truly spontaneous interactions with peers; figuring out how to engage a child's interest requires skill. With the mediation of an adult, however, peer interactions can help with the fundamentals. For example, the teacher or aide can sometimes include one other peer in a little game that mobilizes interaction between the two children at the basic levels of looking, engaging, and exchanging toys. The two might bat a balloon, shake a Slinky, be partners in a tickle or chase game, splash in a small pool, or build and knock down towers. In other cases, the teacher might enlist a "peer therapist" or "peer play partner" who would be encouraged to pursue the child and coached to engage and interact with her. Later these child peers, who are naturals at reaching out and persisting, may become buddies who are happy to have play dates.)

At the start, however, there's no substitute for a one-on-one approach, coordinated between home and school. The home and school plans must be part of one integrated program, which means that teachers and parents need to meet at least once a week to share insights about what works for the child and to coach each other on effective techniques. If a school excludes parents from observing or helping out in the classroom, or if parents don't share with the school what is going on at home, the adequate educational program federally mandated for children is undermined. While pursuing the best program for their child, parents also need to be aware when a teacher is overextended and to work with that teacher to find solutions and support and to lobby for more funding or professional assistance if necessary. It is also helpful for parents of children with ASD to meet regularly with each other.

An important component of the combined home-school team approach is input from a professional who is trained in basic DIR/Floortime approaches and who can help promote these spontaneous and semistructured problem-solving interactions. In an ideal system, an occupational therapist should be available to work on motor and sensory processing capacities and a speech pathologist to work on the language and auditory processing capacities. Other specialists, such as biomedical and mental health professionals and visual-spatial processing specialists, may need to be consulted to help teachers carry out the program. This may be difficult to arrange, but most school systems already have speech pathologists and occupational therapists available. Some school systems and families may be fortunate enough to have a very gifted teacher or parent who learns enough about the different processing areas and basic DIR/Floortime techniques to be the primary one who works with the child, periodically consulting with professionals in the various disciplines to get further ideas and to monitor the child's progress.

However gifted a particular therapist is, an hour a week is only an hour a week. Sessions with therapists are helpful for identifying what parents and educators should be working on and for showing what the child is capable of; but what really counts is what is done every single day, for hours a day, with a child. Depending on the parents' abilities and the availability of volunteers, this model can be expensive or inexpensive; the key thing is that someone is working with the child on mastery of the fundamental building blocks.

The lack of trained teachers and aides in the classroom is cited as a justification for rejecting this kind of learning. One way to make it work is by finding volunteers from the community. Parents have to be invited into the classroom on a regular basis, not just on special days. Grandparents and other volunteers can be trained to tailor learning interactions to individual differences. There need to be more opportunities for undergraduate students and other talented individuals in teaching positions. Involvement of family, students, and neighbors from the community should be actively sought and welcomed in the classroom. (The main criterion when evaluating potential aides is how competent they are at getting a continuous flow of interaction going with the child and stimulating progress in the fundamentals.)

In addition, if a child is working on the fundamentals but is not yet a creative and logical thinker, it would be ideal to have a half-day program at school, with the other half of the day spent working with caregivers at home, especially parents or other family members. The more intimate relationships are the ones that hold the most value for the child. Along these lines, it is helpful for children with ASD to have a consistent teacher over several years, because it takes time for them to get comfortable interacting with a new adult. Ideally, you also want to preserve the same classroom setting over this time, so the child can be as relaxed as possible.

The Thinking-Based Approach to Education

Once the fundamentals are mastered, the focus shifts to promoting creative and logical thinking. Why is this goal important? Which should come first: helping the child learn creative and then logical thinking, or helping him recognize shapes, learn scripted social phrases, and sit in a circle quietly and listen to the teacher read a story? This issue has produced an enormous amount of confusion in the educational system in this country (and in other countries as well). Society has tended to approach special education through a top-down model in which we look at what older children can do and then apply those goals to younger children. If older children can sit still, while younger ones fidget a lot or walk around, we want to teach sitting. If younger children have trouble with some motor skills that most older children have long mastered, such as stacking blocks, we work on developing those skills. Thus, the history of educating children with special needs has been characterized by a lot of superficial skill building.

As discussed earlier, to advance academically, children have to be able to think. Reading comprehension, social studies, history, higher-level math—all require thinking skills. The same is true of behavior. Behaving like other children really means thinking like them, not simply imitating some of their behaviors. Once children can think, they can figure out many things on their own, such as why they shouldn't push other children, why they have to share, and why it gets dark at night when the sun goes down. Now that we know how thinking develops in a child, we can do better than simply teaching children to do rote tasks.

Every child should learn to identify letters and their associated sounds and to sound out words, for example. But the foundations for understanding what one reads and for relating, communicating, and thinking are the true cornerstones of all academic progress. To promote creative and logical thinking, an educational environment needs to spend time on these foundation-building endeavors and create a physical environment that supports them.

Creative Thinking

To teach creative thinking, we need to involve children in activities that promote creative use of ideas. Ideas can be expressed in words, in dramatic gestures, with toys and dress up, or through art and music.

One of the most effective of these activities is pretend or imaginative play, following the basic principles of Floortime. That means a child is on the floor with a toy, and a teacher or aide is on the floor interacting with the child, engaging the child in a pretend drama, trying to make the drama as complex as possible. Children are encouraged to be symbolic early in life when they are given stuffed animals and pretend bottles to feed their dolly or put their favorite Teletubby to bed. Just about every child engages in pretend-play gestures, even if they have to taste the cookie to see if it is real, and just about every educational program allows for free play and has symbolic toys. Yet very little time is devoted to this important experience in which children have the opportunity to become imaginative and create ideas with the help of affect-based interactions with their teachers. When children are not given the interactive experiences to create ideas and understand emotions in play, they may not get the support to develop understanding of the ideas and feelings of others.

Using Floortime to Develop Symbolic Thinking in the Classroom and at Home

- *Create an inviting environment* for symbolic play and *let your child explore and discover new ideas.* It is essential that she initiate the play based on her interests and curiosity. Every play area can have toys and props related to real life experiences, on the floor or low shelves where the objects will entice the child's curiosity. Is that a stethoscope sticking out of the doctor's kit? Is that a real baby doll on the couch with a bottle nearby? Can I try to go down the toy slide or ride that horse? The child may in fact try to go down the toy slide herself before accepting a figure who fits it!
- *Have the toys the child loves and thinks about.* Toys that represent the child's real world are readily understood, and it is useful, in a conversation or visit with the parent who comes into school to play with the

continues

continued

child, to identify the toys or ideas the child loves. These toys reflect the child's attachments and symbolic level and are the doorways to interaction and elaboration of his ideas. He may love animals, trucks, trains, or food—the important thing is to join the child in his interests and help expand and deepen his ideas through your interactions. Many programs select themes for the class that may or may not be relevant or meaningful to the child. It is far more useful to follow the child's lead in selecting a theme that will engage him.

- *Content does not matter*, but it is important that the class have a range of toys to capture possible interests and concerns of different children. Toys might include pretend food, a doll house and furniture, figures of people who can represent family and friends, figures of favorite characters (such as those from Sesame Street, Barney, Disney films), a playground, a pool, vehicles, a garage, an airport, plastic animals and dinosaurs, a camera, musical instruments, puppets, hats, clothing for dress up, a doctor kit, and a tool kit (including masking tape, rubber bands, and clips to hold toys together). Limit cause-effect toys to those with symbolic potential and keep semistructured materials such as puzzles, play dough, markers, and games in another area. These can be used to develop interaction but may be overrelied on when it is harder to use symbolic toys to organize and sequence a story.

- *Toys constitute a language.* Children may play with toys before they speak and use them to show us their interests and thoughts before they have words.

- *Let the child discover symbols.* Saying "pretend" isn't usually necessary. Just respond to your child's real desires through symbolic (imaginary) actions or gestures and props. Some examples follow:

  - Allow the child to discover what is real and what is a toy. For example, if she tries to go down a toy slide or ride a toy horse, encourage her to go on; if she tries to put on the doll's clothes, do not tell her they don't fit; if she takes her shoes and socks off to put her foot in the pool, ask if the water is cold.

  - If your child is thirsty and asks for a drink while playing, offer him an empty cup or invite him to a tea party.

- If your child is hungry, offer her a piece of the toy pizza pie you are "eating" or ask if she wants ice cream or a cookie.
- If she wants to leave, offer her the keys or a toy car.
- If she lies down on the floor or couch, get a blanket or pillow, turn off the light and sing a lullaby.

- *Encourage representation.* Use a specific set of figures or dolls to represent family members or friends and call them by their names as you play ("Here come Daddy and sister Sarah!"). The child is more likely to accept figures named for other people before he accepts a figure with his name. At first he may experience representing himself as having to give up the object he desires.
- *Be a player.* Get involved in the drama. Be a player and assume a role with your own figure so that you can model natural social language. Play is not an interview or reading a story or describing what you see.

  - Use two voices: one as the parent encouraging, supporting, clarifying, and the other as the other kid or symbolic figure you want your child to play with! Your teacher or parent voice, which should have your natural tone, in a compelling whisper can encourage the child to close the circle ("But you didn't tell Ernie what you want!") and insist your child try to answer the question.
  - Be a partner: help your child negotiate and solve problems with your figure or directly by stepping out of the story for a moment, with your parent or teacher voice, to take his side and help him work things out or be more assertive, or figure out what to do with the hungry alligator as it (you) inches along toward the pirate ship!

- *Encourage role play, dress up, and play with puppets.* Instead of using figures, which may be hard to manipulate, your child may prefer to be the actor in dramatic play. Similarly, a puppet is the extension of one's body and is often easier to execute. Role play may allow for clearer gestures and imitation.
- *Start with symbolic figures* that your child knows and loves, such as those of Disney, Sesame Street, or Blue, to generate symbolic play with simple

continues

continued

feeding, picnics, playground trips, bedtime, and the like. For the more advanced child it might be dinosaurs.

- *Give symbolic meaning to furnishings and other objects in the environment.* When your child climbs to the top of the sofa, pretend he is climbing a mountain, or when he comes down the slide, treat it as if he is sliding into the ocean to see the fish.
- *Substitute one object for another when props are needed.* The ball might be a cake or the spoon a candle.
- *Resume use of gestures for props, along with toys and substitutes.* Just use your hand in a gesture to offer money for the toll or to drink a cup of tea!
- *Elaborate, elaborate, elaborate!* Try to expand the child's idea by expanding its purpose (e.g., driving the car to go to the park or zoo and bring props over) or making use of breakdowns or problems with symbolic solutions.

  - If the car crashes, get the tow truck and mechanic with the tool kit.
  - If the doll falls, hug the boo-boo, get a bandage (masking tape), or rush to the hospital with doctor kit, and so forth.
  - Don't overritualize by doing the same expansion each time.
  - Provide "seat belts" (rubber bands) to keep the figure sitting on the horse or on the chair so things aren't always falling apart and the child can be encouraged to go on with the idea. Masking tape, clips, and Silly Putty can be essential tools!
  - Re-enact familiar scenes your child chooses from books or videos to build better comprehension.

- *Insert obstacles into the play* to challenge and make your child think, be more assertive, learn to negotiate. Be compelling and use affect cues to hold his attention and help him tolerate the dilemma.
- *Use reasoning to deepen the plot!* This can be done through questions in a role you add to the child's; ask to go along or object for some reason. Ask the child to tell you her idea and what she wants you to do. Try to deepen the plot by posing problems; asking what if, if-then, or why questions; asking about feelings and predictions; and the like. Expand reasoning in real life and incidental learning simultaneously with symbolic play.

- *Expand the range of themes and emotions.* The hierarchy of themes and emotions moves from dependency to separation and on to bodily injury, fears, anger, sadness, joy, surprise, jealousy, rivalry, competition, aggression, power, revenge, friendship, loyalty, justice, and morality. Support the child's attempts to explore new ideas borrowed from experiences, stories, videos, and peers, beginning with "bad guy wolf, witches, or Captain Hook" and moving on to bad-guy themes in reality—robbers, kings, wars, and so forth.

- *Drama, drama, drama to convey affect cues!* Match your tone of voice to the affect and theme at hand. Pretend to cry when your character is hurt, cheer loudly when happy, convey anger or fear when needed, exaggerate deceptiveness to help the child figure out what you really mean.

- *Focus on process.* Plan the overall idea with your child, including where the story takes place, what characters and props are involved, what the problems are. As you move through the story, focus on who is in trouble, who is safe, what the other side might feel and do, what the ending will be, how each character feels, and so forth. Identify the beginning, middle, and end of each story idea.

- *Reflect on the ideas and feelings during and after the story is over.* Discuss your child's themes and feelings and elicit the point of the story and the abstraction of what is right or wrong or to be learned from the story. Remember, symbolic play and reflective conversation are the safe way to practice, re-enact, understand, and master the full range of emotional ideas, experiences, and feelings. But symbolic ideas also can generate a lot of anxiety and avoidance. This is discussed in the following chapter.

- *Encourage representation of personal issues.* Encourage the child to role-play potentially challenging situations that he has experienced or anticipates.

- *Build bridges between ideas.* Through conversations, ask for opinions, compare and contrast themes, have debates, change sides, empathize and reflect on how play relates to personal challenges. The child who can do this will be able to move on to higher-level thinking.

- *Always challenge the child to initiate—don't take over.* She is the writer and director of the drama. You facilitate by being an ideal partner who is fun, interactive, and challenging.

Using ideas can also occur in a group situation, such as when it is time for a snack and the teacher elicits choices and opinions and negotiates with the children who gets what and how much. Instead of prescribing snack time, saying, "OK, here's your juice; sit down, be quiet, and drink it," the teacher can use the opportunity to ask, "OK, who is thirsty?" Some children might answer, "Me!" or come over anticipating their juice. If they say nothing, the teacher can point to them and ask, "Are you thirsty? Do you want your juice?" Then they can answer yes or no, or gesture their intent. These children use ideas creatively when they answer a novel question, not one to which they have learned the same answer again and again. It doesn't have to stop there. The teacher may offer choices: "Do you want the red juice or the purple juice? Do you want a cookie or an apple?" "Who can get it?" "Does everyone have a cup?" "Do we have enough?" Now she is getting complex conversations going about what the child wants, noticing what other children want and comparing who may be getting more! (Later, when the child reaches logical thinking, the teacher can ask him to explain why he likes the red juice better than the purple juice.) Creativity is defined by the ability to use ideas generated by one's own emotion. So through something as simple as snack time, we can get creative use of ideas. And it can be fun; the teacher can joke with the kids and ask, "OK, who wants chalk for a snack?" Everyone yells, "Yuck! NO WAY!!" "Who wants chocolate chip cookies?" "YEAH!" everyone says.

If a classroom (whether kindergarten, second grade, or high school) has children who haven't yet mastered the ability to use language creatively—to express their needs and desires and to create imaginary or imaginative scenes—that has to be the first goal. Unless we teach our children to do that, they won't progress to logical thinking. In the typical setting, this should be accomplished in preschool, kindergarten, or first grade through imaginative pretend play and back-and-forth conversations. For children with ASD, this can initially be done one-on-one with a teacher or aide (as described above), then in small groups involving one adult and two children, and then maybe by adding another child when the child with ASD is more comfortable.

In the small-group format, the goal of the teacher or aide is to promote the exchange of creative ideas both between the children and between the adult and the children. In pretend play, the caregiver might ask Allen, "Where is Jessica's car going? Can you tell her where to take the car?" With luck, Allen might say, "Jessica, take car to school." And Jessica might respond, "No! Going to store!" If Allen doesn't answer, the adult can promote a little conflict to generate emotion, saying, "Allen, she said she's going to the store, but you said school." And Allen may say, "No, no, no, school!" to Jessica. If the interaction gets too intense, the adult can insert herself as a character in the drama and say, "I'm a policeman. I say we have to go to school *and* to the store. I'm going to hide something in my hands and the one who guesses which hand it is in, gets to choose where we go first." So now the children have a problem to solve, they are interacting, and one of them gets to make a choice while the other one gets to learn about patience.

The more the children begin to interact with each other, the more the adult can step back and let the children play the drama out together. Once two kids can play creatively together, a third child can enter the mix, with the adult as a negotiator, facilitator, and challenger. If any of the children drifts into parallel play, the adult acts as the provocateur, creating a challenge, conflict, or little game, even if it's a structured game. The more the children interact with each other, the more they'll get the hang of it and be able to play on their own.

For the child who has not yet mastered creative and logical thinking, a fair amount of the school day should be devoted to this activity. Time in a large group should be minimized because it's very hard to get more than three or four children to interact with each other without it getting chaotic. If logistics demand that the adult work with a group of six to eight children, the goal is to get a continuous flow of interaction with the whole group. For example, if the teacher is reading a book, all the children should be encouraged to share their opinions and ask questions. The teacher might have a big picture book and ask each child what he or she sees in the picture. Or the group can sing songs and do rhythmic activity, with the children voting on which song to sing by cheering or raising their hands.

Again, though, for a child with ASD who is still learning to stay engaged and communicate creatively, this kind of group activity should represent no more than 10 percent of the day. Being part of a large group does teach patience, tolerance for others, following instructions, and other laudatory goals, but these goals are secondary. For a child at this stage, the majority of the time should be spent one-on-one or in very small groups. The child who is pretty good at a continuous flow of interaction and is starting to work on creative ideas can spend about half the time one-on-one with a caregiver, and the other half with other children, facilitated by the caregiver.

Logical Thinking

Once a child is using many ideas together imaginatively and is pretend-playing in the different classroom settings with other children and with teachers, the next step is teaching her to use ideas logically. This step builds easily on the work the child is already doing; now, in addition to helping the child generate ideas, the caregiver helps her to "make sense," to respond logically to what others say and do. (Techniques to help the child make sense are discussed in Chapter 9).

When children can answer "why" questions, it's a sign that they have achieved some facility in connecting ideas together. Often it's hard for children with ASD to do this because of auditory processing challenges. Therefore, a teacher or aide needs to challenge them by increasing their motivation. As children continue to do the activities they were doing before—from pretend play to motor activities to routine classroom activities such as snack time and cleanup—everything can involve back-and-forth interaction using words, the teacher always trying to get them to logically connect their words to his words. Rather than a "Do as I say" or "Work quietly" environment, it should be a "Let's discuss" environment; we want an active, vibrant atmosphere with happy children who are chatting all the time, connecting their ideas to the teacher's ideas. Again, a large amount of time should be spent one-on-one until children have a basic ability to connect ideas together logically.

If two or three children are interacting together, whether they're pretend-playing, cutting out shapes, or drawing together, the job of the caregiver is to promote logical conversation. If Ryan and Melissa are playing together and Melissa says, "Beep, beep! Truck is going to school," and Ryan just ignores her, the caregiver can say to Melissa, "I think Ryan didn't hear you." So Melissa might say, "BEEP, BEEP! I'm coming!" and then Ryan might answer, "Can't come here," thus closing the circle.

Whatever the grade, if children have not yet mastered creative and logical thinking, these skills come first. We do not want to move into academic work—reading, math, oral and written expression, and the content areas—until a child is at the five-year-old level of age-expected competency in the developmental stages we have described and in language and visual-spatial capacities. Some children master rote academic skills on their own and are even interested in doing worksheets, but can they have a logical conversation, move in space, and create new ideas? What might appear to be skill in the early grades might be masking constrictions and deficits, which will become apparent when the child is expected to debate a point of view, infer motives, do higher-order math, comprehend literature, and write creatively.

Integrating special-needs children into a regular classroom can be a challenge. Perhaps they can participate only in a few of the activities, such as arts and crafts, drama, recess, gym, and lunch. It's fine for them to participate with the group in these activities, but anytime the thinking, conversation, or activity moves above their level, an adult should work with them one-on-one, perhaps in a corner of the room or in a separate little room. Sometimes other children can be brought in as helpers, with the teacher helping these assistants to adapt the lesson or activity to the developmental level of the special-needs child. This way, children with ASD get the best of both worlds: they get to interact with same-aged peers and feel part of the group while also getting one-on-one work on their fundamentals. (As we said earlier, if the school doesn't have the resources for one-on-one work with a child, the child can spend part of the day at school in appropriate group activities and the rest of the day in a homeschooling program.)

Higher Levels of Thinking

Once children are verbal and have made progress in creative and logical thinking, schools can help them advance to higher levels of thinking: multicausal, gray-area, and reflective thinking. While varying degrees of neurological impairments and various other factors may prevent some children with autism from reaching these levels, a sizable group of them are capable of doing so. How can we promote these higher levels of thinking—so important for adult functioning in a complex society, as well as for higher-level academics—in our educational programs, and what should parents look for in a program?

These abilities are developed best in a school that has a thinking-based philosophy of learning. In other words, whether the child is studying math, reading, science, social studies, or history, the content has to be secondary to the level of thought involved. Facts are used to support thinking; math and science should be learned experientially, based on basic principles. For example, children with sequencing problems often put numbers in the wrong column when they do long division, and therefore get an incorrect answer. They should be taught a sense of quantity so they can estimate the answer, and if they arrive at something way off, they can recognize and correct it. In this way, if they understand the concepts, they can compensate for sequencing problems, such as by using adaptations (writing on graph paper or using a calculator, for example) to get their answers down on paper.

When it comes to multicausal, gray-area/comparative, and reflective thinking, it's rare that any child—even one in a gifted and talented program—is asked to evaluate his own essay, his own arguments. Children with ASD, who need more practice in higher-level thinking, are thought not to be capable of it, so they are taught instead with memory-based approaches and that becomes all they know how to do; it becomes a self-fulfilling prophecy.

Using a thinking-based approach, we match the content to the child's thinking level. In teaching new concepts using this approach, we always introduce the concept in a context familiar to the child; only after the concepts are understood do we gradually expand them to incorporate new vocabulary and sequencing challenges.

Ideally, when children's individual processing challenges make it hard for them to communicate rapidly and in a group, about half their day should be spent one-on-one with an aide or tutor, working on thinking skills in the context of different academic areas. The other half can be spent in group situations, if other group members show patience and respect for the special-needs child's mode of communication—if the others will wait, for example, while the child types out responses to questions. A child with ASD could also be paired with a typically developing child to work on projects at home and during class time, thereby facilitating peer relating and social interactions.

The foundation for these higher levels of thinking begins much earlier, at home, as caregivers create incidental experiences in which children can start to evaluate in long, back-and-forth conversations what they're doing, what other people are doing, and why.

Children with ASD often take everything literally, having trouble reading motives or subtle meanings. A child moves from being a literal, black-and-white thinker to a higher-level thinker through conversation and symbolic play with a wide range of emotions, including negative ones such as loss, disappointment, and anger. Exploring with a child how jealousy, for example, plays into a Disney story helps her to realize that there are complex and multiple causes for anyone's behavior.

Whether at home or school, the goal is not to tell children the motives but to get them to make inferences, to figure it out. They can practice putting themselves in the other person's shoes by enacting both sides of a drama: "OK, if you're the British, how do you feel when the colonists declare independence?" We have to keep deepening the plot. To increase children's motivation, we stay with things that are meaningful to them and try not to structure everything for them, and we involve them in creating ways they, themselves, can learn.

The Physical Environment

Any classroom setting for children with ASD should have *an area that facilitates imaginative play, with dolls, trucks, and cars*. There should be enough toys so that children can follow their interests, but not so many that the children are overwhelmed. There should also be areas of the room where children can strengthen various processing abilities and other skills. *One area of the room should be oriented toward gross motor activities*, so children can practice balance and coordination, left and right integration, and sequencing of many actions in a row. This area might include a balance beam, a rocking boat, big Nerf balls, and components of obstacle courses. In another area, children can draw, work with beads, or use scissors to work on fine motor skills. *An area devoted to visual-spatial processing*, where the child can work with different visual patterns, search for hidden objects, and build things with blocks, might be integrated with the gross motor area. Visual thinking tasks could be arranged on a special shelf near a table where a child might work with a friend and the adult to reverse each others' block designs. Again, many of these activities go together, and the environment may be organized in many different ways. The pretend-play area is a good place to work on auditory processing and language skills, for instance.

There should also be *an area for sensory modulation exercises* that support each child's unique profile. Here there might be toys that make sounds on which the child can turn the volume up or down (not too loud, of course). There can be many different textures available, so that children who are tactilely sensitive can, through pretend play, be encouraged to touch different substances and talk about how they feel (maybe the doll likes or doesn't like it). The same thing can occur in terms of the pressure of physical touch: the caregiver can have a big teddy bear tickle and hug the child. There might also be a mini-trampoline, a mattress to jump on, or a swing for vestibular input. Children who crave sensation or underreact to sensation can benefit from opportunities to generate vestibular input—swinging, jumping, and deep pressure with bear hugs—on an hourly basis. That will help them perform better for the rest of the day.

As children move through the areas of the room, focusing on different skills, the creative use of ideas is encouraged as well. Thus a child going through an obstacle course, for example, may pretend to be Batman or a gymnast. The child can choose which end of the obstacle course to start at and may even help set up the course. And then two children might go through the course together as a team, and maybe try to go through faster than another team. Most experienced teachers will have a reservoir of ways to use a room set up with these features when the goals are clear.

Structuring the Day

How do these principles translate into an educational curriculum? Because autism and other special needs conditions are in a sense defined by differences in the way children process information, ideally, about a third of the day should be spent in one-on-one or small-group work strengthening processing abilities: auditory processing (including comprehension of abstract verbal material), visual-spatial processing and thinking (knowing where your body is in space, how you relate to different objects in space, and how to conserve time and space), motor planning and sequencing, and sensory modulation. (Typical classes such as dance, sports, art, and drama can be integrated into these foundation-building components.) Specific goals should be set by determining the child's current level and then creating an objective for the child to achieve in that ability.

These components should be addressed in roughly twenty-minute increments, repeated throughout the day as needed. For example, twenty minutes spent on Floortime work on the fundamentals, twenty minutes spent on language arts, twenty minutes spent on visual-spatial processing, and twenty minutes spent on regulatory-sensory processing.

Another third of the day should be spent working directly on the higher levels of thinking. As described in Chapter 10, this work begins by creating high-affect situations around issues that are familiar to the child—such as family dramas, sibling rivalries, or peer issues—to teach multicausal, gray-area, and reflective thinking skills.

The other third of the day can focus on thinking-based academics, as described earlier in this chapter—that is, schoolwork that is geared to and that strengthens the child's thinking capacities. This can occur one-on-one, in small groups, or in larger groups (for example, a class discussion about a book). In large-group settings, children with ASD will of course need support from a teacher and an aide to be full participants. Many schools now provide special-education teachers who spend part of the day with the child, in or out of the classroom, and are often assigned to stay with the child for several years as she progresses, thereby recognizing the importance of the developmental aspects of learning and the ongoing relationship necessary to support the child even when teachers and aides change. Children, such as the girl in the case study at the beginning of this chapter, should not be moved ahead to levels of academics beyond their thinking level. To determine this level, we look at whether a child has reached a certain level of thinking and at how broadly he can apply that skill. Can he apply it to math as well as to science? Can he apply it to social interactions with peers as well as in conversations with parents? Can he apply it to negative feelings as well as positive feelings?

The critical decision of whether to use a special-needs setting, an integrated program, or have an aide work with the child in a regular school program can be made when the child begins to show a capacity for continuous back-and-forth signaling and interaction. Many parents will of course encounter frustrations when trying to put together a program for their child within the constraints or requirements of the local school system, especially if only school therapists are involved. In communities whose public schools offer only a highly structured special-needs setting—rather than a proper educational setting for a child who requires interactive, spontaneous peers—parents may have to consider homeschooling to create the appropriate environment for the child. They can bring in peers for daily play and find activities in the community such as dance, sports, arts and crafts, and theater. There are many different ways children can interact in social groups—in addition to peer play dates—that can be part of a home educational program.

Some families may of course choose a private school, in which case they will want to look for the kind of program we have described. However, if neither homeschooling nor private schooling is an option, perseverance and fortitude in making a case to the school system has worked for many families around the country. These families have negotiated with their school districts agreements to have the child in school for half a day with group work and at home doing one-on-one work for the other half. Keep trying to get what you want, and remember that it's what a child does every day that counts—so it's not a good trade-off to have the child in a less-than-ideal school setting in return for a few hours of therapy. It's better to provide a daily program that works for the child. There's power in organization. If policy makers and administrators are hearing from teachers and parents that the way schools address the needs of children with ASD has to change, change will happen. It's got to be a grassroots effort.

Structure of the day for children who have not yet mastered the six fundamental developmental levels (repeat the following sequence throughout the child's day, including time outdoors):

- *Floortime*—twenty minutes
- *Language Arts*—twenty minutes
- *Visual-Spatial Processing*—twenty minutes
- *Regulatory-Sensory Processing*—twenty minutes

When the child is at the five-year-old stage of functional emotional development and language and visual-spatial capacities (i.e., can engage in multicausal thinking and use of ideas), add thinking-based academic work, including reading, math, oral and written expression, and content areas.

Part V

⊠ ⊠ ⊠

Overcoming Difficult Symptoms

Chapter 22

Scripting and Echolalia

Animated, dark-eyed six-year-old Joshua was diagnosed with autism, with a relative strength in remembering words. In addition to his Floortime-oriented home and school program, Joshua had speech therapy for his difficulty with expressive language, and occupational therapy for motor planning and sensory challenges. His parents noticed that he seemed more prone to anxiety and had begun using a lot of scripted language: throughout the day, instead of really engaging with others, he would give a running monologue of language taken from books or television programs. They were worried about this new development and wondered how to address it.

How can we help children who tend to use memorized scripts, to repeat things they hear rather than use language meaningfully, or to be echolalic in their use of words? In addressing this behavior, as well as the other problems discussed in this section, our approach is always to see it as an opportunity to strengthen the foundations for relating, thinking, and communicating. We want to ask ourselves, "How does this behavior reveal some missing piece, some missing step in the pathway to healthy development?"

As we have emphasized before, by focusing on the underlying foundations rather than on the problematic symptom itself, we actually

301

address the symptom more effectively and with more lasting effect. It's rather like helping a person who is tripping and falling all the time: if we hold his hand, he may not fall, but if we strengthen his leg muscles and coordination, not only will he not trip and fall but he'll be able to run, dance, and jump as well as walk.

When children repeat what they read in books, what is read to them, or what they hear on a TV or radio show, or when they just re-peat what their parents say rather than responding in a meaningful way, they are showing us a couple of things. On the positive side, they show us that they can remember what they hear, that they have some strength in their memory for sounds or words (or, if they are reading for themselves, for what they see). Their behavior also reveals the missing piece: it tells us that they are not yet able to take these memorized words and use them to think creatively or logically. In other words, they are not reasoning with these words, but just repeating them.

Desire Is the Key

Most of the children with ASD that we work with have the underly-ing ability to learn to reason with words. The first step is to create in-teractions that challenge these children to go beyond just repeating or using their memory. This always occurs at two levels. Thus, when a child is echolalic or scripting, the first questions to ask yourself are:

1. How deeply engaged is the child in terms of warmth, pleasure, and intimacy? How long can he sustain engagement?
2. Is the child engaging in a continuous flow of back-and-forth emotional gesturing?

If the child is not sustaining pleasurable intimacy for long periods and is not engaged in continuous exchanges of emotional gesturing, we have to do more work on those fundamentals, as described in earlier chapters. Otherwise, we are in a poor position to help the child overcome the ten-dency to use language only in stereotyped or highly structured ways. Of the two abilities, the hardest one to strengthen is the continuous flow of back-and-forth emotional signaling.

Meanwhile, we can also be working on the creative and logical use of language; we don't have to stop working on language or even academic skills if the child is at that level. We can work on all of these at once, but we have to think in a few dimensions at the same time. Sometimes, as we showed in Chapter 8, we have to be playfully obstructive to keep the interaction going.

Let's say a child is repeating what you are saying. You may ask, "Sweetheart, do you want to go outside?" and little Tommy repeats, "Sweetheart, do you want to go outside?" You ask, "Sweetheart out?" and the child says, "Sweetheart out." We want to turn this parroting into a meaningful conversation. So you can take Tommy to the door where he might see other children playing outside; you know he really wants to go outside but is not able to express it yet. You'll say, "Come, let's look," and hopefully looking outside will provide increased emotional interest to go outside. Then you'll position yourself between him and the door and ask, "Do you want Mommy to help you go outside?"

Now, if he just repeats "Mommy go outside," you might really simplify the language and ask, "Go out and play?" and open the door and let him see what "out" and "play" feel like, but then hold his hand and say, "or stay in here?" He might repeat "Go out or stay in here." Then you can physically demonstrate "going out" and "staying here," with more emphasis and affect on the "going out" part. After three or four times, usually the child will take the bait and just say the part of the phrase that reflects his desire: "Go out" or "Go out play." If he doesn't do it the first day, he will do it by the second day if you keep doing this.

Of course, you don't want to frustrate a child to the point of a tantrum, but you want to let affect or desire build up to the point that the child has the feeling of attachment to the particular part of the repetitive phrase that will get him what he wants. It could be having a snack, playing with a favorite truck, or going outside. To do this, you slow down your speech while emphasizing (with high emotion) the part of the phrase in which the child is emotionally invested. This helps the child break the echolalic pattern by the strength of his own desire.

Sometimes, when we use very structured learning techniques with children, such as showing them a picture and teaching them to memorize the word for the object in the picture, we inadvertently encourage echolalia or scripting because the memorization is not associated with the child's emotions. As we have explained, children ordinarily learn language by associating a word with a positive or negative emotional experience. They learn "love" through hugs and cuddling. They learn the word "eat" as they eat applesauce. They learn the words "go out and play" as they are going out to play. If they learn words only through memory—either because we teach that way or because they have a strong memory but have a harder time understanding meaning and therefore favor that way of learning themselves—we have to help them connect their desires to words. We do this by using the word in a situation with heightened emotion—almost going outside, almost getting that apple—and prompting the child with choices. As we said, we give the desirable choice first and the silly choice second, so the child can't just repeat the last thing that was said; he actually has to compare the two choices in his mind.

Meaning Before Grammar

Don't worry if a child's phrasing is awkward; the important thing is that the words convey meaning rather than just being recited. If you ask, "Do you want to go out and play or stay here and sleep?" the child might say, "Play out." That's good enough because it conveys intent and meaning. Don't correct the child or try to get the right nouns, pronouns, and adverbs at this point. Just go with the meaning, and say, "OK, terrific! Let's go! Let's play out!" Adopt the child's phrase because it's meaningful. Then over time, once the child gets hooked on using language meaningfully (a big advance), she will eventually start using it correctly, just from hearing you use it correctly.

If your child has a tendency toward scripting and echolalia, the absolute worst thing you can do (and if you have been doing this, rest assured you can change) is to correct your child's grammar. You don't want to be teaching the difference between "he" and "him" or "I" and "me" right now. That comes later. You may think, "But if I let him use bad grammar, he is just going to learn it the wrong way and then it will be harder for him to learn the right way later." I urge you to put that thinking up on the shelf for a moment; your goal is a worthy one, but the concern is coming too early in the game. It's a bit like saying, "My child doesn't know calculus yet," when he's still learning how to add two and two.

The first goal is to hook the child on using words meaningfully, however clumsily. If we don't do that, if we are trying too hard to get her to use just the right phrase or verb-noun relationship, we get back into this structured, rote way of learning. You can teach the child to memorize a phrase—"Mommy, dear, you look beautiful; would you please take me outside to play?" or "Grandma, I'm so happy to see you; can I give you a kiss?" You might feel very gratified, and you may get a big smile from Grandma, but your child won't be meaning what she says. The goal is a meaningful exchange of gestures (facial expressions, head nods, pointing, showing) and words and phrases.

Once the child is hooked on the meaningful use of language, we can work on the correct grammar. For example, a child may confuse "I" and "you" and, instead of saying, "Mommy, I want to go outside," he may say, "Mommy you go outside." Here, we can play that old "Who's on first?" game and act confused ourselves. We'll say, "OK, I'll go out-side," and we go outside. "No, no Mommy!" "Well, who is going outside?" you ask, pointing to the child and to yourself. The child points to himself. Then you can get behind him and prompt him, say-ing, "I want to go outside! I!" Then he may say, "I want to go outside," so you say, "OK, let's go!" He might make the same mistake the next time, and then you have to go through it with him again. Let him point to himself and learn that "me" is the same thing as "I." When the child is motivated to get himself outside, he wants to learn the right word so that he can tell this slow-thinking person here that it's me, and they have it wrong.

The same thing applies to other elements of grammar; you can ac-tually create interactions that clarify each piece of grammar. Once the

child can have a meaningful ten-minute conversation with words—
however inappropriate the words and grammar, as long as it's not memorized script—then you can start focusing in on the grammar. So don't
jump the gun, be patient, take it step-by-step, build the foundations—
and the correct grammar will come.

For many children it happens naturally; you don't even have to
work on the grammar. The more interactive children are and the
more they can exchange gestures, words, and short phrases, the more
they naturally acquire the correct pronouns, the correct agreement
between nouns and verbs, and the proper use of adjectives and adverbs. Our theory of language acquisition is that children learn the
subtleties of grammar through the way they relate to the world. A
simple example: a child learns the adjective "bigger" because she
wants a bigger piece of cake. First she has to have the sense that there
are big slices and little slices, and she has to have the sense of what
she wants. Then, there is negotiation around slices, around the choice
between little slices and big slices, long before she is even using the
words "cake," "big," or "little." Then she has the experience of eating
a big piece and a little piece and emotionally investing in the bigger
versus the little; then learning the adjective occurs naturally. So most
kids will begin using the correct grammar automatically and spontaneously. But if we do need to work on it, we just create experiences in
which a child has to choose the correct grammar, where she has to
make a bigger-versus-smaller choice or an I-versus-you choice.

Scripting and Stress

Some children, such as Joshua, the boy in the case study that opens this
chapter, can engage warmly and have extensive use of language but
tend toward scripting when under stress. They use scripts in a self-
stimulatory way, to pull away and organize themselves. (Self-stimulatory
behavior in general is addressed in the following chapter.) Whenever
there is a change in a child's pattern—he begins scripting more than
usual, for example—we need to do two things at once. First, we want to

go back to the Floortime basics and work through the developmental levels, starting with calm regulation and rhythmic activity, getting the child re-engaged, back into interactive communication and shared problem-solving, and then back to using language interactively.

At the same time, we want to reduce the factors that are overloading or stressing the child. In the case of Joshua, the addition of a new program to work on his hearing, while serving a reasonable goal, was possibly too stressful, and he was losing more than gaining. In these cases we want to modify the approach and give the child a rest (reducing the activity gradually so it's not a sudden shift), while working on the fundamentals, until we get the child back to his baseline. In other words, with a child with ASD, as soon as you lose the fundamentals, you go back and rebuild them; you never want to give up on the fundamentals in order to address some other aspect of a child's functioning. Once the child is back to his baseline, you can reintroduce the activity—for a third or even a fourth of the time he was spending on it before—and see how well he tolerates it. If he tolerates it well, he can build up to more time—maybe to a half or two-thirds of what he was doing before. But at the first signs of stress, drop back a notch. Often, if you can catch the child at the first signs of overload, you really don't lose anything. You learn something about the child—the right way of pacing new activities for him—and then you can get back to helping him master the new challenge, but maybe in a more gradual way with better self-regulation.

Enriching Language

Some children use language appropriately but in a narrow, stereotyped, repetitive way. They may have eight or ten phrases, such as "Want cookie" or "Go out," but they aren't broadening or enriching their use of words. Here again the key is to go back and ask, Can the child engage in a continuous flow of gesturing? If so, how rich is it? In other words, does the interaction consist simply of rolling a ball back and forth a hundred times, or can you and the child go from activity to activity? Can the child exchange many different facial expressions and sounds? Is she as comfortable taking your hand and showing you things during nature walks as during pretend play at home?

As we showed in Chapter 8, always start by broadening the child's emotional experience and range as the foundation for broadening her use of language. Go on hikes or go to the zoo, the beach, the county fair, the supermarket—and in all these places, follow the child's interests, as Floortime suggests. Do lots of pretending with toys and stuffed animals. If the child doesn't like toys, play act with her, using costumes and imitating characters from a book or TV show. To encourage pretending, try to find things the child really loves to do. What is her passion? Is it eating? Running? Moving? Start with activities that you routinely do at home, and have the dolls or animals copy them, and try to entice the child into pretending that way. In other words, enrich the child's emotional experiences.

If the child isn't ready for such pretend play, start by enriching his sensory experiences—that is, things he sees, hears, smells, touches, and tastes. As you do this, if the child is somewhat verbal, introduce the words to describe these things, and have little dialogues around what you are doing. You can coach and prompt a bit, but be sure it is reciprocal and continuous. Try as best as you can to get into pretending, because that stimulates more creativity and imagination and will ultimately broaden and enrich the child's language production.

When the child uses words to say things like "Mommy—want cookie" but doesn't use language more richly, use his motivation to help him elaborate more rather than just repeating what he wants. For example, you can be a little slow in reacting. Before you get it, you can say, "Oh, great! What kind of cookie? Big one or little one?" and indicate sizes with your hands or offer different choices of cookies—chocolate chip or oatmeal. He may not know what those words mean, so you can show them to him and say, "This one is called chocolate chip and this one is oatmeal; which one do you want? Choc? Or oat?" He may surprise you and say, "Both!" and grab them both and run away. But that's terrific—he's using a new word that you didn't know he knew.

A child can get what he wants through repetition only if you let him, so you have to stay out of the repetitive game by playing dumb. You have to be impish and playful and willing to tease him a little. Always challenge the child with more novelty to keep the conversation going. Try to make a simple one-circle conversation into a five-circle conversation. If you feel that you just can't stimulate richer language or pretend play because you don't have enough imagination yourself (a comment we hear from many parents), take a step back and just watch your child. Children will give you the clue as to what they are passionate about, what interests them the most. So watch and observe.

Chapter 23

Self-Stimulation, Sensation Craving, Overactivity, and Avoidant Behavior

Energetic, with bright eyes and curly hair, three-and-a-half-year-old Kim was babbling all the time, but still was not using words or babbling interactively. Kim's parents tried to play with her using Floortime principles, but found it difficult to engage their daughter, especially when she was excited. Rather than playing, Kim had a tendency to grab her mother's hair and smell it or taste it. Her parents wondered what they could do to discourage this behavior and engage their daughter more.

How do we help children who have a tendency to self-stimulate, who crave sensation and are overactive, and therefore are often very avoidant? Typically, this pattern manifests itself in the following way. At age three, for example, a child moves around a great deal—exploring one toy and then another, but quickly, seeming just to touch one before moving on to the next, often at great speed. While doing this, she may sometimes jump and wave her hands in a self-stimulatory way. As we approach her, trying to talk to her or challenge her into engagement, she turns away from us and goes to the other side of the room. The more we approach her, the more active she becomes, sometimes moving her arms or legs at such a frantic pace that she seems distracted by her own movements. Naturally, most parents find it very difficult to help children with this pattern to move up the developmental ladder.

Creating a Profile

As we pointed out in Chapter 11, the first principle in helping children with this pattern to progress is to identify the particular way their nervous systems work. Let's say Jerry craves sensations. What are the bodily sensations he craves? Perhaps he craves jumping, arm waving, touching various toys. He may crave deep pressure and like to bang into things. He may love being swung around and playing the airplane game.

Next, consider the possibility that in addition to craving certain sensations, the child may overreact to others, such as high-pitched sounds or deep motorized noises, bright lights, or movement. When children with this pattern are overwhelmed (for example by a noisy environment), they go into the sensory-craving mode, rather than becoming cautious and retreating. If we get irritated and yell at them for running around, as adults may do, we may overload them even more.

Another aspect of the child's nervous system to consider is his visual-spatial processing—how well he can map out and negotiate the space in which he is moving. Does he flitter aimlessly from one thing to another, or does he—in his jumping and running around—seem to take in the whole room and explore it systematically? Does he bang into things or navigate skillfully around the room?

Then there is motor planning and sequencing. How skillfully does the child pick up a toy or an object? Does everything seem to be difficult for him to do, with clumsy motions and knocking things over, or is the child occasionally able to sequence two or three movements—picking up an object, exploring it, putting it in something or taking it out of something?

How well does the child understand your gestures or words? For example, sometimes children who are very active and crave sensation may remember whole books that you read to them during the times when you get them quieter. Others may have a very weak auditory memory and need work in that area. And how much does the child enjoy physical closeness and intimacy with you? Does she like to cuddle sometimes, or mainly enjoy roughhousing, climbing over you, or being swung in the air? Or does she prefer to be alone?

Joining the Child

You want to make a profile of your child's preferences and sensitivities, as we described in Chapter 11. Once that is done, the more difficult question is: How do we help this child, who is likely to avoid interaction, calm down, slow down, and begin moving up the developmental ladder? The first step may be challenging for caretakers who prefer being more sedentary! Raise your energy level to match the child's and begin moving around the room in rhythm with him. One little boy was aimlessly jumping around the room during a session with his speech pathologist. We suggested that she just jump with him. When she did so, he gave her a big smile, and all of a sudden they were interacting— she would take three steps, then he would take three steps, and so forth. But this occurred only because she entered into his rhythm and got this little dancing game going.

So one of the first things you can try is to imitate what the child is doing with the idea of making it a twosome: two kangaroos jumping around the room or two ballerinas or two Supermen flying from place to place. Some children become intrigued—they now have a partner in crime, so to speak—and we get some shared attention and relating. Communication through movement is fundamental in human development; we know that dance goes back a long way in our evolution.

As you move with the child, help him do whatever he is trying to do. If he likes jumping and being elevated, hold your arms out so he can jump into them. In one session, as a little boy was being very avoidant and running around the room, his daddy ran around with him and then held his arms out and the child literally jumped into his arms; then daddy swung him and started playing the airplane game. Then the child gestured whether he wanted to go fast or slow, or up or down. He also began using sounds—"uh, uh" for "up" or "d, d" for "down." This child, who hadn't spoken before, was gesturing and beginning to use some words.

So join in the child's activity to create a relationship, and then begin to use gestures so the child, in order to get what she wants, has to gesture purposefully back to you and maybe begin using some words. Many children who crave sensation often have the ability to use single words or short phrases, and they can tell you whether to go up or down, stop or go.

Another strategy that can work for children who are so avoidant that they run away when you try to join them is the Moving Fence game. Remember, all children want to engage and interact; it's just that they don't know how to do it if their nervous system makes it almost impossible for them. The biggest mistake with sensory-craving children is to physically restrain them: they will get upset and have a tantrum, and you will have a double challenge. With Moving Fence, you move around the room with the child, trying to get your arms around her without actually touching her. It's like your arms are hula hoops (you can use a real hula hoop if your arms aren't big enough). Sometimes it's easier to do this when the child moves near a corner of the room or near a wall, so the wall can be part of the fence.

Now the child is in an enclosed little space; you aren't physically touching her, but she has to physically touch you if she wants to get out of that little corral. One of two things often happens. Some children actually enjoy being in the more enclosed space. The options of a big space are overwhelming to them, whereas in a small space they may turn around, start smiling, and engage with you a little more. Other children want to break out and go back to roaming around the room. They may duck under or try to climb over your arms. In that case, if you challenge the child to use a purposeful gesture or sound, you're likely to elicit purposeful gestures such as moving the arm up and, not infrequently, words such as "up," "down," or "open." You can also bring in big dolls or stuffed animals to be a part of the fence. "Mr. Teddy Bear says you have to say the magic word to get out from under my arms."

Another strategy that often works well with a child who craves sensation is to have the child on some type of a platform, such as a wide balance beam or simply a couch. This measure of elevation makes some children a little more focused and purposeful; simply feeling above the ground often supplies some of their need for sensation and promotes a compensatory pattern in which the child focuses, organizes, and concentrates a little more.

Similarly, there are swings that you can have inside your home. The seat holds a child in on all sides so he can swing without risk of falling out—and the child can experience a lot of movement in space. The idea is to get the swing moving and then move with the child—move your face as he is moving back and forth. While in this rhythmic and in some respects more regulated movement, the child is much more available for interacting and for gesturing and exchanging sounds with you.

For children who are too distracted by their own movements to speak, even when they have some words at their disposal, we hold their hands and move them back and forth to the rhythm of our voice. This can help the child regulate and slow down, use words he may have available, and learn new words. Other children can benefit from deep pressure via back rubs and bear hugs, from techniques such as brushing and joint compression (via jumping exercises and direct manipulation with the arms and legs), and rhythmic activity to music or the beat of a metronome. (As a child becomes more verbal and able to follow directions, he may also benefit from the Interactive Metronome, a computerized version of the metronome that gives the child feedback about whether he is on rhythm or off rhythm, but that requires him to cooperate at least a little bit and follow directions. Research shows that this tool helps with attention, sequencing, and the fundamentals of self-regulation and self-organization.)

For some children, wearing a weighted vest is helpful because it gives them a lot of sensory input as they move, so they don't have to move quite as much, which makes things easier for the caregiver too.

The idea behind all these techniques is to harness the child's craving for sensation, using it to bring the child into shared attention, more engagement, back-and-forth gesturing, and hopefully, some problem-solving. If we take advantage of the child's movement to get inter-action cooking, the more we get a continuous exchange going, either with gestures or words, the more regulated she becomes. So the key to regulation, which is necessary for mastering the higher levels of emotional development, is to help the child use movement in an interactive way, rather than just in a self-stimulatory or isolated way.

Other Self-Stimulatory Behavior

In addition to children with the profiles discussed above, there are children who engage in self-stimulatory behavior such as staring at fans, moving their bodies against someone else's body or on the floor in a certain way, making repetitive sounds such as clicking their tongues, and so forth. Self-stimulatory activities often serve a purpose for the child. One purpose is to create a bodily sensation that he finds either organizing or pleasurable. That sensory information—the sight, touch, smell, or movement pattern—produces physiological feedback that the child values at that particular point.

Now, how can we help the child find something better to do that will be even more organizing, pleasurable, and satisfying? One of my (SIG's) first teachers in child development, Reginald Lourie, one of the pioneers of child psychiatry in the United States, had a wonderful saying: "When you want a child to give something up, give him something better." To do this, you have to know what it is he derives from the activity or object you want him to give up.

Let's say a child is making sounds that are disturbing to the other students in class; that child is seeking sensations in his mouth that he finds organizing, pleasurable, or satisfying. To understand what the child seeks from that behavior, observe him and make your best guess. Obviously, if the child is verbal, you can ask him, and if you ask in a supportive, uncritical way, you're likely to get an answer. You can say, "Gee, that looks like fun. That's something you do a lot. You must have a good reason for that." The verbal child may be able to tell you that it feels good or that he's imitating a cartoon figure on television. Many children who don't have ASD but have regulatory, learning, or impulse control problems do many of these things and are able to talk about it. They might say, "This feels good in my mouth; it keeps me paying attention," or "It keeps me from falling asleep." I've even heard adults who have unusual patterns say, "It makes me feel alive; it makes me feel like I'm more in the world."

As adults, most of us have our own favorite little self-stimulatory activities, whether it's scratching our head, or wiggling our toes while we're talking, or fidgeting with our legs, or fooling with a pencil. We all have our little ways of keeping our bodies at what we feel is an optimal level of sensation. We may try to keep these hidden or not too obvious, and some are more successful at that than others. Children who are not as socially sensitive or aware may engage in self-stimulatory behavior more obviously, to the point that it is troubling to others. We want to empathize with the child.

With a preverbal child, who's not able to tell us why he behaves in certain ways, we have to observe when he does it more and when he does it less. For example, if we're engaging the child in a favorite game, does he make more of his clicking sounds than at other times or less? Often we find that when we are interacting well with children, they show less of their self-stimulatory behavior. They may do it more when they're alone, when they're overwhelmed with sensation, when the environment is too demanding, or when they're aimless and uninvolved. Each child has his own context for doing more or less of the self-stimulatory behavior.

By observing when the behavior occurs, we try to infer what meaning it may have for the child. Is it a way of filling up her body with sensation when nothing much is going on, or a way of calming down when she's overloaded or stressed? If you can't find a pattern right away, don't give up. Just be patient and observe a little more. Get help from another parent, sibling, or caretaker if necessary, and get the teacher involved if the child is doing the pattern at school.

Once you know or have a hypothesis about what triggers the behavior, you can offer the child better ways of achieving that same sensation. For a child who's moving his mouth a lot, for example, you might get a harmonica or a little children's flute. Drinking through funny straws that bend in circles is good for oral motor practice, too, as is playing the game where you blow Ping-Pong balls across the table, racing each other. (This obviously would require a child to be more intentional and organized and less aimless.) Try to find games and activities in which the child needs to use lots of mouth movements. If the child is making many sounds and can imitate, you can make up interactive little songs based on the sounds he makes—"tch tch tch tch tch / bop bop bop bop bop / boop boop boop boop boop"— experimenting with different rhythms.

The overall principle is to offer the child experiences that produce the same sort of sensations as the self-stimulatory activity but lead up the developmental ladder of regulation, engagement, and interaction. To work on regulation, start off with basic sensory experiences. In this first stage, begin with the sensation but try to vary it, to expand the child's world of sensory input. If the child is making sounds, encourage him to make different sounds. Or you might offer him different things to chew on, or expand his sensory world by offering different smells and different things to touch.

At the same time, we want to help the child use these primary sensory experiences more interactively. Here, too, we start with shared activity—moving rhythmically with the child while trying to synchronize our sounds with his. If the child likes to touch things, we can do the same thing with touch—expand the world of touch and texture and then touch things together while moving together. If the child likes to look at something that spins, we can move the object from left to right and back and forth to get rhythmic looking together.

Once the child is emotionally engaged in the object or activity with us, we can move to purposeful interaction—for example, the exchange of sounds in a little game. The child says "goo," we say, "ga." The child says, "click-click," and we go "click-click-click-click." Then we could start generating many circles of communication in a row around that same self-stimulatory activity, trying to create a problem to be solved. If a child likes to touch things, for example, we could play a little game where she has to find a favorite "touchy" surface by closing her eyes and feeling around in a basket with lots of objects. A colleague of ours, Rosemary White, OTR/L, gives an activity purpose by creating an interesting result for a child. For example, if a child is touching a smooth window repetitively, she might make a swish sound each time the child touches it; or she might spin herself each time the child spins and see if it gets his attention.

In the case of Kim, the little girl described at the beginning of this chapter, the key is to use her interest in her mother's hair to fuel more interaction and pretend play. One way to do this would be to buy an inexpensive wig and put scents into it with hair spray, for example. Then the mother could put the wig on her own head and, if the girl gets excited, could create a game by asking, "Are you going to get my hair? Are you going to get my hair?" and then "hiding" in another part of the room. Now the girl has to find Mother. Once she does, Mother can ask, "What do you want? Do you want Mommy's hair? Huh-huh-hair?" And the little girl might say, "huh, huh" or make the "h" sound, and now we're getting communication and the beginnings of language. If the girl manages to say "huh" or "hair," Mother can bend down, letting the girl pull at her hair and pull the wig off. And Mother can say, "Oh! You got all Mommy's hair!" This way, we've turned a troubling behavior into motivation and interaction, using the child's desire to touch hair to promote development and, at the same time, give her the satisfaction that she wants.

In this way we work up the developmental ladder. If we're lucky, we may even create symbolic play around the self-stimulatory activity, such as having dolls stare at a fan together and talk about the fan, or having dolls make funny sounds together. And then, if the child is advanced, we can talk with him about what it feels like when he is involved in these activities.

Another principle of intervention at work in these cases is offering the child the opportunity to get involved proactively in activities that bring more sensation into the body. This opportunity can be provided in a regular sensory motor workout that the child does three or four times a day for fifteen to twenty minutes. For an older child who's more coordinated, this can involve playing sports, dancing, running obstacle courses, playing games, or just blowing bubbles or finger painting. In other words, socially sanctioned, organized activities are done proactively to create bodily sensations that the child finds organizing and pleasurable.

The last step we take for a self-stimulatory child is to help his teachers and other caretakers understand his pattern, so they can help reduce incidences of stress or isolation that might overwhelm him and can prevent his being left alone too often. (Children who aren't yet very interactive or verbal need to be engaged with an adult most of the time; at home, alone time should be just five or ten minutes here and there when you have no choice because you're cooking or going to the bathroom.) We also show the child how, if he gets overloaded at school, he can do something that's more socially appropriate than the self-stimulatory behavior but that achieves the same goal, such as having some healthy chewing gum to chew on. Or he can excuse himself to the nurse's station or another part of the room.

Repetitive Behavior—Perseveration

With self-stimulation, the sensations the child experiences are the clues as to how to work with her. With repetitive behavior, or perseveration, the key is the pleasure of the motor activity. The tie-in or overlap between self-stimulation and perseveration is that the motor activity, such as lining up toys or opening and closing a door, has sensory components:

the child is enjoying the sensations of making the same movement repeatedly with his hands. There may be a visual component if the child is opening and closing the door and getting a rhythmic movement pattern. So with repetitive behavior, try to discover what the action is providing for the child. Is it organizing, stress reducing, or just filling up time that is otherwise boring or lonely? Look at the benefits each of the components—sensory, motor, and emotional—provides.

With children who are verbal, or are preverbal but can recognize visual symbols, the perseverative activity may have symbolic components. (For adults, doing a crossword puzzle, for example, is a self-stimulatory, repetitive activity, but it's also highly symbolic and socially acceptable.) We may also discover other components by watching the child. Then, we follow the principles, going back to the baseline of doing the motor activity with the child in an engaged way—lining up toy cars together, for example. Once the child is enjoying being with us, we can make it more interactive—handing cars back and forth. To get into shared problem-solving, we try to make it more complex: we have to search for just the right car or find just where to put it. Or we may offer a competing arrangement for the cars, such as putting them in a circle, prompting the child to shake his head "no" and we start negotiating. Then we can make the activity symbolic by having little dolls ride in some of the cars. If we get to that level and the child is verbal, we can have discussions about it: Which design of car is better? Should we line up cars of one color or another color? As we discuss and negotiate, we're stimulating emotions, engagement, creativity, and logic.

At the same time, we can proactively address the child's enjoyment of certain motor activities more than of others. Does she prefer precise, motor-based activities to activities that involve balance and coordination or that have more unpredictable actions, such as throwing and catching a ball? Slowly, we want to expand the child's motor repertoire through enjoyable motor and sensory workouts three or four times a day that expand balance, left-right coordination, and action sequencing in nonrepetitive ways.

To summarize, whether it's a self-stimulatory or perseverative activity, we want to find out its meaning for the child and use that knowledge to work up the developmental ladder—from regulation all the way to symbolic activity—while expanding the area of the nervous system that's used. Everybody's nervous system is a bit different. The key for children with ASD or other special needs is to use that difference to promote development of all the senses at higher and higher levels. If we remember that principle and always go back to re-establishing regulation, we can use a child's natural interests, however unusual they may appear, for his own benefit.

Chapter 24

Meal Time, Toilet Training, Getting Dressed, and Coping with New Challenges

Carson's parents had been trying for a year to get their four-year-old son, diagnosed with mild autism, potty trained. But, aside from enjoying playing with the flush, the gentle, blue-eyed boy resisted using the big toilet. He could communicate with gestures and short phrases, but did not have enough language for his parents to discuss with him why he should use the potty instead of diapers. They wondered what techniques they could try to help him become comfortable with using the toilet.

M astering new challenges is not always easy for children with ASD (or for any children). In particular, mastering bodily functions such as eating new foods, using the toilet, and dressing themselves can be especially difficult for children with ASD and other developmental challenges because often they don't feel fully in control of their bodies. They may have motor planning problems or overreact to tastes and sensations, and they may fear activities relating to their bodies because of the lack of control they feel.

In this chapter we offer some basic principles that help children not only master new challenges and embrace new experiences, but—in keeping with our overall approach—develop their fundamental capacities for relating, communicating, and thinking. Remember that taking small steps leads to the best kind of progress for children because they're building solid foundations.

The first of these principles is that you can't help children master new challenges unless they feel calm and cooperative and are in a problem-solving mode. By analogy, if we adults are feeling overwhelmed and sense that someone is out to make us do something we don't want to do, are we likely to solve a problem or embrace a new experience? Of course not. On the other hand, if someone helps us when we feel cooperative, calm, and reassured, we are more likely to work with that person toward a new goal. So we want to remove or diminish the anxiety likely to surround any new activity. The child probably has gotten the idea that this is something Mommy and Daddy want him to do, but for a variety of reasons he may not feel ready to do it, doesn't want to do it, or is scared to do it. Or maybe he just doesn't know how yet. So the first goal is to reduce the fear and anxiety and turn it into a pleasurable experience rather than a chore. There is no reason why basic bodily functions, even toilet training, can't be enjoyable and positive.

To this end, make sure you are doing enough daily Floortime so that the child is calm and regulated, as well as assertive and purposeful, and able to get involved in a continuous flow of problem-solving interactions, whatever the activity. If the child can use ideas and words, describe and playact the situation he will have to master, before it becomes real. If the child can connect ideas together and answer "W" questions (who, what, when, where, why), help him comprehend the reasons for the new challenge—why it's important to be able to use the potty (so that he can wear big-boy pants), or why it is important to eat more food (so that he can be strong). This can be addressed in your pretend-playing and in discussions about how it's nice to be like Mommy and Daddy. Try to strengthen reasoning in a more general way so the child begins to connect the things he does with his body to the reasons for it and where it happens.

New Foods and Mealtime Behavior

The goal for all new situations is to see the child take charge of solving the problem. If she resists eating anything except a few particular foods and makes a fuss whenever you put something new on her plate, let her choose the food she wants to eat, as long as it's reasonably healthy and not too time-consuming for you to prepare. A verbal child can tell you why she likes the specific food. When the child is in charge of eating, you have detoxified the situation and it's no longer a power struggle. Then you can empathize with the child's positive feeling of being in charge and having the food she wants, and then also empathize with how hard it is to try something new. Maybe it's scary; maybe it doesn't feel good in the child's mouth; maybe it feels icky to touch—whatever the child's experience is. Then you start cooperative problem-solving, breaking down the new challenge into tiny little steps, always heading toward mastery.

The process depends on the individual child. For example, you might try just a bit of new food every two or three days, perhaps by embedding it in something the child already likes, as by mixing a bit of vegetables into a hamburger or into mashed potatoes. You do it just a little at a time; then next week or for the next few days add a little more or another type of taste. The steps you take depend on the child's unique reactions to sensations, ways of processing information, and style of planning and coordinating actions. How many actions in a row can he do as part of solving a problem? Can he hold a spoon or fork? Can he pick up food and bring it to his mouth, or do you need to help?

You also want to think about how the child reacts to the textures and smells of new foods. The more hypersensitive the child is to tastes, smells, and textures, the more slowly you should expose him to new food and the more you'll want to embed the new food into existing foods. If the child is not so sensitive but has a general fear of anything new, perhaps you can move a little more boldly, taking slightly bigger steps.

If the problem is not the new taste but a child's distractibility and craving for new sensations, meals can be a big challenge. In this case you may have to embed feeding into more action-oriented play. For example, an airplane (a fork) is going up into space, and as the child has her mouth open and is looking at the airplane, one of the airplanes needs to land. "Where is it going to land?" you ask. "It's going to land in your mouth!" It may not be the quiet play at your dinner table you would prefer, but eventually, after many small steps, as the child learns to regulate her activity level, she may be able to sit at the table and actually eat with the rest of the family.

One of the DIR principles is limits. Most children need firm expectations, guidelines, and limits. But the limits can't be punitive; they have to be associated with positive consequences. For example, if your child is sitting at the table and is reluctant to try a new food, maybe if he is willing to try just a tiny bit, he can get up from the chair and play with that wonderful new toy or get an extra story at bedtime. So the limits are coupled with an incentive for him to work with you. He may be annoyed that you're making him try something new to get what he wants, but if you have a firm, calm expectation that he'll try just a tiny bit, he will probably compromise. If you get involved in a power struggle, you're going to lose the game and you might as well wait for another time. (Whenever you're setting extra limits or challenging the child to work harder to try something new, you always want to add more Floortime. In the following chapter, we address limits in more depth.)

It's also a good strategy to let the child get used to the different texture of a food through multiple sensory modalities. While we don't want to encourage children playing with food in general, if a child overreacts to taste and smell and is reluctant to try foods with new textures, let him play with the food at first. Let him make it part of himself, just as babies do. He'll eventually graduate to being neat and responsible, but let him get used to it through his fingers and through smell; then he will be more comfortable tasting it.

You can try special tactics or magic bullets as additions—not alternatives—to this program. For example, when encouraging children to tolerate new tastes, it is sometimes helpful to expose them to firm pressure in the mouth and try various oral motor exercises. An experienced speech pathologist or occupational therapist knowledgeable about oral motor abilities and sensory reactivity can guide you in the use of techniques that may help the child tolerate a wider range of sensation in the mouth, such as massage and exposure to certain types of tastes and smells. This is not something for parents to try on their own without professional guidance.

To summarize, if introducing new foods is a problem, help the child develop as much as possible through Floortime, then work on problem-solving interactions that encourage the child to be assertive and in charge—both overall and in making choices about food. Empathize not only with the child's pleasure at being in charge but also with the challenge of trying a new food. Follow this with a lot of preparation, including advance pretending, and then try the new thing with firm expectations and limits that include a positive reward. The more limits you apply and the more firmness you use, the more Floortime you need in order to keep that cooperative attitude; it's the child's desire to please you that helps him move to the next level of trying something new.

At times or in certain situations, some children with ASD refuse to eat at all. A child might not eat while she is at school, though she eats at home. Whenever a child is not eating in a specific setting, it usually means she is retreating from and shutting down in that setting. An aide, teacher, or parent in that setting needs to interact with the child from the bottom up: getting her attention, engaging her in a relationship that is fun and joyful, getting a continuous flow of communication going. Remember: eating involves using the muscles of the mouth, which may be hard for certain children. So the child has to be engaged and motivated before she will eat. If she is overwhelmed by the environment at school and will not eat, she needs one-on-one interaction all day long, or else she will withdraw—from meals as well as other activities. A school can be an appropriate educational setting for children with ASD only when the educational program is tailored to the needs of the individual child (see Chapter 21).

Toilet Training

Toilet training follows the same basic principles as trying new foods. In general, we prefer to hold off on a big push toward toilet training until children are able to answer "why" questions, because then they can really understand the reasons for doing it and the positive consequences, such as being able to wear big-boy pants like Daddy. For children with ASD such as Carson, the boy described at the the chapter's opening, potty training may come a little later than for other children, because special-needs children may not reach that "why" level until age four or five, or even older. Schools pressure parents to have children toilet trained, but some children aren't ready yet in terms of language and intellectual development. You have to resist pressure from school so as not to overwhelm the child.

However, sometimes children with ASD (particularly those whose visual-spatial learning is at a higher level then their language ability) can toilet train sooner if you demonstrate to them the routine and the benefits of using the big potty. The key is doing it in a relaxed, calming, and step-by-step way, making it fun for the child. Once your basic Floortime exercises are well established and you have an interactive, calm, regulated, and happy child, you can gradually introduce the new experience, helping the child to be purposeful and engaged while getting used to a potty.

You might start with simply visiting the bathroom and playing a bit if the child has been scared of the bathroom. Have a small toy potty in the bathroom for the child to use; he can play with both the real potty and the toy potty and learn to enjoy the bathroom. Help him to relax in the bathroom with music and rhythmic activity. Or the first step might be letting the child sit on his potty in his room or in the TV room; you can make that first step as small as you need to in order to maintain the goal of keeping things calm, regulated, and pleasurable.

It is vital to give the child initiative and control. Let her have mastery over the equipment. Whatever the child's level of language, what makes potty training difficult for the child is the fear of being out of control, of being overwhelmed. So we want to start the process by putting her in control and letting her make choices, such as which potty to approach first. Giving the child choices and that sense of control is vital. While the old psychological theory about potty training determining how controlling people later become is no longer upheld as fully as it once was, there is some truth to it. Children who get scared early on and get into power struggles over their bodies tend to grow into older children who feel the need to control everything and have a harder time trusting. So while moving the child toward toilet training, offer her choices.

At the same time, look at the child's individual differences: is he very sensitive to touch on his backside, so that sitting on the potty is uncomfortable, painful, or cold? Does he feel comfort from the familiarity and pressure of the diaper? Having a piece of fabric on the seat may make it warmer, and that alone may help the child feel more comfortable with it. Another child might be sensitive to sounds and therefore avoid the bathroom because he is scared of the flushing noise. In such cases, you can flush after the child leaves the room, or allow him to play with the toilet and get used to having the flushing sound under his control. Some children are scared of the actual flushing itself; older children who are verbal have often expressed the fear of being flushed down the toilet or losing a part of their body. Some children who still haven't yet formed a sense of reality are scared of what part of their body comes out and gets lost down in this whirlpool of swirling water. The key is to be aware of the source of the child's anxiety and do what you can from a practical point of view to mitigate it.

For a child who is hypersensitive, establishing a gradual pattern or ritual can be helpful. However, remember that doing things in a ritualized, predictable, routine way can sometimes backfire; reinforcing a tendency to rigidity may discourage a child from making an effort to get what she wants by trying something new. Interaction helps children become more flexible, and you can create more interaction by helping children do what they want to do. A hypersensitive child who is scared of the potty may be more comfortable, for example, sitting on the child's potty with a diaper on at first. Simply get her used to defecating or urinating while on the potty in her diaper. Then you can gradually loosen the diaper, and eventually have the diaper inside the potty, and then eventually take it away entirely.

Using the toilet can be especially difficult for children who have motor planning and sequencing problems and thus have a hard time doing two or three steps in a row. The whole act of pulling down their pants, sitting on the potty, getting their body to relax, and then letting go might be very confusing and challenging for them. In this case, work very gradually with the child. Try to make a four-step action sequence into several one-step action sequences. Be soothing; sometimes relaxing music helps, or relaxing conversation may clue the child in to what he is supposed to do.

For some children the challenge is with balance and coordination, and sitting on an adult toilet with their legs off the ground is scary because they feel wobbly. They are worried about falling off or into the toilet. Using a child's potty or having a parent close by and holding his or her hand can provide extra security as a child masters this new skill. Sometimes, holding the child's hand and moving it rhythmically helps her learn to relax the sphincter muscles.

Children with severe motor planning and sequencing problems likely need to have a talented and a well-trained occupational therapist involved in the toilet training to help the parents identify the particular sensory modulation challenges. The therapist can address postural insecurity—how the child feels in terms of balance and coordination—and the child's ability to relax his sphincter and sequence many actions in a row. The therapist can help the parent strengthen those aspects of your child's development even before you approach toilet training.

On the other hand, children who underreact to sensation may have a hard time knowing when they have to urinate or defecate, because their body's sensations don't register well; so they go in their diapers or pants. Helping them identify these sensations becomes important. You can have a few days when the child drinks a lot of water and you check in often to see whether he needs to go a little, a medium amount, a whole lot, or not at all. Sometimes it surprises the child: he thinks he doesn't have to go, and suddenly says, "Mommy, I'm going!" Don't be angry or think the child is deliberately trying to foil you. Just say, "Gee, sometimes it really does sneak up on us," and help him get to the bathroom. As you take that supportive approach, the child will get better and better at identifying the sensations. You can also help an underreactive child become more aware of all sensations—how it feels to be tired, to be hungry, to be happy or sad. As you respect the way he describes his own physical states, he becomes better and better at knowing what it feels like when he has to urinate or defecate.

As stated above, once children begin to answer "why" questions, they begin to understand cause and effect: if I flush the toilet, it will make a noise; if I take off my diaper, I'll tinkle on the floor; if I sit here, I can poop or tinkle in this little potty. This understanding allows you to use discussion to help the child master the new experience. Because the child is now somewhat verbal, she can tell you that she likes the baby potty seat better than the big potty seat, or that she wants to flush the toilet or not flush the toilet. She can even protest, and then you can negotiate: "Well, if you try just a little bit, we can go out and play in the backyard with the hose."

Also, because the child can now pretend-play, you can have the dolls, toy animals, or action figures involved with potty training, both indirectly and directly. You can even get one of those tiny doll toilets that actually make a flushing noise, which kids seem to love playing with. As you are introducing this new experience, be very alert during your Floortime play to themes related to the new challenge. Whatever is an important part of the child's life will come out in her play.

You might see issues of control or of aggression. For example, one little boy started his play with submarines, always secret and beneath the surface. As we played in our sessions, I (SIG) encouraged him to express his feelings, which had to do with submarines fighting one another. He got more comfortable with that theme, and all of a sudden the submarines became battleships with the guns and rocket launchers on deck, out in the open. At the same time, he became more comfortable with urinating in the potty; the act of going to the bathroom had brought up his anxiety about his own aggression, which had been hidden beneath the surface like the submarines and was now out in the open like the battleships. We never addressed toilet training or potties directly in the pretending; he got more comfortable in general with assertiveness, and his power struggles over potty training decreased naturally. He became less negative and was more comfortable with being assertive, making his needs known, and negotiating with his parents.

A procedure that works well in some cases is to let the child walk around without any diapers, with rooms set up in such a way that it doesn't matter if he makes a mess; meanwhile the parent follows the child, carrying a child's potty. As soon as the child begins having a bowel movement or urinating, the parent quickly gets him onto the potty. Some parents report that, in a few days, children get the idea that when they have to urinate or defecate, they use their potty. Of course, some parents find that this technique doesn't work or that they can't tolerate following the child around with a potty.

In good weather, children can get out of diapers while playing outside. Bring a potty outside and see if the child notices when she is about to go and gets on the potty. If you lower the anxiety in the situation and create more chances of success, she may feel, "Wow, maybe I can do this." Being outside releases you from worrying about whether she'll make a mess that is hard to clean up.

Whatever the approach, the main thing is that the child is calm and cooperative and that you help him to be assertive—in this case, to be in charge of his experience in the bathroom—and then gradually challenge him to try something a little bit new. As long as you avoid putting too much pressure on the child and thus creating a power struggle, you can only gain, because in following these procedures, you're helping the child master his general developmental capacities.

We want to make the process one of pleasure and accomplishment for the child overall, not one of fear, even if it takes the child a long time. Remember that the biggest source of humiliation and negative self-esteem for many children is the feeling "I can't control myself." For a child some of those first feelings of embarrassment and humiliation arise around eating, toilet training, or getting basic needs met, whereas some of the best experiences children have—such as learning to tie their shoes, to read, or to dance—come from having a sense of mastery over their own bodies. Eating and going to the bathroom are among the most primary and essential bodily functions, so let's make them experiences of pleasure and mastery.

Getting Dressed

Many parents complain that their children won't cooperate in getting dressed or are very finicky about what they wear. The child won't wear these socks or that shirt or won't put clothes on at all, and the parent has to dress her while hurrying to get her on the school bus or into the car, and the whole morning turns into a power struggle with crying, screaming, and misery for everybody. This problem can be especially acute for children with ASD.

Again, before starting something new such as teaching a child to dress himself, keep doing Floortime until you have a happy, cooperative child and, hopefully, a happy caregiver. Then take into account the child's individual differences. Is he having trouble dressing because he is so sensitive to touch that only certain fabrics feel comfortable? Or does he prefer tighter clothes because they hold him firmly, as opposed to rubbing loosely against his skin? Does he have color preferences because of visual sensitivity?

Remember, a child who is in panic mode is unlikely to cooperate. So if you are rushing early in the morning, you've already lost the ball game. The time to negotiate choices is in the afternoon or evening when you have plenty of time—whenever the child is in her best mood. Say, "Let's pick out your clothes for tomorrow," and lay the choices out in the room. You also want to gradually practice dressing and undressing. It could start through pretend play with dolls, or with the child dressing you and the child exercising choices and control. Make it real collaboration and incorporate pretend play: dressing the dolls and seeing what the dolls like and how they feel. Then begin encouraging the child to take the initiative in small steps; if he puts on just one sock or gets one arm through the shirt the first day, that's terrific! Ask, "Should I help you with the other one?" Let the child direct you as you help him. Take your time; if the child is in school and you have to go to work, you may need to get him up a little earlier so you're not rushed.

The most important thing to remember when trying to get your child to do anything new—whether trying a new food, toilet training, getting dressed, or anything else—is to avoid a power struggle. The child is the boss of her own body, and she will win every time when her body is involved. You can't coerce or force her to do what you want. So when you get frustrated, count to ten, take a deep breath, and relax. Then go back to the basic principles: establish a calm, cooperative, problem-solving attitude around things that your child enjoys and then very slowly bring in the new experience. You have to be your child's trusted partner.

⊠

Chapter 25

Behavior Problems

Five-year-old Tyler, diagnosed with a pervasive developmental disorder and ASD, had always been particularly sweet and kind. However, when his little sister was born, Tyler became very aggressive; by the time she was a toddler, he would regularly hit, push, or kick her and seemed to take great pleasure in making her cry. This behavior continued even during the family's Floortime sessions with both children, and Tyler's parents were at a loss as to how to deal with this development.

All parents want their children to be sweet, kind, empathetic, and well regulated. At the same time, they want them to be assertive, creative, and curious and to be leaders, or at least masters of the challenges at hand. But many parents are faced with children who can be moody, sad or depressed, or exceedingly negative—even to the extent of hitting, pushing, or biting their peers. It is often harder to help children with ASD and other special needs who have these problems, because these children may not be able to communicate easily (verbally or otherwise) about their feelings. It's a frustrating situation for both child and parent.

How do we help children with ASD control their moodiness and aggression, regulate their behavior, and become warm, caring individuals?

The most important principle here is to avoid focusing only on changing the behavior. The temptation is to institute a whole program just to curb impulsivity, aggression, or moodiness and negativism. But if we do this without building the foundations for healthy behavior, the results are unsatisfactory. We may decrease some of the bad behavior, but—like water hitting a dam—it may emerge somewhere else. The child may stop pushing but start biting, or may go from being aggressive to being sad.

A Dual Approach

While helping the child overcome the negative behavior, it is important also to teach him to respect, empathize with, and read the signals of others (so that he knows when it's OK to be a little more assertive and rambunctious and when it's necessary to be more cautious). Rewarding a child for good behavior, using incentives, is part of setting limits and giving guidance. But it doesn't provide the infrastructure that allows a child to figure out how to earn those rewards or how to respond to a complex social situation. For this, the child needs lots of practice in emotional signaling. If we give the child this practice while working on the problematic behavior through rewards and limit-setting, we build the cornerstones of communicating, thinking, and relating in a healthy way. That's a tall order, but to do one without the other leaves the job incomplete.

To accomplish these two goals at the same time, we need to understand how ordinarily developing children learn to regulate their behavior and moods. It's not impossible for children with ASD or processing problems to learn these basic skills; a child's unique pathway to this learning depends on how his biology and nervous system operate.

Typically, children learn to regulate their moods and behaviors through interactions and relationships. An infant exhibits global, extreme patterns: the baby gets excited and cries or maybe even gets a bit aggressive or impulsive. As we described in Part II, usually, somewhere between five and ten months of age, babies become more interactive. They begin reading the facial expressions of parents or other caregivers, and there's an exchange of emotional signals: Mommy smiles, baby smiles; Mommy frowns, baby frowns.

At about nine months of age, this interaction gets complicated. The baby begins looking angry and making angry sounds like "RRRRRR, RRRRRR"; he is hungry and wants to eat now. Daddy sees this, and instead of letting the baby's anger escalate to a tantrum, says, "Ooooh! Is my little boy upset?" in a very soothing tone of voice, and then says, "Maybe you want this," offering the food the baby wants. The baby sees that and hears Daddy's soothing voice, and suddenly his sounds go from "RRRRRR, RRRRRR" to "Ah, ah." And he reaches for and takes the food, maybe with a big smile, and Daddy smiles back and the back-and-forth signaling continues.

At fourteen months, when the baby is crawling and toddling, he may reach for a forbidden object. Mother may say, "No, no," and baby goes, "RRRRRR, RRRRRR," escalating toward a tantrum. In a calm, soothing voice, Mommy asks, "How about this instead?" and offers an alternative. There is a negotiation with nods and different sounds and motor gestures as Mommy offers different alternatives; most of the time, the baby modulates. He doesn't have a tantrum because he is communicating his desires, and his mother is communicating back—"I can give you something to make you feel better, and there are other things you can have." Even when parents have to set a limit without an alternative, they can use a soothing tone of voice to counterregulate.

When a baby is getting upset, aggressive, or overstimulated, we can down-regulate, or soothe the child with our tone of voice, facial expression, and gestures. This soothing has to occur as part of a rhythm of interaction so the baby learns to regulate his agitation. When a baby seems sad and gloomy, on the other hand, a little inward looking and sluggish, with no bounce or energy or big smiles, we can "up-regulate," or energize, pulling him into a game of smiling and giggling. We may do it with sounds, with different types of touch, or with different types of movement.

For children with ASD and related processing problems, this is a much harder process. For example, children who crave sensation—touching everything, banging into things, wanting to be involved in everything—may be relatively impervious to pain. When they fall, they don't react very much; they get up and continue toddling around, ready to bang into the next object or person. When a child's nervous system craves sensation (many children are born with this pattern, while others develop it as they learn to crawl and walk), regulation is harder because the child is so active.

The parent has to help contain the child and also direct her into constructive, energetic interaction; the child may not respond to a lower-key approach. So as this child reaches for the lamp, you might have to say, "Oh no, buddy! NO, NO, NO!" and point as if you were the corner policeman directing traffic. The child may object with a loud "RRRRRR, RRRRRR, RRRRRR," but with your vocal tone and gestures, you can still offer alternative, constructive ways of interacting. You might have a big bean bag the child can jump into or a soft and squishy toy she can throw with you. Whatever it is, you do it in a regulated, coordinated way with a back-and-forth rhythm.

As this sensation-craving child gets older, you might play games in which you vary the speed of the interaction and the volume of sounds in order to teach the child to regulate herself with noise and movement by modulating intensity all the time. With great effort, in this way the child becomes both well-regulated and assertive. She may still be a bit of a risk taker, but she will have some control over her actions.

Another challenge is presented by children who get overloaded easily with too much noise or touch or from other children bumping them or brushing against them. When children get overloaded, they tend to push, bite, scream, or throw a tantrum. In these cases, we use the same principle as above, but with a different dynamic: we do much more soothing and regulating, offering alternative ways for the child to express feeling overloaded. Once the child can talk, we can help him use words; but before that, we can encourage him to indicate what is bothering him by pointing, for example.

In typical development, mastery of this emotional signaling system enables children to use symbols and words constructively. If the child doesn't establish this signaling system, he remains in the all-or-nothing reaction mode of infancy, with catastrophic emotions and behaviors.

Children with ASD may take longer to develop expressive signaling. In addition to over- or underreacting to sensation, they may have motor planning or sequencing problems that make it harder to learn how to signal emotionally because of the number of little actions involved in a row—smiles, head nods, pointing. Children who have auditory-processing and language problems can't hear many sounds or can't distinguish sounds well; they can't make many sounds and eventually can't easily produce words. So that too can interfere with this early signaling system. The harder learning is for the child because of his unique biology, the more important it is to get extra practice in this early signaling system. When children learn to signal and modulate, they learn how to regulate their behavior.

Dangerous and Aggressive Behavior

In the case of a child three years of age or older with severe developmental delays who behaves aggressively or violently or who gets very sad, immediate action may be called for. First, figure out the child's developmental level: in ordinary interactions, whether or not she is using words, can the child be engaged and make gestural contact—movements, body posturing, facial expressions, changing vocal tones—in rhythm with you for fifty to sixty circles of communication in a row? About 95 percent of the time, we find that children who have impulse control problems have not fully mastered this stage, even children who are verbal and abstract in their thinking and doing very well in certain academic subjects at school. A child can master this earlier stage partially and move on in development, but if it's not mastered fully, she may be left with a lot of problems with impulse control and mood regulation. See Chapter 7 for many ways to get that system strengthened.

Setting Limits

At the same time, though, if the child is behaving aggressively or impulsively, you may have to set limits. Helping a child learn to follow rules and to stay safe are understandable goals. Sometimes adults may get up-set or have overly harsh policies, and the need for compliance takes the form of strapping children with ASD into chairs, physically forcing them to walk to the bathroom, or imposing other types of restraint or compulsion. Dangerous (as opposed to noncompliant) behavior needs to be dealt with immediately with firm but gentle limits based on the child's developmental level, not his actual age. Just as we should pro-vide each child with the least restrictive environment, we should also use the *least restrictive, developmentally appropriate* tactics to teach each child to control his behavior and be sensitive to the needs of others.

Ultimately, we want the child to learn to set limits for himself, to understand what's appropriate and inappropriate, and to respect the needs of other people. How does a child learn that it's appropriate to push on the football field but not in the classroom? Children learn limits by reading their caregivers' emotions and signals in a continu-ous flow of interaction. For example, if you put your hand up like a traffic cop—Stop!—the child learns to recognize what that means, even if he doesn't understand the word "stop." Or if you just use your voice to say, "Uh oh! " or "Uh, uh uh!" your child is likely to pick up the message or signal in your voice and has to figure out what it is you want him to stop. It is important not to alarm the child with harsh gestures, or he may jump from the frying pan into the fire if he gets too scared or tends to react to fear with aggression.

The key to teaching limits to children with ASD is to do it in a way that is meaningful for the child. If she is hypersensitive to touch or sound or is easily overloaded, she needs soothing, gentle limits, such as a time-out in which we sit with her and talk in a soothing tone of voice, without getting angry. A child who is more sensory-seeking and rambunctious may need a firmer time-out and may need to be physi-cally constrained. She needs to know that you mean business and that there will be consequences if she crosses the line—that is, hits or hurts people or breaks things. You don't want to make the line too severe for little things like talking loudly or not playing properly with a toy, be-cause then you're controlling the child too much.

For the child with language problems, you have to explain very clearly why the limits are being set and help the child respond. Always try to have a conversation with the child so he understands what is going on. If the child is not verbal, you can show him pictures; if he can't yet use symbolic pictures, you can use gestures, pointing to what he broke or where he hit Mommy and shaking your head, "no, no," so the child understands why there is a limit. As the child gradually learns how to be a purposeful, preverbal communicator, responding to limits becomes a part of this purposeful communication.

Within the overall context of teaching limits that are appropriate to the child's individual profile, we have an eight-step program for limit-setting when a child is behaving dangerously or aggressively:

1. Increase your affect and your vocal tone to get the child's attention.
2. Add, almost simultaneously, limit-setting gestures, such as holding your hand up to indicate "Stop" or "Whoa" or shaking your head "No."
3. Use tactile support, if needed, by holding the child's hand or providing firm gentle pressure on his body to get him to pay attention and inhibit his action.
4. Then try to distract the child with something that will satisfy his physical impulse. If he wants to squeeze something, instead of squeezing the cat, he can squeeze a Nerf ball. Or if he wants to hit, maybe he can take a foam bat and hit the couch instead of you.
5. If these steps haven't kept the child from getting out of control, you will have to contain him physically. As we noted above, the principle is to use the minimal amount of containment needed to curb the worrisome behavior. Often this may involve holding the child from behind in a big bear hug, gently and firmly to give sensory support and help the child organize, or maybe moving rhythmically with the child while holding his hands. To do this, you have to know your child so you can anticipate when he is about to scratch, hit, or bite. You can go through steps one to four very quickly, all within five seconds, and then—if necessary—contain the child. Then the goal is to keep him contained until you can get him to relax. For some children, however, physically containing them only revs them up. In these cases you may have to simply

distance yourself from the child and encourage him with your voice to calm down. Or you may contain him just long enough to get him into a safe place where you can give him some space to unwind, maybe a space where he can distract himself with soothing music or soothing toys that he likes. Therefore, step five is creating a calming, containing situation for the child according to his individual needs. An occupational therapist trained in sensory integration can be especially helpful in tailoring this step to the child's profile.

6. *After the child is calm,* you can discuss the situation. The principle here is, "Never throw fuel on a fire." So don't talk to the child about how he's "doing a bad thing" while he's in the middle of his tantrum or aggressive behavior, because doing so will overload him. Once he has calmed down, if he's verbal, have a discussion with him: "What happened? Why did you do that?" Make sure you understand the situation from the child's perspective, and then solve the problem with him: "What can we do next time to handle the situation without hitting—using words instead?" and so forth.

7. Next, consider the appropriate sanction. If the child has overstepped the line by breaking something or hitting, for example, it is often appropriate to have a sanction, particularly if it's not the first time the child has done this. The first time you may say, "Well, he didn't know better," and stop with level six. But if it's happened before, you implement a penalty for the child. It could be missing a favorite activity, like a TV show or a dessert. It could be helping remedy the damage or hurt the child caused, like cleaning up what he broke and maybe doing some extra cleaning as well. It could be a time-out, when the child has to interrupt his activity and sit quietly with you in the room. However, avoid isolating the child. Especially for children with ASD, who need to learn how to relate with others, isolation can be counterproductive to the child's development. For a child with ASD, putting him in his room alone is a developmentally negative experience; sitting quietly in the room with you or having a quiet discussion

that interrupts his activity can often be enough. Also avoid taking away developmentally useful activities, such as a play date with a peer. Families have different ideas about the best sanctions; it's not so important what the sanction is as long as the parents or adult caretakers agree with each other, because if the child senses discord between the parents, it will make him anxious. Whatever they are, the sanctions shouldn't be a surprise to the child. The family constitution—about what is not permissible in terms of hitting, biting, pushing, breaking—should be negotiated far in advance and, for the child who can read, even posted on the refrigerator. For the child who is not verbal, both the no-no's and the penalties can be shown in pictures and demonstrated through gestures. Then, after the child is calm, you can say, "Sweetheart, I know you're not going to like this, but you did cross the line; what do you think is appropriate based on what we talked about before?" So the child participates in anticipating with you what the sanctions are going to be. You can be the "good cop" who doesn't like the sanctions either, but they are necessary if the child has overstepped the boundaries, and they will help him feel secure in the long run. Sanctions at school may be different from the ones at home; the teacher and aide should agree on them.

8. The ongoing goal is to help the child improve at two-way communication, particularly gestural communication, so as to prevent the need for the seven previous steps. For instance, the child can grimace, shake his fists, and learn to say "I'm mad!" instead of hitting. With a child who tends to cross the line, you can work on this by building his sense of responsibility and understanding of rules in smaller, less charged situations. Look for opportunities to have the child do things such as pick up his toys. Maybe if you pick up three toys, and he picks up one, he gets to do something he really wants to do. The next time, he picks up two, and you pick up two; eventually, he's picking up three, you're picking up one, and later still, he's picking up all four. Gradually help the child become responsible through gestural interaction, or through verbal collaboration if the child is using words: "Come on—let's put all the Legos back in

the box!" Make it into a game to get interaction going, and establish rules to the game ("The yellow ones go in first!") so the child learns to follow cues and rules. In your semistructured or problem-solving play, include lots of rule-based games, treasure hunts, and so forth in which the child has to follow your guidelines and cues. Even Floortime gives you opportunities for limit-setting interactions whenever the child wants to do something dangerous or inappropriate. Giving points or stars that lead to special privileges for good behavior can also help a child who can understand this system learn to follow rules and limits.

Helping a Child Learn Self-Regulation and Empathy

Try as best you can to be reflective and aware of your own emotions as you work with your child. Try to be relaxed and playful, and tailor your interactions to the child in terms of her sensory reactivity, motor planning capacity, language and auditory processing skills, ability to understand what she sees, and so forth. Tone of voice is especially important when interacting with children with ASD. When trying to get a continuous flow of communication going, it is easy to fall into a shrill, desperate tone instead of a compelling, energized one. You don't have to speak loudly to achieve the latter tone. A shrill monotone, though loud and capable of getting the child's attention temporarily, doesn't pull the child in. Instead, speak with feeling—with intensity and animation—but very softly.

A regulated individual is one who can respond to his environment with appropriate behavior. In the gym you can be rambunctious. In church or synagogue you need to be quiet. At home you can be one way, but if you are at a new friend's house, you need to be another way. As we noted in Chapter 9, to be able to perceive and take your clues from the environment, you have to interact with that environment continuously. To understand the world and figure out the rules, you have to tune in consistently, and the way you do that is through communication. Whatever specific intervention techniques parents are using, it's essential for the child with ASD to be involved in a continuous flow of emotional signaling in order to become reality based.

Empathy and caring come from sensing the emotions of other people, and the only way to sense others' emotions is to read their signals. And to be assertive in a healthy way, you have to be able to sense what the environment is telling you—when it's appropriate to roughhouse and yell, when it's appropriate to be extra cautious or quiet—and read the emotional cues of others. To have successful relationships with peers, you have to be able to judge what they are willing to do and what they aren't willing to do at any moment in time. Many of the aggression problems in peer play come from an inability to read emotional signals.

When a child is aggressive—such as Tyler, the little boy in the case study that opens this chapter—and seems to enjoy hurting others, the thing to remember is that the child does not yet necessarily share the values you want to instill, such as being nice to others and wanting to make others happy. The child has his own belief system, his own reasons for behaving as he does. In such cases a parent or caregiver also has to examine the atmosphere at home and assess the level of empathy and warmth that characterizes the family environment. A child who seems to enjoy seeing other people unhappy or sad may need to work on the emotional signaling around issues of dependency and warmth—cuddles, hugs, flirtatious glances. The family's availability to the child for the tender side of life, for lots of warm interactions on a daily basis, may need to be explored.

Sometimes a child who can ordinarily signal his feelings and negotiate and regulate himself will regress to the preinteractive level when faced with a new frustration or challenge, such as the birth of a sibling. In such cases, the idea is to give the child, through one-on-one Floortime, extra practice in dealing with the situation. The parent or caretaker can help the child restore his basic abilities by creating scenarios that frustrate the child, similar to those the child might encounter. For example, Daddy can playfully hide a toy the child wants and say, "I'm not going to let you play with this; it's my turn!" As the child gets annoyed and his frustration begins to escalate a little, the parent should be soothing and interactive—saying, "Well, let's see, could you play with this instead?"—stretching the child's ability to negotiate a bit before he starts to shove or hit. This should be a very gradual, gentle process, done of course in the context of the child's individual profile. If the problem is a new sibling, the parent can incorporate a doll who serves as the troublesome sibling, and then introduce the real brother or sister, starting with a few minutes of combined play and then gradually increasing it.

Again, our approach is to work on the immediate issues by imposing limits and consequences and granting rewards, while also working on the foundational piece of emotional signaling through soothing, regulating interactions. If there are two parents in a family, both parents should be involved, as well as any siblings, educators, or therapists who care for the child. This approach works for children with ASD or circumscribed learning problems, as well as for those who just have behavioral problems and no learning, language, or communication problems.

Negativism

Sometimes the problem is not so much that the child is aggressive as that he is negative; he says, "No, no no" to everything. We expect this at a certain point of typical development (around age two); what it tells us is that the child has a sense of who he is. Depending on the degree to which the child can communicate, we actually want to accept a "no" and then find out what he is saying "no" to in order to get interaction. You want to get to the reasoning behind the "no"—he doesn't want to eat spaghetti but he does want to eat a hot dog. Usually, if the child is saying "no" a lot, it indicates that he needs more choices. He has to have a vote. The "no" is his vote. The issue is whether it is negotiable or not, whether you can give him some kind of choice around the issue. In the DIR approach, we fight only the essential battles; we don't want to control everything the child does, and if he has an opinion, we will welcome it. So pick your battles around "no."

Sometimes you can be playful about negativity, or you can turn it into a problem-solving situation: "Well if everything is 'no,' then what are we going to do?" Approach it as an opportunity to have a debate, a longer conversation in which you get to the level of reasons. After you give the child a chance to tell you why he doesn't want to do something, you can empathize with him and then soothingly let him know, "Well, honey, we have to do it now." If children are anxious in a particular situation, or if they are prone to anxiety in general, then they may not like surprises and may become very controlling, and use "no" to handle their anxiety. Then you can be playful: "OK, yes sir, yes general!" and offer lots of support and coax him into it, if it is crucial that he do something.

You can even give the child an award for being the best "No" person or the best "I can't do it" person in the whole wide world. There is nothing better for a child than to be the best at something, and even to be the best at "No" or "I can't" is still terrific. As you help a child characterize what she is doing in a fun way like this ("You are the best 'no' guy in the world!"), if she can understand that, it takes the edge off and turns the interaction from being a hostile power struggle into a warm and fun game. Once you've changed the tone, you can play with the child a bit: if her favorite thing is a chocolate chip cookie, you can say, "Gee, would you like a chocolate chip cookie? Yes or no, but remember you are the 'no' person and you're only allowed to say 'no.'" And now he is in a dilemma, and you have a little twinkle in your eye. The key is to counter negativism with soothing warmth and lots of interaction, even around the negativism itself.

Problems as Opportunities

The key is to think of the problematic behavior as an opportunity to build strengths. We want to ask ourselves not just how to change the behavior, but what missing piece can be built into the child's developmental foundations so he won't need to act that way. For example, the child who has a tantrum when confronted with transitions may not yet have the flexibility to deal with rapid change in his environment. Typically, children who don't handle transitions well have trouble with maintaining a flow of back-and-forth gesturing, so they tend to have a fragmented pattern of relating to others. Instead of using gestures in a continuous way to negotiate a transition, they fall victim to the tantrum. (We discuss tantrums, or meltdowns, in Chapter 27.) Therefore, in these cases we often have to work in basic Floortime on developing long chains of interaction, helping the child to anticipate and master transitions through communicating his needs ("Slow down—I need to adjust to the noise in this room") through gestures. As he masters this missing foundation piece, he also becomes more able to deal with change and won't need to have as many tantrums.

Chapter 26

Coping with Feelings

Six-year-old Tara, diagnosed with Asperger's Syndrome, had a hard time dealing with negative emotions. She would get particularly upset if she, or anyone she cared about, cried, and would try to resist crying even if she hurt herself. She also couldn't stand to watch movies or hear stories in which anything upsetting happened to the main characters, and tended to get angry instead of letting herself be sad. Her parents wondered how they could use Floortime to help Tara deal with sadness.

How do we help children with ASD become aware of and learn to deal with feelings, especially strong feelings, in a constructive and helpful way? There are a number of steps to becoming more familiar with one's feelings; being able to label, identify, and discuss them; and most important, being able to use feelings as a tool in social interaction (that is, reading and responding to other people's feelings) and avoiding getting overwhelmed by and acting out feelings, especially "negative" ones such as anger, sadness, despair, worry, and fear. These intense feelings are difficult for children with ASD to deal with, and they need constructive ways of coping with them.

Observing children with ASD, we see some two-year-olds who, when they want to be close, can only come up and hug you, while others can flirt, smile, and make cute little sounds to woo you. Some toddlers can only hit or bite when they are angry, while others can indicate their anger with a stern voice or a hand gesture. They can negotiate by pointing to what they want and making angry movements indicating that they better get it now, and you can negotiate with them by indicating that they have to wait a bit.

This ability to signal feelings—rather than just expressing them as catastrophic and overwhelming events that take over one's whole body, such as by biting, hitting, or becoming self-absorbed and withdrawing—is the first step in coping with feelings. Once we have helped the child master this first stage, she is ready for a second stage in understanding and coping with feelings—applying words, symbols, or pretend sequences to the feeling during play. For example, dolls can hit or hug each other, and the mommy doll can ask the baby doll, "What made you mad?" or "What do you want?" Now the child has a higher-level way of expressing and coping with the feeling. If the child is angry with another child, she can satisfy some of the anger by having one doll hit another doll.

Anger

Many parents worry that if they playact a feeling—such as aggression—with their child, the pretending will actually encourage more aggression. But nothing could be further from the truth, because if you don't help the child use imagination or words to express the feeling, he is left only with acting it out. The feeling is there; anger and fear are a part of life just as love, curiosity, and other warm feelings are. When the child can translate these feelings into ideas, he doesn't have to express them through behavior or to inhibit them, which would result in tension, anxiety, and compulsiveness.

Therefore, expressing a feeling in play—particularly a strong negative feeling—is helpful. However, there is a difference between a child just repetitively hitting a doll, breaking its legs off, or using it for destructive action, and the child creating a make-believe scenario in which the doll is angry because some other doll took its toy. When the child is just hitting or breaking the doll, he isn't pretending; he's just using the doll in a direct expression of aggression, as if he were hitting another person or breaking a plate. The child is still operating in the all-or-nothing mode.

Acting out a drama of aggression might mean inventing a story in which someone takes the child's toy and the child is angry but then the two make up. Or a drama in which the mommy doll isn't paying attention to the baby doll and the baby doll gets mad, and then something else happens. Real make-believe involves creating a story with increasing depth and detail. So if the child is only repetitively acting out a feeling, help him develop more depth and complexity by giving the characters reasons for what they do.

You don't have to make the story nice. If the child is playing out a scene in which two soldiers are battling or two teachers are arguing, don't try to change the content, but deepen it. Ask, "Why are they arguing?" "What happens next?" If you do that empathetically, the child will eventually come around to playing out other feelings besides anger—warmth, love, or cooperation. If you just try to change the drama and say, "Aren't they going to be nice to each other?" or "Let's fix the little doll whose leg is broken," then you are controlling the drama and it's not coming from the child. True pretend play means you follow the child's lead, helping her to deepen and thicken the plot, and she will eventually create emotional balance and range.

We want to help children experiment with aggression in pretend play and get comfortable with it, because this is how they become healthily assertive. At the same time, we want to keep the aggression regulated and modulated with character development. If the child's doll is mad at your doll and wants to belt it on the nose, ask, "Why do you want to hit me? What did I do to you?" If the child starts banging the dolls or becomes more physically aggressive, slow down the action. Make your voice mellow and soothing; while continuing with the aggressive theme, move to a more regulating emotional tone.

After the child learns to pretend and can answer "why" questions, you can have reality-based conversations in which you can help the child explore and label his feelings. "Did you enjoy playing with Johnny?" you may ask, or, "When Mary took your toy, how did you feel?" If the child shares that he felt happy or felt angry, you can ask follow-up questions, such as, "Gee, what did you do when you felt so angry?" As the child describes the feeling and describes what he did as a result, he learns to connect a feeling with the behavior that follows it. Simply being curious about the child's day and his feelings and behavior helps the child to develop the ability to express and cope with feelings. We often overlook the value of simple chitchat—conversation that can occur in the car, in the bathtub, during dinner, and so forth. Children love this kind of conversation if you're interested in their life, as long as you aren't controlling the talk or asking factual questions about schoolwork.

Beyond the ability to hold reality-based conversations lies a higher level of expressing and coping with feelings. At this level we can play the Thinking About Tomorrow game, in which we help the child anticipate feelings that might occur the next day. In this way, the child prepares for what's going to happen, so he's not surprised by it. This is a great technique for children who are having trouble with certain feelings, who tend to get sad or behave aggressively at school, or who get too excited and shout out answers before other children, or push or shove other children in their excitement.

To play this game, we extend the reality-based conversations by saying, "Gee, let's think about what's going to happen tomorrow. Can you tell me about some good things that are going to happen, or things that you are going to like?" Let the child talk about something enjoyable and then ask, "Is anything going to happen later today or tomorrow that might be hard, that might be something that you wish wouldn't happen?" Maybe the child will say that she hopes that her brother won't bully her, or that the teacher won't give a test, or that the noise won't be too loud in the classroom.

If she can't come up with something, you can suggest possibilities. For example, "Yesterday you told me that your teacher didn't give you enough of a snack during snack time. Do you think that will happen again?" or, "Yesterday you told me about the child on the playground who wouldn't let you play with his ball," and so forth. The goal is to help the child anticipate a challenging situation. Once you find something, and the child can describe it a little bit—even with your help—see if she can actually picture it as if it's a TV show. Sometimes children need to close their eyes to do this; other times they can do it with their eyes open. Some children want to draw it with crayons or with pencils and pens. Other children want to playact it. Whatever the medium, help the child describe how she feels in that situation. See if you can help her to become a poet of her feelings, to describe them in detail and depth.

Thus if the child says, "I was just mad," you can ask, "Well, what did that feel like, that mad feeling?" Use the child's exact words—don't translate it into "anger" or something else. Ask, "What did that mad feeling feel like inside?" "Well, I just got mad." "Try to describe it. We all get mad in different ways; what did it feel like for you?" And eventually the child might say, "Well, my muscles were tense," or, "I felt like I wanted to hit," or, "My stomach hurt," or, "I felt like I was going to explode." The better and the richer the description, the more the child learns to use words to describe the feeling—whether anger, love, or fear—the better understanding the child will have of his own feelings. Some children describe feelings only in action words like, "I wanted to hit." Others describe feelings in terms of their quality: "Well, I was just very, very, very angry. It felt like I was, you know, mad and furious." Still other children may describe the consequences or the scene that happens around the feeling. Don't worry about how the child describes it; just get him to describe it more richly.

Also, help the child to describe how he thinks the other person involved in the situation will feel. Let's say the child is having a conflict with another child over who gets to use the computer. You can ask, "Well, what do you think Sally is feeling when you two are fighting?" This is the beginning of teaching a child to be empathetic. Or if the child describes a situation in which he is mad at Mommy (you), after he describes his own feelings, you can ask, "Well, how do you think Mommy feels when you want her to pay attention to you but she also needs to pay attention to your little brother?" Don't say how Mommy really feels, just find out how the child thinks Mommy feels. And you can ask Socratic questions, such as "Well, is that the only way you think Mommy might feel? What about other possibilities?"

Once the child has described his own feelings and the other person's feelings, then ask him to describe what he usually does when those feelings arise—the typical behavior associated with that feeling. The child may say that he pushes, shoves, runs away, hides in his room, and so forth. Then help the child explore why he tends to do that—that is, he might run off because he doesn't want to fight, or may tend to push and shove because he "doesn't want anybody to get the best of me."

Next, explore what else the child might do when he's in that situation or has that feeling. What are the other possibilities? How else might he cope with the feeling? You don't have to get the child to promise to do it, and we don't want children to copy a pat phrase. We hear too many children say, "I know I should use my words instead of hitting," but it's just what they've been told to say; they aren't really convinced of it. Then they go back the next day and hit another child. Often a child says to us something like "When Johnny bullies me on the playground, I know I should just walk away," but the child has a mischievous grin on his face. So one of us says, "Well, you don't seem convinced that that's the best thing to do." Then the child says, "Well, no—if I do that the other children will make fun of me and say I'm a wimp, so I can't do that. But that's what my parents want me to say, so I say it." So you have to help the child brainstorm about what other alternatives might work for him given his picture of the social context.

If the child doesn't come up with any good alternatives, ask for more: "What else could you do? There must be something you can do that won't get you into trouble or force you to leave." Keep brainstorming until she comes up with a good idea that she finds workable, and then you can say, "That sounds like a good idea." She probably won't implement that idea the first time the situation happens again, but just raising it as a possibility gets it in her mind. If the child is having a particularly difficult time, and you have had lengthy discussions in which she understands her feelings and routine behavior and has pictured alternatives, then you can guide her by offering some positive consequences for electing to use one of the good alternatives rather than responding in her usual way.

If the situation is not about aggressive behavior but one in which the child needs better strategies for coping with fear, anxiety, or sadness, the alternative behavior itself may be its own reward for the child. For example, if a child gets fearful and anxious around other children, help him identify some children he can play with who don't make him scared. Or identify a teacher or helper at school who is comforting. Also, work on ways for the child to calm himself. Similarly, with sad feelings, help the child identify what's causing the sadness and steps he can take to feel better. Perhaps he feels sad when his parents don't have much time for him. How can he let his parents know that he wants some of their time? Maybe he has to communicate a little more forcefully that they need to look up from the computer or the newspaper. While all children want their parents to recognize when they're sad and need a little more nurturing, it's very helpful for children to learn to assert and express themselves. If the parents respond when the child is a little more assertive, then the child really feels that he can do something about the sad feelings—he doesn't have to feel so helpless.

The Thinking About Tomorrow game—which builds on the ability to regulate emotions, to playact them, and talk about them realistically— not only teaches the child to cope with feelings but also develops his language, cognitive, and social skills, as well as his capacity to use interactions with family members and with peers in increasingly healthy ways. Obviously, for children with severe language and relationship problems, making each of these steps—from learning to interact with emotional signals, to using pretend play, to having reality conversations, to playing the Thinking About Tomorrow game—represents enormous progress. As children get better at coping with and expressing their feelings, the process becomes self-reinforcing. It won't happen overnight—it may take many years—but this is the kind of progress we can encourage.

Using pictures or symbols can help nonverbal children express feelings. Many computer-based and augmentative communication strategies can also help to promote children's abilities to express their feelings constructively. What is important when using these tools is not to be satisfied with an all-or-nothing label. Encourage the child to describe the quality of the feeling by asking questions such as, How angry are you? How sad are you? How excited are you? And don't just make it an exercise at a table; help the child use the picture, the symbol, or the electronic device to express the feeling when she is actually having it—then it's just like using words.

As the child does that, use your own emotional expressions—vocal tone, facial expressions, and body posture—to help the child express the quality of the emotion through her own emotional expressions, even if she has to use the electronic device to say the word. When individuals with hearing difficulties use sign language, there is great emotional expressiveness. For example, the sign for "I'm annoyed" can be done gently, indicating a little annoyance, or with an angry move of the hand, indicating extreme annoyance. Similarly, when the child is using augmentative modes, encourage her to be as expressive as possible by being animated in your responses.

Anxiety

For some children with ASD, particularly those who overreact to sensation, the problem is that they are anxious and fearful and always thinking about the worst things that can happen. They get easily overloaded by their own awareness and are very reactive to their own emotions. Their need for certainty is an attempt to regulate that feeling of being overwhelmed.

To begin with, we want to help children with this pattern to become calmer and more regulated through self-calming activities such as relaxing their muscles, deep breathing, and picturing comforting images. It's also important for the home environment to be soothing. The more anxious and scared the child is, the more comforting the parents and the environment should be. If the child is verbal, ask for his input: "What can we do or plan tomorrow to make the day more enjoyable, so that you're less scared?" The idea is to negotiate a comforting rhythm. At the same time, because these children are so focused on details, they may not be very good big-picture thinkers. The Thinking About Tomorrow game is especially useful in developing big-picture thinking.

Also, children who worry easily often are less comfortable with the aggressive side of life; angry feelings are harder for them because they're scary. You can encourage them to be more comfortable with these feelings and to reduce their fears by talking about situations that annoy or upset them. If a teacher punishes the child, and the child thinks the teacher was being unfair, you can ask, "Gee, what are you feeling? I know you wouldn't do it, but if you were the king of the world, what would you like to do to get even with your teacher?" Children, especially if they're verbal, will understand the difference between this kind of fantasy talk and actually planning an action and will become more at ease with their angry feelings.

Fear of Feelings

Like Tara, the little girl in the case study above, many children with ASD and other developmental disorders tend to be scared of feelings, such as sadness, because their feelings overwhelm them and then they get embarrassed at being out of control. In this situation, we want to help the child feel accepted for his feelings. As we remain engaged, soothing, and accepting, the child learns to relax a bit more with feelings. Then, encourage the child to describe his feelings in more detail, through pretend play and conversation. So if the child says, "Oh, I don't want to cry," you can ask, "You don't? What does it feel like when you don't want to cry? It must be hard to try to stop crying when your body wants to cry." In other words, empathize with the child's attempt to contain the feeling and help him become better at describing the conflict he is having. As you do this, make sure you are continuing to regulate and soothe the child and stay in emotional contact.

The next critical step, as with children who are anxious, is to help the child become more comfortable with assertiveness. Many children who say they don't want to cry or don't want to be sad haven't yet gotten comfortable with the assertive side of life, which includes coping with aggression and anger. We want to help the child participate in constructive actions, getting ideas from him and encouraging him to assert himself: "Gee, what can we do to help you feel better?"

At the same time, look for opportunities in pretend play to help the child express and cope with angry and aggressive feelings. Children with developmental challenges may be particularly scared of aggression because, if they have motor challenges, for example, they may be less confident that they can control their anger, or if they have language challenges, they can't express everything they'd like to. Even the fear of crying or of showing feelings can underlie their fear of angry feelings that get out of control. So encourage the child to play out anger with dolls: if he indicates that the dolly is angry, well, what does the doll feel like doing? Also, pay attention to how you typically interact with him: if the child gets a little assertive, do you tend to quash the attempt or insist that he be "nice"? Or do you welcome debate in which the child can express his opinions strongly? While we don't want the child to use bad words or be disrespectful, we want him to feel confident in expressing his thoughts and feelings strongly in a healthy debate. Provide practice for regulated assertiveness.

Emotional Range and Balance

Emotional range and balance are two vital capacities for healthy functioning that are not easy to achieve together. When we talk about children or adults being healthy, we usually mean people who show a broad range of human emotion, can regulate and control those emotions, and can regroup if they lose their equilibrium—people who are "balanced." How do we promote and support emotional range and balance in children with ASD?

The first principle is that caregivers should accept all the different emotions from the child's earliest infancy. In other words, don't assume that certain emotions are good and other emotions are bad; this is the way constrictions get established. If a caregiver believes that children should never show assertiveness or anger and be only compliant and sweet, the child will become either impulsively angry all the time or passive and cautious. Similarly, if a caregiver has the idea that children shouldn't cry or be scared, the child will only become more scared and anxious and less likely to work out his fears. If the caregiver feels that children shouldn't be needy or dependent, important components of intimacy may be quashed, and the child may actually become needier or deny his neediness and manifest pseudoindependence, rather than real self-sufficiency.

Therefore, we need to be accepting of all the emotions. If you have a toddler experimenting with assertiveness, enjoy that assertive interaction and work with the child. If she is pointing to a toy up on the shelf and assertively trying to climb up on a table to get it, instead of taking her down and saying, "No!" ask, "How can I help you?" Interact with her, encouraging her to signal to you with gestures that she wants to be picked up. Then pick her up so she can reach for the toy. That way assertiveness becomes a safe, collaborative effort, not a rebellion that has to be put down. The key is to accept the emotion, then engage it and interact with the child around it.

That takes us to the second general principle: Provide structure and guidance so the child doesn't get overwhelmed by his emotions. We want to engage the emotions not in a way that overstimulates or scares the child, but in a regulated way with inherent limits. To go back to the example of the child who wants to climb up on a dangerous table to get a toy, we help the child do that in a safe and secure way. If the child is trying to do something that is beyond his ability and is dangerous, we set a limit—even if it means that the child gets temporarily frustrated.

Let's say a child wants a hug. Of course you hug him and exchange a lot of warm words and gestures. But if he wants to keep on hugging while you're trying to make dinner, and is becoming a nuisance and wants all the attention for himself, then you may have to sit him on the counter so he can be near you while you work, giving him an occasional kiss between tasks. You thus find a compromise centered on that same emotion of joyful intimacy, letting the child be close to you but also setting limits on his exuberance. In this way he learns regulation through the exchange of emotional signals, and later through the exchange of words as well as gestures. (Many children with ASD require interacting on the level of gestures as well as at the level of words, even after they are verbal. We don't want to lose the exchange of gestures as part of our engagement and regulation of all the emotions.)

Another general principle in helping a child to develop emotional range and balance is to know both his unique profile and your own. For example, children who overreact to sensation are generally scared by loud, assertive voices or too much roughhousing, whereas children who underreact to sensation may crave these kinds of experiences but have a harder time experiencing sadness without feeling aggressive and, therefore, getting out of control. So for a child who is more cautious because of sensory overreactivity, you'll need to help her broaden her range of assertiveness gradually, in a secure way. She may not want to play a vigorous ball game right away; instead you can start with a gentle patty-cake game; over several months, this may lead to a little wrestling match. Similarly, a rough-and-tumble child may have a harder time relaxing and getting comfortable with closeness. You may have to begin by running with him while holding hands and then downshifting to some rhythmic activity that is a little quieter, until eventually you are just lying on the floor together giving each other back rubs. So each child needs to be drawn into the full range of emotions through his or her own window of individual differences.

Meanwhile, you have to pay attention to your own profile. You may not have special challenges in the way you process sensations, but you may have differences in your emotional makeup based on how you were brought up. Some caregivers are comfortable with being warm and intimate but not with showing "ugly" emotions such as anger; whereas others feel awkward being gentle or "needy" and are prone to loud debating and playing rougher games. Ask yourself which emotions you feel comfortable with and which are more difficult for you. Often, parents and children can learn to experience new emotions together as they move up the developmental ladder. We have seen many parents experience deep levels of intimacy and empathy for the first time in their lives with their children, and new levels of assertiveness because their children are learning to be assertive and they realize they need to get more comfortable with it too.

Chapter 27

Meltdowns and Regressions

A meltdown is, technically, the process of being completely disregulated by one's feelings. How do we help the child who is on the floor, yelling and maybe banging his head, or trying to hit or bite Mommy or Daddy, or running around crying uncontrollably—especially if he is a child with ASD whose limited language makes it difficult to talk him through the episode?

Even more challenging is figuring out why a child is experiencing a regression in which he is more self-absorbed or impulsive or less communicative than he was earlier. First let's look at meltdowns.

First Steps

The key principle when a child is in the middle of a meltdown is actually very simple, yet it is often not followed: focus on helping the child calm down. This is not the time to lecture the child on why he is responsible for the situation because he ate all that candy or took a toy from his sister. This is also not the time to yell. Sometimes the child's meltdown leads to a contagion of meltdowns: parents try the calm approach for about two seconds; then, since they are tired and hungry and have just come home from work and are stressed out, they too melt down. Or Daddy sees Mommy yelling at his little boy, so he starts yelling at Mommy for making it worse. Then, if there is a sibling in the family, she sees everyone yelling and screaming, and she gets scared and starts crying. Now we have a four-party meltdown. This may sound absurd, but it is not untypical. *So let there be only one meltdown at a time.*

When a child is having a meltdown, just assume (because it is true) that she can't hear you, can't understand what you are saying, and is feeling out of control. Everyone feels badly about losing control. Don't try to punish the child or set limits in the middle of the meltdown. That just adds fuel to the fire. This doesn't mean that you let her get away with having bitten her brother or having hit you. It just means that the sanctions and the limit-setting will come after everyone has settled down. There will be plenty of time to talk about it and to have consequences—but not at the moment of the meltdown.

Another common mistake is ignoring the meltdown. Some people have the idea that this prevents "rewarding" the child for having the meltdown, but it is an overly simplistic, deplorable strategy. For many children with ASD, the challenge is to get them more engaged in relationships. The best way to solidify the child's sense of trust and intimacy is to show that you are available to help him when he feels overwhelmed. So we don't want to turn our backs on children who are having meltdowns. Extinguishing the tantrum is a small goal compared to convincing the child that he is loved and that he can rely on you.

In no instance is it appropriate to shut the child in his room and give him the message that you're not willing to be there with him while he's upset. However, at certain times, the best way to calm a child might be to diminish the sensory input and give him a little space—maybe staying across the room so he doesn't have to look at you. For each child, we figure out what is going to help him calm down. For some children, it is rhythmic rocking and a calm, soothing voice. For other children, it may be just talking them through it with your voice. Even if they can't understand your words, just calmly repeating "It's OK, we can calm down, sweetheart" and giving them a couple feet of space will help them settle down. Other children might do better if you mostly keep quiet and just occasionally nod your head and say, "I know it's hard; let's settle down."

As we discussed in Chapter 25, if the child is trying to hurt someone, you may have to contain him with a firm bear hug from the back and apply firm pressure until he settles down a little bit, so he doesn't hurt himself or anyone else. It's important to keep children safe while they are having meltdowns. This is more difficult as they get older. Seven- or eight-year-olds can be quite strong, and teenagers are even stronger. (For teachers who are confronted with kids having meltdowns at school, if the children are big and can be aggressive during a meltdown, and you are not a very big person, there needs to be a big strong person available—someone who can be both gentle and firm with an aggressive child. Just the presence of that person keeps everyone feeling secure. He or she might be a volunteer, aide, or teacher who has some training in how to deal with these situations.)

If the child is upset because she is being denied something, the key is not to give in necessarily, although negotiation, discussion, and compromise are always options before the tantrum starts. Rather, the protocol is "Let's calm down and then we'll talk about it." We believe in free speech. There should be no punishments for crying, yelling, or screaming, because after all, we are trying to help children with ASD to be communicative and express emotion. But the line is crossed if children try to hurt themselves, hurt others, or break things. Then, eventually, there should be a penalty associated with the behavior, but the first critical step is to help the child calm down.

After the child calms down, the penalty should be introduced, whether it is loss of an activity or TV privileges (which should be minimal anyhow for children with ASD), assignment to the extra cleanup crew, a time-out, or whatever you think appropriate. The only no-no for the sanctions is isolation. (See Chapter 25 for a more in-depth discussion of limit-setting and sanctions.)

Warning Signs of Meltdowns

Some parents tell me that meltdowns come out of nowhere. However, most kids build up to them gradually, and if we spot the warning signs, we can help a child get regulated before the critical point. The signs may be subtle—a tightening of the child's jaw, a different look in his eyes, a change in body posture or vocal tone. Or there may be a particular situation that tends to bring on a meltdown, such as not winning a game or another child taking his toy.

If you see a meltdown beginning, if you see the child escalating from zero, to twenty, to thirty, and you know he gets overloaded at sixty, intervene at the first sign of buildup. The way to intervene is to alert the child to what is happening in a soothing voice: "Sweetheart, I can see you are getting a little upset." Or shift the activity to something more regulating and soothing. Or if the child needs to win the game, say (if he's verbal), "Do you really want to win? What do we need to do so you can win the game?" Let him know you're on his side. For the child who is not yet fully logical, you can create your own imaginative game out of a real game, as long as you are explicit about what the new rules are. If the child keeps changing the rules so he can win, you can joke about it: "Oh, I see: we're not playing 'throw the ball in the basket,' we're playing 'Johnny gets a point every time he throws, but I have to get the ball in the basket to get a point.'" That will usually make the child smile. You're making the rules explicit and acknowledging the child's fundamental desire to win. Don't worry that he's not getting a realistic picture of how games work; the important thing is that he is learning how to communicate, how to identify his own wishes, and how to be logical. These are the tools he will need to eventually adapt to reality and play real games.

If the child is preverbal, you can use gestures to show that you understand what she wants to do and to redirect her attention to an activity that is more soothing and regulating. If the child is overstimulating herself by running round and round, you can introduce a slower, more rhythmic movement pattern, such as dancing to slow music or gently tossing a ball back and forth.

Warding Off a Meltdown

Rather than thinking of a tantrum or meltdown as bad or manipulative behavior on the part of the child with ASD, we see it as an indication of real helplessness. The child is feeling so disorganized that all she can do is kick, scream, or sob. The fact is, young children don't have a lot of control over life. And they aren't always able to understand why they can't do what they want to do, or have to do things they don't want to do.

How do we help a child deal with all the inevitable no's when he is not yet equipped developmentally to understand the reasons behind them? An important point is that you don't always have to say "no" right away, even if ultimately the answer will be "no." Many tantrums are triggered by children realizing they're not going to be able to do what they want to do. You know you aren't going to get to the park, you know you aren't going to give the child the candy bar, you know you aren't going to let him delay going to bed forever; but you can give the child a chance to vote, and this can be a good strategy to pre-empt meltdowns that come from feeling helpless.

Let your child express her fantasy or wish. There is no rush to say "no" unless, of course, there is some immediate danger. Find out why the child wants what she wants: "Oh, you want to go to the park? What are you going to do there? Are you going to go on the swing or the slide first? Who are you going to see in the park? When you go, do you want to take bubbles or balls?" Just a chance to talk about what she wants can be soothing to a child. If you encourage the child to have ideas, to make a plan, she feels as though you understand her, and trusts that she will get to go there eventually ("We'll go there after we finish our errands") and may be able to tolerate some of the frustration and delays that often cause tantrums.

If the child is preverbal, one often helpful strategy is to draw the things he wants to do. Little sketches of the swing set or slide can, if accompanied by your supportive, soothing voice, help him handle the delay. If he's anxious about a new, unknown situation, drawings can help him deal with his anxiety.

In our DIR/Floortime model the tantrum, like any other behavior, should be used as a basis for improving communication and negotiation. Rather than always saying "No"—which cuts off communication—we want to help the child master shared problem-solving. For example, if the child is trying to open the door to go outside, rather than saying,

"No, it's raining," and risking a tantrum, you could ask, "Do you want to open the door and go out?" If the child nods his head, you could say, "Let's look out the window and you can show me what you want to do." At the window, you can point and show him that it's raining. You can open the window, put your hand out, and invite the child to put his hand out and feel the water, and explain, "It's raining, you see, we'll all get wet." You might even let him step outside for a minute and get a bit wet. If he still wants to go out and play ball, maybe you can offer to play with a Nerf ball inside, and say, "Let's do this now and then later we can go outside." So instead of saying "No," you try to preempt the meltdown by negotiating and compromise. Sometimes it doesn't work. But ultimately, the long-term solution to tantrums or meltdowns is improving the child's ability to communicate and solve problems with you.

If you finally have to say "No," at that point the child may have a little meltdown. So be it. The child would have had a meltdown ten minutes ago anyhow, and the meltdown will be significantly less severe after you've had a complete exchange, because at least the child knows he's been understood. You knew what he wanted, and you're trying your best to explain to him why that wish can't be met at the moment.

You won't always be in a situation that lends itself to talking to the child right away after a meltdown. In cases where you're not, if the child is verbal, often it's worth coming back to the event later on, and saying something like "Wow, we had a hard time today" or "I was thinking about what happened this morning." You can revisit the experience and help the child explore what happened and how she can solve a similar problem in the future.

Factors That May Contribute to Meltdowns and Regressions

This section looks at regressions and meltdowns together because the same possible contributing factors need to be considered. Determining the contributing factors to both requires a systematic approach. Obvious factors include conflicts and overstimulation of the child by too much activity and various physical and emotional changes.

There are other, less obvious reasons. For example, some children are very sensitive to chemicals, such as those in some new polyurethane floor covering and in fresh paint. Adults may just get headaches or a bit irritable when exposed to a strong chemical, but a sensitive child can get more reactive to emotional stresses that he could ordinarily handle. Changes in diet and nutrition can also be a factor; for example, when a child goes to more than one birthday party over a few days and gets more sugar or more chemicals in his food than usual. Some children are highly sensitive to sugar—or more precisely, to the change in adrenaline levels caused by an infusion of glucose into the bloodstream. Eating a lot of fast food, as when the family is traveling, can pose a problem because fast food contains preservatives and other chemicals. Changes in the child's environment (stronger lighting, increased noise levels in the neighborhood) or seasonal changes or allergies can affect him. Do an inventory of each of the child's senses and consider if there has been any change in what the child is taking in.

Medication can also be a factor; if the child is on antibiotics, the sugar and chemicals in the liquid can cause disregulation. Sometimes the illness itself—a particular bacteria or virus, or a nonsymptomatic strep throat (a blood test for antibodies can identify this)—may lead to disregulation. Updating the child's biomedical evaluation can be helpful if she is having more frequent meltdowns, or a regression, with no discernible cause. Some children have subtle irregularities that can only be picked up in an extended-sleep EEG.

Also, changing family dynamics, both dramatic (a death in the family, a new baby) and subtle (a visit from relatives, parents under stress at work), can of course be factors. Another very frequent cause of difficulties is a change in the school environment. For example, the school days may be getting longer, or a bully may be harassing the child, or perhaps a favorite aide has left. A child who tends to get overloaded by noise or visual stimulation and melts down as the morning or day goes on may need to go for a walk with an aide every hour or so for a sensory break. Certain sensory activities, such as games involving jumping or throwing, played for fifteen minutes out of every hour, can also help children regulate. If these solutions aren't sufficient, you may decide that the child should have a shorter school day for a while. Of course, all of the chemical factors that can be problems at home need to be considered at school.

Identifying contributing factors has implications, obviously, for prevention. The key is to set up an environment in which the child does not feel overwhelmed. Parents may ask, "Doesn't my child have to learn to deal with all environments?" Yes, eventually. As a child becomes capable of gestural signaling and language, he can alert a parent or caregiver when the environment is getting too overwhelming for him. This allows him to be exposed to a broader range of experiences. As he becomes highly verbal and reflective and can talk about his feelings and anticipate his reactions, he can adjust to even more challenging situations. But in the short run, we want to try to prevent overload for a child with a sensitive system.

In addition to identifying and changing contributing factors, perhaps most important when confronting frequent meltdowns or a regression is to *go back to the basics*. The child may be feeling not only overwhelmed but also lost. He may be experiencing a decreased sense of where he is in *physical space* (cannot picture Mom in the next room), in *time* (when will he get to go home?), and in *organized thought* (a lot of fragmented ideas rather than logical patterns). The child feels more lost and more anxious, and the pattern cycles. The key is to help the child reestablish his security by working on the basics. This means more time in calm, regulated interactions that emphasize engagement, two-way exchange of gestures, problem-solving interactions, and so forth—up to the highest level the child can mobilize. It may be necessary to shorten the school day, increase Floortime, monitor interactions with siblings more closely, or explore biomedical factors. A child under stress may often have more meltdowns and tend to regress. As contributing factors are explored, it is wise to go back to the basics.

Chapter 28

Developing Social Skills

Will, a bright ten-year-old diagnosed with Asperger's Syndrome, was integrated into a regular classroom, where he was doing well academically but was having trouble making friends. Although his parents were able to engage him during Floortime, Will's tendency was to retreat into his books, videos, or computer games. His parents hated to see their son's loneliness and wanted to help him develop the ability to make friends with his peers.

Children with ASD and other special needs very often have a hard time when more advanced social skills are required. By fourth, fifth, or sixth grade, even if they've made remarkable progress up until that point in language and academic skills, many of these children start having significant difficulties. Many people assume that this is the nature of ASD, that even "high functioning" children with ASD will always face this problem. But, as we have shown in earlier chapters, this is not the case. There is a subgroup of children with ASD who can develop high levels of social skills—empathizing with others, reading emotional signals, negotiating with peers—and can even become gifted in this arena.

The fact that this is possible, even for a subgroup, changes the expectations for all children. Even children who move along more slowly because of greater neurological problems can make progress in the important areas—warmth, compassion, closeness with others—so that the social skills they do develop become more natural and meaningful, even though they may not be at age-expected levels. To think systematically about the development of social skills in autistic children, it helps to go through each of our six stages and the three advanced stages, and show how—as we help a child master each milestone—he or she simultaneously develops social skills.

Remember that in our DIR approach, we're not focusing on a particular behavior, such as looking at someone's face, saying, "Hello," or knowing how to answer the phone. Instead, we're focusing on helping such skills develop in the way they do in a child without challenges. No one teaches a typically developing child explicitly to say, "Hello." The child picks that up in his daily life. He hears his parents saying it. He feels a warm feeling when he sees someone, he's seen people who seem to have that same warm feeling say "hello," or use some other social greeting. The smile is natural when you feel warm and happy, so when Uncle Charlie—who's always fun to play with—comes over, two-year-old Ben gives Uncle Charlie a big smile, maybe a hug, and if he's verbal, maybe a "hi," and they're off and running and playing together. The behavior occurs naturally through interactive learning, a little imitation, and a lot of reciprocal use in social contexts.

Thus in typical development, emotion selects the behavior—the hug or the big smile—and then gives a word like "Hi" real warmth and real meaning. Therefore, the first principle is that for healthy social development, you have to build the foundations from the bottom up. You don't become an eight-year-old who can be out on the playground negotiating with three different children simultaneously—one of whom is making fun of you, another of whom is welcoming you to play soccer, and the third of whom is flirting with you—by learning specific behaviors. You've got to go back and learn things in the way they're ordinarily learned in healthy development.

If a child has ASD or another developmental problem, however, we have to create that typical learning pattern in a different way, by tailoring the interactions to the child's nervous system. We give the child much more practice, and we create heightened states of emotionality so as to help him use his emotions and connect them to his behavior. As the child moves up the developmental ladder, he automatically learns the appropriate behavior.

Attention

Whether a child is one month old or five years old, to see the faces, actions, and behavior of other people and hear the intonations in their voices (and thereby learn appropriate social skills), she must be calm, focused, and attentive and have an awareness of her physical sensations. With a five-year-old who hasn't fully mastered this stage, the basic principle is the same as with infants. In Floortime, parents encourage the child to look at them, to enjoy seeing their faces and hearing their voices. Again, start with the child's interest. If he is doing a puzzle, maybe his mother hides a piece in her hand so that the child focuses on her smiling face when he reaches for it, and has to pay attention to see which hand it is in. Now we have a moment of what our colleague Peter Mundy calls "joint attention," which is the ability to look at the toy and at the parent and act with both of them at the same time. The child is taking an emotional interest in the mother because she is a part of what he is trying to do.

Engagement

To be social, you've got to engage and be comfortable with others, to fall in love with the world of humans. That comes first with your caregivers. Again, Floortime play develops that pleasurable interaction. Now we're going beyond simple attention to encourage that gleam in the child's eye, the big smile. If the child is playing with toy soldiers, you might take soldiers and make them dance—something that may amuse the child. You want to become an enticing human plaything for her—maybe your leg is a mountain that the soldiers have to march up. Depending on the child's unique profile, you might give her more sound cues or more visual cues. Instead of interrupting or competing with the activity, you become part of it. If she's preoccupied with the computer, you might play a computer game with her, which makes it more fun.

Communication

Once children arrive at purposeful communication, they're starting to build social skills in the way they're normally considered. We've discussed in earlier chapters how to get those long chains of interaction going in which you and the child are exchanging gestures and sounds. Just as a parent does this back-and-forth babbling with a typical eight-month-old baby, we can do it with an autistic five-year-old who's not yet verbal. You're always encouraging the child's curiosity, interest, and persistence to see how many circles of interaction you can get without the child getting too frustrated or annoyed. You want it to be pleasurable, but with a little oomph.

Shared Problem-Solving

Shared problem-solving is the beginning of complex social negotiation. At this stage, we want to create interactions that mediate between the child and the satisfaction of his goal, for example, setting up obstacle courses that require the child to work with you to get the piece of candy he wants. You want to focus as much on nonverbal cues as on language, because mastery of social interactions depends on a subtle reading of emotional cues and signals. What distinguishes a "socially acceptable" eight-year-old from one who's not is the ability to read the subtle cues of other children, as opposed to not knowing when a joke has worked or not worked.

If a child can't do four to five dozen circles of gesturing in a row (with or without words) as part of a complex interaction, she is not yet ready to master complex social situations, because these situations require reading a series of emotional signals such as facial expression, voice intonation, body posture, and so forth. The meaning of the words is really the icing on the cake. Routinely, what we've found with older children who are quite verbal but are having social problems, even children who have never been diagnosed with autism, is that they lack full mastery of this level: they can't carry on a continuous exchange of subtle and complex emotional and social signals. So the child needs to work on it through long stretches of play with parents and then with peers, to give her a lot of practice in reading and responding to these signals.

You are your child's first friend and play partner. When you play with your child, it's very important to play like the kids you want your child to be playing with. You want to act and speak like a kid—"Hey, no, it's mine! What do you want? That's not fair!"—bringing that high level of affect that children have and using the social language a child would use. (If you need to communicate as a parent, you can switch to your parental voice.) This way, your child learns that interacting at this level is fun, that he can make his desires and thoughts known and can learn to get his way.

At dinnertime, the family can spend a few minutes not talking and see how much they communicate with their gestures. If someone wants something, he may point to it, indicate how much he wants, or object to someone else getting too much. Simply pantomiming, not talking, will help a child look at and pay attention to the other person.

Using Ideas Creatively and Spontaneously

To be socially competent, a child has got to use ideas in a special way. Simply scripting ideas and memorizing phrases is in many respects counterproductive. The more social difficulties the child has, the more we have to approach her through heightened pleasure and heightened opportunities for spontaneous interaction. Occasionally, some fundamentals can be taught in structured ways, such as doing oral motor work to help the child use more sounds, but this should be only a small part of the work. Otherwise, you may just be reinforcing a pathway that is already neurologically easier for the child, rather than building the new pathway that she needs. Social skills can't be learned from the top down. The approach has to be from the bottom up, no matter what the child's age.

Pretend play is a great vehicle for developing ideas and building language, and language is also built off the child's natural needs and desires. As described earlier, a lot of vocabulary can be built around helping the child figure out how to get an object of desire. In doing that, we're teaching a child to use ideas and words based on his emotions. As the child begins using ideas creatively, you start introducing four or more peer play dates a week in which the caregiver facilitates the two children playing with each other. Now the child is not only reading the other child's emotional and social gestures but also beginning to use words meaningfully: "My toy. No touch!" The words may seem negative or impolite, but the child is talking from the heart, and he's using language meaningfully. If he says, "Look over there," and takes a cookie behind your turned back, that's a good thing at this stage.

Later, he'll learn how to become more politic in order to work the playground, or the cocktail circuit when he's an adult, but first he has to be able to use language meaningfully. He can't use scripts. If he starts using scripts with his peers, they'll know something is different about him. Meaningful use of language is necessary for telling jokes; telling somebody you want them to come over to your house to play; laughing at a cartoon with someone; saying, "No, no, you've got to do it this way," when you're playing a game; and dealing with the teasing that all children experience.

As the child begins to have play dates, it's very important for the parent to be her mediator and partner. You could hold her hand as you're playing Red Light–Green Light with the other child, for example, so as to help the children stay connected as long as possible. One method that often helps is anticipating the play date with your child, asking her, "What are some things you may enjoy doing?" You can talk this over and even draw little pictures: "Oh, will you play on the swing?

Run in the sprinkler? Will you want a snack?" It doesn't matter if you ever do any of these things during the play date, because the principle really is to follow the spontaneous flow and interest. But if you get stuck or if it doesn't seem as if the kids are connecting, it may help to bring the child back to the ideas that she had before. Anticipating the play date also helps the child create the concept of a friend; even if the child is still preverbal, she can have the visual images of that friend. You can take pictures of the child doing things with her friend and create a little book, "My Friend, David," or "My Friend at School." Always have some kind of interaction represented in the pictures so it becomes a way to talk about what the child enjoyed with her friend and what she might like to do next time; it gives the child a way to look back at the experience as well as look forward to the next one.

Sometimes parents ask if, during the play dates, the children should always take turns in the play. Taking turns is an important social skill, and many games involve the custom, but if you always try to regulate the interaction through turn taking, it can really dampen the spontaneity and the child's ability to express what he feels. So rather than always taking turns—because you can do it forever and never really interact—try to think of ways the children can negotiate, such as by trading: "Hey, do you want this? What will you give me for it?" This will help the child to put himself in the other child's place. Sometimes they won't be able to work it out. It's very important to make sure children have support when, in fact, they and their friends disagree, or they just have to wait, or neither of them gets to the point where they actually do what they thought they wanted to do. Then you can encourage them to talk about their feelings and to understand the consequences of not recognizing what their friends want or not being understood by their friends.

Social groups for older kids to practice the meaningful use of language have to focus on natural, spontaneous conversation, even if that conversation at first seems awkward and maybe even off-color. Correcting the child and saying, "No, don't say that, say this" is completely the wrong thing to do. Instead, get any kind of conversation going, and then allow the child, through the interaction, through the facial expressions of the other person, to figure out what's bringing the other person pleasure and what's annoying him, what gets the response the child wants. Thus through trial and error and feedback, he begins learning how to socialize his language.

One kind of group experience that has built-in support and in which it's easy to heighten the emotion is drama: having a drama club, whether it's an actual drama class or just a play date with several children coming together and creating or playacting a story they all know. This approach works very well once children are sharing symbolic ideas. Another way to help children learn to read and respond to social signals is through games that are gestural—that don't even use language—such as charades or games you can buy such as *Kids on Stage* or *Step on It*.

Using Ideas Logically

Once a child can use ideas spontaneously and creatively, she can then start to use them more logically—answering "why" questions and connecting ideas together. Now a child can say to another child, "Come on, Nintendo is more fun than Monopoly; let's play Nintendo," or, "We'll play this first, and then we'll play your game." To get to this stage, the child has to practice connecting ideas together with caregivers and then in peer play dates. Learning to read the ideas of the other person, compare them to your ideas, and debate the ideas is part of the foundation of social negotiation. This can be practiced, for example, in a game of hide-and-seek: three children have to decide where to hide together, and you're going to find them, but they have to negotiate and help each other so they don't give themselves away.

An aspect of social skills is learning to follow rules. This has to be coupled with understanding the reasons for things—logical thinking— and feeling that you belong. So, for example, if the child wants to have dinner, he has to help set the table. It's important to encourage children to do this kind of "work," which is really just participating in the family's real-life experiences. They then begin to understand that there are rules and that they have to follow these rules if they're going to be members of society.

Higher Levels of Thinking

The gray-area, comparative, and multicausal thinking discussed in Chapter 10 is vital to dealing with what we call "playground politics"—knowing one's position in the larger social network. To negotiate at this stage, a child not only has to be able to communicate with other children using ideas creatively and spontaneously, and to read their non-verbal gestures, but also has to be able to size himself up vis-à-vis this complex larger group. This ability builds on all the foundations discussed above, so those have to be solid.

Finally, we aim for the advanced level of social skills we call thinking from an internal standard or thinking about thoughts, which—in typical development—we don't see until ages ten to twelve: "My friends want me to tease Charlie, but I think it's wrong, so I'm not going to do it, even if they give me a hard time for a while." This ability to evaluate her own thoughts, feelings, and behavior allows a child to negotiate more complex social situations and reflect on what she is doing. This stage also builds on all the previous ones.

As mentioned, when we give children with ASD multiple opportunities to practice social skills in a natural, spontaneous way, with heightened emotion and with fine-tuning to suit their nervous system, a subgroup of these children can master these higher levels. Children who can't quite master this highest level may still develop some social skills through this program. They can learn to be warm and engaging, read emotional signals, and flirt with their parents naturally and spontaneously, for example. They may still have some of the rigidities and some of what's often described as "social awkwardness," but these are in proportion to their biological and neurological challenges. They might be held back by cognitive and language difficulties, but they still can develop in a warm, spontaneous, and joyful way.

Appendix A

Outcome Studies of the DIR Model

Review of Two Hundred Cases of Children with Autistic
Spectrum Disorders Receiving the DIR/Floortime Approach

In this study (Greenspan and Wieder, 1997), we looked systematically at the cases of two hundred children whom we had seen for consultation or treatment over an eight-year period. The children had varying presenting impairments (see Table A.1), all diagnosed on the autistic spectrum by two or three other evaluation teams.

The children were treated with methods based on the developmental model described in this book. In reviewing the original diagnoses of these children and their subsequent progress over two to eight years after the start of intervention, we divided the children into groups as indicated in Table A.2.

The "good to outstanding" group did better than any current prognosis for children with autistic spectrum diagnoses would have predicted. After two or more years of intervention, these children became warm and interactive, relating joyfully with appropriate, reciprocal preverbal gestures; could engage in lengthy, well-organized, and purposeful social problem-solving and share attention on various social, cognitive, or motor-based tasks; used symbols and words creatively and logically, based on their intent and desires, rather than using rote sequences; and progressed to high levels of thinking, including making inferences and experiencing empathy. Some children in this group developed precocious academic abilities two or three grade levels above their ages.

They all mastered basic capacities such as reality testing, impulse control, organization of thoughts and emotions, differentiated sense of self, and ability to experience a range of emotions, thoughts, and concerns. Finally, they no longer showed symptoms such as self-absorption, avoidance, self-stimulation, or perseveration. On the Childhood Autism Rating Scale (CARS), they shifted into the nonautistic range, although some still evidenced auditory or

Table A.1 Presenting Conditions of Two Hundred Cases of Children with Autistic Spectrum Disorders

Functional Developmental Component	% of Patients with Mild to Severe Impairment	Description of Functional Developmental Component
Presenting functional, emotional, developmental level	24	Partially engaged and purposeful with limited use of symbols (ideas)
	40	Partially engaged with limited complex problem-solving interactive sequences (half of this group evidenced only simple purposeful behavior)
	31	Partially engaged with only fleeting purposeful behavior
	5	No affective engagement
Sensory modulation	19	Overreactive to sensation
	39	Underreactive to sensation (with 11% craving sensation)
	36	Mixed reactivity to sensation
	6	Not classified
Motor planning dysfunction Low muscle tone	52	Mild to moderate motor planning dysfunction
	48	Severe motor planning dysfunction
	17	Motor planning dysfunction with significant degree of low muscle tone
Visual-spatial processing toys, dysfunction	22	Relative strength (e.g., good sense of direction)
	36	Moderate impairment
	42	Moderate to severe impairment
Auditory processing and language	45	Mild to moderate impairment with intermittent abilities to imitate sounds and words or use selected words
	55	Moderate to severe impairment with no ability to imitate or use words

Table A.2 Floortime Intervention Outcomes

Good to outstanding	58%
Medium	25%
Ongoing difficulties	17%

visual-spatial difficulties (which were improving) and most had some degree of fine or gross motor planning challenges.

The second group made slower and more gradual progress but still made significant gains in their ability to relate and communicate with gestures, entering into long sequences of purposeful interaction but not necessarily a continuous flow. They could share attention and engage in problem-solving. They developed some degree of language and could talk in phrases; many could answer "why" questions. However, they still had significant problems developing their symbolic capacities. They, too, became very warm and loving; in fact, the first thing that changed was their relatedness and ability to show affection. But they had less sophisticated or abstract thinking skills. Some of these children had more involved neurological challenges to begin with. Like the first group, the children in this group no longer evidenced self-absorption, avoidance, self-stimulation, or perseveration.

A third group—those who had the most complicated neurological pictures, including other neurological disorders such as seizure disorders—made very slow progress. While most eventually learned how to communicate with gestures or simple words and phrases or both, they continued to have difficulties with attention and with sequences of gesturing, and still evidenced self-absorption, avoidance, self-stimulation, and perseveration. However, many were making progress in their ability to relate warmly to others, and their problematic behaviors decreased. Of this last group, eight children were wavering or losing abilities.

Because all the children in this study were brought to us by their families, who were motivated to work with this approach, this was not a representative population of children with ASD. However, it is reasonable to assume based on our observations that a subgroup of children with ASD can make enormous progress. Only future clinical trial studies will determine what percent of children are in this subgroup.

We observed that children who made progress tended to improve in a certain sequence. First, within several months, they began showing more emotion and pleasure in relating to others. Contrary to the stereotypes of autism, they seemed eager for emotional contact; the problem was that they had trouble figuring out how to achieve it. They seemed grateful when their parents helped them express their desire for interaction. After parents learned to draw them out by being playfully obstructive, even children who had been very avoidant and self-absorbed began seeking out their parents for relatedness and taking the initiative.

Overall, 83 percent of the children, including some in the third group, initially showed improvement in the range and depth of their engagement and expression of emotions, particularly pleasure. Once engaged, many then moved from simple to complex emotional and motor gestures, which in turn led to the emergence of functional symbolic capacities. Presymbolic communication always preceded creative symbolic elaboration and the expressive use of language. Many children went through a transitional stage of using scripted words and then became increasingly creative with their gestural interactions. Children who remained rigid in their gestural interactions often remained stereotyped in their use of language. Flexibility in nonverbal interactions led to the spontaneous and creative use of language.

Once they became more symbolic, many of the children could not stop talking, as if they were excited to use their new abilities. Their ideas were at first jumbled and occasionally illogical and scripted; over time, however, over half of the children could use their symbols creatively and logically. Most of the children learned to express their own ideas much more quickly than they learned to understand the ideas of others. Eventually, if their caretakers and therapists focused on rapid, two-way, symbolic communication, challenging the children to process incoming information in long, back-and-forth exchanges, children learned to comprehend the ideas of others and express abstract "why" ideas.

The children in the "good to outstanding" outcome group became creative and logical and then became able to hold spontaneous, affect-driven, two-way symbolic communication. This allowed them to differentiate their internal worlds and develop logical thinking, impulse control, and an organized sense of self. For many, this was a two-step process. First, they learned to hold islands of logical dialogue. Over time, they learned to integrate and expand these islands, and a cohesive sense of self and capacity for logic emerged, along with their ability for functional logical exchanges, two-way thinking, problem-solving, and working with others. In consequence, their academic abilities also improved, as did their peer relationships, though the latter required a great deal of practice. With appropriate dynamic and secure academic environments, many of the children in the first group developed average to superior academic skills; however, those in overly structured academic settings tended to remain more rigid, concrete, and rote.

This pattern of progress occurred in the context of a comprehensive DIR/Floortime intervention, as described in this book, with the following elements:

1. Home-based, developmentally appropriate interactions and practices (Floortime), including the following:

   A. Eight to ten 20–30 minute Floortime sessions a day
   B. Semistructured problem-solving, five to eight 15-minute (or longer) sessions a day
   C. Spatial, motor, and sensory activities (15 or more minutes, four or more times a day), integrated with pretend play as appropriate, including running, jumping, spinning, swinging, and deep pressure; perceptual motor challenges; visual-spatial processing and motor planning games
   D. Four or more peer play sessions per week

2. Speech therapy, typically three or more times a week
3. Sensory integration-based occupational therapy or physical therapy, or both, typically two or more times a week
4. Daily educational program: either an integrated program or a regular preschool program with an aide for those who can interact, imitate gestures or words, and engage in preverbal problem-solving; or for children not yet able to engage in preverbal problem-solving or imitation, a special education program focusing on engagement, purposeful preverbal interaction and problem-solving, and training in imitating actions, sounds, and words
5. Biomedical interventions, including consideration of medication, to enhance motor planning and sequencing, self-regulation, concentration, or auditory processing and language
6. Consideration of nutrition and diet, as well as technologies geared to improving processing abilities

Detailed Study of Twenty Cases

As part of the above study, we also studied in detail twenty of the children in the first group who had made the most progress, using videotape analysis to compare them to children with no challenges at all who were functioning both emotionally and intellectually at or above age level. We also compared these two groups with a group of children who continued to have chronic problems in relating and communicating.

The twenty children we studied ranged in age from five to ten years old, had all started intervention between two and four years of age, and had received between two and eight years of intervention or follow-up consultation or both. At the time of outcome, all were attending regular schools, enjoyed relationships with friends, and participated in community activities. Many had been assessed for cognitive abilities using standardized tests and were functioning in the superior range.

Using our Functional Emotional Assessment Scale (FEAS) and the Vineland Adaptive Behavior Scales, we found that the children who never had challenges and the twenty children originally diagnosed with ASD were indistinguishable and differed from the "problem" group. The Functional Emotional Assessment Scale (FEAS) (Greenspan, DeGangi, and Wieder, 2001. Also see the Greenspan Social Emotional Growth Chart, Psychological Corp., Harcourt Assessment, Inc.) is a reliable, validated clinical rating scale that can be applied to videotaped interactions between infants or children and caregivers in order to measure emotional, social, and intellectual functioning.

On the Vineland Scales, all the children scored higher than age level in the communication domain, with 60 percent scoring one to two years higher than age level. In the socialization domain, 90 percent of the children received scores two to three years ahead of age level, which is particularly notable given that children with autistic spectrum diagnoses typically continue to evidence significant social impairments even when there is some progress in language and cognition. The scores for daily living improved somewhat less in comparison to the other two domains; because of motor planning difficulties that affect daily living, self-care skills are often more challenging for this population.

Finally, the adaptive behavior composite scores, which average the three domains, were all above age level except for one case, a child who had significant motor difficulties. None of the children presented maladaptive behavior patterns. Overall, the longer the child was in treatment and the older he was, the higher his scores relative to his age, suggesting that children continued to function progressively better as they grew older.

For the FEAS ratings, each child in each of the groups was videotaped interacting with a caregiver for fifteen or more minutes. A reliable judge blind to the identity of the children used FEAS to rate the children on the functional emotional developmental capacities (FEDC) described in this book. As stated above, the intervention group was indistinguishable from the normal control group. Both groups were significantly different from the group with continuing difficulties. Table A.3 shows the scoring breakdown for each of the groups, with 76 representing the top of the scale.

These findings on the FEAS clinical ratings are especially important because they reliably rate subtle, high-level personality functions (such as quality of intimacy, emotional expressiveness and reciprocity, creativity and imagination, and abstract, flexible thinking, as well as problem-solving and reality testing) that are expected to be relatively permanently impaired in children with an autistic spectrum diagnosis, even those who make considerable progress in their language and cognitive abilities. The fact the intervention subgroup was comparable to a peer group without developmental disorders suggests, at a minimum, that a sub-

Table A.3 FEAS Outcomes

	N	Mean FEAS (76 is optimal %)	Range
Floortime intervention group	20	74.8	70–76
Normal comparison group	14	74.9	65–76
Continuing significant difficulties	12	23.7	<20–40

group of children initially given an autistic spectrum diagnosis can develop sustainable patterns of healthy emotional, social, and adaptive behavior.

Long-Term Follow-up Study

Subsequent to the study described above, we did a ten- to fifteen-year follow-up study of sixteen children who were in the "good to outstanding" group of the original two hundred cases (Greenspan and Wieder, 2005). This study attempted to determine if a subgroup of children initially diagnosed with ASD could—with an optimal developmentally-based program—go beyond expectations for high-functioning ASD; learn to be interactive, empathetic, creative, and reflective thinkers; and continue their gains.

At the time of the study, these children (all males) were between the ages of twelve and seventeen. This follow-up was comprehensive, addressing the full range of emotional, social, and sensory-processing variables in addition to traditional cognitive and academic outcomes. The study showed that the children in this group had developed high levels of empathy and were often more empathetic than their peers. Some became very talented in music and writing, including poetry. Most were outstanding students, excelling in many academic areas; others were average students; a few struggled academically with learning disabilities because of executive functioning and sequencing problems. As a group, they showed the expected range of mental health problems, often depending on family circumstances (a few were anxious or depressed as adolescents). Importantly, however, they coped with the stresses of puberty and family concerns while maintaining their core gains in relating, communicating, and reflective thinking and making further progress as well. For this subgroup of children, the core deficits and symptoms of ASD were no longer observed ten to fifteen years after they initially presented.

For this study we conducted parent interviews and asked parents to complete a functional emotional developmental questionnaire (FEDQ) through which they could rate the children's development in the various domains described below. We also rated our impressions of the children independently, using videotapes made by parents, our direct interviews with the children, or audiotapes recorded via telephone. We also collected school reports and obtained IQ tests when available (most parents indicated there was no need to have their children tested for IQ). Finally, to provide an objective assessment, we administered the Achenbach Scales (Achenbach, 1991), a child behavior checklist (CBCL) that rates competence and clinical syndromes.

All the children received comprehensive intervention programs, as indicated in Table A.4. The average number of different interventions was eight, the children were between ages two and eight and a half, and the duration of intensive interventions was two to five years. All the children received DIR/Floortime consultations from one of the authors, and all did Floortime at home. Families polled said that they did an average of nine hours of Floortime each week (as the children got older, that amount of time diminished), for an average of almost five years. When asked which interventions were most effective, parents reported that Floortime at home, Floortime therapy with their child and a therapist, and play dates were the most significant interventions.

We asked the parents to rate their children on the six core developmental capacities and three higher-order abstract capacities using the FEDQ (Greenspan and Greenspan, 2002). The questions are based on the functional emotional developmental levels (FEDL) described in this book and are designed to assess the emotional, social, and intellectual capacities of the child. The clinicians (the authors and a research assistant) rated the children separately from the parents, using parallel rating scales; their ratings were very close to the parent responses for all the core capacities (see Table A.5). The clinicians also rated (based on the interviews) the level of empathy (whether it was compared to peers or to siblings), creativity, and skills of the children, to cover the full range of these children's competencies.

The parents also completed the Achenbach Scales. On the social competence scales, 94 percent of the children were in the normal range; 88 percent were in the normal range for activities and for school competence. In terms of clinical syndromes (signs of anxiety, depression, withdrawal, socially acting out, or aggression), 75 percent fell into the normal range. With regard to other challenges, 94 percent showed no difficulties in attention.

In terms of processing abilities, all two hundred children in the original study had significant problems with motor or sensory processing and all had some motor planning challenges. Parents of the sixteen children in this study reported that most of the sensory reactivity challenges were resolved; overall, an impressive 88 percent resolved auditory, visual, tactile, and vestibular hypersensitivities with the benefit of maturation, treatment, and activities. Challenges

Table A.4 Comprehensive Intervention Profiles

	% of Children in the Study
DIR consultation	100
Floortime at home	100
Floortime therapy	56
Play dates	75
Speech and language therapy	100
Occupational therapy	100
Auditory integration therapy (AIT)/Tomatis	100
Visual-Spatial Therapy	19
Biomedical	38
Cognitive/Educational therapy	13/13
Nutrition	44
Diet	13/25
Meds at school age	25
Family therapy at school age	13
Adolescent psychotherapy	19
Other interventions	19

Table A.5 Clinician and Parent Independent Ratings, Functional Emotional Developmental Levels

	Clinician Mean*	Parent Mean*
Self-regulation	6.7	6.7
Relationships	6.9	6.5
Purposeful communications	6.8	6.9
Complex sense of self	6.4	6.8
Representational thinking	6.4	6.6
Emotional thinking	6.4	6.4

*On a scale of 1–7, with 1 being the lowest score and 7 being the highest.

with fine motor planning were manifest in part with difficulties in executive functioning. The children also had difficulties managing time (related to sequencing) and following multiple complex directions. However, they had greater strength in verbal sequencing, or the ability to organize and elaborate on verbal ideas (in contrast to motor execution). Memory was an important asset, and 60 percent were described as big-picture thinkers and were able to maintain long logical sequences. Overall, we still saw affect (emotional interests) driving improved sequencing capacities and attention to details.

Finally, in the academic realm, parents reported that this group of young people was gifted in math, science, and the arts and enjoyed a wide range of activities at school. In reviewing school report cards obtained from nine of the children, we found that 83 percent of this group were receiving all As and Bs in programs that included honors and advanced placement classes.

The children in this follow-up study progressed out of their core symptoms and, more important, their core deficits. They became warm, related, and sensitive young people with competence in a full range of activities. Although, like other adolescents, they were not immune to mental health problems such as anxiety and depression, they did not evidence the deficits or symptoms of ASD. Their progress illustrates the crucial importance of comprehensive and intensive DIR intervention during the early years, focusing on the fundamental capacities for relating, communicating, and thinking. It also shows that progress can continue into the adolescent years and likely beyond.

Short-Term Changes

In addition, we conducted a study looking at short-term changes occurring in children with ASD who received DIR/Floortime consultation (Greenspan and Breinbauer, 2005). We looked at ten cases in detail for this pilot study.

Based on our clinical observation that children often showed changes in their ability to engage and interact by the end of the first consultation (because parents were learning how to bring out the highest level of the child's current capacities), our goal with this pilot study was to confirm our hypothesis that many children could operate at a higher level than they typically did if parents harnessed the children's natural emotional interest by following their lead and facilitating interactions. We also wondered if the children would sustain this change and build on it to make further gains as evidenced in a re-evaluation many months later.

First, we observed (by scoring videotapes) the changes occurring in the child's functional emotional developmental capacities (as described in this book) during the first session, before and after parents received coaching on DIR/Floortime strategies. We also scored the tapes during a follow-up visit one to two years later. Both children and caregivers were rated. The results showed significant changes between the first half and the postcoaching, second half of the first session, in both the child's and the caregiver's functioning. The follow-up session showed that these changes continued in a positive direction.

This pilot study of ten cases suggests that the DIR/Floortime approach works on the very processes it purports to address and helps to explain the mechanisms through which children with ASD can change and learn to master the building blocks of relating, communicating, and thinking. The study also shows the value of coaching caregivers in bringing out the child's highest levels in order to help ascertain the child's range, which is necessary for organizing an appropriate intervention program. We will soon replicate this pilot effort with a larger sample.

Overview of Research Support for the DIR Model

(The following is adapted in part from Stanley I. Greenspan, M.D., *Research Support for a Comprehensive Developmental Approach to Autistic Spectrum Disorders and Other Developmental and Learning Disorders: The Developmental, Individual Difference, Relationship-Based Model*, available at www.icdl.com.)

As we have described in this book, children with ASD typically have challenges at two levels: first, in the basic foundations of relating, communicating, and thinking; and second, symptoms such as repetitive behavior, self-stimulation, and self-absorption. Modern developmental, relationship-based approaches for children with ASD and other disorders of relating and communicating—such as the DIR model—attempt to help children master both levels at the same time. In contrast, older approaches—such as behavioral ones, including the widely used ABA–Discrete Trial—tend to focus on changing surface behaviors and symptoms without sufficient attention to underlying individual differences or the missing basic foundations of relating and thinking. As described in Chapter 20 of this book, while early reports on behavioral approaches suggested positive educational gains for children with ASD, later, more definitive studies have shown only modest educational gains and little to no emotional or social gains for highly structured behavioral approaches (McEachin, Smith, and Lovaas, 1993; Smith, Groen, and Wynn, 2000; Smith, 2001; Shea, 2004).

National Academy of Sciences Report

The National Academy of Sciences (NAS), in its report "Educating Children with Autism" (National Academy of Sciences, Committee on Educational Interventions for Children with Autism, NRC, 2001), states that there is research support for a number of approaches, including DIR/Floortime and behavioral interventions, but that there are no proven "relationships between any particular intervention and children's progress" (page 5) and "no adequate comparisons of different comprehensive treatments" (page 8). The report concludes that effective interventions vary depending on an individual child's and family's needs.

The NAS analysis further indicates that behavioral interventions are moving toward naturalistic, spontaneous types of learning situations that follow the child's interests, and note that "studies have reported that naturalistic approaches are more effective than traditional discrete trial at leading to generalization of language gains to natural contexts" (Koegel, Camarata, Valdez-Menchaca, and Koegel, 1998; McGee, Krantz, and McClannahan, 1985).

The NAS points out that these contemporary behavioral approaches are becoming increasingly similar to developmental, relationship-based approaches that focus on working with children's and families' individual patterns with the goal of creating learning relationships that build the foundations (which have often been missing or dysfunctional) for relating, communicating, and thinking. The academy cites ten comprehensive programs with some evidence of being effective. Three are based on developmental, relationships, and family support; two are highly structured behavioral programs; and four involve combined elements including a movement toward more naturalistic teaching methods. As indicated earlier, one of the programs has its own unique educational framework. One of the models cited by the analysis as illustrative of developmental, relationship-based models is the Developmental, Individual Difference, Relationship-Based (DIR/Floortime) approach that we describe in this book.

In analyzing the research on the different models cited by the NAS, it's useful to look at the types of gains observed and reported for the different models. For example, behavioral approaches have tended to focus on educational outcomes as measured by structured performance-based tests and change in surface symptoms (such as perseveration and self-stimulation). Relationship-based, developmental approaches have tended to focus more on relationships, social skills, and meaningful, spontaneous use of language and communication. The DIR/Floortime approach is unique in showing gains not only in the basic social and emotional functioning of relating, interacting, and communicating meaningfully but also, for a subgroup of children, in the attainment of capacities often thought to be beyond the reach of children with autistic spectrum disorders. These include the capacities for making inferences, engaging in high levels of empathy, and enjoying age-expected peer relationships.

Research on the Components of the DIR Model

The article "Evaluating Effective Interventions for Children with Autism and Related Disorders: Widening the View and Changing the Perspective," by Elizabeth Tsakiris, M.Ed. (Interdisciplinary Council on Developmental and Learning Disorders Clinical Practice Guidelines Workgroup, SIGC, 2000) reviews the research support for each of the different component parts of the DIR model. This review shows that a great deal of research supports the importance of the different elements that constitute the DIR/Floortime model, including relationships and emotional/social interactions in facilitating emotional and cognitive development. There is also a great deal of support for interventions that work with auditory processing and language functioning. There is significant support (but less than for the two areas listed above) for interventions that focus on motor planning and sequencing, executive functioning, sensory modulation, and visual-spatial processing.

In a recent study on the new Bayley Scales Kit of Infant and Early Childhood Development, which includes the Greenspan Social-Emotional Growth Chart, a parent questionnaire on the DIR functional emotional developmental capacities (FEDCs) was field-tested on a representative sample of 1,500 infants and young children and found to discriminate between children with problems and disorders and those without. The study also validated the age predictions of the DIR FEDCs and showed that the early FEDCs precluded the later ones, including language and symbolic thinking (see Appendix B for details). (See Psychological Corporation, Harcourt Assessment, website www.harcourt assessment.com, for more information and to obtain a manual with the data.) Furthermore, in a recent national health survey given to over 15,000 families, the federal government's National Center for Health Statistics used questions from the DIR FEDC and found that it identified 30 percent more infants and children at risk (most of whom were not receiving services) than prior health surveys (Simpson, Colpe, and Greenspan, 2003). This was the first time emotional variables were used in this national health survey.

Many studies show that emotionally salient learning interactions result in more integrated learning than impersonal ones (Greenspan and Shankar, 2004).

Additional Research on Developmental Relationship-Based Approaches

In addition to the studies described in the first part of this appendix, a considerable amount of research is emerging on relationship-based approaches that either are an application of or employ a number of the same fundamentals as the DIR model. These are showing very positive results for children with ASD. Following are several examples of recent studies. (These are brief summaries; for more information please see sources cited.)

Michigan PLAY Project.   Rick Solomon, M.D., has analyzed the results of a community-based application of the DIR/Floortime model in his Michigan PLAY Project. He found significant gains for a group of children with ASD in social, cognitive, and language functioning, and demonstrated that the DIR/Floortime model can be applied to a large community with public funding at low cost (Solomon, Necheles, Ferch, and Bruckman, 2006).

The Play and Language for Autistic Youngsters (PLAY) Project, based in southeastern Michigan, is a multifaceted statewide autism training and early intervention center. The PLAY Project Home Consultation (PPHC) program trains parents of children with autistic spectrum disorders using the DIR model. In this program, trained home consultants make monthly half-day visits to families' homes to teach parents how to provide intensive one-on-one, play-based services to their young children with autism. The program is paid for with a combination of fee-for-service and foundation grant funding; average cost per family per year was between $2,500 and $3,000. A detailed training manual is also used to train parents in the PLAY Project approach.

Sixty-eight children completed the eight-to-twelve-month program. Parents were encouraged to deliver fifteen hours per week of one-to-one interaction. The following measures were administered before and after intervention to assess changes in children's behavior and development as well as in parents' behavior and satisfaction with the services:

- The Functional Emotional Assessment Scale (FEAS) ratings
- Clinical ratings related to the six functional emotional developmental levels
- Fidelity (via daily logs kept by parents)
- Client Satisfaction Survey

Based on FEAS scaled scores, 45.5 percent of children made good to very good functional developmental progress over the study period. No statistical relationship was found between initial ASD severity and FEAS total or FEAS scaled scores. Based on clinical scores, 52 percent of children made very good clinical progress over the study period, with 14 percent making good progress. Of the sixty-eight families, fifty completed satisfaction surveys. Of these, 70 percent were very satisfied with the PLAY Project, 10 percent were satisfied, and 20 percent were somewhat satisfied. None were dissatisfied.

The program appears to be an efficient and cost-effective way to teach families in a community-based setting. The study found that a large majority of parents are capable of interacting with their young autistic children in a reciprocal and contingent manner. Indeed, by the time of the first video evaluation, 85 percent of parents were rated as appropriately interactive. (While the families were self-selected and highly motivated and skilled at interaction, the children in the sample did represent the typical range of severity along the autistic spectrum.)

Case Western Reserve Study.　　Gerald Mahoney, Ph.D., and Frida Perales, M.Ed., of the Mandel School of Applied Social Sciences at Case Western University have conducted a number of studies on developmental relationship-based approaches. Their most recent study looked at the effects of relationship-focused (RF) early intervention on children diagnosed either with pervasive developmental disorders (PDDs)—including autism—or developmental disabilities (DDs) (Mahoney and Perales, 2005).

Subjects included fifty mother-child pairs, with all of the children between the ages of twelve and fifty-four months. Each of the children with PDDs had severe regulatory problems as well as deficits in communication and cognitive development; the children with DDs had significant delays in cognitive or communication development. The one-year intervention was conducted through weekly individual sessions that helped mothers use responsive teaching (RT) strategies (an RF intervention) with their children. Parents also reported spending an average of 15.1 hours each week using the techniques at home.

Both groups of children made significant improvements in cognitive, communication, and socioemotional functioning. However, children in the PDD group made statistically greater improvements on the developmental measures than children in the DD group. The intervention also appeared to be very effective at promoting children's development: the entire sample of children made more than a 60 percent increase in their rate of cognitive development. Additionally, in language development, 70 percent of the children made expressive language improvements, and 80 percent made receptive language improvements.

University of Colorado model. Another model based on a developmental and relationship framework, which was not founded on the DIR model but emerged from similar developmental concepts, began in 1981 at the University of Colorado's Health Sciences Center as the "Playschool Model." In 1998 the center shifted the focus to home and preschool environments involving typically developing peers as well. A number of studies on this model have shown significant gains in emotional, social, and cognitive development (Rogers and DiLalla, 1991; Rogers, Hall, Osaki, Reaven, and Herbison, 2000).

Ongoing outcome studies. Continuing studies of the effects of the DIR/Floortime intervention are being conducted at the Harris Research Institute at York University under the direction of Stuart Shanker, D. Phil., and at the Rebecca School in New York City, under the direction of Gil Tippy, Ph.D.

At the Harris center, two types of studies are being done.

1. Two groups of thirty children each who are receiving the DIR/Floortime Approach are being studied. The age range is from three to seven years. The first group has demonstrated positive social and emotional gains

over the first year. Brain imaging of those parts of the brain that process emotions (such as the anterior cingulate and the fusiform) was done at the beginning of the study and one year later. These images showed changes in a positive direction.

The second group is still in the process of being studied, but early indications are that they will show similar, if not even greater, gains. At the outset of this study of this second group, brain imaging showed differences in functioning between these children and that of neurotypical children. Such imaging will be repeated at the end of the study.

These preliminary findings are part of a larger study that will have more definitive results in the near future.

2. A follow-up study is also being conducted at the Harris Center. The follow-up study is in two groups: In the first (already completed) there are sixteen children from middle and late teen years. Brain imagining of five of these children also showed changes in the areas of the brain that process emotions. A new group of over sixty-five late teens and young adults with similar outcomes is currently being studied in depth. This group of teenagers, who have done very well with DIR/Floortime intervention when they were younger and are no longer receiving interventions, show healthy patterns of social, emotional, and intellectual functioning similar to, or in some cases even better than, neurotypical peers. They are highly empathetic, have lots of friends, and are doing well in regular schools. We have also been able to use brain imaging studies on a number of these children who are willing to be tested, and they demonstrated that the areas of the brain that process emotions were similar to those of neurotypical children. This is highly significant because the research literature suggests that individuals with autistic spectrum disorders show continuing differences in these same areas of brain functioning.

At the Rebecca School, sixty children from ages four through fourteen years are being studied over a one- to two-year period using the DIR/Floortime Approach. These children are showing positive social and emotional gains.

In summary, current research supports the focus of modern developmental, relationship-based approaches to working with children with ASD on strengthening or constructing the functional developmental capacities for relating, communicating, and thinking by creating emotionally meaningful learning interactions tailored to each child's and family's developmental profile.

Appendix B

How Autism Develops

The DIR Theory

The Developmental Pathways Leading to Autism

What follows in this section is a summary of the theory of the development of autism as presented in The First Idea *(Greenspan and Shanker, 2004).*

Autism and ASD

According to the observations we have made of a range of infants, young children, and their families (Greenspan, 1979, 1992, 2001; Greenspan and Shanker, 2004, 2006) the development of symbol formation, language, and intelligence is based on a series of critical emotional interactions early in life. When these interactions are not mastered, these abilities do not develop. Biological factors present in autism can make it difficult for a child to participate in these interactions. We have observed that children with ASD have not fully mastered these critical early interactions (Greenspan et al., 1987; Greenspan, 1992; Greenspan and Wieder, 1998, 1999).

Therefore, we hypothesized that it would be possible to help children who (because of their unique biologies) lack critical symbolic, language, and intellectual abilities to make progress in developing them with an intervention that creates special opportunities for the necessary formative emotional experiences. These special opportunities would work with the children's unique biologies and on each of these formative emotional interactions. As indicated in Appendix A, our studies have shown that with appropriate intervention, most of the children with ASD made progress and a subgroup of children with ASD were able to develop these abilities beyond prior expectations (Greenspan and Wieder, 1997).

The challenge we face worldwide is growing. A variety of studies estimate that the rate for autism is between 2 and 4 per 1,000 children, and that the rate for ASD is higher. The Centers for Disease Control (CDC), looking at a number of studies, has put the rate at approximately 1 per 166 for ASD (Bertrand et al., 2001). These estimates are much higher than those of ten to fifteen years ago. Some believe that the current rates reflect improved diagnosis, while others believe that the rates of autism and ASD have risen dramatically.

A Multifactor, Cumulative Risk Model

Although many have assumed that autism is a unitary disorder relating to an as-yet-unidentified genetic pattern, with multiple forms of expression (that is, phenotypes), current research suggests a multipath, cumulative risk model. A great deal of research supports a genetic component to autism. The new hypothesis considers the possibility that there are multiple pathways—each with a different genetic pattern and later risk factors and challenges. Within this model, different genetic patterns and pre- and postnatal developmental processes may predispose a child to autism, or create vulnerabilities to cumulative pre- and postnatal challenges such as infectious illnesses, toxic substances, and factors that can precipitate autoimmunity. Postnatal factors such as experiential or physical stress may also contribute to the behavioral patterns symptomatic of autism and ASD.

We distinguish primary and secondary features of ASD. The former involve deficits in the ability to interact with emotional signals, gestures, and vocalizations; difficulty in maintaining these exchanges in order to engage in social problem solving and create emotionally meaningful ideas; and difficulty in processing auditory, visual-spatial, and other sensory input, and in planning and sequencing actions. Secondary features derive from the primary ones and involve the problems typically associated with ASD, as well as symptoms such as self-absorption, perseveration, and self-stimulation.

These challenges can be intensified by inappropriate interventions and improved by appropriate ones tailored to the child's unique developmental profile. Research on the causes and treatment of ASD should address identifying and classifying clinical subtypes so that findings may be applied more appropriately to specific children.

The Core Psychological Deficit in Autism

The autism-specific developmental deficits that have been suggested include deficits in the following abilities: empathy and seeing the world from another person's perspective (theory of mind [Baron-Cohen, 1994]); higher-level abstract thinking, including making inferences (Minshew and Goldstein, 1998); joint attention, including social referencing and problem-solving (Mundy, Sigman, and Kasari, 1990); emotional reciprocity (Baranek, 1999; Dawson and Galpert, 1990); and functional (pragmatic) language (Wetherby and Prizant, 1993). Neuropsychological models that have been proposed to account for the clinical features of autism further elaborate these autism-specific developmental deficits (Greenspan, 2001; Sperry, 1985; Baron-Cohen, 1989; Baron-Cohen, Leslie, and Frith, 1985; Bowler, 1992; Dahlgren and Trillingsgaard, 1996; Dawson, Meltzoff, Osterling, and Rinaldi, 1998; Frith, 1989; Klin, Volkmar, and Sparrow, 1992; Ozonoff, 1997; Pennington and Ozonoff, 1996).

Our clinical work and research (Greenspan, 2001; Greenspan and Shanker, 2004; Greenspan and Shanker, 2006), however, suggest that all the abilities or deficits listed above stem from an earlier capacity (that is, they are downstream phenomena). This earlier capacity is an infant's ability to connect emotions or intent to motor planning and sequencing and to sensations and, later, to emerging symbols (Greenspan, 1979; 1989; 1997a), making the inability to make this connection the core psychological deficit of autism. We hypothesized that the biological differences associated with ASD may express themselves through the derailing of this connection, leading to both the primary and secondary features of ASD.

A child's capacity to make this connection typically becomes more apparent between nine and eighteen months of age, as the child moves into complex chains of emotional reciprocity. For this to occur, the child needs to have a desire (that is, affect) and then to connect that desire to an action plan. Together, these elements allow the child to create a pattern of meaningful social problem-solving interactions. On the other hand, action without desire becomes perseverative, aimless, or self-stimulatory; it is hard for a child to progress beyond simple motor patterns if she cannot connect them to her desires. In the DIR approach, we create situations of high affect tailored to the infant's unique biology to help children with ASD take purposeful action, exchange emotional signals, and interact with others. Through this process, a child's motor planning and meaningful action improve.

This connection between desire and purposeful action enables a child to exchange emotional signals, which— if the exchange becomes sufficiently complex—leads to the ability to modulate emotions and actions, separate perception from action and symbols, the integration of different processing capacities, and the meaningful use of language. (Without this connection, symbols are often used repetitively, as in scripting and echolalia.) With these abilities, the child can interact flexibly with others and with his environment, which enables associative (as opposed to rote) learning.

Affect-based interactions, social problem-solving, and the meaningful use of symbols are the foundations of the capacities (described above) that distinguish typically developing children from children with ASD. We have observed that infants and toddlers developing autistic patterns do not progress sufficiently from simple to complex patterns of engagement and interaction. In the review of two hundred children described in Appendix A, we observed that approximately two-thirds of the children who developed ASD had this unique type of biologically based processing deficit in the ability to connect emotions and intent to motor planning and sequencing and symbolic capacities. However, they differed with regard to other processing deficits (namely, auditory, motor planning, visual-spatial, and sensory modulation).

We call the hypothesis that explores the connection between affect, motor planning and sequencing, and sensory experience (as well as other processing capacities) the Affect Diathesis Hypothesis. It asserts that a child uses his affect (or emotion) to provide intent for his actions and meaning for his symbols and words. Through many affect-based, problem-solving interactions, the child develops higher-level social, emotional, and intellectual abilities.

The Early Roots of Autism

Because the unique processing deficit described above occurs early in the first months of life, it can undermine the child's essential emotional and cognitive learning experiences. By the time the child is twelve to twenty-four months old, her difficulty with purposeful, interactive communication during this critical age may intensify her difficulties, causing her to withdraw and become aimless or repetitive or both (no matter how competent her parents). By the time she receives professional attention, what appears to be a primary biological deficit may, therefore, actually be one factor in a dynamic process. We are currently conducting studies to help identify children at risk for ASD early, as the problems begin, in order to institute preventative intervention. To this end, we have further developed our theory on the relationship between affect and motor planning.

The Sensory-Affect-Motor Connections

In healthy development, an infant connects the sensory system to the motor system through affect (for example, seeing and turning to look at a caregiver's smiling face and wooing voice). All sensation has both physical and affective qualities (Greenspan, 1997b; Greenspan and Shanker, 2004, chapter 2). The infinite variations in the affective aspect of sensation enable a person to use emotion to code, store, and retrieve information. The ability to create links between the physical and emotional qualities of sensation and motor behavior allows the growing infant to begin to perceive and organize patterns, such as seeing mother and reaching for her. These purposeful units grow into larger patterns, multiple back-and-forth problem-solving interactions. By the second year of life, these patterns lead to a sense of self as the purposeful agent and a sense of others, and ultimately enable a child to form and give meaning to symbols and develop higher levels of thinking.

When biological factors (or severe deprivation or abuse) interfere with the formation of a primary connection among the sensory system, affect, and the motor system, behavior is not strongly linked to affective qualities of sensation. Therefore, infants with this deficit evidence more aimless behavior and cannot initiate or take part in the back-and-forth pattern of communication that would allow them to negotiate the developmental steps that lead to emotional and intellectual abilities. Our observations suggest that for many children with ASD sensory-affect-motor connections are relatively compromised.

We have formulated a number of stages in this Affect Diathesis Hypothesis through which the connection between sensation, affect, and motor behavior progresses (see Greenspan and Shanker, 2004, chapter 2), allowing us to identify infants at risk for ASD. At each stage, we can assess the presence, absence, or compromise of the sensory-affect-motor connection (as described in Chapter 3 of this book). Because the compromise to this connection is not all-or-nothing in children at risk for ASD, early intervention can help. Creating states of heightened pleasurable affect tailored to the child's unique motor and sensory-processing profile helps to develop and strengthen the connection between sensation, affect, and motor action, which leads to more purposeful affective behavior, which in turn leads to reciprocal signaling, a sense of self, symbolic functioning, and higher-level thinking skills. Such regulated emotional interaction helps a child to use all his senses, along with his motor and language abilities, together (for example, in looking, listening, and moving all at once while engaging in meaningful social problem-solving). To be regulating, these emotional interactions must be tailored to a child's individual processing differences (the DIR/Floortime model).

How Affect Transformations and the Affect Diathesis Hypothesis Explain Pattern-Recognition, Joint Attention, Intention Reading, Theory of Mind, and Higher-Level Symbolic Thinking

The following is abstracted from Greenspan and Shanker, 2006.

It is important to take a closer look at each of the early stages of affective interaction to observe how these lead to the capacities thought to be essential for healthy emotional and intellectual growth and to be relatively compromised in ASD.

As indicated earlier, the early stages of emotional interaction involve the infant's emerging capacity to experience sensations in a more and more affectively textured manner. This occurs through the infant's caregivers providing opportunities for progressively more complex emotional interactions. These emotional interactions are, in essence, experienced by the infant as a unique type of sensation—one that comes to have, over time, an almost infinite variety of affective qualities. These affect patterns give rise to, and then orchestrate, a large range of cognitive and social processes.

In the first stage the child begins to forge sensory-affect-motor connections (from birth to three months). Pleasurable, regulating affective experiences, along with growing motor control, enable a baby to begin to respond with actions such as reaching toward a pleasurable touch and turning away from an unpleasant one. In this manner, motor responses quickly move beyond reflexes and become part of a sensory-affect-motor pattern. That is, affect serves as a mediator between sensation and motor response, connecting the two together. This basic unit of sensory-affect-motor response becomes more and more established through infant-caregiver interactions.

To form these connections, a baby must experience positive, regulated affects or emotions, and caregivers must tailor interactions to the baby's unique biological profile. Should a caregiver fail to recognize the child's negative reactions or respond appropriately to a child's overtures, the child may become subdued and withdrawn or adopt defensive behaviors such as gaze-aversion or straining to turn away (Spitz, 1965; Tronick, 1989). By no means, then, is a child's ability to recognize social and communicative patterns or to engage in mutual gaze hardwired. Rather, the caregiver must engage in a variety of subtle affective behaviors, both soothing and arousing, that are finely tuned to the child's individual sensory proclivities, in order to promote the development of these capacities (Greenspan, 1997b).

In the second stage of affective transformation, the child develops a more intimate relationship with her caregiver (two to five months), whom she can now distinguish from other adults. Positive, often joyful, emotions enable her to coordinate gazing, listening, and moving in synchronous and purposeful interactions. Through these affective interactions, she begins to discern patterns in her caregivers' voices and affect signals and to discriminate their emotional interests and recognize the emotional significance of facial expressions or vocalizations. The child's ability to recognize social and communicative patterns and to organize perceptions into meaningful categories is grounded in this ability to engage in and form this emotional relationship and learn to recognize affective patterns.

In the third stage of affective transformation, the child begins to master purposeful two-way interactions (four to ten months). For this to happen, caregivers need to read and respond to the baby's emotional signals and challenge the baby to read and respond to theirs. Through these interactions, the baby begins to engage in back-and-forth emotional signaling. Different motor gestures—facial expressions, vocalizations, arm movements—become part of this signaling, which now harnesses a broad range of emotions, sensations, purposeful movements, and emerging social patterns. By eight months, many of these exchanges usually occur in a row. The infant is now using purposeful affective signaling to orchestrate the different components of her central nervous system (CNS) in an integrated manner and form higher-level cognitive, communicative, and social skills—for example, reaching out to be picked up.

Through these increasingly complex interactions—the endless smiles, head nods, friendly gestures, animated movements, and so forth that she encounters in her countless interactions with her caregivers—the child is learning to read and respond to the social and emotional cues of others as well as to communicate her own. These meaningful patterns involving the back-and-forth reading of and responding to emotional signals enable the toddler to begin forming for herself the social patterns, cultural norms, and rules that characterize her family, community, and culture. This capacity is a vital building block of what we later call pragmatic language.

In the fourth stage of affective transformation, shared social problem-solving, the child learns to sustain a continuous flow of back-and-forth affective communication in order to collaborate with a caregiver in solving affective, meaningful problems (nine to eighteen months). In these complex interactions the infant is further developing the capacity to read and respond to a broad range of emotional and social signals as a basis for forming patterns that include a growing sense of self as well as social and cultural norms.

This process involves all the senses, as well as the capacity for continuous flow of affective interaction needed to imitate complex social interactions, such as putting on Daddy's shoes, looking at Dad for approval (that is, joint attention), and walking around in a manner that is strangely reminiscent of Daddy's gait as he comes home from work. These complex interactive processes constitute affective patterns, as the infant comes to recognize all the behaviors her father does and what she does in response as a pattern of interaction. While the toddler who has not mastered the continuous flow of affective signaling may be capable of limited and isolated visual or vocal pattern recognition, meaningful, affective complex pattern recognition—which includes multiple senses, actions, and social interactions—is a component of the larger capacity for shared social problem-solving.

These long chains of coregulated affective gesturing enable the child to recognize various patterns involved in satisfying her emotional needs. She learns, for example, how to solicit a caregiver's assistance to obtain some out-of-reach desired object and enter into finely tuned, back-and-forth interactions (through vocalizations and facial expressions) in a coregulated solution of the problem (for example, multiple joint-attention interactions). She learns what different gestures or facial expressions signify; the connection between, on one hand, certain kinds of facial expressions, tones of voice, or behavior and, on the other, an individual's mood or intentions; and so on. This ability to read the patterns of others and, through recognition of one's own patterns, form a sense of self, is the basis for what is called intention reading or theory of mind.

This ability is also essential if a child is to have and act upon expectations—to know when to expect different kinds of responses from his caregiver, or to know what love, anger, respect, shame, and so forth feel like. It is equally essential if the toddler is to know what others are thinking or feeling or to grasp their intentions. The ability to recognize the intentions of others does not come out of the blue. Rather, pattern recognition, intention reading, and joint attention emerge from and require mastery of all of the earlier stages of affective transformation outlined above; these capacities are downstream effects of the emotional capacities that have been developing in the first three stages of functional emotional development and reach a more complex configuration in the critical fourth stage of affective transformation.

Understanding the complexity of this process has enabled the formulation of interventions such as the DIR model that are tailored to the child's biological profile and vulnerabilities and increase the likelihood of his achieving some relative mastery of these critical early affective transformations and the subsequent abilities for joint attention, theory of mind, and higher levels of language and symbolic thinking (Greenspan and Wieder, 1998).

The theory just outlined was tested on a representative population of over 1,500 children whose parents were administered the Greenspan Social-Emotional Growth Chart (Greenspan, 2004). Mastery of the early stages of affect transformation was found to be necessary for children to progress to the subsequent stages, and the first four stages were required for the capacities for symbol formation, pragmatic language, and higher-level thinking (including theory-of-mind capacities such as empathy) and for social referencing and joint-attention capacities (such as reciprocal, shared social problem solving). (For a description of this study, see the new Bayley Scales Kit and manual at www.harcourtassessment.com. Also see Greenspan and Shanker, 2006; Bayley, 2005).

This data set provides support for the model presented in this appendix and opens the door to further research on what occurs in the central nervous system when these early emotional interactions are compromised.

The Neurodevelopmental Pathways Leading to Autism

The following is abstracted from the working paper "Clinical Clues to the Neurodevelopmental Pathways Leading to Autism" by Stanley I. Greenspan, M.D., and Stuart G. Shanker, D.Phil.

Clinical observations of the developmental pathways leading to ASD that we have been describing help to explain recent neuroscience findings on individuals with autism and to separate primary factors from downstream effects. In turn, these findings provide support for the DIR model and the Affect Diathesis Hypothesis.

In the last section, we explained why the primary biological deficit in ASD is hypothesized to originate with a neurologically based compromise in the connection between affect, sensory perception, and motor patterns. We described how this first level of affect organization sets the stage for a number of additional levels, each involving transformations of affect and new levels of integration of sensory, affect, and motor patterns, and how the fourth stage—coregulated, reciprocal affect exchanges (or affect signaling)—enables a toddler to engage in creating emotionally meaningful patterns and shared social problem-solving. These, in turn, often involve affective, language, motor, and visual-spatial patterns—all orchestrated by the child's affective goals and interactions.

We are now involved in ongoing research that involves looking at video-tapes of infants who were later diagnosed with ASD. We are confirming that when the initial connection between affect, perceptions, and motor patterns is weak, as seen in children with ASD, due to a neurological deficit, the subse-quent stages leading up to this fourth stage of shared problem-solving either do not occur or occur partially or weakly. We have recently analyzed videotapes of children diagnosed with ASD at ages two to five and carefully rated videotapes from early infancy through the early years of life. We found that the children had marked difficulty in sustaining motor patterns that required affective sup-port. For example, their ability to focus and attend was brief and reactive rather than sustained and directed by their own affective interest. Similarly, their ability for engagement with joy and pleasure was fleeting and reactive. By the time they reached the stage where reciprocal affective interactions were expected, they could engage only in a few back-and-forth interactions, rather than the expected sustained interactive reciprocal patterns; they also lacked initiative. At the critical fourth level of shared social problem-solving, the children who later were diagnosed with ASD demonstrated a marked deficit.

In observing these tapes, we also found that the degree to which the infant and toddler lacked mastery in each of these critical affective steps corresponded to the degree to which they evidenced symptoms such as self-absorption, perse-veration, scripting, or self-stimulation. Often clear symptoms emerged during the latter part of the fourth stage. (See Tables 3.1 and 3.2 in this book.)

Recent neuroscience research on individuals with ASD supports these clin-ical observations. More important, however, these observations provide a co-herent theory that explains a range of findings on children with ASD.

Summary of New Biological Findings on Infants and Children with ASD

Research by Martha Herbert, building on work by Margaret Bauman that demonstrated differences in a number of areas of the brain in individuals with ASD, shows that at around nine months of age the white matter in the central nervous system (CNS) grows abnormally, especially in the frontal lobes, cere-bellum, and association areas. These are parts of the CNS where processing and ordering of information at higher levels tends to occur. In addition, the nonverbal areas in the right hemisphere also tend to demonstrate excessive white matter, and the pathways connecting left and right sides of the brain are not as well developed as would be expected.

Research by Eric Courchesne has demonstrated that individuals with ASD tended to have smaller head circumferences at birth, but then showed rapid growth in circumference (Courchesne et al., 1994). The pattern continues, with some spurts and slow periods, until around age five. By mid-adolescence, however, individuals with ASD tend to have a smaller head circumference, as more typically developing adolescents are catching up. Ruth Carper demonstrated that the frontal lobes tended to have the largest size increase. At the same time, however, the functioning neuronal networks in the frontal lobes were less well developed.

Marcelle Just found that individuals with ASD used parts of the brain that process shapes to remember letters of the alphabet—that is, they used a sensory region to deal with conceptual challenges (Just, Cherkassky, Keller, and Minshew, 2004). He suggested, based on this and related work, that one of the central characteristics of individuals with ASD was difficulty with different parts of the brain communicating with each other. He found that local networks tended to be overconnected and long-range networks tended to be underconnected.

Philip Teitelbaum, in looking at videotapes of infants later diagnosed with ASD, observed that they had difficulty in orchestrating basic motor planning sequences involved in rolling over, sitting up, crawling, and walking (Teitelbaum and Teitelbaum, 1999).

Carlos Pardo-Villaminzar found inflammation in areas of the brain where others had reported excess white matter. He also found activated microglia (a cell associated with inflammation) in the spinal fluid of a number of children with ASD.

These important findings suggest areas for further investigation, such as CNS pathways that connect the different regions of the brain together to enable the mind to work as a cohesive unit (rather than as independent components). However, at present there is no cohesive theory to explain these diverse findings, including the excessive white matter and the irregular pattern of head growth.

New Biological Findings and the Affective Transformations and Developmental Pathways Leading to ASD

The model we have been presenting as, on one hand, a description of the different levels of affect transformation characterizing the growth of symbols, language, and intelligence and as, on the other, a hypothesis for understanding the developmental pathways leading to autism suggests an explanation for, and is supported by, these diverse findings. According to our Affect Diathesis Hypothesis, the pivotal biological deficit occurs at the first stage of affective organization where there's a relative failure of the connection between sensation-affect and basic motor patterns. The sensory-affect-motor connection forms early in infancy and proper interactions with the human environment enable the infant to undergo a series of affective transformations, each involving higher and higher levels of organization and connectivity between the different areas of the CNS. Each transformation also utilizes the different parts of the CNS that are later observed to be impaired in individuals with autism.

For example, as an infant begins coordinating looking and listening (for example, looking towards mother's voice), the parts of the CNS related to pleasurable affect are working together with the parts responsible for looking and listening and, often, early vocalization. A little later, as the infant begins back-and-forth emotional cueing with purposeful hand gestures, vocalizations, and large-muscle movement patterns, such as sitting up, turning over, and initial crawling, additional parts of the central nervous system are utilized in an orchestrated manner under the guidance of the child's affect. Now the parts of the CNS dealing with affect, perception (including perception of sound sequences and spatial relationships), movement, balance, and coordination are all working together.

As described in the first part of this appendix, when the initial sensory-affect-motor connection is not strong (as we hypothesize is the case for children with ASD), the infant is unable to fully engage in the types of interactions that enable the different parts of the CNS to work together and therefore to organize and connect at higher and higher levels. In this dynamic explanation, biological differences and experiential differences interact with each other. Key experiences are necessary for the central nervous system to develop properly. Therefore, we observe the neurologic findings reported earlier. Some of these findings are likely downstream effects.

The overgrowth of white matter and uneven patterns of head growth are also accounted for in this model. Ordinarily, the development and "pruning" of the CNS is dependent on appropriate experiences with the human environment. As indicated earlier, however, meaningful interactions with caregivers, as well as with the physical environment, depend on an infant forming a sensory-affect-motor connection. Without the affective connection, comprehending feedback from the environment and, therefore, learning from the environment are compromised. (Evolutionarily, environment-based learning enables humans to develop differently in different social, cultural, and physical environments.) When this process is interrupted because of a primary biological deficit in the sensory-affect-motor connection, the expected pruning does not occur, and the brain does not develop the interconnectivity necessary for healthy growth.

Infants are endowed with the potential for a variety of CNS growth patterns. When environmentally mediated learning and pruning do not occur, it is not surprising that the original omnipotential connectivity of the CNS results in overgrowth in some areas and, at the same time, lack of critical connectivity. Each area of the brain is in a sense growing on its own, taking in information in a disorganized, uncoordinated, or unorchestrated manner. This is what we see clinically when we observe children with ASD.

The uneven pattern of head circumference growth may be secondary to the irregular white matter growth. Initially, there is overgrowth because of lack of pruning. Then there is compromised growth due to the lack of growth-producing interactions with the human environment and the development of critical cortical capacities. The findings about the frontal lobes being underdeveloped is especially critical because the frontal lobes depend on and also facilitate the complex, multistep, affect-mediated, shared problem-solving that occurs at the critical fourth stage of affective transformation. The inflammatory responses seen in the same areas of the brain where there is overgrowth of white matter may be secondary to the overgrowth (or the initial deficits in the sensory-affect-motor connection may be, in part, related to an inflammatory process).

Implications for Neuroscience Research

The developmental model described above suggests that an important focus for developmental neurobiological research should be on the processes that contribute to the formation of connections in the CNS between affect and the perception of sensation and motor patterns. These investigations should explore prenatal, perinatal, and early postnatal phases of CNS development. A focus on the earliest possible deficits will enable the field to separate primary deficits from downstream effects.

This focus will also likely prove helpful to investigating the mechanisms responsible for the sequence of downstream effects (with an awareness that these may be influenced by the lack of appropriate experiences, due to the primary deficit and the likely environmental responses to it). It will be essential to investigate whether interventions that focus on harnessing the infant's affect, in the context of using multiple sensory pathways and related motor responses in an affectively meaningful and orchestrated manner, significantly improve the infant's ability to utilize the different parts of his CNS together and, therefore, form the connective pathways that appear to be derailed in older individuals with ASD.

Appendix C

Neurodevelopmental Disorders of Relating and Communicating

A work group of the Interdisciplinary Council on Developmental and Learning Disorders (ICDL) has developed the current classification of neurodevelopmental disorders of relating and communicating (NDRC). The group members include Serena Wieder, Ph.D., Lois Black, Ph.D., Griffin Doyle, Ph.D., Barbara Dunbar, Ph.D., Barbara Kalmanson, Ph.D., Lori-Jean Peloquin, Ph.D., Ricki Robinson, M.D., M.P.H., Ruby Salazar, LCSW, Rick Solomon, M.D., Rosemary White, OTR, Molly Romer Witten, Ph.D., and Stanley I. Greenspan, M.D. For a fuller description of this diagnostic framework, see ICDL-DMIC Diagnostic Classification Task Force, 2005, from which this appendix has been abstracted.

Introduction

Neurodevelopmental disorders of relating and communicating (NDRC) involve problems in multiple aspects of a child's development, including social relationships, language, cognitive functioning, and sensory and motor processing. This category includes earlier conceptualizations of multisystem developmental disorders (MSDD), as characterized in *Infancy and Early Childhood* (Greenspan, 1992) and *Diagnostic Classification: 0–3 (DC 0–3)* (Diagnostic Classification Task Force, 1994). Additionally, it includes the *DSM-IV-R* category of pervasive developmental disorders (PDDs), also referred to as autism spectrum disorders (ASDs). The main distinction between NDRC and the earlier conceptualizations is that the NDRC framework enables a clinician to more accurately subtype disorders of relating and communicating in terms of the overall level of social, intellectual, and emotional functioning and the associated regulatory and sensory-motor processing profile. This helps differentiate the profiles that children who are commonly considered on the autism spectrum present and helps define the variations seen among the children with the same diagnosis. This differentiation is important for both intervention planning and research.

Since the description of MSDD in *DC 0–3* and PDD in *DSM-IV-R*, the framework has been broadened to allow consideration of the full range of disorders of relating, communicating, and thinking. Thus, the large degree of individual variation in infants and young children who ultimately evidence common features of difficulties in forming relationships, communicating at preverbal and verbal levels, and engaging in creative and abstract reflective thinking can be captured. These children typically evidence a type of static encephalopathy (that is, nonprogressive central nervous system dysfunction) that interferes with the expected progression of these core capacities. Children within this broad category, however, show wide variation in the degree to which they relate to others and master early communicative and thinking skills, as well as in their most basic ways of processing sensation (for example, some are sensory overresponsive and others are sensory underresponsive; some have relatively strong visual memory, while others have relatively weak visual memory). Therefore, we believe it is important to have the broadest possible conceptual framework within which to capture the full range of individual variation.

As we look at this full range (that is, at all possible subtypes), we discover numerous biological and overall developmental pathways that are associated with these types of challenges. For example, difficulty in connecting affect to perception and motor action, and subsequent difficulty in relating, communicating, and thinking, may be the result of several neurodevelopmental pathways, each with its own genetic or constitutional-maturational variations. Therefore, we suggest a broad category of NDRC to facilitate advances in research, evaluation strategies, and clinical intervention programs.

As this discussion suggests, NDRC can be more fully understood from the perspective of a developmental biopsychosocial model. Applying the DIR model to NDRC has enabled the development of a classification system that attempts to capture individual subtypes based on a more complete understanding of the developmental pathways that lead to significant challenges in relating, communicating, and thinking. These pathways, characterized by individual processing differences, include:

- *Auditory processing and language:* the way we receive information and comprehend and express it
- *Motor planning and sequencing:* how we act on our ideas or on what we hear and see
- *Visuospatial processing:* the ability to make sense of and understand what we are seeing
- *Sensory modulation:* the ability to modulate or regulate sensation as it is coming in

We propose four types of NDRC that cluster the major profiles we have observed in children with significant challenges in relating, communicating, and thinking. Each type highlights the varied features of the subgroup, but it is important to remember that these types and their associated features are on a continuum. We see movement within each type as well as from one type to another as the child receives intervention and makes progress. Each type is described below. These illustrations highlight the main features and quality of the relationships and functioning and are not complete.

Types of NDRC

Type I: Early Symbolic, with Constrictions

Children with Type I disorders exhibit constrictions in their capacities for shared attention, engagement, initiation of two-way affective communication, and shared social problem-solving. They have difficulty maintaining a continuous flow of affective interactions before intervention and can open and close only four to ten circles of communication (back-and-forth interactions with a caregiver) in a row. Often, the child also evidences perseveration and some degree of self-absorption. At initial evaluation, one sees islands of memory-based symbol use such as labeling pictures or repeating memorized scripts, but the child does not display a range of affect expected for his age and has difficulty integrating symbol use with other core developmental capacities and engaging in all processes simultaneously.

With a comprehensive intervention program (see Chapter 20) that emphasizes a continuous flow of affective interactions; the creative use of ideas (see Chapters 7 and 8); and strengthening motor planning, sensory modulation, and visual-spatial thinking. Often one sees such a child rapidly move from perseveration and self-absorption toward sustained engagement, affective interactions, and reactive thinking. Interactions include spontaneous use of language and maintaining the flow of interactions at the levels of two-way problem-solving communication, creating ideas, and building bridges between ideas. Even when language is delayed, the child is able to sequence complex gestures (signs) and use toys to convey symbolic ideas until language is strengthened with an emphasis on affective interactions and creativity. The child can then move toward abstract and reflective levels of symbolic thinking. These capacities enable him to develop healthy peer relationships and participate in typical activities (see Chapters 9 and 10).

Eventually, with appropriate intervention, children with Type I difficulties can usually participate fully in a regular academic program. Often an aide may be required for a period of time to help with regulatory-sensory processing and related attentional challenges. In addition, because academic skills and abstract thinking depend on processing abilities, educational interventions to address specific learning difficulties may be required.

Type II: Purposeful Problem-Solving, with Constrictions

Children with Type II disorder, when seen initially (often between ages two and four years), have significant constrictions in the third and fourth core developmental capacities: purposeful, two-way presymbolic communication and social problem-solving communication. They engage in only intermittent interactions at these levels, completing two to five circles of communication in a row. Other than repeating a few memorized scripts from favorite shows, they exhibit few islands of true symbolic activity. Initially their engagement has a global, emotional quality. They often evidence a profile of moderate processing dysfunctions in multiple areas.

They require a comprehensive program that emphasizes improving reciprocal affective interactions, shared problem-solving, and initiative, as well as multiple sensory and motor processing capabilities (see chapters 6 and 7). Over time, they can learn to engage with real warmth and pleasure. They gradually but steadily improve their capacities for purposeful interaction and shared social problem-solving, learning to initiate and sustain a continuous flow of affective interactions. The slow development of this continuous flow prevents a more robust development of symbolic capacities; these also improve but tend to rely on imitation of books and videos as a basis for language and imaginative play. They do not display an age-appropriate depth and range of affect, and their abstract thinking is very limited and focused on real-life needs. As the children gradually progress through each new capacity, they begin creating ideas and may even reach toward building bridges between ideas in circumscribed areas of interest. They tend to gradually become more and more engaged, happier, and communicative.

Although many children in this group make continuous progress, most cannot participate in all the activities of a regular classroom with a large number of children. They can, however, benefit from appropriately staffed inclusion or integrated programs or from special-needs classrooms in which language development is emphasized and the other children are interactive and verbal.

Type III: Intermittently Engaged and Purposeful

Children in this group are initially very self-absorbed. Their engagement with others is extremely intermittent. They display limited purposeful two-way communication, usually in pursuit of concrete needs or basic sensory-motor experiences (such as jumping or tickling). They may be able to imitate or even initiate some rote problem-solving actions, but they usually evidence little or no capacity for shared social problem-solving or for a continuous flow of affective exchange.

Multiple severe processing dysfunctions, including severe auditory processing and visuospatial processing difficulties and moderate-to-severe motor planning problems, impede the continuous flow of purposeful communication and problem-solving interactions. With a comprehensive program that emphasizes shared attention engagement, and purposeful affective interactions (the basics) coupled with a great deal of sensory processing and motor planning work built into interactions, plus the use of gestural and, where possible, symbolic communication as appropriate, children with Type III difficulties can become more robustly engaged in pleasurable relationships and activities, but their capacity for a continuous flow of affective interactions improves very slowly. Over time, they can increase their islands of presymbolic, purposeful, and problem-solving behavior. These islands may, at times, also involve the use of words, pictures, signs, or two- to three-step actions or gestures to communicate basic needs. Receptive understanding of often used phrases in routines or when coupled with visual cues or gestures can become a relative strength.

Some children in this group have severe oral-motor dyspraxia and either do not speak or only use a few words; they may, however, learn to use a few signs or to communicate using pictures or a favorite toy. Some children with severe motor planning problems show a far more advanced understanding of their world than anyone first believed, once they master using pictures, another symbol system, or learn to type. With a program that emphasizes two-way meaningful communication, they may progress and evidence the pattern described for other subgroups.

Children in this group require very individualized educational approaches and may eventually learn to read words and to understand visuospatial concepts. It is important that they be included in educational programs that encourage social activities and the development of friendships, as well as meaningful communications.

Type IV: Aimless and Unpurposeful

Children in this group are initially passive and self-absorbed or very active and sensory seeking; some exhibit both patterns. They have severe difficulties with shared attention and engagement unless they are involved in sensory-motor play. They tend to make very slow progress. Developing expressive language is quite challenging.

With a comprehensive intervention program similar to the one outlined for children with Type III challenges coupled with special attention to factors that may precipitate regressions, motor planning difficulties, and the use of multiple modes (including augmentative technologies) of communication, children with Type IV difficulties can become warmly engaged and intermittently interactive through the use of gestures and action games, and over time they can learn to solve problems.

Some children learn to complete organized sequences of the sort needed to play semistructured games or carry out self-help tasks, such as dressing and brushing teeth. Many such children can share with others the pleasure they experience when they use their bodies purposefully to skate, swim, ride bikes, or play ball. These meaningful activities can be used to encourage shared attention, engagement, and purposeful problem-solving.

Children in this group have the most severe challenges in all processing areas. Many have special challenges in motor planning, including oral-motor dyspraxia. As a consequence, their progress is very uneven. They have the most difficulty with complex problem-solving interactions, expressive language, and motor planning. They may have periods of progression and regression. Regressions may occur for reasons that are currently unknown, although sometimes they appear to occur because the environment is not sufficiently tailored to the child's processing profile.

Intensive, one-on-one educational approaches need to focus on strengthening engagement and early forms of two-way communication. Both visual and motor pathways—and sensory experiences that are emotionally very salient—must be explored to help the children focus, learn, and progress.

Regulatory-Sensory Processing
Profile for Each NDRC Subtype

Each subtype, in addition to being characterized by its functional emotional developmental capacity, should also be characterized by its regulatory-sensory processing profile. For research purposes, this profile can be simplified. For example, most children with NDRC (including autism spectrum disorders) evidence challenges in language and visuospatial thinking, but differ enormously in their auditory memory and visuospatial memory capacities, as well as their motor planning and sensory modulation capacities. Therefore, these features that capture important clinical and, most likely, developmental pathway differences must be highlighted. Tables C.1 and C.2 summarize both the subtypes and the regulatory-sensory processing profile in terms of these dimensions.

Table C.1 Overview of Clinical Subtypes of NDRC and Related Motor and Sensory-Processing Profile

Type I. Intermittent capacities for attending and relating; reciprocal interaction; and, with support, shared social problem-solving and the beginning use of meaningful ideas (i.e., with help, the child can relate and interact and even use a few words, but not in a continuous and stable age-expected manner).

Children with this pattern tend to show rapid progress in a comprehensive program that tailors meaningful emotional interactions to their unique motor and sensory-processing profile.

Type II. Intermittent capacities for attention, relating, and a few back-and-forth reciprocal interactions, with only fleeting capacities for shared social problem-solving and repeating some words.

Children with this pattern tend to make steady, methodical progress.

Type III. Only fleeting capacities for attention and engagement; with lots of support, occasionally a few back-and-forth reciprocal interactions; often no capacity for repeating words or using ideas, although may be able to repeat a few words in a memory-based (rather than meaningful) manner.

Children with this pattern often make slow but steady progress, especially in the basics of relating with warmth and learning to engage in longer sequences of reciprocal interaction. Over long periods of time, often they gradually master some words and phrases.

Type IV. Similar to Type III, but with a pattern of multiple regressions (loss of capacities). May also evidence a greater number of associated neurological challenges, such as seizures and marked hypotonia.

Children with this pattern often make very slow progress, which can be enhanced if the sources of the regressive tendencies can be identified.

Table C.2 Overview of Motor and Sensory Processing Profile

Children with NDRC (which includes children with ASD) tend to evidence widely different biologically based patterns of sensory reactivity, processing, and motor planning. These differences may have diagnostic and prognostic value. The child's tendencies can be briefly summarized in the framework outlined below. (Almost all the children with an NDRC diagnosis evidence language and visuospatial thinking challenges.) Patterns listed are ones that tend to differ among the children. (See ICDL *Diagnostic Manual* for a fuller description.)

Sensory Modulation

- Tends to overrespond to sensations, such as sound or touch (e.g., covers ears or gets dysregulated with lots of light touch)
- Tends to crave sensory experience (e.g., actively seeks touch, sound, and different movement patterns)
- Tends to underrespond to sensations (e.g., requires highly energized vocal or tactile support to be alert and attend)

Motor Planning and Sequencing

- Relative strength in motor planning and sequencing (e.g., carries out multiple-step action patterns, such as negotiating obstacle courses or building complex block designs)
- Relative weakness in motor planning and sequencing (e.g., can barely carry out simple movements and may tend to simply bang blocks or do other one- or two-step action patterns)

Auditory Memory

- Relative strength in auditory memory (remembers or repeats long statements or materials from books, TV, records, etc.)
- Relative weakness in auditory memory (difficulty remembering even simple sounds or words)

Visual Memory

- Relative strength in visual memory (tends to remember what is seen, such as book covers, pictures, eventually words)
- Relative weakness in visual memory (difficulty remembering even simple pictures or objects)

References

Achenbach, T. M. 1991. *Integrative guide to the 1991 CBCL/4–18, YSR, and TRF Profiles*. Burlington: University of Vermont, Department of Psychiatry.

Baranek, G. T. 1999. Autism during infancy: A retrospective video analysis of sensory-motor and social behaviors at 9–12 months of age. *Journal of Autism and Developmental Disorders* 29:213–224.

Baron-Cohen, S. 1989. The theory of mind hypothesis of autism: A reply to Boucher. *British Journal of Disorders of Communication* 24:199–200.

———. 1994. *Mindblindness: An essay on autism and theories of mind*. Cambridge, MA: MIT Press.

Baron-Cohen, S., A. M. Leslie, and U. Frith. 1985. Does the autistic child have a "theory of mind"? *Cognition* 21:37–46.

Bayley, N. 2005. *Bayley Scales of Infant and Toddler Development*. 3rd ed. (Bayley III). Bulverde, TX: Psychological Corporation.

Bayley, P. J., J. C. Frascino, and L. R. Squire. 2005. Robust habit learning in the absence of awareness and independent of the medial temporal lobe. *Nature* 436:550–553.

Bertrand, J., A. Mars, C. Boyle, F. Bove, M. Yeargin-Allsop, and P. Decoufle. 2001. Prevalence of autism in a United States population: The Brick Township, New Jersey, Investigation. *Pediatrics* 108:1155–1161.

Bowler, D. M. 1992. Theory of mind in Asperger's Syndrome. *Journal of Child Psychology and Psychiatry* 33:893.

Carper, R. A., and E. Courchesne. 2005. Localized enlargement of the frontal cortex in early autism. *Biological Psychiatry* 57(2):126–133.

Courchesne, E., N. Akshoomoff, B. Egaas, A. J. Lincoln, O. Saitoh, L. Schreibman, et al. (1994). *Role of cerebellar and parietal dysfunction in the social and cognitive deficits in patients with infantile autism*. Rep. No. Paper presented at the Autism Society of America Annual Conference. Las Vegas, NV.

Dahlgren, S. O., and A. Trillingsgaard. 1996. Theory of mind in non-retarded children with autism and Asperger's syndrome: A research note. *Journal of Child Psychology and Psychiatry* 37:763.

Dawson, G., and I. Galpert. 1990. Mother's use of imitative play for facilitating social responsiveness and toy play in young autistic children. *Development and Psychopathology* 2:151–162.

Dawson, G., A. Meltzoff, J. Osterling, and J. Rinaldi. 1998. Neuropsychological correlates of early symptoms of autism. *Child Development* 69:1276–1285.

Diagnostic Classification Task Force, 1994. *Diagnostic classification: 0–3: Diagnostic classification of mental health and developmental disorders of infancy and early childhood.* Arlington, VA: ZERO TO THREE: National Center for Clinical Infant Programs.

Frith, U. 1989. *Autism: Explaining the enigma.* London: Blackwell.

Furth, H. G., and Wachs, H. 1974. *Thinking goes to school: Piaget's theory in practice.* New York: Oxford University Press.

Greenspan, J., and S. I. Greenspan. 2002. Functional emotional developmental questionnaire (FEDQ) for childhood: A preliminary report on the questions and their clinical meaning. *Journal of Developmental and Learning Disorders,* 6:71–116.

Greenspan, S. I., 1979. *Intelligence and adaptation: An integration of psychoanalytic and Piagetian developmental psychology.* Psychological Issues Monograph Series, nos. 47–48. New York: International Universities Press.

———. 1989. *The development of the ego: Implications for personality theory, psychopathology, and the psychotherapeutic process.* New York: International Universities Press.

———. 1992. *Infancy and early childhood: The practice of clinical assessment and intervention with emotional and developmental challenges.* Madison, CT: International Universities Press.

———. 1997a. *Developmentally based psychotherapy.* Madison, CT: International Universities Press.

———. 1997b. *The growth of the mind and the endangered origins of intelligence.* Reading, MA: Addison Wesley Longman.

———. 2001. The Affect Diathesis Hypothesis: The role of emotions in the core deficit in autism and the development of intelligence and social skills. *Journal of Developmental and Learning Disorders* 5:1–45.

———. 2004. *Greenspan Social-Emotional Growth Chart.* Bulverde, TX: Psychological Corporation.

Greenspan, S. I., and C. Breinbauer. 2005. *Short-term changes in emotional, social, and intellectual functioning in children with ASD with the DIR-Floortime approach.* Working paper.

Greenspan, S. I., G. A. DeGangi, and S. Wieder. 2001. *The functional emotional assessment scale (FEAS) for infancy and early childhood: Clinical & research applications*. Bethesda, MD: ICDL (www.icdl.com).

Greenspan, S. I., and S. Shanker. 2004. *The first idea: How symbols, language and intelligence evolved from our primate ancestors to modern humans*. Cambridge, MA: Perseus Books.

———. 2006. The developmental pathways leading to pattern-recognition, joint attention, language and cognition. *New Ideas in Psychology*, February.

Greenspan, S. I., and S. Wieder. 1997. Developmental patterns and outcomes in infants and children with disorders in relating and communicating: A chart review of 200 cases of children with autistic spectrum diagnoses. *Journal of Developmental and Learning Disorders* 1:87–141.

———. 1998. *The child with special needs: Encouraging intellectual and emotional growth*. Cambridge, MA: Perseus Books.

———. 1999. A functional developmental approach to autism spectrum disorders. *Journal of the Association for Persons with Severe Handicaps (JASH)* 24:147–161.

———. 2005. Can Children with Autism Master the Core Deficits and Become Empathetic, Creative, and Reflective? A Ten to Fifteen Year Follow-up of a Subgroup of Children with Autism Spectrum Disorders (ASD) Who Received a Comprehensive Developmental, Individual-Difference, Relationship-Based (DIR) Approach. *The Journal of Developmental and Learning Disorders* 9.

Greenspan, S. I., S. Wieder, A. Lieberman, R. Nover, R. Lourie, and M. Robinson. 1987. Infants in multirisk families: Case studies in preventative intervention. *Clinical Infant Reports*. New York: International Universities Press.

Herbert, M. R., D. A. Ziegler, N. Makris, P. A. Filipek, T. L. Kemper, J. J. Normandin, H. A. Sanders, D. N. Kennedy, and V. S. Caviness Jr. 2004. Localization of white matter volume increase in autism and developmental language disorder. *Annals of Neurology* 55:530–540.

ICDL-DMIC Diagnostic Classification Task Force. 2005. *Interdisciplinary Council on Developmental and Learning Disorders Diagnostic manual for infancy and early childhood mental health disorders, developmental disorders, regulatory-sensory processing disorders, language disorders, and learning challenges*. Bethesda, MD: ICDL (www.icdl.com).

Interdisciplinary Council on Developmental and Learning Disorders Clinical Practice Guidelines Workgroup, SICC. 2000. *Interdisciplinary Council on Developmental and Learning Disorders' clinical practice guidelines: Redefining the standards of care for infants, children, and families with special needs*. Bethesda, MD: ICDL (www.icdl.com).

Just, M. A., V. L. Cherkassky, T. A. Keller, and N. J. Minshew. 2004. Cortical activation and synchronization during sentence comprehension in high-functioning autism: Evidence of underconnectivity. *Brain* 127:1811–1821.

Klin, A., F. R. Volkmar, and S. Sparrow. 1992. Autistic social dysfunction: Some limitations of the theory of mind hypothesis. *Journal of Child Psychology and Psychiatry* 33:861–876.

Koegel, J. K., S. M. Camarata, M. Valdez-Menchaca, and R. I. Koegel. 1998. Setting generalization of question-asking by children with autism. *American Journal of Metal Retardation* 102:346–357.

Lovaas, O. I. 1987. Behavioral treatment and normal educational and intellectual functioning in young autistic children. *Journal of Consulting and Clinical Psychology* 55:3–9.

Mahoney, G., and F. Perales. 2005. Relationship-focused early intervention with children with pervasive developmental disorders and other disabilities: A comparative study. *Developmental and Behavioral Pediatrics* 26(2):77–85.

McEachin, J. J., T. Smith, and O. I. Lovaas. 1993. Long-term outcome for children with autism who received early intensive behavioral treatment. *American Journal on Mental Retardation* 97:359–372.

McGee, G. C., P. J. Krantz, and L. E. McClannahan. 1985. The facilitative effects of incidental teaching on preposition use by autistic children. *Journal of Applied Behavior Analysis* 18:17–31.

Minshew, N., and G. Goldstein. 1998. Autism as a disorder of complex information processing. *Mental Retardation and Developmental Disabilities* 4:129–236.

Mundy, P., M. Sigman, and C. Kasari. 1990. A longitudinal study of joint attention and language development in autistic children. *Journal of Autism and Developmental Disorders* 20:115–128.

National Academy of Sciences, Committee on Educational Interventions for Children with Autism, NRC. 2001. *Educating Children with Autism*. Washington, DC: National Academies Press.

Ozonoff, S. 1997. Causal mechanisms of autism: Unifying perspectives from an information-processing framework. In D. Cohen and F. Volkmar, eds., *Handbook of autism and pervasive developmental disorders*, pp. 868–879. New York: Wiley.

Pennington, J., and S. Ozonoff. 1996. Executive functions and developmental psychopathology. *Journal of Child Psychology and Psychiatry* 37:51–87.

Rogers, S., and D. DiLalla. 1991. A comparative study of the effects of a developmentally based instructional model on young children with autism and young children with other disorders of behavior and development. *Topics in Early Childhood Special Education* 11:29–47.

Rogers, S. J., T. Hall, D. Osaki, J. Reaven, and J. Herbison. 2000. The Denver model: A comprehensive, integrated educational approach to young children with autism and their families. In J. S. Handleman and S. L. Harris, eds., *Preschool education programs for children with autism, 2nd ed.*, pp. 95–133. Austin, TX: Pro-Ed.

Shea, V. 2004. A perspective on the research literature related to early intensive behavioral intervention (Lovaas) for young children with autism. *Autism* 8:349–367.

Siller, M., and M. Sigman. 2002. The behaviors of parents of children with autism predict the subsequent development of their children's communication. *Journal of Autism and Developmental Disorders* 32:77–89.

Simpson, G. A., L. Colpe, and S. I. Greenspan. 2003. Measuring functional developmental delay in infants and young children: Prevalence rates from the NHIS-D. *Paediatric & Perinatal Epidemiology* 17:68–80.

Smith, T. 2001. Discrete trial ABA approaches. In *New approaches to help the most challenged children learn to communicate and talk*. Tysons Corner, VA: ICDL.

Smith, T., A. D. Groen, and J. W. Wynn. 2000. Randomized trial of intensive early intervention for children with pervasive developmental disorder. *American Journal of Mental Retardation* 105:269–285.

Solomon, R., J. Necheles, D. Ferch, and D. Bruckman. In press. Program evaluation of a pilot parent training program for young children with autism: The PLAY Project Home Consultation Program. *Autism*.

Sperry, R. W. 1985. Consciousness, personal identity, and the divided brain. In F. Benson and E. Zaidel, eds., *The dual brain*, pp. 11–27. New York: Guilford.

Spitz, R. 1965. The first year of life: A psychoanalytic study of normal and deviant development of object relations. New York: International Universities Press.

Teitelbaum, P., and O. Teitelbaum. 1999. *Motor indicators of autism in the first year*. Paper presented at the Interdisciplinary Council on Developmental and Learning Disorders' Third Annual International Conference on Autism and Disorders of Relating and Communicating. McLean, VA.

Tronick, E. Z. 1989. Emotions and emotional communication in infants. *American Psychologist* 44:115–123.

Vargas, D. L., C. Nascimbene, C. Krishnan, A.W. Zimmerman, and C.A. Pardo. 2005. Neuroglial activation and neuroinflammation in the brain of patients with autism. *Annals of Neurology* 57(1):67–81.

Wetherby, A. M., and B. M. Prizant. 1993. Profiling communication and symbolic abilities in young children. *Journal of Childhood Communication Disorders* 15:23–32.

The Greenspan Social-Emotional Growth Chart and Questionnaire is available from the Psychological Corporation, and is also part of the 2004 Bayley Scales package, available from Harcourt Press Inc. at www.harcourtassessment.com.

For more information about getting started with DIR/Floortime and to locate one of the approximately 40,000 clinicians trained in the approach, as well as the hospitals and schools using the model, visit the Floortime Foundation website (www.floortime.org) and the ICDL website (www.icdl.com).

About the Authors

Stanley I. Greenspan, M.D., is Clinical Professor of Psychiatry and Pediatrics at George Washington University Medical School and Chairman of the Interdisciplinary Council on Developmental and Learning Disorders. He is a founding president of Zero to Three: The National Center for Infants, Toddlers and Families, a supervising child psychoanalyst at the Washington Psychoanalytic Institute, and former director of the Mental Health Study Center and Clinical Infant Development Program at NIMH. Considered the world's foremost authority on clinical work with infants and young children with developmental and emotional problems, his work is the basis for regional networks and guides their care. A recipient of the American Psychiatric Association's high honor for child psychiatric research, Greenspan is the author or editor of more than thirty-eight books, translated into over a dozen languages, including *The First Idea* (coauthored with Stuart Shanker, D.Phil), *The Growth of the Mind*, *Building Healthy Minds*, *The Challenging Child*, *The Child with Special Needs* (coauthored with Serena Wieder, Ph.D.), *Infancy and Early Childhood*, *Developmentally-Based Psychotherapy*, and (with T. Berry Brazelton, M.D.) *The Irreducible Needs of Children*.

Serena Wieder, Ph.D., is a clinical psychologist in private practice, specializing in the diagnosis and treatment of infants and young children with developmental and emotional disorders. Associate Editor of the *Journal of Developmental and Learning Disorders*, she is on the faculty of the Washington (D.C.) School of Psychiatry and is Associate Chair of the Interdisciplinary Council on Developmental and Learning Disorders. Dr. Wieder is coauthor with Dr. Greenspan of *The Child with Special Needs*.

Index